ORIGEN

THE SONG OF SONGS
COMMENTARY AND HOMILIES

ANCIENT CHRISTIAN WRITERS

THE WORKS OF THE FATHERS IN TRANSLATION

EDITED BY

JOHANNES QUASTEN, S. T. D.
Catholic University of America
Washington, D.C.

JOSEPH C. PLUMPE, Ph.D.
Pontifical College Josephinum
Worthington, O.

No. 26

ORIGEN

THE SONG OF SONGS
COMMENTARY AND HOMILIES

TRANSLATED AND ANNOTATED
BY
R. P. LAWSON

NEWMAN PRESS

New York, N.Y./Ramsey, N.J.

Nihil Obstat:
    J. Quasten
       Cens. Dep.

Imprimatur:
    Patricius A. O'Boyle, D.D.
      Archiep. Washingtonen.
       die 2 Nov. 1956

Library of Congress
Catalog Card Number: 57-11826

ISBN: 0-8091-0261-7

PUBLISHED BY PAULIST PRESS
Editorial Office: 1865 Broadway, New York, N.Y. 10023
Business Office: 545 Island Road, Ramsey, N.J. 07446

PRINTED AND BOUND IN THE UNITED STATES OF AMERICA

CONTENTS

v

CONTENTS

ORIGEN

THE SONG OF SONGS
COMMENTARY AND HOMILIES

INTRODUCTION

During the past few decades the great Alexandrian whose name appears on the present volume, has received justice immemorially due, a completely new appraisal of his contribution to the Christian life and the thought of the early Church. For far too long he was ignored for the best he gave and gave so zealously, for too long he was regarded only as a philosopher or a humanist or a speculative theologian. This was made possible only by the utter neglect through the centuries of those works in which this great theologian speaks to us as a master mystic, one who has exerted tremendous influence on Christian spirituality and piety, and to whom monasticism through the ages is greatly indebted for inspiration.

In our day this unbalanced judgement of Origen has in great part been corrected. For this change in approach to the great wreckage of his literary remains—and such it is considering that so much survives only in the versions of his translators Rufinus and Jerome—we are indebted to the monographs of Völker[1] and Lieske,[2] de Lubac[3] and Daniélou,[4] Lebreton[5] and Bertrand,[6] and most recently, Crouzel.[7] As a result of these enquiries the hitherto neglected works of Origen are seen in an entirely new light. It is against the background of this newly awakened interest in the mystical writings of Origen that we here offer a first English translation of his great *Commentary* and his two *Homilies on the Canticle of Canticles*.

Unfortunately, neither the *Commentary* nor the *Homilies* survive in the original text. Of the former only a few

Greek fragments have come to light, and of the latter not one Greek line is known. The present translation is based on the Latin version of the *Commentary* made by Rufinus, and of the *Homilies* made by St. Jerome. The reader will further bear in mind that in the case of the *Commentary* the Latin version reproduces only a large fragment of the original work: whereas Rufinus translated three books (according to best manuscript tradition—see below), we know that the original Greek text comprised ten books.[8]

THE COMMENTARY ON THE CANTICLE OF CANTICLES

According to Eusebius (*Hist. eccl.* 6.32.2), Origen composed the first five books of his great *Commentary* in Athens about the year 240, and wrote the other five somewhat later at Caesarea in Palestine. Most of the Greek fragments that remain are found in the catena-commentary on the Canticle of Canticles ascribed to Procopius of Gaza.[9] This catena and the Origen fragments it contains receive special attention in a monograph by the late Cardinal Faulhaber.[10] These fragments and the two or three small pieces discovered in other catenas may be found below the Latin text in the edition by Baehrens, and in the present volume appear in English translation, in smaller print and at the foot of the page, in the respective places of concurrence with the translated Rufinian version.

The Latin translation by Rufinus offers the long prologue to the *Commentary* and the first three books of the same. In the earlier editions of the *Commentary* the division between Book Three and (a part of) Book Four is warranted only by a minority of the manuscripts, and a statement by Cassiodorus contradicts it.[11] The translation was made in Sicily about the year 410 while Alaric was expanding his conquest of Italy into Calabria. Origen's exegesis in Book One covers only the first four verses of the Canticle; in Book Two he treats 1.5–14; in Book Three, 1.15–2.15.

If we compare the recovered Greek fragments of the *Commentary* with the translation of Rufinus, it is quite obvious that, here as elsewhere, his version is extremely free; and this so much so that throughout the great areas for which we have no Greek remains, we can never be quite certain whether or not he is offering a mere paraphrase of the original, or to what extent he may have expanded or abridged or even changed or 'corrected' what Origen had set down. This free treatment of the original text becomes particularly apparent in passages in which Rufinus deals with Scriptural difficulties arising from a Latin version or reading, or in which he adverts to etymologies or other matters affecting the Latin reader only. It is however hardly necessary now to say that Rufinus ought not to be blamed for this, as he has been often in the past. He is not trying to interpolate or falsify his author, and there is in him no dishonesty. On the contrary, as a translator of the 5th—and not the 20th—century he candidly pursued certain quite legitimate and laudable aims, and followed carefully an adopted methodology which it is unreasonable and unfair to adjudge by modern norms or canons of translation.[12]

Certainly the work that remains to be done toward a true estimate of Rufinus as a translator of Origen is very formidable. A great deal of research at its best is still required to enable us to establish, on the basis of a comparative study of the Latin translations of Origen's exegetical commentaries and homilies with *all* that remains in Greek of his Scriptural output, to what extent, or with what exclusions, the Rufinian versions reproduce what Origen really said or wrote. We should likewise note here that the Greek fragments themselves—and here we speak especially from our experience with the fragments reproduced in translation in their places in the present volume—present the problem of trustworthiness. The problem is especially acute with regard to fragments derived, as in the case of the present *Commentary*, from catenas : are these fragments true and unchanged quotations from the original—are they not sometimes drastic condensations of the original? [13] At all events, the student of Origen who reads the three books that Rufinus rescued of his monumental *Commentary*, will agree that the opinion which F. Barth gave concerning the two *Homilies* on the Canticle, holds also for the former : 'But all in all it is the genuine Origen we have before us, and that, too, in the full maturity of his theological thinking.' [14] And, whatever liberties Rufinus may have taken with the Greek text, in his version we still have a work the reading of which confirms Jerome's judgement on the original, that while in his other works Origen far surpassed all other authors, in his *Commentary on the Song of Songs* he surpassed himself. [15]

Origen was not the first Christian writer to compose a commentary on the Canticle of Canticles. Before him Hippolytus of Rome had undertaken the task. Much less was Origen the last ancient Christian writer to essay an explication of the Song : he was followed by Athanasius, Gregory of Nyssa, Theodore of Mopsuestia, Theodoret of Cyrus, Maximus Confessor. But, though almost all borrowed from him, none equalled him in richness of thought and depth of mystical conception. His *Commentary* is indeed the first great work of Christian mysticism. It is a work that, notwithstanding what it has lost in the translation by Rufinus, stirs the soul even to-day and through its concept of the Church becomes a profoundly inspirational experience to the reader. The exquisite picture that the great Alexandrian portrays of his beloved Church is so vivid and so rich in colour that we moderns begin to see how a one-sided over-emphasis on the legal and hieratic character of the Church has tended in our own times to take from her fair countenance the blood and life that ought to give it hue and colour. Small wonder that for too many to-day she stands only for an organization, rather than for what she was familiarly in Origen's thought of her—Our Lord and Saviour's mystical Bride!

If we reflect upon the full import of Origen's exegesis of the Canticle of Canticles, we cannot but be very certain that for the Fathers there was no treatise *De Ecclesia*. In the Old Testament there was no book so inviting, so rich in materials for delineating the Church foreshown for so long, as this love-song inspired by the Holy Spirit. Already the Synagogue had identified the bride of this Song with Yahweh's chosen people Israel; and so the thought quite readily suggested itself to the Fathers that the bride should be sought in God's new people, in the mystery of its nuptial union with Christ, as is set forth by the Apostle in his Letter to the Ephesians (5.32). As a matter of fact, all the Greek exegetes of the Canticle have been very partial to the ecclesiological interpretation, or have at least tolerated it.[16] This also holds of those writers who, in the few remains that we have of their commentaries, appear to be guided primarily by ascetic interests and so would have the bride to be the Christian soul. The sole exception is the jejune rationalist Theodore of Mopsuestia: he regards the Song as Solomon's reply to the opponents of his marriage with the Egyptian princess, and refuses to grant it any allegorical significance. When the first interpreter of the Canticle of Canticles in the West, St. Hippolytus, saw in the bride the Church and extolled the saving fecundity of her mystical union with Christ, he with Origen of the East blazoned a way that was to be followed by the Fathers of the Church for centuries to come.

Origen was the first Christian scholar to systematize allegorical interpretation of Scripture. This becomes especially apparent in his *Commentary on the Song of Songs*. He is convinced that the Holy Spirit has veiled the form and shape of the mysteries in Holy Writ, and that He did not wish these to be accessible to the grasp of all (Bk. 1, p. 74). Indeed, in Book Three (pp. 218–28) there is a regular excursus on the pneumatic interpretation of Scripture. Taking as his authority Wisdom 7.17–21, he teaches the reader that not all that is found in Scripture is to be understood wholly in the literal sense: there is much that becomes clear only if it is given a transferred or a figurative meaning. The examples which he adduces further to illustrate this are entirely apposite: thus, for instance, 1 Corinthians 4.15, where St. Paul states that he begot his converts through the Gospel; or when there is frequent talk of the 'snares of the devil.' Here Origen opposes the exegetical method which, taking support from a misguided respect for the Word of God, would interpret it with absolute word-for-word literalness. In the first words of this excursus Origen has us invoke God the Father 'to the intent that we may utter not the things that the ear of the flesh perceives, but those that are contained within the Spirit's will' (p. 218). Referring to the *occulta et manifesta* of Wisd. 7.21, he states that 'each of the manifest things is to be related to one of those that are hidden; that is to say, all things visible have some invisible likeness and pattern' (p. 220). Origen practically gives us the cosmological-theological key to his exegesis when he says: 'So . . . all the things in the visible category can be related to the invisible, the corporeal to the incorporeal, and the manifest to those that are hidden; so that the creation of the world itself, fashioned in this wise as it is, can be understood through the divine wisdom, which from actual things and copies teaches us things unseen by means of those that are seen, and carries us over from earthly things to heavenly. But this relationship does not obtain only with creatures; the Divine Scripture itself is written with wisdom of a rather similar sort' (p. 223).

Origen then draws the conclusion: If there are hidden relations between the seen and the unseen, between earth and heaven, flesh and soul, body and spirit, and if the world takes its origin from their uniting into one, then Sacred Scripture too has a visible and an invisible element. In the letter, visible to all, it has a body; in the hidden meaning inherent in it, it has a soul; and it has a spirit in the element of heaven of which it offers an image. Here we have the Platonic tripartite man—body-soul-spirit—applied to the Word of God, in which Origen sees an incarnation of the Holy Spirit. The letter of Scripture is a symbol of what is directly intelligible—hence it is, as it were, body of the Divine Spirit; but if we approach the matter more profoundly, it is likewise a symbol of what is intelligible indirectly, of the Spirit, therefore, in His own invisible, heavenly spirituality. If the Logos in His Incarnation is God-Man, so, too, in the mind of Origen the incarnation of the Pneuma in Holy Scripture is divine-human. The invisible, inscrutable mystery that it contains is divine, while its body, the fact that in its garb of the written word it is a subject of sense-perception, makes it human.

Applied to the Canticle of Canticles, this yields, first, the carnal or direct sense, which sees in it only a minnesong or lofty lyric; second, the indirect sense, of which the pneumatic component hymns the mystical nuptials of Christ and the Church, while its psychic counterpart has for its theme the bridal union of the Logos and the human soul.[17]

THE CHURCH AS THE BRIDE OF CHRIST

When Origen applies the bride-bridegroom relationship to the union obtaining between God and Israel or between Christ and His Church, his exegesis moves entirely within the pale of Old and New Testament thought. It is to be noted, however, that in his *Commentary* the psychic interpretation more and more displaces the pneumatic, the parent Christ-Church concept; for, having its ground in the latter, the bridal Logos-Soul relationship is always its individual fruition and realization. Just as Christ makes manifest the human visibleness of the Word, so the Church is the visible society of the individually sanctified. 'The Church, you must observe, is the whole assembly of the saints. So it must be the Church as a corporate personality who speaks and says: "I am sated with the gifts that I received as betrothal presents . . ."' (Bk. I, p. 59). Now if Christ is the Bridegroom of the Church in the visible sphere, so, too, the Word hidden in the figure Christ is the Bridegroom of the individual souls hidden in the common figure of the Church.

But the relationship of God with Israel is not seen as a union between Yahweh and the Chosen People. Rather, we see the Synagogue—an immature, undeveloped bride, a child-bride, indeed, a bride with a history of sin—looking with great longing for her Bridegroom Jesus Christ, who is hastening to her over hill and mountain to grant her ardent desire—*Let Him kiss me with the kisses of His mouth* (1.2). But this yearning was not to be satisfied at once. For some time to come, the young bride must be content with the company of the friends of the Bridegroom—the angels and the patriarchs and the prophets—and receive through them His kisses, the kisses of the teachings and exhortations of the Old Testament (*Hom.* 1.2, p. 269). While this is transpiring, the Bridegroom rests on His couch (1.7), that is to say, the time for His coming has not yet arrived (though for Origen He and His Church are present from the beginning). Their becoming in Revelation, their birth in the Crib and on the Cross, their onward course together through the space of time to ultimate perfection—these are for him but the entry into and the exit out of the world of space and time, in other words, they are but their history.

The ointments with which the young bride is familiar are the words of the Law and the Prophets. As she awaits the arrival of the Bridegroom, she is instructed, though incompletely, in the right service of God. From the first beginning of time till its fulfilment in Christ, she is permitted to listen to the voice of her Lover only as it speaks to her in the words of the Prophets; it is not given to her to see Him. It is but natural that we should hear her lament—in touching words she pleads with the Father of her Bridegroom, that He send Him to her at last, beseeching Him

to have compassion at last upon my love, and to send Him, that He may now no longer speak to me only by His servants the angels and the prophets, but may come Himself, directly, and *kiss me with the kisses of His mouth*; that is to say, may pour the words of His mouth into mine, that I may hear Him speak Himself, and see Him teaching (Bk. 1, p. 60).

Thus speaks the Bride chosen from all eternity, the Bride of the God-Man Jesus Christ; and even as her plaint is heard, the Bridegroom suddenly stands before her, breathing the sweet odours of His divine gifts. Each odour reveals a virtue that adorns Him. She receives the blissful kiss of Christ's endowment with grace, and, with her hand in His, steps forth now to the glorious springtime of redeemed humankind.

But it is not the *Ecclesia ex circumcisione* alone that Origen sees represented in the Canticle of Canticles: the *Ecclesia ex gentibus* is found there too. The Marriage of Solomon the prince of peace remained the unparalleled model of the Israelite ceremonial of marriage that saw the bride received by the bridegroom seated on the nuptial dais. At the same time the Queen of Sheba, who came from afar to feast her eyes on the magnificent splendour of Solomon and to receive from the largess of his wisdom, is regarded by Origen as a clear presage of the Church that comes to Christ from pagan lands to drink from the fountain of His Wisdom. The extraordinary confidence and hope that this Church places in the Saviour, which hope gave her the determination and strength to ignore all the hardships of the journey, stand in marked contrast to the stubborn incredulity of the Jews, and on the Day of Judgement her strong faith will bring shame and condemnation upon that people. She portrays the *Ecclesia ex gentibus*, the Church that has expended her youth in 'dark' paganism and is now cleansing herself in the waters of the fountain of life, the Church of the Gentiles—eager to believe, ready for sacrifice.

And as Solomon generously shared his wisdom with the Queen, so also does the Church of the Gentiles receive wisdom from the new Solomon: in Christ's Revelation she is enlightened on numerous questions and problems which pagan philosophy had never been able to solve for her—e.g. concerning God and creation, concerning the immortal soul and judgement. Only when these questions have been answered, does human life take on its full and real meaning. Again, the Queen of Sheba came laden with rich gifts: in like manner the Church *ex gentibus* does not come empty-handed—she brings with her many a noble gift of her ancient culture. Full of sorrow and repentance, she opens up her heart to the Saviour, just like the Queen when she told Solomon all that was on her mind; and she hears Him speak to her, forgiving her and teaching her. She marvels at the palace which Divine Wisdom has built in the mystery of the Incarnation. She tastes of the food of the Obedient One, who said: *My meat is to do the will of Him that sent me* (John 4.34—see p. 98 ff.). She gazes in wonder at the garment of those of whom it is said: *As many of you as have been baptized in Christ, have put on Christ* (Gal. 3.27—*ibid.*), she gazes at the cupbearers who pour out the wine of Christ's doctrine for the guests at His table, and awe-filled she witnesses the Sacrifice of devout prayer (*ibid.*). All this amazes and fascinates the Church of the Gentiles. Attracted by the true word of Christ's Revelation, her journey to the Prince of Peace has not been in vain: she finds that all her expectations are surpassed.

Such, in brief, is the outward appearance of the Church that comes up from the steppe of paganism to receive from her Bridegroom the living water that is to turn her arid lands into the fruitful paradise of the Second Adam and the second Eve; and to her is given in turn the mission of becoming the Mother of God's people resurrected to new life through Baptism.[18]

From what has been said we already gather one of the central ideas of Origen's ecclesiology, and this aligns him with a tradition also followed by his master Clement of Alexandria: the concept of a pre-existent church, the Church that was present from all time, even before man was created. It is a concept which occupies his thoughts again and again and lends them fresh inspiration. 'For you must please not think,' he writes in the *Commentary*, 'that she is called the Bride or the Church only from the time when the Saviour came in flesh; she is so called from the beginning of the human race and from the very foundation of the world—indeed, if I may look for the origin of this high mystery under Paul's guidance, even *before* the foundation of the world. For this is what he says: "... *as He chose us in Christ before the foundation of the world, that we should be holy and unspotted in His sight, predestinating us in charity unto the adoption of sons* "' (Eph. 1.4 f.—p. 149). Here the commentator argues the eternity of the Church from the mystery of predestination. Origen is aware, of course, that the consummation of the bridal union of the Logos and the Church takes place only in the Incarnation. But the Church is *Sponsa Christi* from the creation of mankind, she has been such even before the creation of the world. In the last analysis, this thought gives us the key to the *Commentary* of the great Alexandrian.

THE SOUL AS THE BRIDE OF CHRIST

In the *Commentary* Origen's spiritual interpretation of the Canticle is everywhere conjoined with the psychic interpretation—in fact, this latter becomes increasingly prominent as the discussion moves on. It must not be separated, however, from the former: rather, we should speak of the parallelism of the relationship between the Divine Word and the Church and between the Word and the Soul. But more than a parallel is involved: at the base of it is the intimate relationship of being between the Church and the individual soul. As has already been suggested, the Church is identical with the *coetus omnium sanctorum*. Origen states clearly, simply, '*We* are the Church'—*Ecclesia . . . nos sumus* (*Hom.* 2.3—p. 287).[19] He shows throughout how he is saturated with the idea of the compenetration of the life of the Church and the life of the soul, of the mystery of the Church and our life under grace: in the final analysis, the two—inseparable—stand for true participation in the Divine-Human nature of the Logos.

From the beginning Christ has been to the Church her life and soul, and through the Church He is the same to each individual. And what has been fulfilled in the Church as a result of her bridal union with Christ, the same is effected in every soul entering into bridal relations with Christ. In her Old Testament pre-existence He has prepared the Church, step by step, and brought her to perfection: thus, too, He unfolds the divine life of grace in her every member, the individual soul. Day by day, in His mystical communion with her, He enlightens her until she achieves perfection in holy nuptials with the Logos. Through His grace He leads her on and on, from a knowledge of self to the struggle against sin, to practices of asceticism, to the mystical ascent, until at last she is admitted to the *spiritalis amplexus* of mystical union with the Logos:

The soul is moved by heavenly love and longing when, having clearly beheld the beauty and the fairness of the Word of God, it falls deeply in love with His loveliness and receives from the Word Himself a certain dart and wound of love. . . . If, then, a man can so extend his thinking as to ponder and consider the beauty and the grace of all the things that have been created in the Word, the very charm of them will so smite him, the grandeur of their brightness will so pierce him as with *a chosen dart*—as says the prophet (Isa. 49.2)—that he will suffer from the dart Himself a saving wound, and will be kindled with the blessed fire of His love (Prol.—p. 29 f.).

These are Platonic reminiscences in which Christ and the Church appear as Eros and Psyche.[20] At the same time it becomes quite obvious how much is owed to Origen's *Commentary* by the later mystics through the Middle Ages, with whom concepts such as the *scintilla animae* and the spiritual marriage play a prominent rôle.[21]

THE TWO HOMILIES ON THE CANTICLE OF CANTICLES

The church historian Socrates reports that Origen as a rule preached on Wednesday and Friday.[22] His homilies on the Gospel of St. Luke are reported to have been given on Sundays,[23] and his apologist Pamphilus writes that he preached almost daily.[24] His renown as an instructor and preacher equalled his reputation as a writer. Already in the year 216 when he had come to Palestine, though he was only about thirty and still a layman, the bishops of Caesarea, Jerusalem, and other cities requested him to preach to their congregations. At his death he left homilies on almost all the books of Scripture. Unfortunately, the homilies fared particularly badly and for the most part they have perished. Of 574 known homilies only 21 have survived in Greek, and 388 no longer exist even in Latin translation.

The two *Homilies on the Canticle of Canticles* are of the number that survive in Latin version. As has already been

stated, they were translated by St. Jerome, who also prefixed them with a prologue addressed to Pope Damasus.
If the reader applies himself seriously to the contents of
these *Homilies*, he will soon discover how important they
are for a deeper insight into the religious thinking of
Origen. The fact that his homilies were quite generally
ignored inevitably had disastrous results in the history of
the study of Origen. Scholars who more or less confined
their research to the more theoretical of his theological
works, such as the *De Principiis* and the *Contra Celsum*,
have, as has been amply shown by Völker,[25] drawn a
completely distorted picture of this Man of Steel who
ranks first among the Church's first great teachers. For a
comprehensive appraisal of his theology, and especially
his doctrine on grace, his homilies are indispensable. With
a view, therefore, of making a small contribution to a more
equitable judgement on the theology of Origen, we here
add a first English translation of both *Homilies* to the
version of the *Commentary on the Canticle of Canticles*.

The *Homilies*, very likely written down by Origen himself, seem to have been given only a few years after the
composition of the *Commentary*—probably before 244.[26]
Obviously, in content they show very considerable
affinity with the *Commentary*. That the *Commentary* had
gone before and served him well as he explained the
Song of Songs to the faithful will be readily seen, for
instance, in his exegesis of the ἀπόδεσμος τῆς στακτῆς of
Cant. 1.13 in *Homily* 2.3 as compared with that in Book
Two (p. 163) of the *Commentary*. But there is this marked
difference that in the *Homilies* the identification of the
Bride in the Canticle of Canticles with the universal
Church is entirely predominant. In the introduction to
the *First Homily* (§ 1) he states very clearly: 'Christum

sponsum intellige, *Ecclesiam sponsam sine macula et ruga*'
(Eph. 5.27); whereas at the beginning of Bk. 1 of the *Commentary* he writes: 'Spiritalis vero intelligentia ... vel de
Ecclesia ad Christum sub sponsae vel sponsi titulo *vel de
animae cum Verbo Dei coniunctione* dirigitur.' True, the
occasional application to the individual soul is not entirely
wanting in the *Homilies*; but the application is quite
secondary, while in the *Commentary* it assumes increasing
prominence. The theme of the holy marriage between
Christ and the soul is little more than alluded to in the
Homilies, but in the *Commentary* it is always present with
the representation of the nuptials of Christ and the Church
—in fact, it appears as its inseparable counterpart.

Possibly this is why Jerome chose to begin with a
translation of the *Homilies*, while intending to give a
version of the *Commentary* later, an intention which is
actually asserted for Jerome by Rufinus in the preface to
his translation of the *Peri archon*.[27] The *Homilies* were to
serve as an introduction, so to speak, to the reading of
the *Commentary* when it too appeared in Latin version.
He was thus giving the reader a foretaste of this nuptial
mysticism as fully developed in the greater work. Jerome
may well be reflecting this as his original purpose when
in the preface addressed to Pope Damasus he writes that
since he was not taking it upon himself to translate the
difficult *Commentary*, he is offering in the *Homilies* not
the 'meat' (*cibum*) of the larger work, but only a 'taste'
(*gustum*) of it. This is in excellent agreement with his
further statement, also cast in the figure of St. Paul (1 Cor.
3.1 f.), that Origen wrote these *Homilies* for 'little ones'
still in the 'nursing' stage of their faith. And here there is
also an unmistakable allusion to the Prologue of the
Commentary. There Origen states clearly that he has

written the same, not for such as are still children in the
faith and fed with the 'milk' of Christ's teaching—*qui
lacte in Christo aluntur, non cibo forti*, but for such as take
'strong meat': *In verbis enim Cantici Canticorum ille cibus
est, de quo dicit Apostolus, 'perfectorum autem est solidus cibus'*
(Heb. 15.12, 14—Prol., p. 22).

St. Jerome composed his translation of the *Homilies*
while he was at Rome in or about the year 383. As for the
character of his translation, he himself states in the Prologue to Pope Damasus that he rendered them *fideliter
magis quam ornate*. Certainly he is a very much more
accurate and faithful translator than Rufinus.

⁊   ⁊   ⁊

The present English translation of Origen's *Commentary*
and *Homilies* was made from the critical edition published
by W. Baehrens in Vol. 8 of Origen's Works—with the
series number 33—in the Berlin collection: *Die griechischen
christlichen Schriftsteller der ersten drei Jahrhunderte* (=GCS),
in Leipzig in 1925. The history of the manuscript tradition
of the Latin versions by Rufinus and Jerome and special
problems are discussed by the editor in his foreword.
Attention may be called to what Baehrens has to say about
the Greek fragments (XXVII f.): these in some instances
caused considerable difficulty to the translator, and some of
them obviously are not in good state; as Baehrens indicates,
he was prevented from editing these, particularly the Procopius fragments, definitively. I have not adopted for
translation the catena-fragment published by Ghislerius for
the reason that, as Baehrens himself (who prints it among
the 'Nachträge,' p. LIV) remarks (XXVIII), its place in the
Commentary is very doubtful.

An excellent French translation of the *Homilies*, with a

reprint of the Latin text by Baehrens, appeared recently as Vol. 37 of the series *Sources Chrétiennes*: Dom O. Rousseau, *Origène, Homélies sur le Cantique des Cantiques* (Paris 1954). To my knowledge, the *Commentary* itself has not been translated into a modern language before; though selections taken from here and there have been offered in English by Tollinton,[28] in French by Bardy,[29] in German by von Balthasar.[30]

PART ONE

THE COMMENTARY

FROM THE LATIN TRANSLATION BY RUFINUS

PROLOGUE

1. *The Song of Songs a Drama of Mystical Meaning*

It seems to me that this little book is an epithalamium,[1] that is to say, a marriage-song, which Solomon wrote in the form of a drama and sang under the figure of the Bride, about to wed and burning with heavenly love towards her Bridegroom, who is the Word[2] of God. And deeply indeed did she love Him, whether we take her as the soul made in His image, or as the Church. But this same Scripture also teaches us what words this august and perfect Bridegroom used in speaking to the soul, or to the Church, who has been joined to Him.[3] And in this same little book that bears the title *Song of Songs*, we recognize moreover things that the Bride's companions said, the maidens who go with her, and also some things spoken by the Bridegroom's friends and fellows. For the friends of the Bridegroom also, in their joy at His union with the Bride, have been enabled to say some things—at any rate those that they had heard from the Bridegroom Himself. In the same way we find the Bride speaking not to the Bridegroom only, but also to the maidens; likewise the Bridegroom's words are addressed not to the Bride alone, but also to His friends. And that is what we meant just now, when we said that the marriage-song was written in dramatic form. For we call a thing a drama, such as the enaction of a story on the stage, when different characters are introduced and the whole structure of the narrative consists in their comings and goings among themselves. And this work contains these things one by one in their own order, and also the whole body of it consists of mystical utterances.

But it behoves us primarily to understand that, just as in childhood we are not affected by the passion of love, so also to those who are at the stage of infancy and childhood in their interior life—to those, that is to say, who are being nourished with milk in Christ, not with strong meat, and are only beginning *to desire the rational milk without guile*[4]— it is not given to grasp the meaning of these sayings. For in the words of the Song of Songs there is that food, of which the Apostle says that *strong meat is for the perfect*; and that food calls for hearers *who by ability have their senses exercised to the discerning of good and evil*.[5] And indeed, if those whom we have called children were to come on these passages, it may be that they would derive neither profit nor much harm, either from reading the text itself, or from going through the necessary explanations. But if any man who lives only after the flesh should approach it, to such a one the reading of this Scripture will be the occasion of no small hazard and danger. For he, not knowing how to hear love's language in purity and with chaste ears, will twist the whole manner of his hearing of it away from the inner spiritual man and on to the outward and carnal; and he will be turned away from the spirit to the flesh, and will foster carnal desires in himself, and it will seem to be the Divine Scriptures that are thus urging and egging him on to fleshly lust![6]

For this reason, therefore, I advise and counsel everyone who is not yet rid of the vexations of flesh and blood and has not ceased to feel the passion of his bodily nature, to refrain completely from reading this little book and the things that will be said about it. For they say that with the Hebrews also care is taken to allow no one even to hold this book in his hands, who has not reached a full and ripe age. And there is another practice too that we have received from them—namely, that all the Scriptures should be delivered to boys by teachers and wise men, while at the same time the four that they call *deuterōseis*[7]—that is to say, the beginning of Genesis, in which the creation of the world is described; the first chapters of Ezechiel, which tell about the cherubim; the end of that same, which contains the building of the Temple; and this book of the Song of Songs—should be reserved for study till the last.

2. The Theme of the Song of Songs

Before we come to consider the things that are written in this book, therefore, it seems to me necessary to say a few things first about love itself, which is the main theme of this Scripture; then about the order of the books of Solomon, among which we find that this one is put third; then about the name of the book itself, why it is entitled *The Song of Songs*; and, lastly, for what apparent reason it is written in dramatic form and, like a story that is acted on the stage, with dialogue between the characters.

Among the Greeks, indeed, many of the sages,[8] desiring to pursue the search for truth in regard to the nature of love, produced a great variety of writings in this dialogue form, the object of which was to show that the power of love is none other than that which leads the soul from earth to the lofty heights of heaven, and that the highest beatitude can only be attained under the stimulus of love's desire. Moreover, the disputations on this subject are represented as taking place at meals, between persons whose banquet, I think, consists of words and not of meats. And others also have left us written accounts of certain arts, by which this love might be generated and augmented in the soul. But carnal men have perverted these arts to foster vicious longings and the secrets of sinful love.

You must not be surprised, therefore, if we call the discussion of the nature of love difficult and likely to be dangerous also for ourselves, among whom there are as many inexperienced folk as there are people of the simpler sort; seeing that even among the Greeks, who seem so wise and learned, there have none the less been some who did not understand what was said about love in the sense in which it was written, but took occasion from it to rush into carnal sins and down the steep places of immodesty, either by taking some suggestions and recommendations out of what had been written, as we said above, or else by using what the ancients wrote as a cloak for their own lack of self-control.

Lest, therefore, the like should happen to us, and we too should interpret in a vicious and carnal sense the things the ancients wrote with good and spiritual intent, let us stretch out our hands, alike of body and soul, to God; that the Lord, who *gave the word to them that preach good tidings with great power,*[9] may by His power bestow the word also on us; so that we, out of these things that have been written, may be able to make clear a wholesome meaning in regard to the name and the nature of love, and one that is apt for the building up of chastity.

In the beginning of the words of Moses, where the

creation of the world is described, we find reference to the making of two men, the first *in the image and likeness of God,* and the second *formed of the slime of the earth.* [10] Paul the Apostle knew this well; and, being possessed of a very clear understanding of the matter, he wrote in his letters more plainly and with greater lucidity that there are in fact two men in every single man. He says, for instance: *For if our outward man is corrupted, yet the inward man is renewed day by day;* and again: *For I am delighted with the law of God according to the inward man;* [11] and he makes some other statements of a similar kind. I think, therefore, that no one ought any longer to doubt what Moses wrote in the beginning of Genesis about the making and fashioning of two men, since he sees Paul, who understood what Moses wrote much better than we do, saying that there are two men in every one of us. Of these two men he tells us that the one, namely, the inner man, is renewed from day to day; but the other, that is, the outer, he declares to be corrupted and weakened in all the saints and in such as he was himself. If anything in regard to this matter still seems doubtful to anyone, it will be better explained in the appropriate places. But let us now follow up what we mentioned before about the inner and the outer man.

The* thing we want to demonstrate about these things

---

* J. A. Cramer, *Catenae Graecorum Patrum in Novum Testamentum* 8 (Oxford 1844) 115 f.: [12] There are certain instances in which the same name is given to things happening to the outer man and to the inner, instances which have analogy with each other. For example, with regard to age, the word 'child' is applied to the outer man, and the child gaining increase of stature grows into the 'youth,' until, being called a man, he becomes a 'father.' Now I use these names on account of what is written by John in the Catholic Epistle, having arranged these three names accordingly. But in a manner synonymous and analogous to the use of these three names as applied to the outer

is that the Divine Scriptures make use of homonyms; that is to say, they use identical terms for describing different things. And they even go so far as to call the members of the outer man by the same names as the parts and dispositions of the inner man; and not only are the same terms employed, but the things themselves are compared with one another. For instance, a person is a child in age according to the inner man, who has in him the power to grow and to be led onward to the age of youth, and thence by successive stages of development to come to the perfect man [13] and to be made a father. Our own intention, therefore, has been to use such terms as would be in harmony with the language of Sacred Scripture, and in particular with that which was written by John; for he says: *I have written to you, children, because you have known the Father; I have written to you, fathers, because you have known Him who was from the beginning; I have written unto you, young men, because you are strong, and the word of God abideth in you, and you have overcome the wicked one.* [14] It is perfectly clear; and I think nobody should doubt that John calls these people children or lads or young men or even fathers according to the soul's age, not the body's. Paul too says somewhere:

---

man, I would say that a person can similarly be a 'child' in his inner man, however old he might be; the use of the word 'child' as to the outer man is parallel. Even so someone can be a 'youth' according to *the hidden man of the heart* (1 Peter 3.47), and in the same way one can be a 'man' and a 'father' inwardly. John indeed speaks thus: *I write unto you, little children, because you know the Father; I have written unto you, fathers, because you know Him who is from the beginning; I write unto you, young men, because you are strong, and the word of God abideth in you, and you have overcome the wicked one* (1 John 2.12–14). It is clear, I think, and consistent with the actual fact, that he means that he is writing these things to those who are *spiritually* 'children' and 'young men' and 'fathers.' And Paul says somewhere: *I could not speak to you as unto spiritual, but as unto carnal; as unto little ones in Christ. I gave you milk to*

I could not speak unto you as unto spiritual, but as unto carnal, as unto little ones in Christ. I gave you milk to drink, not meat.[15] A little one in Christ is undoubtedly so called after the age of his soul, not after that of his flesh. And finally the same Paul says further: *When I was a child, I spoke as a child, I understood as a child, I thought as a child; but, when I became a man, I destroyed childish things.*[16] And again on another occasion he says: *Until we all meet . . . unto a perfect man, unto the measure of the age of the fullness of Christ:*[17] he knows that those who believe will *all meet unto a perfect man* and *unto the measure of the age of the fullness of Christ.*

So, then, just as these different ages that we have mentioned are denoted by the same words both for the outer man and for the inner, so also will you find the names of the members of the body transferred to those of the soul; or rather the faculties and powers of the soul are to be called its members. We read in Ecclesiastes, therefore: *The eyes of a wise man are in his head;*[18] and again in the Gospel: *He that hath ears to hear, let him hear;*[19] and in the prophets likewise: *The word of the Lord that was made in the hand of Jeremias the prophet,*[20] or whoever it happens to be. The passage that says: *Let not thy foot stumble,*[21] is another instance of the same; so also is: *But my feet were moved a little*

---

drink, not meat (1 Cor. 3.1 f.). Now the same name is used here for one who in his soul is a little one in Christ, as when the same Paul in another place says: *When I was a child, I spoke as a child, I understood as a child, I thought as a child.* Then, since he did not remain in childhood, he says: *But when I became a man, I put away the things of a child* (1 Cor. 13.11). Similarly I hear him say: *until we all meet . . . unto a perfect man, unto the measure of the age of the fullness of Christ,* for he knew that believers all *meet unto a perfect man* and to *measures* of mental *age* (Eph. 4.13). Now just as there are these synonymous and analogous expressions, applicable both to the inner man and the outer man, so you may find the names of the limbs of the body used metaphorically with reference to the soul.

less.[22] The womb of the soul also is plainly designated where we read: *Lord, from fear of Thee we have conceived in our womb.*[23] So likewise who is puzzled when it is said that *their throat is an open sepulchre,* and again: *Cast down, O Lord, and divide their tongues,* and also when it is written: *Thou hast broken the teeth of sinners,* and again: *Break Thou the arm of the sinner and of the malignant?*[24]

But what need is there for me to collect more examples of these things, when the Divine Scriptures are full of any number of evidences? It is perfectly clear that in these passages the names of the members can in no way be applied to the visible body, but must be referred to the parts and powers of the invisible soul. The members have the same names, yes; but the names plainly and without any ambiguity carry meanings proper to the inner, not the outer man. Moreover, this material man, who also is called the outer, has food and drink of like sort with himself— that is to say, corporeal and earthly; but in the same way the spiritual man, who also is called the inner, has for his proper food that *living Bread which came down from heaven,* and drinks of the water that Jesus promises, saying: *Whosoever shall drink of this water, which I will give to him, shall not thirst for ever.*[25]

The same terms, then, are used throughout for either man; but the essential character of the things is kept distinct, and corruptible things are offered to that which is corruptible, while incorruptible things are set before that which cannot be corrupted. It happens in consequence that certain people of the simpler sort, not knowing how to distinguish and differentiate between the things ascribed in the Divine Scriptures to the inner and outer man respectively, and being deceived by this identity of nomenclature, have applied themselves to certain absurd fables and silly tales. Thus they even believe that after the resurrection bodily food and drink will be used and taken—food, that is, not only from that True Vine who lives for ever,[26] but also from the vines and fruits of the trees about us.[27] But concerning these we shall see elsewhere.

Now then, as the foregoing remarks have shown, one person is childless and barren according to the inner man, while another has plenty of offspring. And we notice that the saying: *The barren hath borne seven, and she that hath many children is weakened,*[28] is in accord with this; as also is that which is said in the blessings: *There shall not be one among you that is childless or barren.*[29] This being so, it follows that, just as there is one love, known as carnal and also known as Cupid by the poets,[30] according to which the lover sows in the flesh; so also is there another, a spiritual love, by which the inner man who loves sows in the spirit.[31] And, to speak more plainly, if anyone still bears the image of the earthy according to the outer man, then he is moved by earthly desire and love; but the desire and love of him who bears the image of the heavenly according to the inner man are heavenly.[32] And the soul is moved by heavenly love and longing when, having clearly beheld the beauty and the fairness of the Word of God, it falls deeply in love with His loveliness and receives from the Word Himself a certain dart and wound of love. For this Word *is the image* and splendour *of the invisible God, the Firstborn of all creation, in whom were all things created that are in heaven and on earth, seen and unseen alike.*[33] If, then, a man can so extend his thinking as to ponder and consider the beauty and the grace of all the things that have been created in the Word, the very charm of them will so smite him, the grandeur of their brightness will so pierce him as with *a chosen dart*—as says the prophet[34]—that he will

suffer from the dart Himself a saving wound, and will be
kindled with the blessed fire of His love.

We must realize also that, just as an illicit and unlawful
love may happen to the outer man—as that, for instance,
he should love a harlot or adulteress instead of his bride or
his wife; so also may the inner man, that is to say, the soul,
come to attach its love not to its lawful Bridegroom, who
is the Word of God, but to some seducer or adulterer.
The prophet Ezechiel plainly states this fact under the
same figure, when he brings in Oolla and Ooliba to represent Samaria and Jerusalem corrupted by adulterous
love; the actual passage in the prophetic scripture declares
this plainly to those who desire a deeper understanding of
it.[35] And this spiritual love of the soul does flame out, as
we have taught, sometimes towards certain spirits of evil,
and sometimes towards the Holy Spirit and the Word of
God, who is called the faithful Spouse and Husband of the
instructed soul, and from whom indeed the Bride derives
her title, particularly in this piece of Scripture with which
we are now dealing; this, with the Lord's help, we shall
explain more fully when we come to expound the actual
words of the book.

It seems to me, however, that the Divine Scripture is
anxious to avoid the danger of the mention of love
becoming an occasion of falling for its readers; and, to
that end and for the sake of the weaker ones, it uses a more
respectable word for that which the wise men of the world
called desire or passion—namely, charity or affection.[36]
For instance, it says of Isaac: *and he took Rebecca and she
became his wife, and he loved* (dilexit) *her*; and again the
Scripture speaks in the same way about Jacob and Rachel:
*But Rachel had beautiful eyes and was fair of face, and Jacob
loved* (dilexit) *Rachel and said, 'I will serve thee seven years*

for Rachel thy younger daughter.' [37] And the unchanged force of this word appears even more plainly in connection with Amnon, who had a passion for (adamavit) his sister Thamar; for it is written: *And it came to pass after this that Absalom the son of David had a sister who was very fair of face, and her name was Thamar, and Amnon the son of David loved* (dilexit) *her.* The writer has put 'loved' here in place of 'had a passion for.' *And Amnon,* he says, *was so troubled that he fell sick because of Thamar his sister, for she was a virgin, and Amnon thought it a serious thing to do anything to her.* And a little later, with reference to the outrage that Amnon did to Thamar his sister, the Scripture says thus: *And Amnon would not listen to what she said, but overpowered her and humbled her and slept with her. And Amnon hated her with an exceeding great hatred, for the hatred with which he hated her was greater than the love* (dilectio) *with which he had loved* (dilexerat) *her.* [38]

In these places, therefore, and in many others you will find that Divine Scripture avoided the word 'passion' and put 'charity' or 'affection' instead. Occasionally, however, though rarely, it calls the passion of love by its own name, and invites and urges souls to it; as when it says in Proverbs about Wisdom: *Desire her greatly* (adama) *and she shall preserve thee; encompass her, and she shall exalt thee; honour her, that she may embrace thee.* [39] And in the book that is called the Wisdom of Solomon it is written of Wisdom herself: *I became a passionate lover* (amator) *of her beauty.* [40] I think that the word for passionate love was used only where there seemed to be no occasion of falling. For who could see anything sensuous or unseemly in the passion for Wisdom, or in a man's professing himself her passionate lover? Whereas had Isaac been spoken of as having a passion for Rebecca or Jacob for Rachel, some

unseemly passion on the part of the saints of God might
have been inferred from the words, especially by those
who do not know how to rise up from the letter to the
spirit. Most clearly, however, even in this our little book
of which we are now treating, the appellation of 'passionate love' has been changed into the word 'charity' in the
place where it says: *I have adjured you, O daughters of Jerusalem, if you find my Nephew, to tell Him that I have been
wounded by charity.*[41] For that is as much as to say: 'I have
been smitten through with the dart of His "passionate
love."'

It makes no difference, therefore, whether the Sacred
Scriptures speak of love, or of charity, or of affection;
except that the word 'charity' is so highly exalted that even
God Himself is called Charity, as John says: *Dearly beloved,
let us love one another, for charity is of God; and everyone that
loveth is born of God and knoweth God; but he that loveth not
knoweth not God, for God is Charity.*[42] And although some
other time might be more suitable in which to say something about these words that, by way of example, we have
cited from John's Epistle, it seems not unreasonable to
touch briefly on the matter in this context too. *Let us love
one another*, he says, *for charity is of God*; and a little later:
God is Charity. In saying this, he shows both that God Himself is Charity, and that He who is of God also is Charity.
For who is of God, save He who says: *I came forth from
God and am come into this world?*[43] If God the Father is
Charity, and the Son is Charity, the Charity, that Each
One is, is one; it follows, therefore, that the Father and
the Son are one and the same in every respect. Fittingly,
then, is Christ called Charity, just as He is called Wisdom
and Power and Justice and Word and Truth.[44] And that is
why the Scripture says that *if charity abideth in you, God*

abideth in you [45]—God, that is to say, the Father and the Son,
who also come to him who has been perfected in charity,
according to the saying of Our Lord and Saviour: *I and
my Father will come to him and will make our abode with him.* [46]

We must understand, therefore, that this Charity, which
God is, in whomsoever it exists loves nothing earthly,
nothing material, nothing corruptible; for it is against its
nature to love anything corruptible, seeing that it is itself
the fount of incorruption. For, because God, *who only hath
immortality and inhabiteth light inaccessible,* [47] is Charity, it is
charity alone that possesses immortality. And what is immortality, except the life eternal which God promises to
give to those who believe in Him, the only true God, and
in Jesus Christ, whom He has sent? [48] And for that reason
we are told that the thing which in the first place and
before all else is acceptable and pleasing to God, is that a
man should love the Lord his God with all his heart and
with all his soul and with all his powers. [49] And because
God is Charity, and the Son likewise, who is of God, is
Charity, He requires in us something like Himself; so that
through this charity which is in Christ Jesus, we may be
allied to God who is Charity, as it were in a sort of blood
relationship through this name of charity; even as he, who
was already united to Him, said: *Who shall separate us from
the charity of God which is in Christ Jesus our Lord?* [50]

This charity, however, reckons all men as neighbours.
For on that account the Saviour rebuked someone, who
thought that the obligation to behave neighbourly did not
apply to a righteous soul in regard to one who was sunk
in wickedness; and for that same reason He made up the
parable that tells how a certain man fell among robbers, as
he was going down from Jerusalem to Jericho, and blames
the priest and the Levite, who passed by when they saw

the man half-dead, but approves the Samaritan who showed mercy. And, by means of the reply of him who raised the question, He affirmed that the Samaritan was the neighbour of the man, and said: *Go, and do thou in like manner.*[51] By nature, indeed, we are all of us neighbours one of another; but by the works of charity a man who has it in his power to do service to another who has not that power, becomes his neighbour. Wherefore also our Saviour became neighbour to us, and when we were lying half-dead from the wounds the robbers had inflicted on us, He did not pass us by.

We must recognize, therefore, that the charity of God is always directed towards God, from whom also it takes its origin, and looks back towards the neighbour, with whom it is in kinship as being similarly created in incorruption. So you must take whatever Scripture says about charity as if it had been said with reference to passionate love, taking no notice of the difference of terms; for the same meaning is conveyed by both. But if anyone should remark that we speak of 'loving' money and harlots and such-like evils, using the same word as that which has obvious reference to charity, you must understand that in such contexts we speak of charity by an improper use,[52] and not according to its basic sense. To take another example, the word 'God' is used primarily of Him *of whom are all things, and by whom are all things, and in whom are all things;*[53] so that it declares plainly the virtue and nature of the Trinity. But by a secondary and so to speak improper usage Scripture describes as gods those to whom the word of God came, as the Saviour affirms in the Gospels.[54] And the heavenly powers also seem to be called by this name when it is said: *God hath stood in the congregation of gods; and, being in the midst of them, He judgeth gods.*[55]

And by a third usage, false rather than improper, the daemonic gods of the Gentiles are so styled when Scripture says: *All the gods of the Gentiles are devils.*[56]

Thus, then, the name of charity belongs first to God; and for that reason we are bidden to love God with all our heart and all our soul and all our strength—Him, that is, from whom we have the very power of loving. And this command undoubtedly implies that we should also love wisdom and right-doing and piety and truth and all the other virtues; for to love God and to love good things is one and the same thing. In the second place, we are bidden also to love our neighbour as ourselves by a use of the word that is, as it were, derived and secondary. And the third usage is that by which 'loving' money, or pleasure, or anything that is connected with corruption and error, is called charity by a misnomer. So it makes no difference whether we speak of having a passion for God, or of loving Him; and I do not think one could be blamed if one called God Passionate Love (*Amorem*), just as John calls Him Charity (*Caritatem*). Indeed I remember that one of the saints, by name Ignatius, said of Christ: 'My Love (*Amor*) is crucified,'[57] and I do not consider him worthy of censure on this account. All the same, you must understand that everyone who loves money or any of the things of corruptible substance that the world contains, is debasing the power of charity, which is of God, to earthly and perishable objects, and is misusing the things of God by making them serve purposes that are not His; for God gave the things to men to be used, not to be loved.

We have discussed these matters at some length because we wanted to distinguish more clearly and carefully between the nature of passionate love and that of charity;

lest perhaps, because Scripture says that God is Charity, the charity and love that is of God should be esteemed to be in our every attachment, even to corruptible things. And we have seen that though charity is truly the possession and the gift of God, His work is not always appropriated by men for the things of God and for what God wills.

At the same time we ought to understand also that it is impossible for human nature not to be always feeling the passion of love for something. Everyone who has reached the age that they call puberty loves something, either less rightly when he loves what he should not, or rightly and with profit when he loves what he should love. But some people pervert this faculty of passionate love, which is implanted in the human soul by the Creator's kindness. Either it becomes with them a passion for money and the pursuit of avaricious ends; or they go after glory and become desirous of vainglory; or they chase after harlots and are found the prisoners of wantonness and lewdness; or else they squander the strength of this great good on other things like these. Moreover, when this passion of love is directed on to diverse skills, whether manual crafts or occupations needful only for this present life—the art of wrestling, for example, and track running—or even when it is expended on the study of geometry or music or arithmetic or similar branches of learning, neither in that case does it seem to me to be used laudably. For if that which is good is also laudable—and by that which is good we understand not anything corporeal, but only that which is found first in God and in the powers of the soul—it follows that the only laudable love is that which is directed to God and to the powers of the soul.

And that this is the case is shown by Our Saviour's own

statement when, having been asked by a certain person what was the greatest commandment of all and the first in the Law, He replied: *Thou shalt love the Lord thy God with thy whole heart and with thy whole soul and with all thy powers; . . . and the second is like unto it: Thou shalt love thy neighbour as thyself;* and He added: *On these two commandments dependeth the whole Law and the Prophets*, showing thereby that true and perfect love consists in keeping these two, and that the entire Law and Prophets hang on them. And the other injunction: *Thou shalt not commit adultery, thou shalt not kill, thou shalt not steal, thou shalt not bear false witness*, and whatever other commandment there may be is summed up in the words: *Thou shalt love thy neighbour as thyself.*[58]

This will be better explained as follows. Suppose, for instance, that there is a woman with an ardent passion of love for a certain man who longs to be admitted to wedlock with him. Will she not act in all respects and regulate her every movement in a manner designed to please the man she loves, lest maybe, if she acts against his will in something, that excellent man may refuse and scorn her society? Will this woman, whose whole heart and soul and strength are on fire with passionate love for that man, be able to commit adultery, when she well knows that he loves purity? Or murder, when she knows him to be gentle, or theft, seeing she knows him to be pleased with generosity? Or will she covet other people's goods, when all her own desires are absorbed in passionate devotion for that man?

That is the sense in which every commandment is said to be comprised in the perfection of charity, and the strength of the Law and the Prophets to depend on it. Because of this good gift of charity or love, the saints are neither straitened in tribulation, nor utterly perplexed in doubt, nor do they perish when they are cast down; but *that which is at present momentary and light of their tribulation worketh for them above measure an eternal weight of glory.*[59] This present tribulation is not described as momentary and light for everyone, but only for Paul and those who resemble him in having *the* perfect *charity of God in Christ Jesus poured out in their hearts by the Holy Spirit.*[60]

In the same way also it was the love of Rachel that kept the patriarch Jacob from feeling the searing of either heat by day or cold by night through seven long years of toil.[61] So too do I hear Paul himself, enkindled by the power of this love, declare: *Charity beareth all things, believeth all things, hopeth all things, endureth all things; charity never falls.*[62] There is, therefore, nothing that he who loves perfectly would not endure; but there are many things that we do not endure, simply because we have not got the charity that *endureth all things.* And, if we are impatient under certain burdens, it is because we lack the charity that *beareth all things.* In the struggle that we have to wage with the devil, too, we often fall; undoubtedly because the charity that *never falls* is not in us.

The Scripture before us, therefore, speaks of this love with which the blessed soul is kindled and inflamed towards the Word of God; it sings by the Spirit the song of the marriage whereby the Church is joined and allied to Christ the heavenly Bridegroom, desiring to be united to Him through the Word, so that she may conceive by Him and be saved through this chaste begetting of children, when they—conceived as they are indeed of the seed of the Word of God, and born and brought forth by the spotless Church, or by the soul that seeks nothing bodily, nothing material, but is aflame with the single love of the Word of

God—shall have persevered in faith and holiness with sobriety. [63]

These are the considerations that have occurred to us thus far regarding the love or charity that is set forth in this marriage-hymn that is the Song of Songs. But we must realize how many things there are that ought to be said about this charity, what great things also about God, since He is Charity Himself. For, as *no one knoweth the Father but the Son, and he to whom it shall please the Son to reveal Him,* so also no one knows Charity except the Son. In the same way also, *no one knoweth the Son,* since He Himself likewise is Charity, *except the Father.* Further and in like manner, because He is called Charity, it is the Holy Spirit, who proceeds from the Father, who alone knows what is in God; just as the spirit of man knows what is in man. Wherefore this *Paraclete, the Spirit of Truth who proceedeth from the Father,* goes about trying to find souls worthy and able to receive the greatness of this charity, that is of God, that He desires to reveal to them. [64]

3. *The Place of the Song of Songs among the Works of Solomon*

Now, therefore, calling upon God the Father, who is Charity, through that same charity that is of Him, let us pass on to discuss the other matters. And let us first investigate the reason why, when the churches of God have adopted three books from Solomon's pen, the Book of Proverbs has been put first, that which is called Ecclesiastes second, while the Song of Songs is found in the third place. [65] The following are the suggestions that occur to us here.

The branches of learning by means of which men

generally attain to knowledge of things are the three which
the Greeks called Ethics, Physics and Enoptics; these we
may call respectively moral, natural, and inspective. Some
among the Greeks, of course, add a fourth branch, Logic,
which we may describe as rational.[66] Others have said
that Logic does not stand by itself, but is connected and
intertwined throughout with the three studies that we
mentioned first. For this Logic is, as we say, rational, in
that it deals with the meanings and proper significances
and their opposites, the classes and kinds of words and
expressions, and gives information as to the form of each
and every saying; and this branch of learning certainly
requires not so much to be separated from the others as to
be mingled and inwoven with them. That study is called
moral, on the other hand, which inculcates a seemly
manner of life and gives a grounding in habits that incline
to virtue. The study called natural is that in which the
nature of each single thing is considered; so that nothing
in life may be done which is contrary to nature, but
everything is assigned to the uses for which the Creator
brought it into being. The study called inspective is that by
which we go beyond things seen and contemplate somewhat of things divine and heavenly, beholding them with
the mind alone, for they are beyond the range of bodily
sight.

It seems to me, then, that all the sages of the Greeks
borrowed these ideas from Solomon, who had learnt them
by the Spirit of God at an age and time long before their
own; and that they then put them forward as their own
inventions and, by including them in the books of their
teachings, left them to be handed down also to those that
came after.[67] But, as we said, Solomon discovered and
taught these things by the wisdom that he received from

God, before anyone; as it is written: *And God gave under-standing to Solomon and wisdom exceeding much, and largeness of heart as the sand that is on the seashore. And wisdom was multiplied in him above all the sons of men that were of old, and above all the sages of Egypt.*[68] Wishing, therefore, to distinguish one from another those three branches of learning, which we called general just now—that is, the moral, the natural, and the inspective, and to differentiate between them, Solomon issued them in three books, arranged in their proper order. First, in Proverbs he taught the moral science, putting rules for living into the form of short and pithy maxims, as was fitting. Secondly, he covered the science known as natural in Ecclesiastes; in this, by discussing at length the things of nature, and by distinguishing the useless and vain from the profitable and essential, he counsels us to forsake vanity and cultivate things useful and upright. The inspective science likewise he has propounded in this little book that we have now in hand—that is, the Song of Songs. In this he instils into the soul the love of things divine and heavenly, using for his purpose the figure of the Bride and Bridegroom, and teaches us that communion with God must be attained by the paths of charity and love. But that in laying down these basic principles of true philosophy and establishing the order of the subjects to be learnt and taught, he was neither ignorant of the rational science nor refused to deal with it, he shows plainly right at the beginning of his Proverbs, primarily by the fact that he made *Proverbs* the title of his book; for the word pro-verb denotes that one thing is openly said, and another is inwardly meant.[69] The ordinary use of proverbs shows us this, and John in his Gospel writes of the Saviour saying: *These things have I spoken to you in proverbs; the hour cometh when I will no more speak to you in proverbs, but will show you plainly of the Father.*[70]

So much in passing for the actual title. But Solomon goes on forthwith to discriminate between the meanings of words:[71] he distinguishes knowledge from wisdom, and instruction from knowledge, and represents the understanding of words as something different again, and says that prudence consists in a person's ability to grasp the shades of meaning in words. He differentiates, moreover, between true justice and right judgement; but he mentions a certain perspicacity as being necessary for those whom he instructs—meaning, I believe, the astuteness of perception by which crooked and fallacious lines of thought may be seen for what they are, and shunned accordingly. And he says, therefore, that subtlety is given by wisdom to the innocent, doubtless lest they should be deceived in the Word of God by sophistic fraud. And in this also it seems to me that he has in mind the rational science, whereby the content of words and the meanings of expressions are discerned, and the proper significance of every utterance is reasonably defined. Children in particular are to be instructed in this science; he enjoins this when he says: *to give perception and the faculty of thought to the younger child.* And because he who is instructed in these matters inevitably rules himself reasonably, because of what he has learned, and preserves a better balance in his life, Solomon says further: *He who understandeth shall acquire government.*

But after all this, knowing that there are different modes of expression and sundry forms of speech in the divine words, whereby the order of living has been transmitted by the prophets to the human race, and realizing that among these there is one figure called a parable, another that is known as dark speech, others that have the name of riddles, and others again that are called the sayings of the wise, he writes: *Thou shalt also understand the parable, and dark speech, and the sayings of the wise, and riddles.* Thus, by these several means, he expounds the rational science clearly and plainly; and, following the custom of the ancients, he unfolds immense and perfect truths in short and pithy phrases. And, if there is anyone who meditates day and night on the law of the Lord, if there is anyone who is as the mouth of the just that meditates wisdom,[72] he will be able to investigate and discover these things more carefully; always provided that he have first sought and knocked at Wisdom's door, beseeching God to open to him and to make him worthy to receive the word of wisdom and the word of knowledge through the Holy Spirit, and to make him a partaker of that Wisdom who said: *I stretched out my words and ye did not hear.*[73]

And rightly does he speak of 'stretching out his words' in the heart of him to whom God had given largeness of heart, as we said above. For the heart of a man is enlarged, when he is able, by taking statements from the Divine Books, to expand by fuller teaching the things that are said briefly and in enigmatic ways. According to this same doctrine of the most wise Solomon, therefore, it behoves him who desires to know wisdom to begin with moral instruction, and to understand the meaning of the text: *Thou hast desired Wisdom: then keep the commandments, and God will give her to thee.*[74] This, then, was the reason why this master, who was the first to teach men divine philosophy, put at the beginning of his work the Book of Proverbs, in which, as we said, the moral science is propounded—so that when a person has progressed in discernment and behaviour he may pass on thence to train his natural intelligence and, by distinguishing the causes and natures of things, may recognize the vanity of vanities[75] that he must forsake, and the lasting and eternal things that he ought to pursue. And so from Proverbs he goes on to Ecclesiastes, who teaches, as we said, that all visible and corporeal things are fleeting and brittle; and surely once the seeker after wisdom has grasped that these things are so, he is bound to spurn and despise them; renouncing the world bag and baggage, if I may put it in that way, he will surely reach out for the things unseen and eternal which, with spiritual meaning verily but under certain secret metaphors of love, are taught in the Song of Songs.

This book comes last that a man may come to it when his manner of life has been purified, and he has learnt to know the difference between things corruptible and things incorruptible; so that nothing in the metaphors used to describe and represent the love of the Bride for her celestial Bridegroom—that is, of the perfect soul for the Word of God—may cause him to stumble. For, when the soul has completed these studies, by means of which it is cleansed in all its actions and habits and is led to discriminate between natural things, it is competent to proceed to dogmatic and mystical matters, and in this way advances to the contemplation of the Godhead with pure and spiritual love.

I think, moreover, that this threefold structure of divine philosophy was prefigured in those holy and blessed men on account of whose most holy way of life the Most High God willed to be called *the God of Abraham, the God of Isaac, and the God of Jacob.*[76] For Abraham sets forth moral philosophy through obedience; his obedience was indeed so great, his adherence to orders so strict that when he heard the command: *Go forth out of thy country, and from thy kindred, and out of thy father's house*, he did not delay, but did as he was told forthwith. And he did more even than that: even on hearing that he was to sacrifice his son, he does not hesitate, but complies with the command and, to give an example to those who should come after of the obedience in which moral philosophy consists, *he spared not his only son.*[77] Isaac also is an exponent of natural philosophy, when he digs wells and searches out the roots of things.[78] And Jacob practises the inspective science, in that he earned his name of Israel from his contemplation of the things of God, and saw the camps of heaven, and beheld the House of God and the angels' paths—the ladders reaching up from earth to heaven.[79]

We find, moreover, that for this reason those three blessed men made altars to God,[80] as it was fitting that they should—that is to say, they hallowed the results of their philosophy, no doubt that they might teach us that these fruits must be ascribed, not to our human skills, but to the grace of God. Further, they lived in tents[81] to show thereby that he who applies himself to divine philosophy must have nothing of his own on earth and must be always moving on, not so much from place to place as from knowledge of inferior matters to that of perfect ones.[82] And you will find that this order, which we have pointed out in regard to the books of Solomon, appears in just the same pattern in many other things in the Divine Scriptures too; but it would take too long for us to follow these up, with another matter on hand.

If, then, a man has completed his course in the first subject, as taught in Proverbs, by amending his behaviour and keeping the commandments, and thereafter, having seen how empty is the world and realized the brittleness of transitory things, has come to renounce the world and all that is therein, he will follow on from that point to contemplate and to desire *the things that are not seen*, and *that are eternal.*[83] To attain to these, however, we need God's mercy; so that, having beheld the beauty of the Word of God, we may be kindled with a saving love for Him, and He Himself may deign to love the soul, whose longing for Himself He has perceived.

4. *The Title 'Song of Songs'*

We must now pass on to our next point, and discuss the actual title of 'The Song of Songs.' You find a similar phrase in what were called *the holies of holies* in the Tent of the Testimony, and again in the *works of works* mentioned in the Book of Numbers, and in what Paul calls *the ages of ages.*[84] In other treatises we have, as far as we were able, considered the difference between *holies* and *holies of holies* in Exodus, and between *works* and *works of works* in the Book of Numbers;[85] neither did we pass over the expression *ages of ages* in the passages where it occurs.[86] Rather than repeat ourselves, therefore, we will let those comments suffice.

But we must now enquire for the first time what are the songs in relation to which this song is called 'The Song of Songs.' I think they are the songs that were sung of old by prophets or by angels. For the Law is said to have been *ordained by angels in the hand of a mediator.*[87] All those, then, that were uttered by them, were the introductory songs sung by the Bridegroom's friends; but this unique song is that which the Bridegroom Himself was to sing as His marriage-hymn, when about to take His Bride; in which same song the Bride no longer wants the Bridegroom's friends to sing to her, but longs to hear her Spouse who now is with her, speak with His own lips; wherefore she says: *Let Him kiss me with the kisses of His mouth.*[88]

Rightly, then, is this song preferred before all songs. The other songs that the Law and the prophets sang, were sung to the Bride while she was still a little child and had not yet attained maturity. But this song is sung to her, now that she is grown up, and very strong, and ready for a husband's power and the perfect mystery. It is said of her for this reason: *My perfect dove is but one.*[89]

As the perfect Bride of the perfect Husband, then, she has received the words of perfect doctrine. Moses and the children of Israel sang the first song to God, when *they saw the Egyptians dead on the seashore*, and when they saw *the strong hand* and the high arm *of the Lord, and believed in God and Moses His servant.* Then they sang, therefore, saying: *Let us sing to the Lord, for He is gloriously magnified.*[90] And I think myself that nobody can attain to that perfect and mystical song and to the perfection of the Bride which this Scripture contains, unless he first marches *through the midst of the sea upon dry land* and, with *the water becoming to him as a wall on the right hand and on the left*, so makes his escape *from the hands of the Egyptians* that he *beholds them dead on the seashore* and, seeing the strong hand with which the Lord has acted against the Egyptians, believes in the Lord and in His servant Moses.[91] In Moses, I say—in the Law, and in the Gospels, and in all the Divine Scriptures; for then he will have good cause to sing and say: *Let us sing unto the Lord, for He is gloriously magnified.*

A man will sing this song, however, only when he has first been freed from bondage to the Egyptians; but after that, when he has traversed all those things that are written in Exodus and in Leviticus, and has come to be admitted to the divine Numbers, then he will sing another, a second song, when he has emerged from the valley of Zared, which means Strange Descent, and has come to the well of which it is written: *And the Lord said to Moses: 'Gather the people together, and I will give them water to drink from the well.'* For there he will sing and say: *Consecrate the well to Him. The princes dug it, the kings of the Gentiles hewed it out in their kingdom, when they had the rule over them.*[92] But we have already treated more fully of these matters, as far as the Lord gave us, in treating of the Book of Numbers.[93] We must proceed, then, to the well which has been dug by princes and hewn out by kings, on which no common person labours, but all are princes, all are kings—royal and princely souls, that is to say, who search to its depths the well that holds the living water.[94]

After this song we come to that in Deuteronomy, of which the Lord says: *And now write you the words of this song and teach it to the children of Israel, and get them to know it by heart; that this song may be unto me for a testimony among the children of Israel.* And see how great a song and of what sort it is, for which it is not enough that it be sung on earth alone, but heaven too is called upon to listen to it! For it says: *Hear, O heaven, and I will speak: and let the earth give ear to the words of my mouth!* Observe what great and what momentous things are said. *Let my speech,* it says, *be looked for as the rain, and let it come down as the dew upon the grass and as falling snow on the hay; because I have invoked the Name of the Lord,* and so forth.[95]

The fourth song is in the Book of Judges. Of it Scripture says that *Debbora and Barac son of Abinoem sang it in that day, saying: 'Bless ye the Lord for that which the princes undertook, and that which the people purposed. Hear, O ye kings, give ear, ye governors,'* and so forth.[96] But he who sings these words must be himself a bee, whose work is such

that kings and commoners alike make use of it for purposes of health. For Debbora means bee, and it is she who
sings this song; but Barac sings it with her, and his name
means a flash.[97] And this song is sung after a victory,
because no one can sing of perfect things until he has
conquered his foes. That is why we sing in this same song:
*Arise, arise, O Debbora, rouse up the people in their thousands.
Arise, arise, sing a song; arise, O Barac.*[98] But you will find
further discussion of these questions too in the little
addresses that we published on the Book of Judges.[99]

Following these, the fifth song is in the Second Book of
Kings, when *David spoke to the Lord the words of this song,
in the day that the Lord delivered him out of the hand of all his
enemies, and out of the hand of Saul, and he said: ' The Lord
is to me as a rock and a defence and my deliverer; my God will
be my keeper.'*[100] If, then, you also have been able to reflect
as to who are these enemies whom David vanquishes and
overthrows in the First and Second Books of Kings, and
how he became worthy to receive the help of the Lord
and to be delivered from enemies like that, then you
yourself also will be able to sing this fifth song.

The sixth song is in the First Book of Paralipomenon,
when David has just appointed Asaph and his brethren to
sing the praises of the Lord; and the song begins like this:
*Praise ye the Lord and confess Him, and call upon Him by His
name; make known His will among the peoples. Sing ye to Him
and chant a hymn, relate all His wondrous doings that the Lord
hath done,* etc.[101] You must know, however, that the song
in the Second Book of Kings is very much like the seven-
teenth Psalm; and the first part of the song in the First
Book of Paralipomenon, as far as the place where it says:
And do no evil to my prophets, resembles Psalm 104, while
the latter part of it, after this passage, shows a likeness to

the opening verses of Psalm 95, where we read: *Sing to the Lord, all the earth,* down to the place where the psalmist says, *because He cometh to judge the earth.*

If, therefore, we are to finish our enumeration of the songs, it will be obvious that the book of the Song of Songs must be put in the seventh place. But, if anyone thinks that the song of Isaias [102] should be numbered with the others—though it does not seem very suitable that the song of Isaias should be put before the Song of Songs, seeing that Isaias wrote much later—if, notwithstanding, anyone is of opinion that the prophetic utterances are to be adjudged according to their content rather than their date, he will then add that song as well, and say that *this* song that Solomon sang is the Song of Songs not only in relation to those that were sung before it, but also in respect of those that followed it in time. Whereas if anyone opines further that we ought to add from the Book of Psalms whatever is there called a song, or a song of a psalm, [103] he will gather together a multitude of psalms that are older in time. For he will add to the others the fifteen Gradual Songs [104] and, by assessing the virtue of each song separately and collecting from them the grades of the soul's advance, and putting together the order and sequence of things with spiritual understanding, he will be able to show with what stately steps the Bride, as she makes her entrance, attains by way of all these to the nuptial chamber of the Bridegroom, passing *into the place of the wonderful tabernacle, even to the House of God with the voice of joy and praise, the noise of one feasting.* [105] So she comes, as we said, even to the Bridegroom's chamber, that she may hear and speak all these things that are contained in the Song of Songs.

Before we come to the actual text of the book, we may

make this further enquiry. Why is it that Solomon, who served the will of the Holy Spirit in these three books, is called *Solomon, son of David, who reigned in Israel* in Proverbs, while in the second book the name Solomon does not appear and he says merely: *The words of Ecclesiastes, the son of David, king of Israel in Jerusalem*, calling himself son of David and king of Israel as in the first book, but writing 'words' here in place of 'proverbs,' and calling himself Ecclesiastes, where formerly he gave his name Solomon? And whereas in the former he mentioned only the nation over which he reigned, here he mentions both the nation and the seat of government, Jerusalem. But in the Song of Songs he writes neither the name of the nation, nor the place where he reigns, nor even that he is the king at all, nor yet that he had David for his father; he only says *the Song of Songs that is Solomon's own*.[106] And although it is difficult for me both to be able to examine the differences in these books and arrive at any explanation of them, and also to expound them clearly and commit them to writing when they have been thus searched out, nevertheless, as far as our own intelligence and our readers' apprehension allow, we will try to unfold these matters briefly.

It is, I think, unquestionable that Solomon is in many respects a type of Christ, first in that he is called the Peaceable,[106a] and also because *the queen of the south . . . came from the ends of the earth to hear the wisdom of Solomon*.[107] Christ is thus called the Son of David, and reigns in Israel; He reigns also over those kings from whom He gets the title *King of kings*. Again, He *who, being in the form of God, . . . emptied Himself, taking the form of a servant*,[108] that He might gather the Church into one flock, is Himself the true Ecclesiast; for an ecclesiast takes his title from his function of assembling the ecclesia. And then again, who is so truly Solomon—that is, Peaceable, as Our Lord Jesus Christ, *who of God is made unto us wisdom and justice and peace*? [109] Therefore in the first book, Proverbs, where he grounds us in ethical teaching, Solomon is called king in Israel—not in Jerusalem, as yet; because, although we be called Israel by reason of faith, we have not yet got so far as to reach the heavenly Jerusalem. When, however, we have made further progress, and have attained to fellowship with *the Church of the firstborn that is in heaven* [110] and, having rid ourselves more thoroughly of our old natural concerns, have come to recognize the heavenly Jerusalem as our celestial Mother, then Christ becomes our Ecclesiast too, and is said to reign not in Israel only, but also in Jerusalem. And when the perfection of all things has been achieved and the Bride, who has been perfected—in other words, the whole rational creation—is united with Him, *because He hath made peace through His blood, not only as to the things that are on earth, but also as to the things that are in heaven*, then He is called Solomon only, *when He shall have delivered up the kingdom to God and the Father, when He shall have brought to nought all principality and power. For He must reign until He hath put all His enemies under His feet and death, the last enemy, is destroyed.* [111] Thus, when all things have been pacified and subjected to the Father, and God is all in all, then He will be called Solomon and nothing else— that is, the Peaceable, only.

Fittingly, therefore, and for the same reason as before, we find in this little book that was to be written about the love of the Bridegroom and the Bride, neither 'Son of David,' nor 'king,' nor any other term patent of a corporeal connotation; thus the Bride now perfected may say of Him with reason: *And if we have known Christ after the*

flesh for a while, but now we know Him so no longer.[112] Let
no one think that she loves anything belonging to the
body or pertaining to the flesh, and let no stain be thought
of in connection with her love. So the Song of Songs is
simply Solomon's; it belongs neither to the Son of David,
nor to Israel's king, and there is no suggestion of anything
carnal about it. And let it not surprise you, seeing that
Our Lord and Saviour is One and the Same, that we
should speak of Him first as a beginner, in Proverbs; then
as advancing, in Ecclesiastes; and lastly as more perfect in
the Song of Songs, when you see the same things written
in the Gospels where He is said, for us and among us, to
advance. *Jesus advanced*, it is written, *in age and wisdom with
God and men.*[113]

It is, I think, because of all these things that neither 'Son
of David' nor 'King of Israel' is written; and also for this
further reason that in the Song of Songs the Bride had
progressed to the point where there was something greater
than the kingdom of Jerusalem. For the Apostle says there
is a heavenly Jerusalem, and speaks of believers coming
thither; but the same Paul calls this Bridegroom, to whom
the Bride now hastens, *the High Priest*, and writes of Him
not as being in heaven, but as *passing into* and beyond all
the heavens; whither also His perfected Bride follows Him;
cleaving to Him and *joined to Him*, she has ascended
thither, for she has been made *one spirit* with Him.[114]

Hence too it seems to me that this was the reason why,
when He said to Peter, who could not follow Him at first:
Whither I go, ye cannot come now, He added: *but thou shalt
follow hereafter.*[115] And we gather from the Book of
Numbers that there may be something greater than Israel
too. For there the whole of Israel is numbered and
reckoned in twelve tribes, as under a fixed number; but

the tribe of Levi, being of greater eminence than the others, is accounted extra to this number and never thought of as being one of Israel's number; for the writer says: *This is the visit of inspection in which the children of Israel were reckoned according to their households; the whole visitation of them yielded a total of six hundred and three thousand, five hundred and fifty. And the Levites were not included in this number, as the Lord commanded Moses.*[116] You see how the Levites are set apart from the children of Israel, as being of greater eminence, and are not reckoned among their number.

Further, the priests are described as being more eminent than the Levites; for this same Scripture tells us that *the Lord spoke to Moses, saying: 'Bring the tribe of Levi and make them stand in the sight of Aaron the priest, to minister to him.'*[117] Do you see how here too he both speaks of the priests as superior to the Levites, and once more makes the Levites appear as more eminent than the children of Israel?[118]

We have thought fit to discuss these matters rather more carefully, because we wanted by their means to demonstrate the reason why, in the very titles of his books, Solomon differentiated as necessity required, and signified one thing in Proverbs, another in Ecclesiastes, and yet another in the Song of Songs, as the title in each case shows. And the fact that in the Song of Songs, where now perfection is shown forth, he describes himself neither as son of David, nor as king, enables us to say further that, since the servant has been made the lord, and the disciple as the master,[119] the servant obviously is such no longer: he has become as the lord. Neither does the disciple figure as a disciple when he has been made as the master; rather, the sometime disciple is in truth as the master now, and the sometime servant as the lord. This line of thought may be applied also to the case of the king and those over whom he reigns, *when the kingdom will be delivered up to God and the Father.*[119a]

But let us not overlook the further fact that some people write the title of this little book as *Songs* of Songs. That is, however, incorrect; it is called the Song of Songs in the singular, not in the plural.

Let these remarks on the actual heading or title of the book suffice for introduction. Now, with Our Lord's help, let us go on to consider the beginning of the work itself; yet—not to leave anything out—there is one other point about the title and heading of the book that seems to some people to require investigation. For *The Song of Songs, which is Solomon's own,* is taken by these persons as meaning *the* Song of the Songs of Solomon, as though he signalized this one song among his many songs. But how shall we accept an interpretation like this when, in the first place, the Church of God has not adopted any further songs of Solomon to be read; and, in the second place, the Hebrews, by whom God's utterances were transmitted to us, have in their canon no other than these three books of Solomon that we also have in ours?[120] Those who advance this view, however, urge in its support that in the Third Book of Kings we are told that Solomon's songs were many; they cite this to prove that this song is one of many. The passage in question runs: *And God gave to Solomon understanding and wisdom exceeding much and largeness of heart as the sand that is on the seashore. And Solomon became exceeding wise, surpassing the wisdom of all the ancients and of all the sages of Egypt, and surpassing Gethan the Zarite and Henan and Chalcat and Darala; and Solomon spoke three thousand parables, and his songs were five thousand.*[121] They would, therefore, reckon this Song, of which we are treating, as

of the number of these five thousand songs; but as to
when or where those songs were sung, the churches of
God have no experience, nor have they even any knowledge of them.

It would be toilsome and irrelevant to the matter in hand
for us to enquire how many books are mentioned in the
Divine Scriptures, of which nothing whatever has been
handed down for us to read. Nor do we find that the Jews
made use of lections of this kind; for either the Holy
Spirit saw fit to remove them from our midst, because they
contained some matters beyond human understanding; or
else—in the case of those scriptures that are called apocrypha—because many things were found in them that
were corrupt and contrary to the true faith, our pre-
decessors did not see fit for them to be given a place, or
admitted among those reckoned as authoritative.

It is beyond us to pass judgement on such matters. But
it is common knowledge that the apostles and evangelists
borrowed and put into the New Testament many things
that we read nowhere in the Scriptures that we account
canonical, but that are found none the less in the apocryphal writings, and are quite obviously taken from them.[122]
Not that the apocryphal writings are to be given a place
in this way: we must *not overpass the everlasting limits
which our fathers have set.*[123] But it may be that the apostles
and evangelists, being filled with the Holy Spirit, knew
what was to be taken out of those writings and what must
be rejected; whereas we, who have not such abundance of
the Spirit, cannot without danger presume so to select.

In regard to the text before us, therefore, we keep to the
statement which we explained above, especially as the
writer himself makes a clear distinction by saying: *The
Song of Songs that is Solomon's own.* For, if he had meant us

to understand that this is the Song of Solomon's Songs, he would surely have said: The Song of the Songs that are Solomon's, or A Song from among the Songs of Solomon. But now his saying *that is Solomon's* shows that this Song, which we have in hand and which he was about to sing, is Solomon's, and for that reason has the title that he gave to it.

Let us now proceed to the consideration of the things that follow.

BOOK ONE

(On Cant. 1.2–4—Vg. 1.1–3)

I

'Let Him kiss me with the kisses of His mouth.' (1.2a—Vg. 1.3a)

LET HIM KISS ME WITH THE KISSES OF HIS MOUTH. It behoves us to remember the fact to which we drew attention in our introduction—namely, that this little book which has the semblance of a marriage-song is written in dramatic form. And we defined a drama as something in which certain characters are introduced who speak; and from time to time some of them arrive upon the scene, while others go or come, so that the whole action consists in interchange between the characters. This book, therefore, will be like that all through; and, reading it along those lines, we shall get from it according to our powers a simple record of events. And the spiritual interpretation too is equally in line with that which we pointed out in our prologue; the appellations of Bride and Bridegroom denote either the Church in her relation to Christ, or the soul in her union with the Word of God.[1]

Reading it as a simple story, then, we see a bride appearing on the stage, having received for her betrothal and by way of dowry most fitting gifts from a most noble bridegroom; but, because the bridegroom delays his coming for so long, she, grieved with longing for his love, is pining at home and doing all she can to bring herself at last to see her spouse, and to enjoy his kisses. We understand further that the bride, seeing that she can neither be quit of her love, nor yet achieve what she desires, betakes herself to prayer and makes supplication to God, whom she knows to be her Bridegroom's Father. After this manner, then, let us consider her, *lifting up holy hands without anger or contention, . . . in decent apparel with modesty and sobriety,*[2] adorned with the worthiest of ornaments, such as befit a noble bride, and aflame with longing for her Spouse, vexed by the inward wound of love, pouring out her prayer to God, as we have said, and saying concerning her Spouse: 'Let Him kiss me with the kisses of His mouth.'

This is the content of the actual story, presented in dramatic form. But let us see if the inner meaning also can be fittingly supplied along these lines. Let it be the Church who longs for union with Christ; but the Church, you must observe, is the whole assembly of the saints.[3] So it must be the Church as a corporate personality who speaks and says: 'I am sated with the gifts which I received as betrothal presents or as dowry before my marriage. For of old, while I was being prepared for my wedding with the King's Son and the Firstborn of all creation,[4] His holy angels put themselves at my service and ministered to me, bringing me the Law as a betrothal gift; for *the Law*, it is said, *was ordained by angels in the hand of a mediator.*[5] The prophets also ministered to me. For they it was who uttered all the things that were to tell me and to show me about the Son of God, to whom they were desiring to betroth me, when all these so-called betrothal gifts and dowry presents should have been taken away. Moreover, in order to enkindle me with love and longing for Him, they with prophetic voice proclaimed to me about His coming; filled with the Holy Spirit, they foretold His countless acts of power and His mighty works. His beauty also they described, His charm and gentleness, that I might be inflamed beyond all bearing with the love of Him by all these things. But, since the age is almost ended and His own presence is not granted me, and I see only His ministers ascending and descending upon me, because of this I pour out my petition to Thee, the Father of my Spouse, beseeching Thee to have compassion at last upon my love, and to send Him, that* He may now no longer speak to me only by His servants the angels and the prophets, but may come Himself, directly, and kiss me with the kisses of His mouth—that is to say, may pour the words of His mouth into mine, that I may hear Him speak Himself, and see Him teaching. The kisses are Christ's, which He bestowed on His Church when at His coming, being present in the flesh, He in His own person spoke to her the words of faith and love and peace, according to the promise of Isaias who, when sent beforehand to the Bride, had said: *Not a messenger, nor an angel, but the Lord Himself shall save us.*[6]

As the third point in our exposition, let us bring in the soul whose only desire is to be united to the Word of God and to be in fellowship with Him, and to enter into the mysteries of His wisdom and knowledge as into the chambers of her heavenly Bridegroom; which soul has

---

* Procopius, *Comm. in Cant. Cant.* 1.2 (MG 17.253 A): 'Let Him not court me through His prophets,' she says, 'but hold converse with me Himself, in the spiritual sense.' It is in this sense that John says: *Our hands have handled of the Word of life* (1 John 1.1). Thus she speaks as though she had heard the prophet say: *The king has greatly desired thy beauty* (Ps. 44.12); and elsewhere: *As the bridegroom shall rejoice over the bride* (Isa. 62.5).

already received His gifts—that is to say, her dowry. For, just as the Church's dowry was the volumes of the Law and the Prophets, so let us regard natural law and reason and free will as the soul's betrothal gifts. And let the teaching, which comes down to her from her masters and teachers, following on these gifts of her natural endowment, be to her for her earliest instruction. But, since she does not find in these the full and perfect satisfaction of her desire and love, let her pray that her pure and virginal mind may be enlightened by the illumination and the visitation of the Word of God Himself. For, when her mind is filled with divine perception and understanding without the agency of human or angelic ministration, then she may believe she has received the kisses of the Word of God Himself.

For this reason, then, and for the sake of these kisses, let the soul say in her prayer to God: 'Let Him kiss me with the kisses of His mouth.' For as long as she was incapable of receiving the solid and unadulterated doctrine of the Word of God Himself, of necessity she received 'kisses,' that is, interpretations, from the mouth of teachers. But, when she has begun to discern for herself what was obscure, to unravel what was tangled, to unfold what was involved, to interpret parables and riddles and the sayings of the wise along the lines of her own expert thinking, then let her believe that she has now received the kisses of the Spouse Himself, that is, the Word of God.[7]

Moreover, the plural, 'kisses,' is used in order that we may understand that the lighting up of every obscure meaning is a kiss of the Word of God bestowed on the perfected soul. And it was perhaps with reference to this that the prophetic and perfected soul declared: *I opened my mouth and drew breath.*[8]

And let us understand that by the 'mouth' of the Bridegroom is meant the power by which He enlightens the mind and, as by some word of love addressed to her—if so she deserve to experience the presence of power so great—makes plain whatever is unknown and dark to her. And this is the truer, closer, holier kiss, which is said to be granted by the Bridegroom-Word of God to the Bride— that is to say, to the pure and perfect soul; it is of this happening that the kiss, which we give one to another in church at the holy mysteries,[9] is a figure.

As* often, therefore, as we find some problem pertaining to the divine teachings and meanings revealed in our heart without instructors' help, so often may we believe that kisses have been given to us by the Bridegroom-Word of God. But, when we seek the meaning of something of this sort and cannot find it, then let us make this prayer our own and beg from God the visitation of His Word, saying: 'Let Him kiss me with the kisses of His mouth.' For the Father knows each single soul's capacity and understands the right time for a soul to receive the kisses of the Word in lights and insights of this sort.

2

'*For Thy breasts are better than wine.*' (1.2b—Vg. 1.1b)

FOR THY BREASTS ARE BETTER THAN WINE, AND THE FRAGRANCE OF THINE OINTMENTS IS ABOVE ALL SPICES. Taking the story that is being acted first, you must under-

---

* Procopius, *Comm. in Cant. Cant.* 1.2 (MG 17.253 A): Whensoever we inquire into something and we receive divine instruction, let us reckon that we have been kissed by the Bridegroom's mouth; whenever we are at a loss, let us betake ourselves to prayer and say: 'Let Him kiss me with the kisses of His mouth!'

stand that the Bride has poured out her petition with hands uplifted to God the Father, and has prayed that the Bridegroom might come to her now and bestow on her the kisses of His own mouth. While she is thus praying to the Father, she is ready to add to this very prayer in which she said: 'Let Him kiss me with the kisses of His mouth,' some further words of prayer, and to say that, even as she began to utter those words, the Bridegroom was present and standing by her as she prayed, and that He revealed His breasts to her, and appeared as Himself anointed with splendid ointments, possessed of fragrance such as befits a Spouse. The Bride, having seen that He, for whose coming she was praying, was already present, and that even as she spoke He offered her the thing for which she asked, and that the kisses that she had demanded had been given her, is rendered thereby glad indeed; and, moved deeply by the beauty of His breasts and by the fragrant odour of Himself, she alters the form of her prayer from that which she intended, in order to adapt it to the fact of her Spouse's presence. Whereas she had said before: 'Let Him kiss me with the kisses of His mouth,' she now continues, speaking to the Bridegroom's present Self: 'Thy breasts are better than wine, and the fragrance of Thine ointments is above all spices.'

So much in passing for the literal meaning which, as we said before, is woven in form of a play.

And now let us enquire what the inner meaning holds. We find the ground principle of the heart [10] described in the Divine Scriptures by different words according to the cases and circumstances that are being discussed. Sometimes it is simply called 'the heart,' as, for example: *Blessed are the clean of heart*, and: *With the heart we believe unto justice*. [11] But if the occasion be that of a meal, and the appearance and order of those reclining at table are being described, it is called the 'bosom' or 'breast'; as, for instance, where John speaks in the Gospel about the *certain disciple whom Jesus loved,* that he reclined *in His bosom* or *on His breast*; he indeed to whom Simon Peter *beckoned and said: 'Ask who it is of whom He speaks.'* And after that, *leaning on Jesus' breast he saith to Him, 'Lord, who is it?'* [12] We are undoubtedly given to understand that John on this occasion reposed on the ground of Jesus' heart and amid the inward meanings [13] of His teaching, there seeking and searching *the treasures of wisdom and knowledge that are hid* in Christ Jesus. [14] And indeed I think the term 'the bosom of Christ' is not unfitting, if it be taken as denoting the place of holy teachings.

The ground of the heart [15] is, then, as we had begun to say, denoted in the Holy Scripture by a variety of terms. There is a further instance in Leviticus, where *the little breast of separation* and *the shoulder* are set aside for the priests out of the sacrifices; for here too the intention in thus passing over other men is that the little breast that is set apart, and the shoulder, should be the ground of the heart and the glory of works among the priests. We have explained this more fully in dealing with the Book of Leviticus, as far as the Lord deigned to give us power so to do. [16]

On the analogy of the foregoing, therefore, let us understand the ground of the heart as being denoted by the breasts in the passage before us, since it is evidently a drama of love; the words spoken will then mean: 'Thy heart, O Bridegroom, and Thy mind—that is, the teachings that are within Thee, or the grace of teaching—surpass all the wine that is wont to gladden a man's heart.' [17] For just as it seems fitting to speak of their 'heart' with regard to those of whom the Lord says that *they shall see God*,[18] while with reference to those reclining at table 'bosom' or 'breast' is used, doubtless because of the behaviour of those persons and the nature of the meal, and again in respect of the priests the words 'little breast' and 'shoulder' are used with mystical meaning: so in this present passage, where the behaviour and conversation of lovers is described, I think that this same seat of the heart is very happily called 'breasts.'

The Bridegroom's breasts are good, therefore, because treasures of wisdom and knowledge are concealed in them. The Bride, moreover, compares these breasts to wine, and that in such a way as to point the breasts' superiority. By wine is meant the ordinances and teachings which the Bride had been wont to receive through the Law and Prophets before the Bridegroom came. But when she now reflects upon the teaching that flows forth from the Bridegroom's breasts, she is amazed and marvels: she sees that it is far superior to that with which she had been gladdened as with spiritual wine served to her by the holy fathers and prophets, before the Bridegroom came; for they also had planted vineyards of this sort and cultivated them—Noe, for example, first, and Isaias *on a hill, in a fruitful place*.[19] So, realizing now that the instructions and the knowledge that are to be found in the Bridegroom are of high eminence, and that a much more perfect teaching than that of the ancients issues from His breasts, she says: 'Thy breasts are better than wine'—better, that is to say, than the teaching with which she was gladdened by them that were of old.

For we must understand Ecclesiastes as referring to this wine of the ancients when he says: *I said in my heart, 'Come, and I will stir thee with gladness, and look thou on that which is good.'* And the same Ecclesiastes says in another place concerning the same vineyards: *I enlarged my work: I built me houses, I planted me vineyards; I made myself gardens and orchards,* and so forth. And there are certain ministers of this mystical wine who are called wine-pourers; for again the same person says: *I made me singing men and singing women and, in the gladness of the sons of men, men that pour out the wine, and women too.*[20]

Let us then see if in this matter, as in others, we can perceive the Saviour mingling the new things that flow from His own breasts with the wine of the ancients, on the occasion when Mary and Joseph searching *found Him in the Temple, sitting in the midst of the doctors,* both *hearing them and asking them questions, and all . . . were astonished at His answers.*[21] But perhaps the glory of this figure is fulfilled in the place where, *going up into a mountain, He taught the people and said: 'It was said to them of old, " Thou shalt not kill. . . ." But I say to you, whosoever is angry with his brother without reason shall be held guilty'*; and, *'It was said to them of old, " Thou shalt not commit adultery." But I say to you, whosoever shall look on a woman to lust after her has already committed adultery with her in his heart.'*[22]

In so far, therefore, as this teaching of His surpasses that which was given of old, thus far also does the Bride perceive and declare that 'His breasts are better than wine.' But the fact that *the Son of Man came eating and drinking, and they say, 'Behold a man that is a glutton and a wine-drinker,'*[23] is no less relevant to this. And it was the same, I think, with that wine that was drunk at Cana at the wedding feast; for when that ran short, He Himself made another wine of which the chief steward testified that it was very good and far superior to that which had been used up, when he said: *'Every man at first setteth forth good wine; and, when men have well drunk, then that which is worse. But thou hast kept the good wine until now.'* [24]

And there is also the case of Solomon, who for the wisdom that he had received of God earned the admiration of the queen of Sheba. She had come to try him with questions. Listen to what Scripture says about the things at which that same queen marvelled in regard to him. *And the queen of Sheba*, it says, . . . *saw all the wisdom of Solomon, and the house which he had built, and the magnificence of his entertainment, and the apartments of his servants, and the order of his ministers, and his raiment, and his wine-pourers, and his burnt offerings that he offered in the House of the Lord; and she was dumbfounded*, and so forth. [25] Now mark here how she, who *came from the ends of the earth to hear the wisdom of Solomon*, [26] among other things wonders at *the meats of his table* and *his wine-pourers*, and is said to have been dumbfounded at them. I doubt if we may think that the queen, who had come from the ends of the earth with the intention of hearing Solomon's wisdom, was so lacking in sense as to marvel at bodily meats and that ordinary wine and the cup-bearers in the king's employment. For what was there in those things, which almost all men have, that the queen should consider worthy of admiration? It seems to me that she marvelled rather at the meats of his teaching and the wine of the judgements which were uttered by him through the divine wisdom.

The same thing surely appears in the story that Jeremias tells about the sons of Jonadab, the son of Rechab, who, on being summoned to drink wine at the time when the sins of the people were prevailing and the captivity was threatening because of the national iniquity, said that their father Jonadab had commanded them not to drink wine, neither they nor their children for ever, and not to build

houses either, nor to sow seed, not to plant vineyards, but
to live in tents all the days of their life. And the Lord looks
on them with favour because they kept their father's
commandment and refused to drink wine.[27] For because
of the people's sins and iniquities *their vine was of the vine
of Sodom and their vine-shoots of Gomorrha; their grapes were
grapes of gall and their cluster bitter; their wine was the poison
of asps and the frenzy of dragons.*[28]

The sons of Jonadab, then, are accounted worthy of
praise because they refused to drink and take such wine—
that is to say, teachings poisonous and alien to the faith of
God. And perhaps the reason why God destroyed the vineyards of the Egyptians was, as it is written in the Psalm,
in order that they might not produce that kind of wine.[29]

If,[*] therefore, we have understood the different sorts of
wine and have perceived that they correspond to the
diversity of teachings, we must take what the Bride says
here, 'Thy breasts are better than wine,' as referring to
good wine, not to bad. For the Bridegroom's teachings
are preferred in comparison not with bad ones, but with
good. She had tasted good wine before, in the Law and
the Prophets, in that by musing upon them the Bride had
prepared herself, as it were, to receive gladness of heart,
and had made herself ready and able to receive also that

---

[*] Procopius, *Comm. in Cant. Cant.* I.I (MG 87.2.1548 D.—Procopius assigns the extract to Apollinaris, not to Origen): There being
many sorts of wine in the Scriptures, some better, some worse, here
the 'breasts' of the Bridegroom are compared with the better (they
would not be compared with the worse). The Bride, therefore, while
rejoicing in these many diverse wines and having in them a means of
preparation for receiving the 'breasts' of the Bridegroom which are
better than these former wines, says these words to show how she
values these latter more highly than the 'wine' in the Law and the
Prophets.

more excellent and all-surpassing doctrine that was to come to her hereafter through the breasts of the Bridegroom Himself. That, therefore, is why she says: 'Thy breasts are better than wine.'

See now if we can fit into this pattern that Gospel parable which says: *The Kingdom of Heaven is like unto a treasure hidden in a field. Which a man having found, hid it, and for joy thereof goeth and selleth all that he hath, and buyeth that field.*[30] This, treasure, then, is hidden, not in some desert place, nor in the woods, but in a field. And it is certainly possible that the field has in it vineyards to produce wine, that it has the treasure for the sake of which the finder spent all that he possessed and bought that field. He, then, who bought that field, can say that the treasure which is in the field is better than the wine which is in it. And in the same way also the Bridegroom is good, and the breasts of the Bridegroom, who is hidden like a treasure in the Law and the Prophets, are better than the wine that those contain—that is to say, the teaching in them that is open and rejoices all who hear. The breasts of the Bridegroom, therefore, are good, because treasures of wisdom and knowledge are hidden in Him; and these, when they have been opened and revealed to the eyes of the Bride, will seem to her much more excellent than was that wine of the Law and the teaching of the Prophets, which she had before.

But if we ought to understand these things according to a third interpretation,[31] with reference to the perfect soul and the Word of God, then we may say in this connection that as long as a person is a child and has not yet offered himself wholly to God, he drinks the wine which that field produces, which holds within itself the hidden treasure too; and he is gladdened by the wine he drinks. But, when he has offered and vowed himself to God and has been made a Nazirite,[32] and has found the hidden treasure and come to the very breasts and fountains of the Word of God, then he will no longer drink wine or spirit,[33] but with reference to these treasures of wisdom and knowledge that are hidden in the Word of God, he will say to Him: 'Thy breasts are better than wine.'[34]

3

' *The fragrance of Thine ointments is above all spices.*' (1.3a— Vg. 1.2a)

The Bridegroom has, however, certain ointments also, and with their fragrance the Bride has been delighted; so she says: THE FRAGRANCE OF THINE OINTMENTS IS ABOVE ALL SPICES. Spices are a species of medicament. The* Bride had the use and the knowledge of spices—that is, of the words of the Law and the Prophets, by which, though only to a moderate extent, she was instructed and practised in the service of God before the Bridegroom came, she being then as yet a little child and under tutors, governors, and pedagogues; for, says the Scripture, *the Law was our pedagogue to Christ.*[35] All these things, then, were the spices with which, as we have seen, she was nourished and made ready for her Spouse. *But when the fullness of the time was come,* and the Bride was grown up, and the Father had *sent His Only-begotten Son into this world, anointed with the Holy Spirit,*[36] then, having perceived the fragrance of the

---

* Procopius, *Comm. in Cant. Cant.* 1.2 f. (MG 87.2.1549 A): Notice how she uses the word 'perfume' with reference to our evangelical citizenship; but, when referring to the bondage of the Law, she uses the word 'spices,' showing the excellent and spiritual nature of the former, but the grossness of the latter.

divine ointment and realizing that all the spices she employed before are vastly inferior when set beside the sweetness of this new and heavenly ointment, she says: 'The fragrance of Thine ointments is above all spices.'

And since the same Christ is called Priest as well as Bridegroom—Priest indeed, because He is the *Mediator of God and men* and all creation, on whose behalf, moreover, He was made *the propitiation*, in that *He offered Himself as a sacrifice* for the sin of the world; but Bridegroom because He is united to the *Church not having spot, or wrinkle, or any such thing*[37]—because of this, you must consider whether perhaps the priestly ointment, that is commanded in Exodus[38] to be compounded by the perfumer's art, may not contain the meaning of this ointment, of which the Bride perceives the fragrance here, and at which she marvels; and you must consider whether it is not because those spices, that made up the ointment with which Aaron is said to have been anointed, were earthly and of material substance, whereas this ointment, with which the Bride beheld her Spouse anointed, is spiritual and heavenly, that she says: 'The fragrance of Thine ointments is above all spices.'

Let us see, then, how that ointment was made up. *And the Lord*, the Scripture says, *spoke to Moses, saying: 'Take thee five hundred shekels weight of flower of chosen myrrh, and two hundred and fifty shekels of sweet cinnamon, and two hundred and fifty shekels of sweet reed, and five hundred shekels of cassia, according to the holy shekel, and a hin of olive oil; and thou shalt make of that oil by the perfumer's art the ointment for the holy unction.'*[39]

The Bride had of course heard these things mentioned in the Law; but now she grasps their meaning and their truth. For she sees that those four ingredients of that ointment symbolized the Incarnation of the Word of God,

who assumed a body compacted out of the four elements; [40] in which body *myrrh* signifies the death He underwent, alike as Priest for the people and as Bridegroom for
the Bride. But the fact that what was written was not
simply 'myrrh,' but 'flower of myrrh,' and 'chosen
myrrh' too, foreshadowed not His death alone, but also
that He was to be *the Firstborn from the dead*, and that those
who had been *planted together in the likeness of His death*
should be not only called, but chosen too.[41] The spotless
cinnamon is doubtless mentioned on account of the Church,
which *He cleansed by the laver of water* and made to be
without spot or wrinkle or any such thing.[42] *Reed* is taken too
because *His tongue is as the reed of a scrivener that writeth
swiftly*; and the smoothness of the pigment denotes the
graciousness of His teaching.[43] And the kind of *cassia*
employed is one that is very hot and burning, so we are
informed; and that either denotes the fervour of the Holy
Spirit, or else is a type of the judgement by fire that is yet
to come.[44]

And the number *five hundred*, or *two hundred and fifty*,
either contains the mystery of the five senses perfected a
hundredfold in Him; or else, as being the pardonable
number fifty multiplied five times, it signifies the remission
of sins that is bestowed through Him.[45]

But all these things are blended together with pure *oil*;
and that shows us either that the cause of the only mercy
was that He, *being in the form of God, took the form of a
servant*;[46] or else that the things of a material nature, which
had been assumed in Christ, were through the Holy Spirit
reduced to one, and made to be all of a single kind, namely
the Person of the Mediator. That material oil, therefore,
could not possibly be called the oil of gladness. But this
oil—that is to say, the ointment of the Holy Spirit with

which Christ was anointed, and at the fragrance of which the Bride, when she perceives it, marvels, this oil is fitly called the oil of gladness; because joy is a fruit of the Spirit, and with it God anointed Him who *loved justice and hated iniquity*. For *therefore*, Scripture says, *hath the Lord His God anointed Him with the oil of gladness above His fellows*.[47] And for this reason the fragrance of His ointments is above all spices.

We shall make use of a like interpretation whenever we transfer these words to every individual soul that is fixed in the love of the Word of God and in desire for Him; a soul that will have traversed in order all the sorts of instruction in which she was exercised and taught before she attained to the knowledge of the Word of God, whether those teachings be based on ethics or on natural philosophy.[48] For all those things were so many spices for that soul, in that by their means an agreeable disposition and improvement of behaviour are acquired, and because in them the vanity of the world is discovered and the deceitful marvels of perishable things are rejected.

All these things were, then, as spices and perfumes, cosmetics as it were of the soul. But when she has come to knowledge of the mysteries and the divine judgements, when she has reached the gates of wisdom itself, of *the wisdom that is not of this world, neither of the princes of this world who come to nought*, but is the very wisdom of God which is discoursed upon among the perfect, and when the mystery that was not made known to former generations has been revealed to the sons of men [49]—when, I say, the soul ascends to recognition of this so great secret, she has cause to say: 'The fragrance of Thine ointments'—that is, the spiritual and mystical meaning—'is above all spices' of moral and natural philosophy.

We must not, however, overlook the fact that in certain versions we find written FOR THY SAYINGS ARE BETTER THAN WINE, where we read 'For Thy breasts are better than wine.' But although it may seem that this gives a plainer meaning in regard to the things about which we have discoursed in the spiritual interpretation, we ourselves keep to what the Seventy interpreters wrote in every case. For we are certain that the Holy Spirit willed that the figures of the mysteries should be roofed over in the Divine Scriptures, and should not be displayed publicly, and in the open air.[50]

4

'*Thy name is as ointment emptied out. Therefore have the maidens loved Thee, have they drawn Thee. We will run after Thee into the fragrance of Thine ointments.*' (1.3b and 4ab—Vg. 1.2b and 3ab)

THY NAME IS AS OINTMENT EMPTIED OUT. THEREFORE HAVE THE MAIDENS LOVED THEE, HAVE THEY DRAWN THEE. WE WILL RUN AFTER THEE INTO THE FRAGRANCE OF THINE OINTMENTS. The literal interpretation, which we followed in treating the foregoing passages, holds good also for that which is before us now, until some change occurs between the characters; the dramatic sequence, which we accepted in this interpretation, in fact requires this. We* may well see in these words a certain prophecy, uttered by the Bride herself concerning Christ, to the effect that at

---

* Procopius, *Comm. in Cant. Cant.* 1.2 (MG 17.253 B): Straightway he prophesies the power of the Name of Christ filling the whole world at His coming, becoming, as Paul says, *to the one indeed the odour of death unto death, but to the others the odour of life unto life* (2 Cor. 2.16). For if it had been *unto life* for all men, the Bride would have said,

Our Lord and Saviour's coming it should come to pass that His name should be so spread abroad throughout the globe and over the whole world, as to make it an odour of sweetness in every place; as the Apostle also says: *We are the good odour of Christ in every place; to the one indeed the odour of death unto death, but to the others the odour of life unto life.*[51]

For, had it been the odour of life unto life for all men, we should surely have read in this place too: 'They have all loved Thee and have drawn Thee.' But now it says that when 'Thy name' has been emptied out as ointment, 'have they loved Thee,' not those little old souls clothed in the old man, nor yet the spotted and wrinkled, but that 'the maidens' have done so—that is to say, the young souls growing up in years and beauty, who are always being made new and renewed from day to day, as they put on the new man, who is created according to God.[52]

For the sake of these young souls, therefore, in their growing and abundant life, He who was in the form of God emptied Himself, that His name might be as ointment emptied out, that He might no longer dwell only in light unapproachable and abide in the form of God; but that the Word might be made flesh, and so these maiden souls at the beginning of their progress might not only love Him, but might draw Him to themselves.[53] For every soul draws and receives to itself the Word of God according to the measure of its capacity and faith. But when souls have thus drawn the Word of God to themselves, and have ingrafted Him into their minds and understandings, and

---

'Therefore have *all* loved Thee,' not only the maidens who were being renewed from day to day, having *neither spot nor wrinkle* (Eph. 4.23, 5.27). And He *emptied Himself* (Phil. 2.7) so that what had been shut in silence, might no longer remain unspoken.

have experienced the pleasantness of His sweetness and odour, when they have received the fragrance of His ointments and have grasped at last the reason for His coming, the motives of the Redemption and Passion, and the love whereby He, the Immortal, went *even to the death of the cross* for the salvation of all men, then these maiden souls, attracted by all this as by the odours of a divine and ineffable perfume and being filled with vigour and complete alacrity, run after Him and hasten to the odour of His sweetness, not at a slow pace, nor with lagging steps, but swiftly and with all the speed they can; even as did he who said: *I so run, that I may obtain.*[54]

But that which is said here: 'Thy name is as ointment emptied out. Therefore have the maidens loved Thee, have they drawn Thee. We will run after Thee into the fragrance of Thine ointments'—the maidens, namely, draw Christ to themselves—this surely must be taken as referring to the churches, which are one Church when perfected, but many 'maidens' while they are still under instruction and advancing on their way. These, then, draw Christ to themselves through faith; for, when Christ sees *two or three gathered together in* the faith of *His name,* He goes thither, and *is in their midst,* drawn by their faith and called forth by their unity of mind.[55]

If, however, on the third interpretation it behoves us to take this passage as referring to the soul that is following the Word of God, to every soul that has been first instructed in ethics and then practised in natural philosophy,[56] then the Word of God is drawn by means of all those things which, as we showed just now, are taught in the aforesaid studies—namely, amendment of manners, knowledge of affairs, and uprightness of conduct. And He is willing to be drawn, and comes very gladly to instructed souls; and He accepts their drawing of Him courteously, and kindly yields thereto.

But let me ask you this: if His Name only, that became as ointment emptied out, had such effect and stirred the maidens so, that first they drew Him to themselves and then, when they had got Him with them, perceived the fragrance of His ointments and ran after Him forthwith; if all these things, I say, were brought about by virtue of His Name alone, what do you think His very Self will do? What strength, what vigour will these maidens get from it, if ever they are able by some means to attain to His actual, incomprehensible, unutterable Self? I think myself that if they ever did attain to this, they would no longer walk or run, but, bound as it were by the bands of His love, they would cleave to Him, and would have no further power ever to move again. For they would be one spirit with Him, and that which is written: *As Thou, Father, in me and I in Thee are one, so may these also be one in Us*, would be fulfilled in them.[57]

In the meantime, apparently, the Bride, who has associated with herself the many maidens—they are said to be numberless a little further on[58]—relates that she is running towards the fragrance of the Bridegroom's ointments under the compulsion of one single sense, the sense of smell alone. This may be because she herself still needs to run and to advance; or it may be that, though she herself is perfected, she is admitting that for the sake of these maidens who do still need to run and to take forward steps, she herself also runs even as did he who, *though not himself under the Law, became under the Law that he might gain those who were under the Law; who also, though he was in the Law of Christ, became without the Law to them that were without the Law, that He might save them that were without the Law.*[59]

This comes about, as we have seen, when as yet they have received only the scent of Him. What, do you think, will they do when the Word of God takes possession of their hearing, their sight, their touch, and their taste as well, and offers excellences from Himself that match each single sense according to its nature and capacity; so that the eye, if it have seen *His glory, the glory as it were of the Only-begotten of the Father*, desires to see nothing evermore but that, nor would the hearing hear aught else except *the Word of life* and *of salvation*? [60]

And the one whose *hands have handled of the Word of life* will nevermore handle anything material, nor anything that breaks and perishes; nor will his palate suffer any other taste, when it *has tasted the good Word of God*, and His Flesh, and *the Bread that cometh down from heaven*. [61] Because He tastes so sweet and so delightful, all other flavours will seem harsh and bitter to him now; and therefore he will feed on Him alone. For he will find in Him all the sweetness that ever he desired; for He adapts and fits Himself to all requirements. Again, to those *who are being born again of incorruptible seed*, He is made *the rational and guileless milk*; while to those who are weak in some respect He offers Himself like healing herbs in friendly and gracious hospitality. [62] And again, to *them who, as they are able, have their senses exercised to the discerning of good and evil*, He presents Himself as *solid food*. But if there are some who have come out of Egypt and, following the pillar of fire and cloud, are entering the wilderness, then He comes down from heaven to them and offers them a small, thin Food, like to the food of angels; so that *man eats the bread of angels*. [63]

He has in Himself many other and indeed innumerable sorts of food besides, the which a man still clothed in skin and flesh and bones and sinews [64] cannot at present take. But he who shall have merited to return and be with Christ, he who, having been found faithful in a little, is placed over many things, that man will be brought to a certain place which, because of the abundance and variety of foods that it contains, is called the Place of Delights; and there he will taste and see the satisfaction of the Lord. That is why he is said to be put in Eden, which means Delights; for there they will say to him: *Delight in the Lord.* [65]

His delighting will not, however, be restricted to the single sense of eating and tasting; he will be delighted in his hearing too, and he will be delighted in seeing, and touching, and smelling. For he will run towards the odour of His ointment. And in this way he who has reached the peak of perfection and beatitude will be delighted by the Word of God in all his senses.

Wherefore we also, from the position where we find ourselves, earnestly beg the hearers of these things to mortify their carnal senses. They must not take anything of what has been said with reference to bodily functions, but rather employ them for grasping those divine senses of the inner man; as Solomon himself teaches us, saying: *Thou shalt find the divine meaning,* [66] and as Paul also writes to the Hebrews, as we remarked before, about the perfect who have their senses trained to discern good and evil. He points out that there are other senses in man besides these five bodily senses; these other senses are acquired by training, and are said to be trained when they examine the meaning of things with more acute perception. For what the Apostle says about the perfect having their senses trained to discern good and evil must not be taken carelessly and in any sense one likes.

To make its meaning clearer, therefore, let us if you like take an example from these bodily senses, and thus we shall come at length to those divine senses which Scripture calls those of the inner man. If, then, the bodily eye has the faculty of sight and there is no obstacle in the way, it will perceive the colours and sizes and qualities of bodies in their entirety and without any deception; for if the power of sight be hindered either by dimness or by any other weakness, so that it thinks a white thing to be red or a black one green, or that a crooked, twisted thing is straight, the mental judgement undoubtedly will be disturbed, and one thing will be done in place of another.[67] And in the same way, if the interior vision, instead of being trained by learning and diligence so as to acquire the power of discerning good and evil through much experience, gets its eyes misted as it were by ignorance and inexperience, or bleary as from the feebleness induced by some disease, it cannot manage to discern good from evil by any means at all. And so it happens that it does bad things instead of good, and rejects the good in favour of the bad. And if you apply this analogy, of which we have treated in regard to the sight of body and soul, to hearing, and taste, and smell, and touch also, and work out the parallel between all the several powers of the bodily senses according to their kind and the corresponding powers of the soul, you will then clearly perceive what training should be undertaken in each case, and what correction ought to be set going.

We have digressed somewhat over this, because we wished to show that the sense of smell, by which the Bride and the maidens perceived the fragrance of the Bridegroom's ointments, denotes not a bodily faculty, but that divine sense of scent which is called the sense of the interior man. This power of perception, therefore, having once picked up the scent of Christ, in so far as it is sound and healthy leads on thenceforward from life unto life. But if, on picking up the scent of Christ, it be not healthy, it casts a man down from death unto death, according to him who said: *For we are the good odour of Christ, to some from life to life, but to others the odour of death unto death.*

Lastly, those too whose business it is to understand the properties of herbs and medicaments, say that there are certain medicaments at the smell of which some animals die instantly; whereas others by the same odour are refreshed and given life. And it seems to be a matter of life unto life for some, and of death unto death for others, with these same discourses and expositions that we now have in hand. For, if the sensual man,[68] as he is called, the man who cannot perceive and understand the things of the Spirit of God, were to hear these matters so interpreted, he would doubtless mock and pronounce them foolish and empty, telling us we are discussing dreams, rather than the causes of things and the divine teachings. For such men, therefore, the effect of this odour of the Song of Songs is from death unto death—from the death of unbelief, that is to say, unto the death of judgement and condemnation. But to those who follow the leading of their subtle spiritual sense and perceive that there is greater truth in the things that are not seen, than there is in those that are seen, and that the things invisible and spiritual are closer to God than are the bodily and visible, this kind of interpretation will doubtless commend itself as that which they should follow and embrace; for they recognize that this is the way of understanding truth that leads to God.

It is small wonder that a man should adjudge these things as foolish and ridiculous, if he be an alien from the faith; but if among those who profess to believe and to accept the authority of the Scriptures, there should be anyone who none the less does not accept a spiritual exegesis on these lines, but scorns and disparages it, let us try to instruct and persuade him from other passages of Scripture, in the hope that perhaps he may return to his senses. Let us talk to him along the following lines.

Scripture says: *The commandment of the Lord is lightsome, enlightening the eyes.* Let him then tell us what sort of eyes these are, that are enlightened by the light of the commandment! And again: *He that hath ears to hear, let him hear!* What ears are these, whose possessor alone is said to hear the words of Christ? And again: *For we are the good odour of Christ unto God*; and, among other passages: *O taste and see that the Lord is sweet!* And what else does it say? *And our hands have handled of the Word of life.*[69] Will a man of this sort, do you think, unless he is actuated by the vice of contention and boasting, fail to be moved by all this evidence, and to see that these things were not spoken about the senses of the body, but about those which, as we have taught you, reside in everyone according to the inner man?[70]

Since by these vices of contention and boasting not only is the inward vision blinded, but the sense of smell also is closed up and the power of hearing stopped, there is good reason for his inability either to hear and see things that are spiritual, or to perceive the odour of Christ which these maidens, in whom this sense of smell was very healthy and vigorous, perceived, who are now running after Him towards the odour of His ointments and, as they run, faint not nor toil, because they are continually renewed and strengthened by the sweetness of the smell of Him who is *from life unto life.*[71]

There is yet another interpretation of these words, 'Thy name is as ointment emptied out; therefore have the maidens loved Thee.' The Only-begotten Son, *being in the form of God, . . . emptied Himself and took the form of a servant.* The emptying out was surely out of the fullness in the which He was. So those who say: *Of His fullness we all have received,*[72] are the maidens who, receiving of that fullness of which He emptied Himself and thereby made His name as ointment emptied out, declare: 'We will run after Thee towards the fragrance of Thine ointments.' For, if He had not emptied out the ointment—that is, the fullness of the Divine Spirit—and humbled Himself even to a servant's form, no one would have been able to receive Him in that plenitude of Godhead, unless perhaps it were the Bride alone; because she seems to indicate that the ointment emptied out furnished cause of love, not for herself, but for the maidens. For her saying: 'Thy name is as ointment emptied out; therefore have the maidens loved Thee,' is as much as to say: 'The maidens indeed have loved Thee, because Thou didst empty Thyself of the form of God, and Thy name became as ointment emptied out; but I have loved Thee, not for the ointment emptied out, but for the ointments' very plenitude.' Her saying: 'The fragrance of Thine ointments is above all spices,' points to this. But, as we explained before, the reason why she herself runs with the maidens after Him is that the perfect always *become all things to all men, that they may gain all.*[73]

5

'The King hath brought me into His chamber. Let us rejoice and be glad in Thee. We will love Thy breasts more than wine. Equity hath loved Thee.' (1.4c–f—Vg. 1.3c–f)

THE* KING HATH BROUGHT ME INTO HIS CHAMBER. LET US REJOICE AND BE GLAD IN THEE.

The Bride had drawn her Bridegroom's attention to the fact that the maidens, attracted by His fragrance, were running after Him, and that she herself likewise was going to run with them; so that in all things she might set them an example. But now, as though she has already attained the reward of her labour in thus running with the runners, she tells us that the King has brought her into His chamber, that she may see there all the royal riches. And this gives her good reason for gladness and rejoicing, in that she has now beheld the secrets of the King and hidden mysteries. This is the literal interpretation, taking the thing as a story told in dramatic form.

But since the reference is either to the Church who comes to Christ, or to the soul that cleaves to the Word of God, how should we understand Christ's chamber and the storehouse of the Word of God into which He brings the Church or the soul thus cleaving to Him—you can take it either way—except as Christ's own secret and mysterious mind? Of this Paul also said: *We have the mind of Christ, that we may know the things that are given us from God.* These

---

* Procopius, *Comm. in Cant. Cant.* 1.4 (MG 17.253 C): *The King hath brought me into His chamber,* that is to say, the sanctuary of the soul worthy of love, or the Church, or the guiding mind of Christ. When Paul entered therein he said: *We have the mind of Christ, that we may know the things that are given us from God.* What are these things? Those

things are those that *eye hath not seen, nor ear heard, neither hath it entered into the heart of man, what things God hath prepared for them that love Him.* So, when Christ leads a soul to understand His mind, she is said to be brought into the King's chamber, *in which are hid the treasures of His wisdom and knowledge.*[74]

It seems to me, however, not without significance that instead of saying 'I was brought in by my Spouse,' or 'by my Nephew,' or using some other of her wonted terms, in this place, because she was about to mention the chamber, she says it is 'the King's' chamber, and does not use some other appellation, such as might perhaps be taken to mean some ordinary person. She named the King in this connection, I believe, to emphasize how very rich this chamber was, being thus royal and filled full with many and vast riches. I think that the man who said he had been rapt to the third heaven, and thence to Paradise, and had heard unspeakable words that it is not lawful for a man to utter, had been close to this King, or following Him.[75] For what words do you think he heard, unless he heard them from the King, and heard them either in the chamber or from just outside? And those words, I believe, were such as to encourage him to press on yet further, and to promise him that if he persevered until the end, he would himself be able to enter the King's chamber, according to the promise that the prophet also gave: *I will give thee dark treasures and hidden ones; I will open to thee things unseen, that thou mayest know that I am the Lord thy God, who call thee by thy name, the God of Israel.*[76]

---

that *eye hath not seen, nor ear heard, neither hath it entered into the heart of man; for these things God hath prepared for them that love Him* (1 Cor. 2.16, 12, 9—cf. Isa. 64.4). For in the 'chamber' of the Bridegroom *are hid all the treasures of wisdom and knowledge* (Col. 2.3). The Bride, then,

The maidens, then, run after Him and into His fragrance, each one of them according to her powers, one faster, one somewhat more slowly, while another runs behind the rest and brings up the rear. They all run, certainly; but she alone is perfect who so ran as to obtain, and alone to receive the prize. This only one is she who says: 'The King hath brought me into His chamber,' whereas formerly, speaking not of herself only, but of many, she had said: 'We will run after Thee into the fragrance of Thine ointments.' She, then, is brought into the chamber, and is made the queen; and she it is of whom it is said: *The queen stood on Thy right hand, in gilded clothing, girt about with divers colours.* But of the maidens who had run behind her and stayed some distance from her as they ran, it is said: *After her shall virgins be brought to the King; her neighbours shall be brought to Thee, they shall be brought with gladness and rejoicing, they shall be led into the temple of the King.*[77]

But we must note in this connection the further fact that, just as the King has a certain chamber into which He brings His queen or bride, so also has the Bride her chamber, the door whereof the Word of God enjoins her, when she has entered it, to shut, and so, with all those riches of hers shut away inside that chamber, *to pray to the Father, who seeth in secret* and perceives what valuables—what virtues of the soul, that is—the Bride has gathered there; so that, seeing her riches, He may grant her prayers. For *to everyone that hath it shall be given.*[78]

The words, 'Let us rejoice and be glad in Thee,' however, seem to be spoken by the maidens, who in them beg

---

anticipating the maidens, was brought in and took her stand as *queen* at the King's *right hand in gilded clothing,* as David says; but as for the maidens, *they shall be brought to the King after her* (Ps. 44.10, 15), and the rest.

and pray the Bridegroom that as the Bride has obtained the things that are perfect and rejoices therefor, so may they likewise merit to fulfil their course and come even to the King's chamber; that, having there beheld and looked on all these things of which she speaks with pride, they also may rejoice as she rejoices, and be glad in Him.

Moreover, the words, WE WILL LOVE THY BREASTS MORE THAN WINE, may also be taken as addressed by the maidens to the Bride; they rejoice with her, because they look forward to becoming partakers of her joy and gladness. The Bride herself, after she has been found worthy to receive kisses from the Bridegroom's own mouth, and to enjoy His breasts, says to Him: 'Thy breasts are above wine.'[79] But the maidens, who had not yet reached that degree of blessedness, nor attained the summit of perfection, nor yet had so produced the fruits of perfect charity in conduct and works as to enable them to say from experience that His breasts are good, these, I say, seeing the Bride delighted and refreshed by the Bridegroom's breasts —that is to say, by the springs of wisdom and knowledge that proceed from them—seeing her drink the cups of heavenly teaching, promise and say, as those who copy her perfection and desire to follow in her steps: 'We*will love thy breasts more than wine.' That is: 'We indeed are not yet so perfect as to love thy breasts more than wine now'—or 'thy breasts that are above wine,' either sense will do—'yet, just because we are maidens, we cherish the hope that we shall reach the age at which we can not only feed from the breasts of the Word of God, and be nourished thereby, but also love Him who thus nourishes.'

---

* Procopius, *Comm. in Cant. Cant.* 1.4 (MG 17.256 A): *We will love Thy breasts more than wine*—that is to say, although now through our weakness we love wine more than Thy breasts, O Bridegroom, when

As we have often said before, these maidens represent souls who, like little children, have received the elements and firstfruits of instruction, and are gladdened, as with a sort of wine, by the schooling only of tutors and governors and of a pedagogue;[80] they are such as have it in their power to love wine, but are not yet of an age to be moved and stirred by love for the Bridegroom's breasts. They promise, none the less, that when the fullness of the times has come and Christ in them has advanced in age and wisdom,[81] and they have begun to perceive what the breasts of the Bridegroom are, and what perfection of the Word of God and what fullness of spiritual teaching is denoted by them, they will then love the Bridegroom's breasts, which now they love after the manner of children, 'more than wine'—that is, they will be apter students of Christ's full and perfect teachings than ever they were of their ordinary studies, or of the teachings of the Law and the Prophets.

EQUITY HATH LOVED THEE.[82] I think this, too, is spoken by the maidens, by way of compensation for the fact that they had only promised to love the Bridegroom's breasts 'more than wine,' and do not so love them at present, nor do they display the full force of charity. The words imply self-blame: the maidens have not yet so cast away iniquity and come to equity, as to be able to love the Bridegroom's breasts more than wine now; and they know that it is wholly unfitting for any trace of iniquity to remain in a person who has reached the perfection of spiritual and

we have been made stronger, *we will love Thy breasts more than wine.* The wine that rejoices the maidens is the things of the Law, the breasts are the perfection of the Bridegroom. By way of apology, then, for not loving now, she says: '*Equity hath loved Thee* (Cant. i.4). But we have not yet made our paths straight.'

mystical teaching. Therefore, because the height of perfection consists in charity,[83] and charity allows nothing of iniquity—and where there is no iniquity, there surely is equity—it is rightly said to be Equity that loves the Bridegroom.

And see if this saying of the Saviour's in the Gospel does not come to the same thing: *If ye love me, keep my commandments.*[84] For if he who loves Christ keeps His commandments, and in him who keeps the commandments there is no iniquity, but equity abides in him, equity then is that which both keeps the commandments and loves Christ. And again, if the person who keeps the commandments is also the person who loves Christ, and it is by equity that the commandments are kept, and equity that loves Christ, then the person who does anything iniquitous neither keeps the commandments, nor loves Christ.

It follows, therefore, that as far as there is any iniquity in us, to that extent precisely are we far from loving Christ, and to that extent also is there in us transgression of His commandments. Let us, therefore, make equity into a sort of straight-edge;[85] so that if there be anything of iniquity in us, by using this ruler and adding thereto the rule of God's commandments, anything crooked or twisted that there may be in us may be put straight by this ruler's edge; so that it may be said of us also: 'Equity hath loved Thee.'

We can also take what it says here, 'Equity hath loved Thee,' as being a similar statement to: 'Justice hath loved Thee,' and Truth, and Wisdom, and Modesty, and all the virtues in turn. And do not be surprised that we speak of the virtues loving Christ, since in other cases we are wont to regard Christ as Himself the substance of those very virtues. You will find this often in the Divine Scriptures, adapted to the context and conditions; we find Him, for example, called not only Justice, but also Peace and Truth.[86] And again, it is written in the Psalms: *Justice and Peace have kissed;* and *Truth is sprung out of the earth, and Justice hath looked down from heaven.*[87] All of which things are both said to *be* Himself, and to embrace Him. Moreover, He is both called Bridegroom and named Bride, as it is written in the prophet: *As a bridegroom hath He decked me with a crown, and as a bride hath He adorned me with jewels.*[88]

BOOK TWO

(On Cant. 1.5–14—Vg. 1.4–13)

I

'I am dark and beautiful, O ye daughters of Jerusalem, as the tents of Cedar, as the curtains of Solomon.' (1.5—Vg. 1.4)

I AM DARK AND BEAUTIFUL, O YE DAUGHTERS OF JERUSALEM, AS THE TENTS OF CEDAR, AS THE CURTAINS OF SOLOMON. In some copies we read: I AM *BLACK* AND BEAUTIFUL.[1] Here again the person of the Bride is introduced as speaking, but she speaks now not to those maidens who are wont to run with her, but to the daughters of Jerusalem. To these, since they have spoken slightingly about her as being ugly, she now makes answer, saying: 'I am indeed dark—or black—as far as my complexion goes, O daughters of Jerusalem; but, should a person scrutinize the features of my inward parts, then I am beautiful. For the tents of Cedar, which is a great nation,' she says, 'also are black, and their very name of Cedar means blackness or darkness. The curtains of Solomon likewise are black; but that blackness of his curtains is not considered unbecoming for so great a king in all his glory.[2] Do not reproach me for my colour, then, O daughters of Jerusalem, seeing that my body lacks neither natural beauty, nor that which is acquired by practice.'[3]

This much is comprehended in the tale enacted, and is the superficial meaning of the story here set forth. But let us return to the mystical exposition.[4] This* Bride who speaks represents the Church gathered from among the Gentiles; but the daughters of Jerusalem to whom she addresses herself are the souls who are described as being *most dear because of the election of the fathers, but enemies because of the Gospel.*[5] Those are, therefore, the daughters of this earthly Jerusalem who, seeing the Church of the Gentiles, despise and vilify her for her ignoble birth; for she is baseborn in their eyes, because she cannot count as hers the noble blood of Abraham and Isaac and Jacob, for all that she forgets her own people and her father's house and comes to Christ.[6]

The Bride knows that the daughters of the former people impute this to her, and that because of it they call her black, as one who has not been enlightened by the patriarchs' teaching. She answers their objections thus: 'I am indeed black, O daughters of Jerusalem, in that I cannot claim descent from famous men, neither have I received the enlightenment of Moses' Law. But I have my own beauty, all the same. For in me too there is that primal thing, the Image of God wherein I was created; and, coming now to the Word of God, I have received my beauty.[7] Because of my dark colouring you may compare me to the tents of Cedar and the curtains of Solomon; but even Cedar was descended from Ismael, being born his second son, and Ismael was not without a share in the

---

* Procopius, *Comm. in Cant. Cant.* 1.5 (MG 17.256 B; Baehrens p. LIII): The Church of the Gentiles says these words to the souls of Jerusalem, or rather to Jerusalem, acknowledging that she is 'black' through having no illustrious nor enlightened fathers; wherefore, she says, she is given up to darkness, but she is 'comely' because of the word which she has received; and she says she is like the curtains of Solomon, which he had, along with his other possessions *in all his glory* (Luke 12.27).

divine blessing.[8] You liken me even to the curtains of Solomon, which are none other than the curtains of the tabernacle of God[9]—indeed I am surprised, O daughters of Jerusalem, that you should want to reproach me with the blackness of my hue. How have you come to forget what is written in your Law, as to what Mary suffered who spoke against Moses because he had taken a black Ethiopian to wife? How is it that you do not recognize the true fulfilment of that type in me? I am that Ethiopian. I am black indeed by reason of my lowly origin; but I am beautiful through penitence and faith. For I have taken to myself the Son of God, I have received *the Word made flesh*; I have come to Him *who is the Image of God, the Firstborn of every creature and* who is *the brightness of the glory and the express Image of the substance of God,* and I have been made fair. What are you doing, then, reproaching one who turns away from sin, which reproach the Law entirely forbids? How do you come to glory in the Law, and yet to violate it?'[10]

Now, however, since we are on the subject of the Church that comes of the Gentiles and calls herself black and yet beautiful, though it may seem a long and toilsome matter to collect from the Divine Scriptures the passages containing types foreshadowing this mystery, and to consider in what way they so foreshadow it, it seems to me that we should not entirely omit the task, but should advert to it as briefly as may be.

First, then, in the Book of Numbers it is written of the Ethiopian woman thus: *And Mary and Aaron spoke, and they spoke against Moses because of the Ethiopian woman, whom he had taken to wife, and said, 'Hath the Lord spoken to Moses only? Hath He not also spoken to us?'*[11] And again in the Third Book of Kings it is written of the queen of Sheba, who *came from the ends of the earth to hear the wisdom of Solomon,*[12] after this manner: *And the queen of Sheba heard of the name of Solomon and the name of the Lord, and she came to try him with parables. And she came to Jerusalem with very great array, with camels carrying spices and very much gold and precious stones; and she entered in to Solomon, and spoke to him all that she had in her heart. And Solomon answered all her questions: there was no question that the king left out and did not so answer. And the queen of Sheba saw all the prudence of Solomon, and the house which he had built, and his meats, and his servants' residence, and the order of his ministers, and his apparel, and his wine-pourers, and his burnt offerings that he offered in the House of the Lord; and she was amazed. And she said to king Solomon:* ' *The report is true which I heard in my own country concerning thy word and thy prudence. And I did not believe them that told me, till I came and saw with my own eyes; and lo, the half hath not been told me! For thou hast added good things beyond everything that I heard in my own country. Blessed are thy women, blessed are thy servants who stand ever in thy sight, and hear all thy prudence! Blessed be the Lord thy God, who hath given thee the throne of Israel! For because the Lord hath loved Israel and willed him to endure for ever, He hath appointed thee king over them that thou mayest do judgement with justice, and mayest judge them.' And she gave Solomon a hundred and twenty talents of gold, and of spices a very great store, and precious stones. There had never come thither such spices, nor in such quantity, as those which the queen of Sheba gave to king Solomon.*[13]

We wanted to quote this story somewhat at length, and to insert it in our exposition, because we know that the correspondence between these matters and the person of the Church, who comes to Christ from out of the Gentiles, is so close that the Lord Himself mentioned this queen in the Gospels, saying that *she came from the ends of the earth to hear the wisdom of Solomon.*[14] He calls her *the queen of the south*, because Ethiopia lies in southern parts; and He says *from the ends of the earth*, in that it is, as it were, situated in the farthest place. But we find further that Josephus also mentions this queen in his *History*;[15] and he gives us the further fact that when she had returned from Solomon, the king Cambyses—so he says—marvelling at her wisdom, which doubtless she had got from Solomon's instruction, bestowed on her the name of Meroe. He relates, moreover, that she held rule not only over Ethiopia, but also over Egypt. And we may adduce further the words of the sixty-seventh psalm with reference to this same type. The writer says there: *Scatter thou the peoples that delight in wars. Ambassadors shall come out of Egypt, Ethiopia shall stretch out her hands to God. Sing to God, ye kingdoms of the earth, sing ye to the Lord!*[16]

And in a fourth passage, from the prophet Sophonias, it is written thus regarding this same figure: *Wherefore wait for me, saith the Lord, in the day of my rising up for witness,* that is to say, *for testimony; for my judgement is upon the gatherings of the nations, that I may lay hold on kings and pour out upon them all the wrath of mine indignation; for with the fire of my jealousy shall all the earth be devoured. For then will I change the speech of the peoples for its generation, that they may all call upon the name of the Lord and serve Him beneath one yoke. From beyond the rivers of Ethiopia will I receive the dispersed ones, and they shall bring me sacrifice. In that day thou shalt not be ashamed, O Saba, for all thy doings wherein thou hast wrought impiously against me.*[17]

And it is written also in Jeremias that the princes of the house of Israel *cast Jeremias into the pit of Melchias, the king's son, which was in the prison house, and let him down with ropes;*

and in the pit there was no water, but mire, and he was in the mire. Now Abdimelech the Ethiopian, an eunuch that was in the king's house, hearing that they had put Jeremias in the pit, spoke to the king and said: 'Lord King, these men have done evil in what they have done against Jeremias the prophet; for they have cast him into the pit, and he will die there of hunger, for there is no more bread in the city.' And the king commanded Abdimelech the Ethiopian himself, saying: 'Take from hence thirty men with thee, and draw him up from the pit, that he die not there.' And what happened then? It was Abdimelech the Ethiopian who drew up Jeremias from the pit. And a little later *the word of the Lord came to Jeremias, saying: 'Go and tell Abdimelech the Ethiopian . . ., saying: ". . . Thus saith the Lord God of Israel: Behold, I bring my words upon this city unto evil and not unto good, and I will deliver thee in that day, and will not give thee into the hands of the men before whose face thou fearest. For I will surely deliver thee, and thou shalt not fall by the sword; but thy life shall be saved for thee, because thou hast put thy trust in me, saith the Lord."'* [18]

These were the passages from the Holy Scriptures that suggested themselves to me at the moment, as being in accordance with this verse of the Song of Songs which we are now considering—namely, the verse in which it says: 'I am dark (*or* black) and beautiful, O ye daughters of Jerusalem, as the tents of Cedar, as the curtains of Solomon.'

So, then, in the Book of Numbers we find Moses taking an Ethiopian wife—that is to say, one who is dark or black; and because of her Mary and Aaron speak ill of him, and say with indignation: *Hath the Lord spoken to Moses only? Hath He not also spoken to us?* [19] Now on careful consideration the narrative here is found to lack coherence. What has their saying, *Hath the Lord spoken to Moses only? Hath*

He not also spoken to us? to do with their indignation about
the Ethiopian woman? If that was the trouble, they ought
to have said: 'Moses, you should not have taken an
Ethiopian wife, and one of the seed of Ham; you should
have married one of your own race and of the house of
Levi.' They say not a word about this; they say instead:
*Hath the Lord spoken to Moses only? Hath He not also spoken
to us?* It seems to me that, in so saying, they understood
the thing Moses had done more in terms of the mystery;
they saw Moses—that is, the spiritual Law—entering now
into wedlock and union with the Church that is gathered
together from among the Gentiles. This is the reason,
apparently, why Mary, who typified the forsaken Synagogue, and Aaron, who stood for the priesthood according
to the flesh, seeing their kingdom taken away from them
and given to a nation bringing forth the fruits thereof, say:
*Hath the Lord spoken to Moses only? Hath He not also spoken
to us?*

Moreover, Moses himself, in spite of all the great and
splendid achievements of faith and patience that are recorded of him, was never so highly praised by God as on
this occasion when he took the Ethiopian wife. It is said of
him, in reference to this: *Moses was a man exceeding meek
above all men that are upon earth.* Further, in this same connection the Lord says concerning him: *If there be among you
a prophet, I will speak to him in visions or in dreams. But it is
not so with my servant Moses, who is faithful in all my house;
mouth to mouth will I speak to him, plainly and not by riddles;
and he has seen the glory of the Lord. Why then were you not
afraid to speak ill of my servant Moses?* [20]

Moses was found worthy to hear all these things, because
of his marriage with the Ethiopian woman. But we have
dealt with these questions more fully in our exposition of

the Book of Numbers; anyone who thinks it worth his
while may look them up there.[21] Now, however, let it
suffice to demonstrate from these things that this 'black
and beautiful' woman is one and the same as the Ethiopian
who is taken in marriage by Moses—that is, by the
spiritual Law, who is undoubtedly the Word of God and
Christ—although the daughters of Jerusalem, namely, that
people and their priests, decry him and speak evil of him
for so taking her.

Now let us look at the passage which we quoted from
the Third Book of Kings about the queen of Sheba, who
also was an Ethiopian; and concerning whom the Lord
bears witness in the Gospels that *in the day of judgement she
shall come together with the men of this faithless generation, and
shall condemn them; because she came from the ends of the earth
to hear the wisdom of Solomon.* And He adds: *A greater than
Solomon is here,*[22] teaching us thereby that the Truth is
greater than the figure of the Truth.

This queen came, then, and, in fulfilment of her type,
the Church comes also from the Gentiles to hear the
wisdom of the true Solomon, and of the true Peace-Lover,
Our Lord Jesus Christ. She too at first comes *trying Him
with riddles and with questions,* which had seemed to her
insoluble before; and He resolves all her perplexity concerning the knowledge of the true God, and concerning
the created things of the world, the immortality of the
soul, and the future judgement, all of which ever remained
doubtful and uncertain for her and for her teachers, at
least for the Gentile philosophers.

She came to Jerusalem, then, to the Vision of Peace,[23]
with a great following and in great array; for she came not
with a single nation, as did the Synagogue before her that
had the Hebrews only, but with the races of the whole

world, offering moreover worthy gifts to Christ, fragrant spices, so the writer tells us—namely, good works that ascend to God in the sweetness of their savour. She came with gold also, with the trained perceptions and the rational habits of mind which she had acquired through this common knowledge of the schools before she came to faith. She brought also precious stones, by which we may understand the adornments of good behaviour. With this pomp, then, she enters in to the Peaceable King Christ and opens her heart to Him, in confession, doubtless, and repentance for her past transgressions. *And she spoke to Him all that was in her heart;* wherefore Christ, who is our peace,[24] *answered all her questions, and there was no question that the King left out and did not so answer.* And, to crown all, when the time of His Passion was near, He spoke to her—that is, to His chosen disciples—as follows: *I will not now call you servants, but friends; for the servant knoweth not what his lord doth; but I have made known to you whatsoever things I have heard of my Father.*[25]

Thus, therefore, is the saying fulfilled that there was no matter which the peace-making Lord did not declare to the queen of Sheba, to the Church that is gathered from among the Gentiles. And, if you look at the constitution of the Church, and consider the way in which her affairs are ordered and governed, then you will see why the queen marvelled at all the prudence of Solomon.[26]

And you may ask at the same time why He spoke of all the *prudence* of Solomon, and not of all his wisdom; for learned men would have us understand prudence in relation to human affairs, and wisdom with reference to things divine. Perhaps the reason is that the Church likewise marvels at the prudence of Christ for a time, while she is yet on earth and lives her life among men; but *when that which is perfect is come*, and she has been translated from earth to heaven, then, when she no longer perceives *through a glass and in a dark manner*, but sees *face to face* in respect of every single thing, then she will see all His wisdom.[27]

She saw, moreover, *the house that He had built*—doubtless the mysteries of His Incarnation, for that is the dwelling that Wisdom has built for herself.[28] *She saw the meats* of Solomon; that means, I think, the meat of which He said: *My meat is to do the will of Him that sent me, and to perfect His work.*[29] She saw also *His servants' residence*, which seems to me to mean the order which obtains in the Church with regard to the seats of bishops and of priests. That she saw also *the orders*—or *stations*—*of His ministers* seems to me to denote the order of deacons who assist at divine worship.[30] And her seeing *His apparel* refers, I believe, to that with which He clothes those of whom it is said: *As many of you as have been baptized into Christ have put on Christ.*[31] And I think *His wine-pourers* means the teachers who mix the Word and teaching of God like wine for the people, so that it may rejoice the hearts of those who hear.[32] And that she saw *His burnt offerings* denotes undoubtedly the mysteries of prayers and supplications.

When, therefore, this black and beautiful one saw all these things in the house of the Peaceable King, that is, of Christ, *she was amazed. And she said to Him: 'The report is true which I heard in my own country concerning Thy word and concerning Thy prudence.* For because of Thy word, which I recognized as the true word, I came to Thee. For all the words that were said to me, and which I heard while I was in my own country, from worldly teachers and philosophers, were not true words. That only is the true word, which is in Thee.'

But perhaps you will think we should enquire why this queen says to the King: *I did not believe them that told me concerning Thee*, since she certainly would not have come to Christ, unless she had believed. Let us, however, see if we can solve this problem thus. 'I did not believe them that told me,' she says, 'for I did not put my trust in those who spoke of Thee, I put it in Thyself—that is to say, I believed not men but Thee, O God. I heard of Thee by means of them indeed, but it was to Thee Thyself that I came, and Thee whom I believed; and with Thee my eyes beheld far more than the things which were being told me.'

For truly, when this black and beautiful one comes to the heavenly Jerusalem and enters the vision of peace, she will see things many more and far more splendid than have been told her now. For *she sees now* as *in a glass and in a dark manner; but then face to face*, when she attains to the things *that eye hath not seen, nor ear heard, neither hath it entered into the heart of man*. And she will see then that what she heard while she was still *in her own country was not the half of them*.[33]

Blessed, therefore, *are* Solomon's *women*; for this doubtless means the souls who become partakers of the Word of God and of His peace. *Blessed are* his *servants, who stand ever in his sight*; it is not those who sometimes stand and sometimes do not stand who are truly blessed, but those who always and unceasingly stand by the Word of God. Such a one was that Mary who sat at Jesus' feet, hearing Him; and the Lord Himself bore witness to her, saying to Martha: *Mary hath chosen the best part, which shall not be taken away from her*.[34]

And finally the black and beautiful one says: *Blessed be the Lord who hath willed to grant Thee (to sit) upon the throne of Israel*. For truly, *because the Lord hath loved Israel and willed him to endure for ever, He hath appointed thee king over him.* Whom? The Peacemaker, undoubtedly. For Christ *is our peace, who hath made both one and hath broken down the middle wall of partition.*[35]

And, after all these things, we read that the queen of Sheba *gave king Solomon a hundred and twenty talents of gold.* This number a hundred and twenty is that which was allotted as the lifetime of those men who lived in the days of Noe;[36] that space of life is granted them wherein they are invited to repent. The same number was also that of the years of the life of Moses.[37] So the Church offers to Christ, in this semblance and weight of gold, not only the whole sum total of her faculties and mental powers; but the metaphor, inherent in this number that includes the span of Moses' years of life, denotes the further fact that her faculties are devoted to the Law of God.

She offers sweet spices too, such spices and in such amount as had never come thither before. You can take these as meaning either prayers or works of mercy, whichever you like. For never had she prayed so rightly as now when she drew near to Christ; and never had she wrought so dutifully as when she recognized that she was doing her acts of piety, not before men, but before *the Father who seeth in secret and will repay* openly.[38] But it is a big undertaking to follow up in different places all these things which you see we have adduced as evidence.—Let that which has been said about the Third Book of Kings suffice.

Let us give some attention now to the passage we cited from Psalm 67, in which the writer says: *Ethiopia shall stretch out her hands to God.*[39] For, if you consider how salvation comes to the Gentiles through Israel's offence, and that it was Israel's failure that opened the way for the Gentiles to come in, you will observe how the hand of

Ethiopia—that is, the people of the Gentiles—outstrips and precedes in its approach to God those to whom first His oracles were given.[40] You will see that this is how the saying is fulfilled, that *Ethiopia shall stretch out her hands unto God*, and that 'black one' becomes beautiful, for all that the daughters of Jerusalem are unwilling that it should be so, and envy and revile her.

And I think that the statement which we quoted from the prophet, in which the Lord received those also who come from places *beyond the rivers of Ethiopia* and bring offerings to God,[41] calls for a like interpretation. For it seems to me that he is said to be *beyond the rivers of Ethiopia* who has been darkened with exceeding great and many sins and, having been stained with the inky dye of wickedness, has been rendered black and dark. And yet the Lord repels not even these; He drives away from Him none who offer *the sacrifices of a troubled spirit and humbled heart* to God,[42] turning to Him with the password of confession and repentance. For thus says Our Lord the Peaceable: *Him that cometh to me I will not cast out.*[43]

Those, however, who, dwelling *beyond the rivers of Ethiopia*, shall even so come to the Lord, bearing sacrifices, can also be taken as denoting those who will come after the fullness of the Gentiles—for which *the rivers of Ethiopia* are a figure—has come in, and then all Israel shall be saved.[44] In this case their being *beyond the rivers of Ethiopia* would refer to their being outside the regions to which the floodtide of the salvation of the Gentiles comes, and after it in point of time. And perhaps that is how this saying also is fulfilled: *In that day thou shalt not be ashamed*, O Israel, *for all thy doings wherein thou hast wrought wickedly against me.*[45]

It remains now to expound only that passage from

Jeremias which relates how Abdimelech, the Ethiopian eunuch, having heard that Jeremias had been put in the pit by the princes of the people, draws him out thence.[46] And I do not think it is unsuitable to say that this foreigner, this man of a dark and ignoble race, who draws forth from the pit of death him whom the princes of Israel had cast therein, represents the people of the Gentiles, which believes in the resurrection from the dead of Him whom those princes had handed over to death and, by its faith, recalls and brings Him back from hell. But I think that this same Ethiopian is said to be a eunuch, because, *He had made himself a eunuch for the kingdom of heaven,* or even because He had in Himself no seed of wickedness.[47] He is also a servant of the king, because *a wise servant rules over foolish lords*; for Abdimelech means 'servant of kings.'[48] And this is why the Lord, forsaking the people of Israel because of their sins, addresses Himself to the Ethiopian and tells him; *Behold, I bring my words upon this city unto evil and not unto good, ... and I will save thee in that day, and will not give thee into the hands of men ..., but will surely deliver thee.*[49] And the reason why he is delivered is that he drew forth the prophet from the pit—that is, that by his faith in the resurrection of Christ from the dead, in a manner of speaking he drew *Him* forth from the pit.

There are thus, as you see, many passages which bear witness to the fact that this dark (or black) and beautiful one behaves freely with the daughters of Jerusalem, and asserts confidently: ' It is true that I am dark (or black) as the tents of Cedar, but I am beautiful as the curtains of Solomon.'

I do not remember anything in Scripture that refers expressly to the curtains of Solomon. But I think they may have to do with his glory, concerning which the Saviour says that *not even Solomon in all his glory was arrayed as one of these.*[50] We do, however, find frequent mention of the word 'curtains' in connection with the 'tabernacle of witness'; as for example when the Lord says: *Thou shalt make also curtains of goats' hair to cover the top of the tabernacle of witness, eleven curtains shalt thou make. The length of one curtain shall be thirty cubits and the breadth four cubits. The measure of all the curtains shall be equal. And thou shalt join five curtains together, and the other six in the same way, and thou shalt fold back the sixth curtain from the front of the tabernacle. And thou shalt make fifty loops in the edge of one curtain, and fifty loops in the edge of the other curtain, with which to join the curtains one to another. Thou shalt make also fifty brazen rings for each, and thou shalt join the curtains with these, and they shall be one whole. And thou shalt fold back from the front of the tabernacle the half of one curtain out of that which remains over of the curtains; and with the other half that is left over thou shalt cover the back of the tabernacle; a cubit on one side and a cubit on the other shall overlap, of the extra length of the curtain; and the tabernacle will be covered on both sides.*[51]

That, I think, is why curtains are mentioned in the Song of Songs, and are said to be Solomon's, by whom is understood the Peaceable Christ.[52] The tabernacle, then, is His; so also are its fittings; especially if we consider that tabernacle which is called *the true tabernacle, which God hath pitched, and not man,* and concerning which the writer says: *For Jesus is not entered into the holies made with hands, the patterns of the true.*[53] So, if the Bride compares her beauty to the curtains of Solomon, she doubtless means the glory and beauty of those curtains which cover that *tabernacle, which God hath pitched, and not man.* But, if it is her blackness (with which, as we have seen, the daughters of Jerusalem

reproach her) that she compares to the curtains of Solomon, we must take these curtains as belonging to this
tabernacle that is called *the pattern of the true tabernacle*, and
as being in fact black themselves, since they were woven of
goats' hair; though they served none the less for the worship and adornment of the tabernacle of God.

But, although the speaker appears as a single person, she
has likened herself in her blackness to the tents of Cedar
and the curtains of Solomon in the plural number. We
must understand, therefore, that a single character appears,
yet there are countless churches scattered all over the
world, and huge gatherings and multitudes of peoples;[54]
just as the kingdom of heaven is said to be one, yet there is
mention of *many mansions in the Father's House.*[55]

It can be said also of each individual soul that turns to
repentance after many sins, that she is black by reason of
the sins, but beautiful through her repentance and the
fruits of her repentance.

And finally, because she who now says: 'I am black and
beautiful' has not remained in her blackness to the end,
the daughters of Jerusalem say later on concerning her:
*Who is this that cometh up, having been made white, and
leaning upon her Nephew?*[56]

2

'*Look not at me, for that I am darkened; for the sun hath looked
down on me.*' (1.6a—Vg. 1.5a)

LOOK NOT AT ME, FOR THAT I AM DARKENED; FOR THE
SUN HATH LOOKED DOWN ON ME. If the explanation we have
constructed above, either concerning the Ethiopian
woman whom Moses took to wife, or in regard to the
Sheban queen of the Ethiopians who came to hear the

wisdom of Solomon, seems to us to fit the facts, this dark (or black) and beautiful one appears now to give good reason for her blackness or darkness, and a proper explanation to those who reproach her for it. She tells them that it is not a natural condition in which she was created, but something that she has suffered through force of circumstance. 'It came to pass,' she says, 'because the sun looked down on me'; and thus she shows that she is not speaking of bodily blackness, because the sun is wont to tan or blacken when it looks *at*, and not when it looks down *on* anyone.

And it is commonly said among the whole of the Ethiopian race, in which there is a certain natural blackness inherited by all, that in those parts the sun burns with fiercer rays, and that bodies that have once been scorched and darkened, transmit a congenital stain to their posterity.[57] But the reverse is the case with the blackness of the soul; for the soul is scorched, not by being looked at by the sun, but by being looked down upon. Its blackness, therefore, is acquired not through birth, but through neglect; and, since it comes through sloth, it is repelled and driven away by means of industry.

And lastly, as I said just now, this same person who is now called black, is mentioned towards the end of this Song as *coming up, having been made white, and leaning on her Nephew*.[58] She became black, then, because she went down; but, once she begins to come up and to lean upon her Nephew, to cleave to Him and suffer nothing whatever to separate her from Him, then she will be made white and fair; and, when all her blackness has been cast away, she will shine with the enveloping radiance of the true Light.[59]

So now, apologizing to the daughters of Jerusalem for her blackness, she says: 'You must not think, O daughters

of Jerusalem, that this blackness which you see in my face
is natural; you must understand that it has come to pass
because the sun looked askance at me. For the Sun of
Justice [60] found me not standing straight; and so He did
not focus His rays on me directly. I am the people of the
Gentiles, who beheld not the Sun of Justice before, nor
stood before the Lord; [61] therefore* He looked not at me,
but looked askance at me; nor did He stand by me, but
rather passed me by. But thou likewise, who art called
Israel, and hast experienced this thyself already, wilt again
and again admit that this is so and say: 'For as when I of old
did not believe, thou wast chosen and didst obtain mercy,
and the Sun of Justice regarded thee, but looked askance
at me and spurned me, as disobedient and unbelieving; so
likewise now, when thou hast become unbelieving and
disobedient, do I hope to be looked upon by the Sun of
Justice and to obtain mercy. And I will bring you the
magnificent Paul, who knew the secrets of heaven, to
testify to you that we thus share this being looked askance
at by the sun, and that I first was so despised by Him by
reason of my disobedience, when thou wast looked upon;
but that now not only has the sun looked askance at thee,
but also a certain partial blindness has befallen thee. This
is what he says: *For as you*—he is clearly addressing the
Gentiles—*in times past believed not God, but now have
obtained mercy through their unbelief; so these also now have not
believed in your mercy, so that they also may obtain mercy.* And
again he says in another place: *That blindness in part has
happened in Israel until the fullness of the Gentiles should come
in.* [62] This blackness, then, for which you reproach me, is

---

* Cf. Procopius, *Comm. in Cant. Cant.* 1.6 (MG 17.256 C): Christ,
whom the Scriptures call the Sun of Justice, looked askance at me,
darkened as I was by sin, because of my unbelief.

in me because the sun has looked askance at me by reason of my unbelief and disobedience. But when I shall stand upright before Him and shall be crooked in nothing, when *I turn aside neither to the right hand, nor to the left,* but *make straight the paths for my feet, walking* before the Sun of Justice *in all His justifications without blame,* [63] then He who is Himself upright will look on me, and there will be in me no crookedness, nor any cause for Him to look askance at me. And then my light and my splendour will be restored to me, and that blackness for which you now reproach me will be banished from me so completely, that I shall be accounted worthy to be called *the light of the world.'* [64]

Yonder visible sun, then, darkens and burns the bodies which come within its range when it is at the zenith; whereas it keeps within its light and does not burn at all those bodies that are distant, and situated further from it when in that position. But the spiritual sun, by contrast, the Sun of Justice in whose wings is healing, we are told, illuminates and surrounds with every brightness those whom He finds upright in heart and standing close to the zenith of His splendour; but must needs look askance at those who walk contrary to Him, and cannot look on them with favour; and it is their own fickleness and instability that brings this about.

For how can those who are turned aside receive that which is straight? It is as if you put a perfectly straight ruler against a curved line; the crookedness of the thing will indeed be patently shown by the ruler, but it is not the ruler that made the line go crooked. It behoves us, therefore, to hasten to straight ways and to stand in the paths of virtue, lest it happen that when the Sun of Justice come straight over us, finding us crooked and turned aside, He look askance at us and we be made black.

And indeed, in so far as we are incapable of receiving His light, thus far also shall we make room for darkness and blackness in ourselves. For this is the very Sun, who both *was the true Light, which enlighteneth every man that cometh into this world,* and Himself *was in the world, and the world was made by Him.* [65] For it was not by that visible light of ours that the world was made; that light is itself a part of the world. The world was made by that true Light, who, as we are told, looks askance at us if we walk contrary thereto.

And, when we thus walk contrary, that Light itself walks contrary to us, in a sense; as it is written in the curses in Leviticus: *And if you walk contrary to me,* it is said there, *and will not obey me, I will bring upon you seven more plagues.* And a little further on: *And if you will not amend, but will walk contrary to me, I also will walk contrary to you;* or, as we read in some copies: *If you walk crookedly with me, I also will walk crookedly with you.* And a little further on He says again, in conclusion: *And because they have walked crookedly in my sight, I also will walk crookedly with them in wrath.* [66]

We have adduced these passages to show in what sense the sun is said to look askance—that is, to look crookedly. And it has plainly appeared that He looks askance at and walks contrary to and crookedly with those who walk crookedly with Him. But* let us not leave undiscussed the point which this present passage suggested—namely, that the sun is seen as having twofold power: by one it gives light, and by the other it scorches; but according to the

---

* Origen, *Philocalia* 27.13 (255.20 ff. Robinson=25.277 f. Lomm.): Note, moreover, the fact that the sun, for all that it is white and shining, seems to be the cause of the blackening, which cause originates not in itself, but, as we have shown, in the one who becomes black. And so

nature of the objects and substances lying immediately under it, it either illuminates a thing with light, or darkens and hardens it with heat. [67]

Perhaps it is in this sense that God is said to have hardened the heart of Pharao, [68] because the substance of his heart was obviously such as to elicit from the Sun of Justice not His illumination, but His power to harden and to scorch; that no doubt was the reason why this same Pharao afflicted the life of the Hebrews with hard works, and wore them out with clay and bricks. [69] And certainly the works that he devised came from a heart as miry and muddy! And, as the visible sun contracts and hardens the substance of clay, so with the selfsame rays wherewith He enlightened the People of Israel and by means of those rays' selfsame properties, the Sun of Justice hardened the heart of Pharao, that harboured muddy devices.

But that these things are so, and that the servant of God through the Holy Spirit is writing here no ordinary story of the human sort is demonstrated also by the fact that when he relates that *the children of Israel groaned*, he says that they did so, not because of the clay, or the bricks, or the straw, but *because of their works*. And again he says, *their cry went up to God*; and this, he says, not because of clay and bricks, but again *because of their works*. Wherefore

---

too, perhaps, *the Lord hardens Pharaoh's heart* (Exod. 9.12), the cause of this being the fact of his *making the life* of the Hebrews *bitter with hard works in clay and brick and with all manner of service* (Exod. 1.14), not in the mountains and hills, but in the plains. For, being a material man through his own wickedness and living according to the flesh in all things, because he happens to be a lover of clay, he wants to make the Hebrews a people of clay also. He does not have his reason clear of clay. And this reason, just as clay is hardened by the sun, was hardened by the beams of God's light watching over Israel.

That a sense something like this underlies the words of the passage, and that it is not the appointed task of God's servant to write mere

he adds that *the Lord heard their groaning*;[70] for assuredly
He hears not the groaning of those who do not cry unto
the Lord by reason of their works.

Although we may seem to have dealt with these matters
at too great length, we adjudged the opportunity afforded
by these passages such as should certainly not be missed;
especially because they bear a certain likeness to this saying
of her who is darkened because the sun has looked askance
at her. And we have shown that this takes place wherever
a sinful condition has previously obtained, and that a
person is darkened or scorched by the sun where the
ground of sin exists. But where there is no sin, the sun is
not said to burn or darken; even as it is written of the just
man in the Psalms: *The sun shall not burn thee by day, nor
the moon by night.*[71] So you see that the sun never burns the
saints, in whom is nothing sinful; for, as we have said, the
sun has twofold power: it enlightens the righteous; but
sinners it enlightens not, but burns, for they themselves
hate the light because they do evil.[72]

And, lastly, it is for this reason too that *our God* is said
to be *a consuming fire*,[73] yet at the same time is called the
Light, in whom there is no darkness.[74] Light is He without
a doubt to the just; and fire to the sinful, that He may
consume in them every trace of weakness and corruption
that He finds in their soul. And, if you look into the matter,
you will find over and over again that in many passages
in Scripture where sun and fire are mentioned, it is not the

---

history, will be clear to one who observes that when *the children of
Israel groaned*, they did so not because of the brick, nor because of the
clay, nor because of the straw, but *because of the works; and their cry went
up to God*, not because of the clay, but—again—*because of the works.*
Wherefore *God* also *heard their groaning* (Exod. 2.23 f.), while not
hearing the groaning of such as cry to Him not because of their works,
but because of clay and their earthly deeds.

visible sun and fire that are meant, but those that are
unseen and spiritual.

3

'*The sons of my mother have fought in me, they have made me
the keeper in the vineyards; my vineyard I have not kept.*'
(1.6b—Vg. 1.5b)

THE* SONS OF MY MOTHER HAVE FOUGHT IN ME,[75] THEY
HAVE MADE ME THE KEEPER IN THE VINEYARDS; MY VINE-
YARD I HAVE NOT KEPT. She, who is dark indeed by reason
of her former sins, but beautiful through faith and change
of heart, now makes this further statement that her
mother's sons fought not against but *in* her; and that
after this war which they waged *in* her, they made her
keeper not of one vineyard only, but of many vineyards.
And the same speaker tells us further that, besides those
vineyards over which she was set by her mother's sons, she
has another one, her own, which she has not kept. That is
the story of the play before us.

Let us now enquire who the mother of the Bride who
tells us this may be; and also who the others, the mother's
sons, may be, who fought in the Bride and, when the war
was over, committed vineyards to her keeping, as though
she could not have so guarded them, had they not fought;
yet, having thus received the care of other vineyards, she
either could or would not keep her own.

Paul says, writing to the Galatians: *Tell me, you that*

---

* Procopius, *Comm. in Cant. Cant.* 1.6 (MG 17.256 C): *The sons of
my mother have fought in me, they have made me the keeper in the vineyards; my vineyard I have not kept.* That is to say, while Christ's disciples
were teaching me, desiring to cleanse me of my former evil thoughts
and the demons fostering them, they 'fought' these 'in me.' They are

*desire to be under the Law, have you not heard the Law? For it
is written that Abraham had two sons, the one by a bondwoman
and the other by a freewoman. But he who was of the bondwoman
was born according to the flesh; but he of the freewoman was
according to promise. Which things are said by an allegory. For
these are the two testaments, the one from Mount Sina engender-
ing unto bondage, which is Agar. For Sina is a mountain in
Arabia, which is likened to the Jerusalem which now is, and is
in bondage with her children. But that Jerusalem which is above
is free, which is the mother of us all.*[76]

Paul thus calls the heavenly Jerusalem both his own
mother and that of all believers. Then in what follows he
adds the conclusion: *So then, brethren, we are not the children
of the bondwoman, but of the free, by the freedom wherewith
Christ has made us free.*[77] Paul, therefore, plainly declares
that everyone who through faith from Christ follows after
liberty, is a son of the freewoman; and he says that this
freewoman is the free Jerusalem, which is above; she it is
who is the mother of us all.

We understand, therefore, both that the Bride is herself
a daughter of this mother, and that those who fought in
her and made her a keeper of the vineyards are her sons.
It appears from this that these, empowered both to wage
war in her and to appoint her keeper of the vineyards,
were not the citizens of some mean and lowly place; so
we can take the sons of the Bride's mother as meaning the
apostles—that is, the sons of the heavenly Jerusalem, who
formerly fought in her who is gathered from among the
Gentiles. They fought that in her they might overcome her

---

sons of the same mother as I—*of the freewoman* (Gal. 4.23), I mean—
adopted as *a remnant according to the election of* grace (Rom. 11.5), while
I have received the testament as of *the Jerusalem which is above* and have
been born again *by promise* (Gal. 4.23–25). It was not that they first

former dispositions of unbelief and disobedience and all pride that exalts itself against the knowledge of Christ; as is said too by Paul: *Destroying counsels and every height that exalteth itself against the knowledge of Christ.*[78] They fought, therefore, not against but in her, that is to say, in her dispositions and her heart, so that they might destroy and drive away all unbelief, all vice, and all the teachings which she had absorbed from the false statements of the sophists,[79] the while she lived among the heathen.

Christ's apostles had, therefore, a great war to wage before they could cast down from the Bride all the towers of untruth and the walls of wrong teaching, before they could overthrow the arguments of iniquity and overcome the evil spirits that wrought and kindled all these in her heart. And when they have thus routed from her all the dispositions of the old unbelief, they do not leave her idle, lest perchance through idleness the old things should creep back, and those that have been driven away return; but they give her a task to perform, they assign to her the charge of the vineyards.

We may take the vineyards as meaning each and all of the books of the Law and the Prophets; for every one of these was *as a plentiful field which the Lord hath blessed.*[80] These, then, do those brave men, when they have won the war, commit to her to guard and keep, for, as we said, they do not leave her idle. In the same way we may take the evangelic writings and the apostles' letters as vineyards, committed by them to her who is gathered from among the Gentiles and for whom they fought, that she may keep and till them.

---

made her a keeper and then fought against her; but, fighting her first, they made her fit to be placed as keeper in the vineyards. They are Moses and the prophets, and each *field* and vineyard of theirs was

But as to her own vineyard, which she says she has not kept, we can call that the learning that everyone used to receive before he came to faith; which learning he, when he believes in Christ, doubtless forsakes and leaves, counting as loss for Christ the things that used to seem to him as gain. Thus does Paul also boast that the observance of the Law and the whole glory of the Jewish system was to him as dung, so that he might be found in Christ, having not his own justification that was of the Law, but the justification that is of God. [81] In this sense, therefore, Paul kept not his own vineyard—that is to say, he did not keep the Jews' tradition after he had received the faith of Christ. And perhaps the reason why he did not keep it was that, although it had been planted by God as a true vine, it had turned into the bitterness of a strange vine, and *their vine was as the vineyard of Sodom, and their vineshoots of Gomorrha, and bitter clusters among them; their wine was the fury of dragons and the incurable wrath of asps.* [82]

And among the Gentiles also there were many teachings of this sort; and, after those wars waged by the teachers to get them to believe in and acknowledge Christ, I think it should be counted an offence for anyone to keep such vineyards and to continue to till a field that has been sown with poisonous and harmful doctrines.

But you should not be surprised that she who is gathered out of the dispersion of the nations and prepared to be the Bride of Christ, has sometimes been guilty of these faults. Remember how the first *woman was seduced and was in the transgression*, and could find her salvation, so the Scripture

---

plentiful, *which the Lord had blessed* (Gen. 27.27); but any man among them who did not keep his own former property, let it become like *the vineyard of Sodom* (Deut. 32.32), and so applies the present word to himself.

says, only in bearing children; which for our present purpose means those who *continue in faith and love with sanctity*.[83] The Apostle, therefore, declares what is written about Adam and Eve thus: *This is a great mystery in Christ and in the Church*; He so loved her that He gave Himself for her, while she was yet undutiful, even as he says: *When as yet we were ungodly according to the time, Christ died for us*; and again: *When as yet we were sinners, Christ died for us*.[84]

So it is not surprising that she *who was seduced and was in transgression*, she who was *ungodly according to the time*, and *a sinner*, should be said to have cultivated such a vineyard at the time she was still undutiful; which vineyard she was obliged to forsake and on no account to keep.

If it is permissible to offer a third explanation, let us refer these words to every soul who, after she has turned to God and come to faith, undoubtedly experiences conflicts of thought and assaults of evil spirits, which strive to call her back to the attractions of her former life and the errors of unbelief. But, lest this should happen, lest the evil spirits should again find foothold in her, God's providence looked forward in such wise as to provide the little ones and those who, being as yet but babes and sucklings in Christ, cannot defend themselves against the wiles of the devil and the attacks of evil spirits, with angel champions and guardians.[85] These are ordained by Him to act as tutors and governors of those who, as we said, are under age and so unable to fight for themselves.[86] And, that they may do this with greater confidence, it is granted them *always to see the face of the Father who is in heaven*. And I think that they are those little ones, whom Jesus has bidden to come to Him and will not suffer them to be forbidden, and who, He says, *always see the face of the Father*.[87]

And you must not think it contradictory if this soul that

is tending Godwards calls these angels the sons of her own mother. For, if the heavenly Jerusalem is the mother of souls, and the angels equally are called heavenly, there will be no inconsistency in her calling these who like herself are heavenly, her mother's sons. It will, on the contrary, seem supremely apt and fitting that those for whom God is the one Father [88] should have Jerusalem for their one mother.

But when she says: 'My vineyard I have not kept,' she seems to indicate that it was praiseworthy not to have kept those habits and customs and the way of life that she practised when she lived after the old man; and this was ever since she fought and conquered by the angels' help and completely drove out of herself *the old man with his deeds*, and was appointed by them to be the keeper of the vineyards—that is, of the divine secrets and teachings, so that from them she may drink wine to gladden her heart. [89]

4

'Tell me, O Thou whom my soul has loved, where Thou feedest, where Thou hast Thy couch in the midday, lest perchance I be made as one that is veiled above the flocks of Thy companions.' (1.7—Vg. 1.6)

TELL ME, O THOU WHOM MY SOUL HAS LOVED, WHERE THOU FEEDEST, WHERE THOU HAST THY COUCH IN THE MIDDAY, LEST PERCHANCE I BE MADE AS ONE THAT IS VEILED ABOVE THE FLOCKS OF THY COMPANIONS. It is still the Bride who speaks, but to the Bridegroom now, not to the daughters of Jerusalem. So from the beginning, where she says 'Let Him kiss me,' down to this place, 'above the flocks of Thy companions,' all the things that have been said are the words of the Bride. But she addresses herself first to God, then to the Bridegroom, and thirdly to the maidens:

standing as it were between them and the Bridegroom, and acting—to use dramatic phraseology—as a sort of chorus-leader, she directs her words sometimes to them, sometimes to the Spouse; and then again she answers the daughters of Jerusalem. This last speech, therefore, is addressed to the Bridegroom; she asks Him where He feeds at the midday, where He keeps His flock: she fears that while she is seeking Him, she may come upon those places where His companions assemble their flocks throughout the time of noon.

It is plain from these words that this Bridegroom is also a shepherd. We had already learnt that He is also a king, for the undoubted reason that He rules over men. But he is a shepherd, because He feeds the sheep; He is the Bridegroom, because He has the Bride, who is to reign with Him even as it is written: *The queen stood at Thy right hand in gilded clothing.*[90] These are the elements in the drama, as far as the historical sense goes.

Let us now search out the mystical meaning; and, if it is necessary to anticipate somewhat matters that we shall have to deal with later, in order to show what sort of people these companions are, let us remember that it is written that *there are threescore queens,* but *only one dove* among them, *only one perfect one,* who shares the kingdom. But the others are of lower rank, those who are called the *fourscore concubines;* yet *the young maidens, who are without number,* come after the concubines in point of dignity.[91] Now all these represent different classes of believers in Christ, associated with Him in different relationships; so that, for instance, taking another figure, we call the whole Church the Body of Christ, as the Apostle does; but in that Body, so he tells us, there are divers members, some of them eyes, some hands, some even feet, and all of them co-ordinated in the members of this Body according to the merit of their several functions and works.[92]

Now, then, we must understand the passage before us on the same lines. In this marriage drama we must take it that some souls who are associated with the Bridegroom in a nobler and more splendid sort of love, have with Him the status and the love of queens; others whose dignity in respect of progress and the virtues is undoubtedly less, rank as His concubines; and others again are in the position of the maidens who are placed outside the palace, though not outside the royal city.[93] And lastly, and after all these, there are, as we remarked above, those souls that are called sheep.[94] And, if we look more closely, we shall perhaps find further that out of all these sheep some are inferior and last of all—those, namely, that are reckoned as belonging to His companions' flocks. For they, too, are said to have some flocks, which the Bride does not wish to meet; and that is why she asks the Bridegroom to tell her where He feeds and where He passes the midday, 'lest perchance I be made,' she says, 'as one that is veiled above the flocks of Thy companions.'

The question is, therefore, whether these companions who are said to possess some flocks, do so as servants of the Bridegroom, acting under Him as the Chief of shepherds, since they are called *His* companions; or whether, since the Bride flees and is afraid, lest perchance she meet the companions' flocks while she is looking for her Spouse, these companions desire to possess something as their own exclusive property in a manner not accordant with the Bridegroom's mind.

But consider whether by her further words, 'lest perchance I be made'—not 'veiled,' but '*as* one that is veiled,' she may not show that one or more of the companions are as brides, wearing the bridal dress and being veiled, *having a veil upon their head*, as the Apostle says.[95] And, to make the figure in this saying clearer, let us again investigate what is said as taking place in the course of the drama. The Bride asks her Bridegroom to show her the place of His private retreat and rest; because, being impatient for love, she longs to go to Him even through the noonday heat—that is, at the particular time when the light is brighter and the splendour of the day perfect and pure—so that she may be near Him, as He feeds or refreshes His sheep. And she earnestly desires to learn the way by which she ought to go to Him, lest perchance, if she have not been taught the windings of this way, she should come upon the companions' flocks and resemble one of those who come veiled to His companions; and, having no care for modesty, she should fear not to run hither and thither and to be seen of many. 'But I,' she says, 'who would be seen of none save Thee alone, desire to know by what road I may come to Thee, that it may be a secret, that none may come between us, and that no vagrant, strange onlooker may fall in with us.'

And perhaps the reason why she asks what are those places where the Bridegroom feeds His sheep, and the reason why she shows to Him the modesty that makes her anxious not to meet the flocks of the companions, is so that He may keep His sheep apart from the companions' and feed them separately, and thus the Bride may not only be seen of Him alone, but also may more privately enjoy the Bridegroom's secret and unspeakable mysteries.

Let us now consider the matter in detail. And notice first that, if we may say that the Lord, whose portion was Jacob and the lot of whose inheritance was Israel, is Himself to be understood as the Bridegroom; then His companions must be those angels, according to whose number the Most High, when He divided the nations and scattered the sons of Adam, appointed the nations' bounds according to the number of the angels of God, as Scripture says.[96] So perhaps the flocks of the Bridegroom's companions may be all those nations that are divided up like herds under angel shepherds; but those are to be called the Bridegroom's flock, of whom He Himself says in the Gospel: *My sheep hear my voice.* For look and note carefully that He says '*my* sheep,' as though there may be others beside which are not His; even as He Himself says in another passage: *Ye are not of my sheep.*[97] All of which things are, of course, highly relevant to this hidden mystery.

If this interpretation is correct, it is fitting also that the Bride should want the flock of each of the companions to be understood as that companion's bride, the bride whom she has described as being 'veiled.' But, because she was sure that she herself was superior to all those, she does not want to seem like any of them; for she knows that she ought to surpass those brides of the companions—or, as the Bride calls them, the 'veiled' ones—in the same measure as her Bridegroom surpasses the companions.

It will be seen, however, that she had other motives for asking what she did. She knows that the Good Shepherd makes it His business to seek for the best pastures for His sheep, and to find green and shady groves where they may rest during the noonday heat; whereas the Bridegroom's companions do not know how to do this, neither do they possess His knowledge and care in choosing their feeding-grounds. That, therefore, is the reason why she says: 'Tell me where Thou feedest, where Thou hast Thy couch in the midday': she desires just that time when the light is poured out on the world more copiously, when the day is pure and the daylight clearer and brighter.

'And then,' says she, 'tell me, O Thou whom my soul has loved, where Thou feedest, where Thou hast Thy couch in the midday, lest perchance I be made as one that is veiled above the flocks of Thy companions.' The Bride has now called the Bridegroom by a new name. For, knowing that He is the Son of Charity—nay, rather that He is Himself the Charity that is of God,[98] she has made a sort of title for Him with the words: 'Thou whom my soul has loved.' Yet she has not said 'Thou whom *I* have loved,' but 'Thou whom *my soul* has loved,' knowing that one must not love the Bridegroom with just any sort of love, but with one's whole soul, and one's whole strength, and with all one's heart.[99]

'Where feedest Thou,' she says, 'and where hast Thou Thy couch?' I think, moreover, that the prophet likewise is speaking of this place, concerning which the Bride desires of the Bridegroom to learn and to be told the whereabouts; set as he is under the same Shepherd, he says: *The Lord ruleth me*—or, as we read in other versions, *The Lord feedeth me*—*and I shall want nothing*.[100] And because he knew that other shepherds through sloth or inexperience assemble their flocks in the drier places, he says about the Lord, this best of shepherds: *In a green place, there hath He set me; He hath brought me up on the water of refreshment*, thus making it clear that this Shepherd provides His sheep with water that is not only plentiful, but also wholesome and pure and utterly refreshing.

And, because he has been changed from his former estate of being a sheep under a shepherd, and has advanced therefrom to rational and higher things, and has achieved this advance as a result of his conversion, he says further: *He hath converted my soul; He hath led me on the paths of justice for His own name's sake.* But, since he had advanced to the point of entering the paths of justice and justice itself inevitably has injustice fighting against it—and he who enters the way of justice *must* experience struggle with those who oppose him—trusting in faith and hope, the prophet says about these conflicts: *For though I should walk in the midst of the shadow of death, I will fear no evils, for Thou art with me.*

After this, as though returning thanks to Him who had instructed him in shepherd lore, he says: *Thy rod and Thy staff*—with which I was appointed to the office of shepherd—*they have comforted me.* Then, when he sees how he has been changed over from shepherd pastures to rational meats and mystical secrets, he goes on to say: *Thou hast prepared a table before me against them that afflict me; Thou hast anointed my head with oil, and Thy chalice which inebriates—how goodly it is! And Thy mercy will follow me all the days of my life, that I may dwell in the house of the Lord unto length of days.* That first life, the pastoral, was a preparatory one, in order that, being set in a green place, he might be brought up on the water of refreshment. But the things that follow have to do with progress and perfection.

And, since we have brought up the subject of pastures and of greenness, it seems fitting to support what we say out of the Gospels also. There too have I encountered this Good Shepherd talking about the pastures of the sheep; there is a passage where He styles Himself the Shepherd, and even calls Himself the Door, saying: *I am the Door. By me, if any man enter in, he shall be saved; and he shall go in and go out, and shall find pastures.*[101]

Him, therefore, the Bride now plies with questions that she may learn and hear from Him in what pastures He keeps His sheep, and in what pleasant places He keeps Himself during the midday heat. And what she calls 'midday' denotes those secret places of the heart in which the soul pursues the clearer light of knowledge from the Word of God; for midday is the time when the sun is at the zenith of its course. So when Christ, the Sun of Justice, shows to His Church the high and lofty secrets of His powers, then He will be teaching her where lie His pleasant pastures and His places of repose at noon. For when she has only begun to learn these things and is receiving from Him the rudiments, so to speak, of knowledge, then the prophet says: And *God will help her in the morning early.*[102] At this time, however, because she is now seeking things that are more perfect, and desiring higher things, she asks for the noonday light of knowledge.

I suppose this is the reason also why it is recorded of Abraham, after the many previous experiences in which God had appeared to Him and taught him on particular matters, that *God appeared to him at the oak of Mambre, as he was sitting at the door of his tent at midday. And lifting up his eyes,* Scripture says, *he saw, and behold, three men were standing over him.*[103] As we believe that these things were written by the Holy Spirit, I take it that it was not for nothing that the Divine Spirit saw fit to commit to the pages of Scripture even the time and hour of the vision; the detail of that hour and time was to add something to the knowledge of *the children of Abraham*—of those, that is, whose duty is *to do the works of Abraham,*[104] and also to hope for those visitations. For he who can say: *The night is passed and the day is at hand; . . . let us walk honestly as in the day: not in rioting and drunkenness, not in chambering and impurities, not in contention and envy,*[105] having gone through all these experiences, will have stepped over this time when the night is passed and the day is at hand, and will be hastening on, not to the beginning of the day, but to midday; so that he too may attain the grace of Abraham. For, if the light of the mind that is in him and the purity of his heart shall be bright and shining, he will have this midday time within himself; and, being set as it were in the noon through this purity of heart, he will see God as he sits by the oak of Mambre, which means From Seeing.

With regard to the time of vision, then, he 'sits at midday' who puts himself at leisure in order to see God. That is why Abraham is said to sit, not inside the tent but outside, at the door of the tent. For a man's mind also is out of doors and outside of the body, if it be far removed from carnal thoughts and carnal desires; and therefore God visits him who is placed outside all these. It is relevant to the same mystery that Joseph likewise, when he had received his brothers in Egypt, feeds them at midday, and at midday they bow down to him with their gifts.[106]

And, in conclusion, I suppose that was the reason why none of the Evangelists wanted to write about the things that the Jews committed against the Saviour, that they were done at midday; although the sixth hour denotes no other time than that of noon, yet no one calls it that. But Matthew puts it like this: *Now from the sixth hour there was darkness over the whole earth until the ninth hour*; Luke says: *And it was about the sixth hour, and there was darkness over all the earth until the ninth hour because the sun was darkened*; and Mark likewise: *And when the sixth hour was come, there was darkness over the whole earth until the ninth hour.*[107] Whence it appears that in the visitation of Abraham and in the banquet of the patriarchs with Joseph there was no need for that time to be denoted under the name of the number six; it was all right for it to be called midday. For the Bride, who was already foreshadowed in them, wanted to learn where the Bridegroom fed and where He had His couch; and therefore she calls the time midday. But the Evangelists, in telling their story, needed not the expression midday, but the number of the sixth hour, manifestly in order to narrate the sacrifice of that Victim who was offered on the day of the Pasch for the redemption of man, who himself was formed by God on the sixth day, after the earth had *brought forth the living creature after its kind, four-footed and creeping things and beasts of the earth.*[108]

For this reason, therefore, in the present passage the Bride desires to be enlightened with the full light of knowledge, lest going astray through lack of instruction she may be made in any respect like those schools of teachers which occupy themselves not with the very wisdom of God, but with the wisdom of this world and of the princes thereof. The Apostle also appears to state this selfsame thing in the passage where he says that *we speak the wisdom of God hidden in a mystery, . . . which none of the princes of this world knew.* And again he signifies the same thing when he says: *For we have received not the spirit of this world, but the spirit that is of God, that we may know the things that are given us from God.*[109]

So, then, the Bride of Christ enquires for His noonday resting-places and asks God for the plenitude of knowledge, lest she appear to be as one of the schools of the philosophers, which are said to be veiled, because with them the plenitude of truth is hidden and veiled. But the Bride of Christ says: *But we behold the glory of God with open face.*[110]

5

' Unless thou know thyself, O good (or fair) one among women,
   go forth in the footsteps of the flocks, and feed thy goats
   among the shepherds' tents.' (1.8—Vg. 1.7)

UNLESS THOU KNOW THYSELF, O GOOD (Or FAIR) ONE
AMONG WOMEN, GO FORTH IN THE FOOTSTEPS OF THE FLOCKS,
AND FEED THY GOATS AMONG THE SHEPHERDS' TENTS.

The* admirable maxim 'Understand thyself' or 'Know
thyself' is said to derive, among others, from one of the
seven men whom popular opinion acclaims as having been
of outstanding wisdom among the Greeks.[111] But Solomon who, as we saw in our Introduction,[112] anticipated all
these sages in time and in wisdom and in the knowledge of
things, says to the soul, as to a woman, and with the implication of a threat: 'Unless thou hast known thyself, O
fair one among women, and hast recognized whence the
ground of thy beauty proceeds—namely, that thou wast
created in God's Image,[113] so that there is in thee an abundance of natural beauty; unless thou hast thus realized how
fair thou wast in the beginning—though even now thou
art superior to other women and art the only one of them
to be called fair, unless thou hast in this wise known thyself
for what thou art—for I would not have thy beauty to
seem good by comparison with that of thine inferiors, but
rather that thou form thy judgement of thyself by looking

---

* Procopius, *Comm. in Cant. Cant.* 1.7 (MG 17.256 D-257 C): That
well-known saying among the Greeks, 'Know thyself,' was anticipated,
so tradition has it, by the wise Solomon. In line with this the soul is
now threatened by her Lover and Bridegroom that unless she guards
the beauty given to her in God's Image, she will be *cast out* from
indoors and put *in the outermost* area to tend *goats on the left hand* (Matt.
25.30, 33). 'Thou shalt tend them at the tents of the shepherds, now of

squarely at thyself and thine own comeliness—unless, I say, thou hast done this, I command thee to go forth and put thyself at the very back of the flocks, and no longer to feed sheep or lambs, but to feed goats, those creatures which, by reason of their wantonness and perversity, will be standing on the left hand of the King when He sits in judgement.[114] And though, when thou wast brought into the royal chamber, I may have shown thee things that are supremely good,[115] if thou know not thyself, I shall show thee also things that are supremely bad, that thou mayest profit from them both, alike by terror of the evil as by desire for the good. For, if thou hast not known thyself, and hast lived in ignorance thereof, not trying to acquire self-knowledge, thou shalt certainly not possess a tent of thine own, but shalt run about among the shepherds' tents, and, in those now of one, now of another, thou shalt feed thy goats, those restless, straying creatures that are appointed for sins.[116] These things shalt thou endure till circumstances and experience teach thee how great an evil it is for the soul not to know herself, nor yet that beauty of hers by which she is superior not to other virgins, but to other women—those, namely, who have suffered corruption and have not kept their maidenhood intact.'

After all those sayings of the Bride, this is what the Bridegroom says at this point in the drama. He speaks with a certain sternness, as giving a warning, and turns the thoughts of the Bride to the care for self-knowledge. But

this one, now of that, like some vagabond, until thou hast been guided by thy experience to the knowledge of thine own conversion.'

The saying can be applied to the Church also. A man knows himself when he knows whether his disposition is good or bad, and whether he is left far behind on the road to virtue, or is *stretching forth to those things that are before, forgetting the things that are behind* (Phil. 3.13); whether he has not yet attained beauty, or been made perfect in it, or

now let us do as we have done before, and apply these things to Christ and to the Church.[117]

In addressing these words to His Bride—that is, to the souls of believers, He makes the height of spiritual health and blessedness to consist in the knowledge and understanding of oneself.[118] I do not think it is possible to explain easily or briefly how a soul may know herself; but as far as we are able, we will try to elucidate a few points out of many.

It seems to me, then, that the soul ought to acquire self-knowledge of a twofold kind: she should know both what she is in herself, and how she is actuated; that is to say, she ought to know what she is like essentially, and what she is like according to her dispositions. She should know, for instance, whether she is of a good disposition or not, and whether or not she is upright in intention; and, if she is in fact of an upright intention, whether, in thought as in action, she has the same zeal for all virtues, or only for necessary things and those that are easy; furthermore, whether she is making progress, and gaining in understanding of things, and growing in the virtues; or whether perhaps she is standing still and resting on what she has been able to achieve thus far; and whether what she does serves only for her own improvement; or whether she can benefit others also, and give them anything of profit, either by the word of teaching or by the example of her actions.

If, on the other hand, she knows herself not to be of a good disposition nor upright in intention, let her in this

---

is only drawing near to its bounds. His duty is to attend to his every action to see how it is begotten in his every thought and word.

And the impure and careless souls he calls 'women.' Neglecting self-knowledge, the soul will be *tossed to and fro and carried about with*

case find out whether she is greatly deficient and far from the path of virtue; or whether she has already been set in that same way, and is trying to follow it, desiring to apprehend the things that are before and to forget those that are behind,[119] but has not yet drawn near or, if she have come near, at least has not as yet attained perfection.

And the soul needs to know herself in another way—whether she does these evil deeds of hers intentionally and because she likes them; or whether it is through some weakness that, as the Apostle says,[120] she works what she would not and does the things she hates, while on the contrary she seems to do good deeds with willingness and with direct intention. Does she, for example, control her anger with some people and let fly with others, or does she always control it, and never give way to it with anyone at all? So too with gloominess: does she conquer it in some cases, but give way to it in others, or does she never admit it at all? It is the same with fear, and all the other things that are patently opposed to the virtues.

And the soul who knows herself needs further to enquire whether she is greatly desirous of glory, or only slightly so, or not in the least. She can tell that from her reactions to praise—if she is greatly delighted thereby, or only mildly so, or not in the least degree; and regarding reproaches—whether they sadden her much, or only a little, or not at all.

For the soul who knows herself, there are, moreover, certain indications in the manner of her giving and receiving—whether she makes her offerings and bestows her

---

every wind of doctrine by the wickedness of men (Eph. 4.14); and she feeds her own *goats on the left hand* everywhere rather than at the side of the Good Shepherd who is the Word. But she—the Word is kind!—though she is not such as yet, is already accounted *fair among women* and

gifts in a spirit of sharing, and as one who likes her equity to be recognized among men; or whether she does so, as it is said, *with sadness or of necessity*,[121] or at any rate as expecting requital from those who hear her or receive gifts from her. So also in the matter of receiving, the soul who knows herself will notice whether she cares nothing for the things that she receives, or whether she rejoices over them as over something good.

Such a soul will take stock also of her mental processes, so as to find out whether she is easily moved by the hearing of some apparent truth and carried away by the skill and grace of its verbal presentation; or whether this seldom occurs or never at all. But we have said enough about that sort of knowledge. Anyone who so desires can think of a host of further ways like these, by which the soul may test her knowledge of herself and, contemplating the beauty which she received at her creation in God's Image, may judge how it may be renewed and restored.

The passage before us, then, enjoins the soul, under the figure of a woman, that she should know herself. It says, 'Unless thou know thyself.' That is to say: 'Unless thou hast guided thine inclinations along the several lines that we have just laid down, distinguishing in every case between what must be done and what must be avoided, between what thou lackest and what thou hast in full, what needs to be amended and what has to be preserved; and if, instead of doing this, thou hast without discrimination chosen to run with other souls on the common human

---

as of the Church of God and as fairer than the little ones therein; for those who are thus called 'women' of the Church are incomparably better than the Gentile souls following after lovers of adverse powers —'women' so-called, but not virgins. Indeed, how can she who looks up to her Creator, fail to be better?

level—which souls here are called women—among whom thou art fair, because thou hast already not only received the kisses of the Word of God, but also hast beheld the secrets of His chamber: if, then, I say, thou hast not known thyself, but, making no distinction, hast preferred to live as do the common people, go forth, then, in the footsteps of the flocks.' [122] That is to say: 'If, after all these things that have been given thee, thou doest nothing of uncommon excellence, neither—since thou knowest not thyself—hast held aloof from the flock's way of life, then be with the rest of the flock. And thou shalt be not only with the flock, but "in the footsteps of the flocks"; he shall become the last and latest, who did not understand his own preeminence.' [123]

And for this reason, when a soul has thus neglected knowledge, she is bound to be *carried about with every wind of doctrine* [124] into the deception of errors, so that she pitches her tent now with one shepherd—that is, with one teacher of the Word—and now with another, and so she is carried hither and thither, tending not sheep, which are guileless creatures, but goats—that is, her wanton, restless, sinful inclinations; [125] for which purpose indeed she has sought these divers teachers. And this will be the punishment of the fault of the soul, who has not tried to know herself and to follow that Shepherd only who lays down His life for the sheep. [126]

This is one way in which the soul ought to get knowledge of herself—namely, in her affections and actions. The other way in which the soul who is beautiful among women is

---

And as for the (command,) 'Go out,' this is the same as a man excommunicated from the Church being *delivered over to Satan for the destruction of the flesh* (1 Cor. 5.5), after having been, as was said to the maidens, introduced by the King into his chamber.

bidden to know herself is more abstruse and more difficult. If she can achieve it, she may hope for all good things; if not, then let her know that she must go forth after the footsteps of the flocks, and feed goats in the tents of shepherds, who are strangers to her. Let us then consider and, so far as we are able, embark on the discussion of this kind of knowledge too.

The Divine Word says by the mouth of the prophet: *Kindle for yourselves the light of knowledge.*[127] Now among spiritual gifts there is one that is indeed the greatest of them all, namely that word of knowledge which is imparted by the Holy Spirit;[128] and the primary object of that knowledge is that which Matthew's Gospel puts in this way: *No one has learnt* (novit) *the Son but the Father, neither hath anyone learnt* (novit) *the Father but the Son, and he to whom it shall please the Son to reveal Him.* But in Luke it runs thus: *No one knoweth* (scit) *what the Son is but the Father, and no one knoweth* (scit) *what the Father is but the Son, and he to whom it shall please the Son to reveal Him.* And according to John we read: *As the Father comprehendeth* (cognoscit) *me, even so do I know* (agnosco) *the Father.* But in the forty-fifth psalm the writer says: *Be still, and know that I am God.*[129]

The supreme function of knowledge is, therefore, to know the Trinity; and, in the second place, to know God's Creation, even as did he who said: *For He hath given me the true knowledge of the things that are, the substance of the world and the virtue of the elements, the beginning and ending and midst of the times,* etc.[130]

For the soul, therefore, these things will include a certain self-perception, by which she ought to know how she is constituted in herself, whether her being is corporeal or incorporeal, and whether it is simple, or consists of two or three or several elements;[131] also, as some would enquire, whether the substance of the soul has been made, or has definitely not been made by anyone; and, if it has been made, how it was made; whether, as some opine, its substance is contained in the bodily seed and originates together with the first beginning of the body; or whether it is introduced from the outside into the womb of a woman, and there united, as a perfect thing, to the body already prepared and formed for it.[132] And, if this be the case, whether it comes as a new creation that has only just been made when the body is seen to have been formed; in which case we should adjudge the reason for its creation to be the need for furnishing the body with a soul; or whether we should think that, having been created some time earlier, it comes for some reason to assume a body. And, if it is believed to be thus drawn into the body for some cause, then the work of knowledge is to determine what that cause may be.[133]

And there is the further question whether the soul puts on a body only once and, having laid it down, seeks for it no more; or whether, when it once has laid aside what it took, it takes it yet again; and, if it does so a second time, whether it keeps what it has taken always, or some day puts it off once more. But if, as the Scriptures lead us to think, the consummation of the world is near and this present state of corruption will be changed into one of incorruption,[134] there seems no doubt that the soul cannot come to the body a second or third time under the conditions of this present life. For, if this other view were accepted, then the world would know no end of such successive re-assumptions.

And the soul, pursuing this knowledge of herself, may further ask if there is some other class of beings, whether there are some spirits of the same sort of nature as herself, and other spirits too, that are not as she, but different from her: that is to say, are there not only some other spirits possessing reason as she does herself, but also some lacking reason? And is her nature the same as that of the angels— for it is generally thought that one sort of rationality cannot by any means differ from another? [135] And, if she is not such as they by nature, will she, if she be worthy, be made so by grace? Or can she not in any case be made like the angels, if the character and make-up of her nature have not received this form? For one would think it possible for that which has been lost to be restored, but not for that to be bestowed which the Creator did not give in the beginning.

And the soul in pursuit of self-knowledge should enquire also, whether her power of reason is changeable and such as can come and go; or whether it never fails when once it has been acquired. But what need is there to recount further reasons why the soul should know herself? That is to say, if she be neglectful about seeking a perfect self-knowledge, she may be commanded to go forth in the footsteps of the flocks and feed the goats, and this not in her own tent but in the shepherds' tents. Everyone who is disposed to follow up such reasons has ready to his hand abundant opportunities to take some of the things we have mentioned, and practise himself therein by the word of wisdom, as his strength permits.

Let us now take it that these words are spoken by the Word of God to the soul that has indeed been set in the path of progress, but has not yet attained the summit of perfection. She is called beautiful because she is advancing; yet to enable her to reach perfection a warning has to be addressed to her, because, unless she knows herself in detail, as we specified above, and exercises herself watchfully in the Word of God and in the divine Law, she will surely gather to herself about those details the notions of all sorts of people, and will follow men who speak nothing of excellence, nothing that is inspired by the Holy Spirit. For this is what it means to follow in the footsteps of the flocks: it is to run after the teachings of those who, continuing sinners themselves, have been unable to provide any remedy for those who sin. He who follows these will be feeding goats that are appointed for sins, and will be going round the shepherds' tents—that is, the various sects of the philosophers.[136]

Consider now more carefully how terrible a thing it is that this figure presages. 'Go forth,' He says, 'in the footsteps of the flocks.' The soul, now within doors and set among the mysteries, because she neglects to know herself and to enquire who she is and what she ought to do and how she ought to do it, and what she should not do, is for that fault of sloth told to go forth; she is turned out by Him who is set over her. So huge a danger is it for the soul to fail to know and understand herself.

But we have given a twofold explanation of what is meant by the soul's knowledge of herself. And it may seem that she is deservedly bidden to go forth—in the sense of being driven out of doors from the inside—if, as on the first interpretation, she neglects to examine her acts and test her progress and review her faults; but, on the other hand, the sentence may be thought severe, if we follow the second explanation, according to which we said that the knowledge she ought to have is that of her own nature and substance and state, both past and future. For where can there easily be found such a soul, so perfect and so very powerful that the reason and understanding of all these things is clear to her?

We shall reply to this that the words before us are not addressed to all souls; the Bridegroom is speaking not to the maidens, nor to the other women, nor to the eighty concubines, nor to the sixty queens, but only to her who alone is said to be the fair and perfect one among all women.[137] It is obvious from this that the words are spoken to certain beloved souls who, although God has given them many graces of perception and understanding, nevertheless neglect parts of this knowledge and take no pains to get to know themselves. The threat of the divine saying that *unto whomsoever much is given, of them much shall be required*,[138] applies, therefore, to them; the humble person shall be accounted worthy of pardon and mercy, but the mighty shall be mightily afflicted.[139]

So, then, if thou, O soul, that art fairer and more notable than others—teachers, for instance—neglectest thyself and continuest in thine ignorance, how will those desiring edification obtain instruction, and how will the gainsayers be refuted and denounced as false?[140] With reason, therefore, is she told, with an implication of threat, 'Go forth in the footsteps of the flocks, and feed thy goats among the shepherds' tents.'

We may compare with this what Moses writes, namely, that if an Israelite woman have committed adultery, she shall be stoned; but, if she be *the daughter of a priest . . . she shall be burnt with fire*.[141] The threat will seem just, therefore, as uttered against those who have the capacity for learning and knowledge, but slothfully neglect to use it; the Bridegroom's anger against such is very just, for He knows that the negligence of one involves the hurt of many.[142] For such a soul will appear also as resembling him who received a penny and hid it in the earth, so that his lord should get no profit on his money; it will resemble also him whom God slew, so we are told, because he was wicked, that is to say, him who, grudging to posterity the seed of natural knowledge that he had received, spilled that seed on the earth.[143]

And further, as we said before, if indeed this saying is of the nature of a warning to the Church, the shepherds must be taken as denoting the princes of this world, in other words those angels under whose charge the other nations are, having been brought to this condition either by lot or by some more secret processes.[144]

But if the warning be referred to the individual soul who neglects to know herself, then the sages and masters of this present age are to be understood, who teach the wisdom of this world.[145] Thus we may understand once and for all how vital it is for a soul—and especially for one who is good and lovely in disposition and awake in her intelligence—to acquire knowledge of herself, and to give heed to the recognition of herself through the study of doctrine and sacred pursuits, and thus to be led by the Spirit of God and the Spirit of adoption.[146]

For if such a soul as this shall have neglected herself and abandoned sacred pursuits, she is bound to give her attention to worldly pursuits and secular wisdom, and to be led by *the spirit of this world again in fear*. And that is just what the Apostle means when he says: *Now we have not received the spirit of this world, but the Spirit that is of God;* and again: *For you have not received the spirit of bondage again in fear, but you have received the spirit of adoption, whereby we cry: Abba, Father.*[147]

These are the points that have occurred to me about this present passage. Now let us turn to what follows.

6

'To my company of horsemen in Pharao's chariots have I deemed thee like, my neighbour.' (1.9—Vg. 1.8)

TO MY COMPANY OF HORSEMEN IN PHARAO'S CHARIOTS HAVE I DEEMED THEE LIKE, MY NEIGHBOUR. The historical sense which the writer seems to give is this: 'Just as, when long ago in Egypt,' he says, 'Pharao advanced in chariots and with horsemen in his pursuit of the people of Israel, and mine'—that is, the horsemen belonging to the Lord, the Spouse—'far outstripped the chariots of Pharao and were superior thereto, for they overcame them and drowned them in the Sea; [148] so likewise thou, my neighbour and my Bride, surpassest all women, and hast come to be compared to my company of horsemen which, by comparison with Pharao's chariots, is considered altogether stronger and more splendid.'

This seems to be the sense of the actual saying, and what the words are trying to express. But let us see now whether, on the mystical interpretation, under the figure of the chariots and four-horse teams of Pharao headed and driven by him for the persecution of God's people and the oppression of Israel, he is perhaps describing souls who are under the dominion of the spiritual Pharao and spiritual wickedness. For it is certain that the evil spirits stir up the temptations and troubles which they arouse against the saints, by means of certain souls who are suitable and convenient for the purpose. Mounting these like chariots, they fiercely attack and assail both the Church of God and individual believers. [149]

But, as to who the horsemen of the Lord may be, we read nothing in the passage in Exodus where Pharao's chariots are overthrown and drowned in the Sea, except the bare fact that the Lord cast Pharao's chariots and his army into the Red Sea. In the Fourth Book of Kings, however, we find that Eliseus says to his servant, who is alarmed at the approach of the enemy who had come with horsemen and chariots: *'Fear not, for there are more with us than with them.' And Eliseus prayed*, Scripture says, *and said: 'Lord, open the eyes of this servant that he may see.' And the Lord opened his eyes and he saw; and behold, the mountain was full of horses and chariots of fire round about Eliseus, which had come down to him.*[150] Again, in the prophet Habacuc we read plainly and clearly about the horsemen of the Lord, and that He mounts His horses. The words of Scripture in that place are these: *Wast Thou angry, O Lord, with the rivers? Or was Thy wrath upon the rivers? Or Thy fury on the sea? For Thou shalt mount Thy horses, and Thy horsemen are salvation.*[151]

Here, then, are the horses of the Lord that He mounts, and also His horsemen. And I myself take both the horses and the horsemen to be none other than those souls who accept the bridle of His discipline, and bear the yoke of His sweetness,[152] and are led by the Spirit of God and, in so doing, find salvation for themselves.

But in the Revelation of John we read that there appeared to him a horse, and sitting upon it One that was faithful and true and judging with justice, whose name, he tells us, is the Word of God. And so he says: *And I saw heaven opened, and behold, a white horse. And He that sat upon him was called faithful and true, and with justice doth He judge and fight. And His eyes were as a flame of fire, and on His head were many diadems, having a name written which no man knoweth but Himself. And He was covered with a garment sprinkled with blood, and His name was called The Word of*

God. And His army was in heaven, and they followed Him on white horses, clothed in fine linen, white and clean.[153]

To reveal to us the meaning of these things, however, so that we may perceive what these visions signify, what the white horse may be, and He who sits thereon, whose name is the Word of God, we need the grace of God. And perhaps somebody will say that the white horse is the body which the Lord assumed, and by which He, who as God the Word was in the beginning with God, so to speak rode about. Another, however, will prefer to say that it denotes the life which the Firstborn of every creature took, and of which He said: *I have power to lay it down, and I have power to take it up again.*[154] And someone else will think that both the body and the life together are called the white horse when they have no sin. Fourthly and lastly, somebody will say that it is the Church which also is called His Body, which appears as a white horse; since she, whom He has sanctified for Himself by the laver of water, has neither spot nor wrinkle.[155] And he will interpret on the same lines also the things which follow, the host of heaven and the army of the Word of God, and the fact that all the followers of the Word of God also are seated on white horses, everyone of them, and are clothed in fine linen, white and clean.

Christ, then, is comparing and likening His Church at once to this white horse, by which He Himself is carried who is called the Word of God, and to this heavenly army that follows Him, also on white horses. Moreover, we can take 'in Pharao's chariots' also to mean either that just as the Lord's company of horsemen surpasses and excels the cavalry and chariots of Pharao, so likewise dost thou, who art the fair one among women, surpass and excel all other souls, who still bear Pharao's yoke and endure his riders;

or it can certainly mean that this 'my company of horse-men,' which has been cleansed by the laver of water and made pure and shining and is deemed worthy to have the Word of God for its rider, has been taken from among the chariots of Pharao. For all believers do come thence; because *Christ came into the world to save sinners*.[156]

We can, therefore, explain the meaning of this phrase in this way: 'I deem thee, my neighbour, like to my company of horsemen that formerly was numbered among Pharao's chariots and now, having been purified by the laver of water, follows me upon white horses.'

Blessed are those souls, in consequence, who have bent their backs to take upon themselves the Word of God as rider and to endure His bridle, so that He may turn them whithersoever He will, and lead them with the reins of His commandments; for they no longer go in their own way, but are led, and led back, in all things according to their Rider's will.

And the fact that the Church is the aggregate of many souls and has received the pattern of her life from Christ, may lead us to suppose that she has received that pattern not from the actual deity of the Word of God—and this obviously is far above those actions and dispositions in respect of which men ought to be given a pattern—but rather that it was the soul [157] that He assumed and in which was the utmost perfection, that was the pattern displayed to men. It will then be the likeness of the same soul which He here calls 'my neighbour,' that the Church—and this is the aggregate of those many souls that were formerly under Pharao's yoke and among his chariots, and now are called the company of the Lord's horsemen—ought to bear.

But you who read this must decide for yourself which

of these two interpretations best suits the phrase in question.

7

'How lovely have thy cheeks become, as are the turtle-dove's, thy neck as necklaces!' (1.10—Vg. 1.9)

HOW LOVELY HAVE THY CHEEKS BECOME, AS ARE THE TURTLE-DOVE'S, THY NECK AS NECKLACES!' The drama seems to have developed in the following manner. After the Bridegroom had used some sternness in cautioning the Bride, impressing on her that if she knew not herself, she must go forth in the footsteps of the flocks and feed, not sheep but goats, she blushed at the severity of the command. And the redness of shame, which then suffused her face, made her cheeks lovely and much fairer than they had been before; and not her cheeks only, but also her neck is now rendered as beautiful as if it were adorned with necklaces of jewels. Further, the beauty of her cheeks is compared to turtle-doves, because birds of this kind are notable both for their noble mien and for their eager speed. So much for the narrative. Now let us look at its significance.

Paul the Apostle, writing to the church of the Corinthians, speaks as follows: *For the body also is not one member, but many. And, if the foot should say, 'Because I am not the hand, I am not of the body,' it would not therefore be not of the body. And if the ear should say, 'Because I am not the eye, I am not of the body,' it would not therefore be not of the body. If the whole body were the eye, where would be the hearing? If the whole were hearing, where would be the smelling? But now God hath set the members, every one of them, in the body as it hath pleased Him.* And, after a further discussion of the matter, he says finally: *Now you are the body of Christ and members severally.*[158] And again, writing to the Ephesians, he says: *Being subject one to another in the fear of Christ, let women be subject to their husbands as to the Lord; because the husband is the head of the wife, even as Christ is the head of the Church. He is the Saviour of the body. But as the Church is subject to Christ, so also let the wives be to their husbands in all things. Husbands, love your wives, as Christ also loved His Church and delivered Himself up for it, that He might sanctify it by the laver of water in the Word, that He might make ready for Himself a glorious Church, not having spot or wrinkle or any such thing, but that it should be holy and without blemish.* And a little further on he says: *For no man ever hated his own flesh, but nourisheth and cherisheth it, as also Christ doth the Church, because we are members of His body,* and so forth.[159]

Therefore, we are taught by these words that the Bride of Christ, who is the Church, is also His Body and His members. If,* then, you hear mention of the members of the Bridegroom, you must understand by it the members of His Church. Among these, just as there are some who are called eyes, doubtless because they have the light of understanding and of knowledge, and others ears, to hear the word of teaching, and others hands to do good works and to discharge the functions of religion:[160] so also are there some who may be called His cheeks. But they are called the cheeks of the face, when integrity and modesty of soul appear in them; these cheeks must, therefore,

---

* Procopius, *Comm. in Cant. Cant.* 1.9 (MG 17.257 C): But Paul speaks of the members of Christ as those of His Bride the Church. It is as if those excelling in the beauty of the other members do not at all consider her face ugly, but rather regard her blushes as the fruit of her modesty.—Those who perhaps were not beautiful before underwent

surely be those members of the Church who cultivate the integrity of chastity and virtue.

Because of these, therefore, it is said to the whole body of the Bride: 'How lovely have thy cheeks become!' And notice that He did not say, 'How lovely are thy cheeks!'— but, 'How lovely have thy cheeks become!' He means to show that previously they were not so lovely. It was only after she had received the Bridegroom's kisses, and after He, who formerly spoke by the prophets, had come and cleansed this Church for Himself in the laver of water and made her to be without spot or wrinkle and given her knowledge of herself, that her cheeks became lovely. For the chastity and virtue and virginity which had not existed before, were spread abroad in a lovely beauty through the cheeks of the Church.

This beauty of the cheeks, however, that is, of modesty and chastity, is compared to turtle-doves. They say it is the nature of turtle-doves that the male bird never mates with any female but one, and the female similarly will not suffer more than a single mate; so that, if one of the pair be killed and the other left, the survivor's desire for intercourse is extinguished with its mate.[161] The figure of the turtle-dove is thus fittingly applied to the Church, either because she knows no union with any other after Christ, or because all the continence and modesty that is in her resembles a flight of many doves.

Let us interpret the Bride's neck in the same way. It must surely denote those souls who receive the yoke of Christ who says: *Take up my yoke upon you, . . . for my yoke is*

---

so great a change, that it was said to the Bride: 'Why were thy cheeks made beautiful, *not having spot or wrinkle* (Eph. 5.27)?' Perhaps by getting to know the one only God; yes, for the turtle-dove also has but a single mate.

sweet.[162] Her 'neck' is so called, therefore, because of her obedience. And her neck has been made 'lovely as necklaces,' and rightly so. For that which the disobedience of the Transgression formerly made shameful,[163] the obedience of faith has now made beautiful and fair.

'Thy neck,' then, 'has been made fair as necklaces'; for we must understand 'has been made fair' with both subjects. By 'necklaces' are meant here the strings or chains of jewels which rest on the nape of the neck; the rest of the adornment depends and hangs down from them over the entire neck. So He has compared the Bride's neck to the ornament that is usually placed on the back of the neck and on the front of it. Our thoughts on this saying are as follows: We have said that subjection and obedience are called the neck; because the neck may be said to receive the yoke of Christ and to offer the obedience of faith in Him. So the adornment of her neck, that is, of her obedience, is Christ. For He himself was first made *obedient unto death*; and, *as by the disobedience of one man*—namely, of Adam—*many were made sinners, so also by the obedience of one*—that is, of Christ—*many shall be made just.*[164] So the adornment and necklace of the Church is the obedience of Christ. But the neck of the Church too, that is, her obedience, has been made like to the obedience of Christ; because His obedience is the necklace of the neck.

Great in this matter, therefore, is the praise of the Bride, great the glory of the Church, when her obedience, patterned as it is on Christ's, equals the obedience of Him whom the Church imitates.

This same sort of necklace is mentioned also in Genesis, as given by the patriarch Juda to Thamar, his daughter-in-law, with whom he had lain as with a harlot.[165] This mystery is not obvious to all. We understand by it that

Christ gave to the Church, whom He had gathered in from the prostitution of many philosophical doctrines, these pledges of future perfection, and put this necklace of obedience on her neck.

8

'We will make thee likenesses of gold with silver inlays, till the King recline at His table.' (1.11–12a—Vg. 1.10–11a)

WE WILL MAKE THEE LIKENESSES OF GOLD WITH SILVER INLAYS, TILL THE KING RECLINE AT HIS TABLE. We have already noted [166] that this little book, being cast in the form of a play, is woven out of interchange of characters; and now the friends and companions of the Bridegroom— who, on the mystical interpretation, can be taken, as also we remarked before, either as the angels or even the prophets, or as the patriarchs [167]—appear as speaking the words quoted to the Bride. For it was not only when the Lord after the baptism of John was tempted by the devil in the wilderness, that the angels came and ministered to Him; [168] before the coming of His bodily presence they always ministered. For the Law itself is said to have been *ordained by angels in the hand of a mediator*; and the Apostle, writing to the Hebrews, says: *For if the word which was received through angels became steadfast. . . .* [169]

These acted, then, as governors and guardians appointed for the Bride while she was yet a little child with the Law as her pedagogue—until *the fullness of the time should come,* and *God should send His Son, made of a woman, made under the Law*, and should lead her who was under governors and guardians and the Law her pedagogue, to receive the kisses [170] of the Word of God Himself, that is, His words and teaching.

Before the time came for these things to happen, therefore, the Bride was being cherished by the service of angels
in many ways; they used in those days to appear to men
and tell them such things as the time and occasion required.[171] For you must please not think that she is called
the Bride or the Church only from the time when the
Saviour came in flesh: she is so called from the beginning
of the human race and from the very foundation of the
world—indeed, if I may look for the origin of this high
mystery under Paul's guidance, even *before* the foundation
of the world. For this is what he says: . . . *as He chose us in
Christ before the foundation of the world, that we should be holy
and unspotted in His sight, predestinating us in charity unto
the adoption of sons.*[172]

And in the Psalms too it is written: *Remember Thy
congregation, O Lord, which Thou hast gathered from the
beginning.*[173] And indeed the first foundations of the congregation of the Church were laid at the very beginning;[174]
and for this reason the Apostle says that the Church is
built on the foundation not of the apostles only, but also of
the prophets.[175] And among the prophets Adam too is
reckoned,[176] who prophesied *the great mystery in Christ and
in the Church,*[177] when he said: *For this cause a man shall
leave his father and his mother, and shall cleave to his wife, and
they shall be two in one flesh.*[178] It is clearly with reference
to these words of his that the Apostle says that *this is a great
mystery, but I speak in Christ and in the Church.*[179]

When, however, the same Apostle says: *For Christ so
loved the Church that He delivered Himself up for it, sanctifying
it by the laver of water,*[180] he is far from showing that she
did not exist before. For how could He have loved her, if
she did not exist? Undoubtedly He loved her who did
exist; she existed in all the saints who have been since time

began. So, loving her, He came to her; and, *as the children were partakers of flesh and blood, He also Himself in like manner was made a sharer of the same,*[181] and delivered Himself up for them. They themselves were the Church whom He loved to the intent that He might increase her in multitude and develop her in virtue and translate her through the love of perfectness from earth to heaven.

The prophets, then, ministered to her from the beginning; so also did the angels. What else was happening when the three men appeared to Abraham as he sat by the oak of Mambre? The angels on that occasion, however, displayed something more than mere angelic ministry, for the mystery of the Trinity was there made known.[182] This was the case also in Exodus, where the angel of the Lord is said to have appeared to Moses in a flame of fire in the bush; but directly afterwards it is written that the Lord and God spoke by the angel, and He is designated as *the God of Abraham, and the God of Isaac, and the God of Jacob.*[183] Some of the heretics reading this passage have said that the God of the Law and the Prophets was much inferior to Jesus Christ and to the Holy Spirit; and they have gone so far in their impiety as to ascribe all plenitude to Christ and the Holy Spirit, but imperfection and weakness to the God of the Law.[184] But more of this another time.

We are setting out now to show in what sense the holy angels who had charge of the Bride while she was yet a child, before the coming of the Lord, are identical with the friends and companions of the Bridegroom, here represented as saying to her: 'We will make thee likenesses of gold and silver inlays, till the King reclines at His table.' They show that they themselves are going to make for the Bride not gold, for they possess none worthy to be given her, but in the place of gold they promise to make her *likenesses* of gold, and not one alone, but many. So they speak also of silver, implying that they have that, but only a small quantity of it; for they promise to make her out of silver not likenesses, but *inlays*. They do not possess enough silver to make a complete solid article of that alone, so they would put only inlays and some little things, like dots, into the thing that they were making for her out of the likeness of gold. These, then, are the ornaments which the Bridegroom's friends, of whom we spoke just now, are making for the Bride.

As to the secret meaning which these things contain, however, and the teaching that these strange words labour to express, let us pray the Father of the Almighty Word and Bridegroom, that He Himself will open to us the gates of this mystery, whereby we may be enlightened not only for the understanding of these things, but also for the propagation of them, and may receive also a portion of spiritual eloquence, according to the capacity of those who are to be our readers.

We have often and in many contexts pointed out that gold symbolizes the perceptive and incorporeal nature;[185] whereas silver represents the power of speech and reason, even as the Lord says through the prophet: *I gave you silver and gold, but you have made silver and golden Baalim.*[186] Which is as much as to say: 'I gave you perception and reason, with which to perceive and worship me, your God; but you have transferred the perception and reason that is in you to the worship of evil spirits.'

We are told, too, that *the words of the Lord are pure words, as silver tried in the fire*; again, in another place *the tongue of the just* is said to be *as silver tried by fire*.[187] And the cherubim are described as golden, because they are by interpretation the plenitude of knowledge. And it is commanded also that a candlestick of solid gold should be put in the Tabernacle of the Testimony;[188] and that, it seems to us, is a type of the natural law in which the light of knowledge is contained. But what need is there to multiply proof texts, when those who will can easily see for themselves from many Scripture passages, that gold is applied to the intellect and mind, whereas silver is referred only to language and the power of speech?

Now, therefore, let us hasten on to contemplate, along the lines that we have just laid down, the sense in which the Bridegroom's friends speak of making 'likenesses of gold and silver inlays' for the Bride. For it seems to me that because the Law which *was ordained by angels in the hand of a mediator*, had *but a shadow of good things to come, not the very image of the things*, and because all the things that happened to those who are described as being under the Law happened in a figure, not in the truth,[189] these things are all of them the likenesses of gold, and not true gold. Let us then take it that true gold denotes things incorporeal, unseen and spiritual; but that the likenesses of gold, in which is not the Truth itself but only the Truth's shadow, denote things bodily and visible. That tabernacle made with hands, for instance, was a likeness of gold, of which the Apostle says: *For Jesus is not entered into the Holies made with hands, the patterns of the true, but into heaven itself.*[190]

The unseen and incorporeal things that are in heaven, then, these are the true; but those that are visible and bodily on earth are said to be the patterns of the true, and not themselves the true. It is these, therefore, that are called the likenesses of gold; and they include the Ark of the Testimony, and the propitiatory, and the cherubim, and the altar of incense, and the table of proposition, and the loaves; likewise the veil, and the pillars, and the bars, and the altar of holocausts, and the Temple itself, and all the things that are written in the Law.[191] All these were likenesses of gold. But the visible gold itself, just because it was visible, was not the true gold, but the likeness of that true and unseen gold.

The friends of the Bridegroom, therefore—that is to say, the angels and the prophets who ministered in the Law and the other mysteries—made these likenesses of gold for the Bride Church. And this, I think, is what Paul understood when he said: *In religion of angels, being in vain puffed up by the sense of the flesh, in the things that he sees.*[192] Thus the whole of the Jewish religion and cult was likenesses of gold.

When, however, a man *shall be converted to the Lord,* and *the veil shall be taken away* from him,[193] then he will see the true gold. Before that Gold came and offered Himself to be known, His friends made likenesses of Him for the Bride, so that she, being warned and aroused by these similitudes, might conceive a longing for the true Gold. For Paul shows that this happened when he says: *Now these things happened to them in figure, and they are written for our sake, upon whom the end of the ages is come.*[194] But do not take this end, of which Paul speaks, in a temporal sense; for the end of time will find many for whom these things were not written, neither will such grasp their significance. You must understand *the end of the ages* rather as the consummation of things;[195] these are the things that are said to have actually happened to Paul and others like him, and to have been written for their sakes.

We have dealt at unusual length with these matters because we wanted to show that when the Bridegroom's friends tell the Bride that they are making for her likenesses of gold inlaid with silver, they mean thereby the things that have been handed down in writing in the Law and

the Prophets by means of figures, and images, and likenesses, and parables.

Among★ these likenesses, however, there are also some
small silver inlays, that is, some tokens of a spiritual
meaning and a rational interpretation; though these are
only very rare and slight. For before the coming of the
Lord scarcely one of the prophets ever disclosed a hint of
any hidden meaning; as, for example, Isaias when he says:
*For the vineyard of the Lord of hosts is the house of Israel, and
the house of Juda, His beloved newly planted vine;* and again
in another place: *The many waters are many nations.*[196] And
Ezechiel, speaking of two sisters called Oolla and Ooliba,
explains that the one is Samaria and the other Juda.[197] It is
passages such as these, the interpretation of which is revealed to the prophets themselves, that are called silver
inlays.

But, when our Lord and Saviour Jesus Christ came,
upholding all things by the word of His power,[198] a sign was
given at His Passion that the things which were concealed
in secrets and mysteries were now to be brought into the
light and come to manifestation. For the veil of the
Temple, by which the hidden and secret parts of the Holies
were curtained off, was rent from the top to the bottom,[199]
thus openly declaring to all men that that which had been
formerly concealed within could now be seen.

As, therefore, what was ministered by angels and prophets was the likeness of gold, with a few small inlays of

---

★ Procopius, *Comm. in Cant. Cant.* 1.10 (ML 17.257 D): At that
time silver was neither plentiful nor scattered abroad: only a few
things were said in secret by the prophets and wise men of old. But
when He dwelt among us, the things in the untrodden parts of the
Temple were gazed upon by anyone who beheld the true *veil rent from
the top to the bottom* (Matt. 27.51), in order that the inner part might be

silver; so have the things delivered through Our Lord Jesus Christ Himself been set in true gold and in solid silver. For this likeness of gold with silver inlays, made by the friends of the Bridegroom, is not promised to last for ever; its time is fixed for it by the speakers themselves as being 'till the King recline at His table.' For when He has laid Him down and slept *as a lion and as a lion's whelp*, and afterwards the Father has aroused Him, and He has risen from the dead,[200] if then there be such as have been made conformable to His resurrection, they will continue no longer in the likeness of gold, that is, in the pursuit of bodily things, but will receive the true gold from Him. For what they seek and hope for is not things visible, but things invisible; not things on earth, but things in heaven where Christ sitteth at the right hand of God. And they will say: *If we have known Christ according to the flesh, but now we know Him so no longer.*[201]

Now, therefore, they will use no longer little inlays of silver, but will use it copiously and freely. For they will understand that Christ was in that likeness of gold, the rock which is said to follow the people and to afford them drink, and that the Sea is Baptism, and the cloud the Holy Spirit, and the manna the Word of God, and the paschal lamb the Saviour, and the blood of the lamb the Passion of Christ, and the veil which is in the Holies of Holies and by which those divine and secret things were covered, is His flesh;[202] and countless other things will lie open to them from His resurrection, not now like a little inlay, but as spread out in all their breadth.

---

gazed upon, when He laid Him down and slept *as a lion and as a lion's whelp and rose again* (Gen. 49.9). And next: Then those who have been made conformable to His resurrection will receive from Him, instead of likeness, gold; they will be surfeited with gold and silver.

But now, however, in order to elucidate the meaning of 'till the King recline at His table,' let us also adduce from the second prophecy of Balaam the passage that refers to Christ. *A star*, he says, *shall rise out of Jacob and a man shall come forth from his seed, and he shall rule over many nations, and his kingdom shall be exalted over Gog, and his kingdom shall increase. For God shall bring him out of Egypt; as the glory of the unicorn he shall lay waste the nations of his enemies, and deprive their bones of strength, and shoot them with his darts. Lying down he shall rest as a lion and as a lion's whelp, and who shall rouse him up?* [203]

So consider these points more carefully, and see in what sense every likeness of gold is said to last for a fixed time— namely, until the King's reclining at His table. But after these things *his kingdom shall be exalted above Gog*—that is, above *the many mansions.*[204] This will happen when it has been translated from earth to the heavenly dwellings. But we have pursued this matter further, as far as the Lord enabled us, in writing on the Book of Numbers.[205]

Let us, however, consider whether the grace of this perfection, which is of the true gold, was given also to the holy fathers and prophets who ministered the Word before the coming of Our Lord Jesus Christ, or whether they understood these matters only as future, and foresaw in the spirit that they would come to pass; so that when the Lord said of Abraham that he desired to see His day, and saw it and was glad,[206] He meant only that in the spirit he had foreknowledge of the things to be. And perhaps it is the latter view that would be supported by that other saying: *Many . . . just men have desired to see the things that you see and have not seen them, and to hear the things that you hear and have not heard them*;[207] although not even they could have lacked the perfection that proceeds from faith. For the things that we believe actually to have happened they, with a greater expectation, believed as going to happen.

As, therefore, the faith of believers since Christ's coming in things that have already taken place has brought them to the summit of perfection, so also did their faith in things to come bring them to the same end. If this be interpreted in relation to the individual soul, we shall get this: As long as the soul is still a little child, and imperfect, and set under tutors and guardians, whether these be the Church's teachers or the angels—whom *the little ones* are said to have, and who *always see the face of the Father who is in heaven*—they make her likenesses of gold because she is not fed with the solid and strong meats of the Word of God, but is instructed by means of likenesses and taught, as we may say, by parables and patterns, just as even Christ Himself is said to have grown in age and wisdom and in grace with God and men.[208]

The soul, then, is instructed by these similitudes and silver inlays are made for her while she is a child.[209] For every now and then particles of light are shed upon the deeper mysteries for those too who are being thus instructed, so that they may conceive desire for higher things; for no one can even desire a thing of which he has no knowledge whatsoever. And, therefore, just as beginners and those who are receiving the rudiments of learning must not have everything unfolded to them all at once, so neither must spiritual and mystical matters be wholly hidden from them; but, as the divine Word says, silver inlays must be made for them and some small sparks of spiritual understanding cast into their minds, so that they may somehow acquire a taste for the sweetness that is so much to be desired; otherwise, as we have said, there would be no desire, if that which is desirable be utterly unknown.

Let no one think, however, that, because we call the soul a little child, she is so essentially; no, she is such only in that she lacks learning; because she has but small understanding and very little skill, do we speak of the soul as little. These likenesses had, therefore, to be made only 'till the king recline at His table'—that is, only until such a soul shall advance sufficiently to receive 'the King reclining at His table' in herself. For this King says Himself: *I will dwell among them, and I will walk among them,*[210] meaning among those, surely, who offer such roomy hearts to the Word of God that He may even be said to walk about in them, that is, in the open spaces of a fuller understanding and a wider knowledge.

That doubtless is the reason too why He is said also to recline at table in that soul, of whom the Lord Himself says by the prophet: *Upon whom shall I rest, but upon him that is lowly and quiet, and that trembleth at my words?*'[211] That King, who is the Word of God, reclines, then, at His table in that soul who has already come to perfection, provided that she have no vice in her, but rather is full of holiness, full of piety, faith, charity, peace, and all the other virtues. Then is it that the King takes pleasure in resting and reclining at His table in her. For it was to this soul that the Lord was speaking when He said: *I and my Father will come and will sup with him, and will make our abode with him.*[212] And where Christ with the Father sups and makes His abode, how does He not also there recline at table? Blessed is that roomy soul, blessed the couches of her mind, where both the Father and the Son, surely together with the Holy Spirit, recline and sup and have their dwelling-place!

With what precious stores, think you, with what abundance are such Guests regaled? Peace is the first food put on there, with it are served humility and patience, clemency likewise and gentleness and—the sweetest of all to Him—cleanness of heart. But charity holds the highest place at this banquet.

On these lines, therefore, on this third interpretation, you will see that the words: 'We will make thee likenesses of gold with silver inlays, till the King recline at His table,' may be applied to any individual soul.

9

'*My spikenard has yielded its* (or *His*) *odour.*' (1.12b—Vg. 1.11b)

MY* SPIKENARD HAS YIELDED ITS (or HIS) ODOUR. What is shown by this next step in the drama seems to be as follows. After the foregoing words were spoken, the Bride came in to the Bridegroom and anointed Him with her ointments; and in some marvellous way the spikenard, scentless so long as it was with the Bride, yielded its odour when it touched the Bridegroom's body; with the result, apparently, not that He has received something from it, but rather that the spikenard has received from Him.

And if we read: 'My spikenard yielded *His* odour,' as we find in some copies, something still more divine emerges: this ointment of spikenard, with which the Bridegroom has been anointed, has acquired not the odour natural to the spikenard, but that of the Bridegroom

---

* Procopius, *Comm. in Cant. Cant.* 1.11 (MG 17.260 A): 'It is my Bridegroom's odour,' she says, 'that my spikenard wherewith I anointed Him, has yielded.' For having *anointed the feet of Jesus with* her own *nard and wiped them with her hair*, she in turn received it back

Himself; and that the nard has wafted His odour back to the Bride. She, in anointing the Bridegroom, has thus received as a gift the odour of His own ointment; and her present words will therefore mean: 'My spikenard, with which I anointed the Bridegroom, has come back to me, bearing with it the Bridegroom's own odour; its natural odour has been mastered by the Bridegroom's fragrance, and it has brought back His own sweetness unto me.'

So much for the dramatic narrative; now let us turn to the spiritual sense.

Let us see the Bride Church in this passage in the character of that Mary of whom it is said with all fitness that she brings a pound of ointment of great price, and anoints the feet of Jesus, and wipes them with her hair.[213] Through the hair of her head she as it were gets that ointment back, and receives it again for herself, steeped in the character and virtue of His body; thus through the hair with which she wiped His feet, she draws to herself the odour not so much of the ointment as of the very Word of God, and what she has put on her own head is the fragrance of Christ, rather than that of the nard. Wherefore she says: 'My spikenard, having been given to the body of Christ, has yielded me back His odour.'

And notice now to what these things refer. *Mary*, the Scripture says, *brought a pound of ointment of spikenard of great price, and anointed the feet of Jesus, and wiped them with the hair of her head. And the whole house*, it says, *was filled with the odour of the ointment.* This surely shows that the odour of the teaching that proceeds from Christ, and the

---

refined by the odour of her Bridegroom. Perceiving the fragrance to have come upon her head, she says: 'my spikenard has yielded me the odour of my Bridegroom!' Wherefore, as from the body of Jesus, her —His disciple's—myrrh *filled the whole house* (John 12.3).

fragrance of the Holy Spirit have filled the whole house of the world, or else the whole house of the Church. Or, indeed, it has filled the whole house of the soul, who has received a share in the odour of Christ, in the first place, by offering Him the gift of her faith as the ointment of spikenard, and then receiving back the grace of the Holy Spirit and the fragrance of spiritual teaching.

What difference, therefore, does it make whether it is the Bride in the Song of Songs who anoints the Bridegroom with ointment, or the disciple Mary in the Gospel who anoints her Master Christ, hoping, as we said, that by that ointment the odour of the Word and the fragrance of Christ will be returned to her, so that she too may say: *We are a good odour . . . unto God?* [214] And, because that ointment was full of faith and of precious, loving intention, Jesus Himself bore witness to her saying: *She hath wrought a good work upon me.* [215]

So likewise, a little further on in the Song of Songs He speaks of the Bride's 'shoots' with the same favour as He shows here to Mary's work: for He says: *Thy shoots are a paradise with pomegranates, cypress with spikenards, spikenard and saffron.* [216] Thus He includes the 'shoots' and gifts of the Bride among these things too.

We have of course observed that in the passage that has just been quoted the plural 'spikenards' was used first, and then the singular. I think the reason for this usage is the same as that for which the merchant of the Kingdom of Heaven buys many pearls at first, until such time as he may find the one pearl of great price. [217] And perhaps His saying 'Thy shoots are a paradise with pomegranates' denotes those fruits with many spikenards, which we gather from the elements of instruction and the prophets' teaching. The shoots and gifts that we gather from the teaching of the

Lord Jesus Christ Himself, however, have not many spike-nards, but only one.

Now let us return to her who says, 'My spikenard has yielded its odour,' and see whether we can still understand in this present passage also—if ever we can contrive to treat adequately and fitly of the Godhead of Christ, and to frame worthy statements concerning His might and majesty—that the Church, or the soul, who can thus openly declare His glory in the words, 'My spikenard has yielded its odour,' will perhaps be justified in doing so. And we need not think it strange that Christ, who is the Fountain, and from whom rivers of living water flow, who is Bread and gives life,[218] should in the same way also be the spike-nard, and yield His odour, and be the ointment which makes those who are anointed by it to be Christs themselves, as it says in the Psalm: *Touch not my Christs.*[219]

And perhaps, as the Apostle says, *for those who have their senses exercised to the discerning of good and evil,*[220] Christ becomes each of these things in turn, to suit the several senses of the soul.[221] He is called the true Light, therefore, so that the soul's eyes may have something to lighten them. He is the Word, so that her ears may have something to hear. Again, He is the Bread of life, so that the soul's palate may have something to taste. And in the same way, He is called the spikenard or ointment, that the soul's sense of smell may apprehend the fragrance of the Word. For the same reason He is said also to be able to be felt and handled, and is called the Word made flesh, so that the hand of the interior soul may touch concerning the Word of life.[222] But all these things are the One, Same Word of God, who adapts Himself to the sundry tempers of prayer according to these several guises, and so leaves none of the soul's faculties empty of His grace.

10

*'A sachet of a myrrh-drop is my Nephew to me, He shall abide
   between my breasts.'* (1.13—Vg. 1.12)

A SACHET ⋆ OF A MYRRH-DROP [223] IS MY NEPHEW TO ME,
HE SHALL ABIDE (or TARRY) BETWEEN MY BREASTS. These are
still the words of the Bride, speaking apparently to the
maidens. She had said before that her spikenard had yielded
her the Bridegroom's odour, and that, by means of the
ointment with which she had anointed Him, she had received the fragrance of His odour. But now she says: 'My
Nephew smells to me like myrrh,' and that not diffused
and dispersed at random, but bound and tied together, so
as to make the sweetness of its odour stronger and more
potent. 'And He,' she says, 'since such He is, tarries and
abides between my breasts, and has His rest and His abode
in my bosom.'

But because the Bride has now for the first time called
Him her Nephew, and because she uses this title for Him
frequently throughout practically the entire book, I think
it well to discuss first the reason for His being so called, and
to explain what 'nephew' means, and whence the name
derives. A person is called 'nephew' when he is a brother's
son. Let us then first enquire who is the Bride's brother,
whose son this 'nephew' is held to be, and see if we can say
that the Bride is indeed the Church of the Gentiles, and her

⋆ Procopius, *Comm. in Cant. Cant.* 1.12 (MG 17.260 AB): 'A sachet
of stacte is my Nephew to me, He shall abide between my breasts.
Having said, "My spikenard has yielded me 'my Bridegroom's'
odour," I now say that my Nephew breathes forth stacte—not diffused nor blown about, but compassed about and giving concentrated
fragrance.' Having the first people for her brother, the Church of the
Gentiles, seeing that *of them was Christ according to the flesh* (Rom. 9.5),

brother—her elder brother, as circumstances show—the former People. Christ is called the son of her brother by the Gentile Church, because He was born of that former People according to the flesh.[224] Her saying, 'A sachet of a myrrh-drop is my Nephew to me,' denotes, therefore, the mystery of His bodily birth; for the body, with which the myrrh of the divine power and sweetness in Christ is bound, does seem to be a 'sachet' in a sense, and as it were a band on His soul.

If, however, these words be taken as referring to the individual soul, the 'sachet of a myrrh-drop' must be understood as the contents of the divine teachings and the intricacy and complication of the propositions of theology;[225] for the articles of our belief are interwoven, and are bound together with the bands of truth. Moreover, the Law declares further that every vessel that is bound is clean, but that which has been loosed and not tied is unclean;[226] and from that type we can see why Christ, in whom was never any impurity, is called a sachet of myrrh. Wherefore the soul must not touch anything that has been loosed and that is not supported by reason and tied together with the truth of dogmas, lest it become unclean. For because according to the Law he that shall touch the unclean shall be himself unclean,[227] if an unreasonable opinion and one that is alien from the wisdom of God has touched a man, it has made him unclean.

And now see if possibly we can take the coming of the

---

she is calling her Bridegroom her brother's son. Aquila, however, has 'Paternal Brother': we should then have to say that the former people is the father of the Gentile Church, seeing that from their Law and Prophets come her birth in God and our first introduction to piety. Accordingly, in this interpretation which regards that people as her father, the Saviour, *made*, like them, *under the Law* (Gal. 4.4), is her Brother.

Son of God in flesh as being here referred to as a 'drop' and described as something small and insignificant. Such is the case when Daniel speaks concerning Him of the small stone that was cut out without hands from the mountain, and thereafter became a great mountain;[228] or as when in the Book of the Twelve Prophets it is said that there will nevertheless be a certain 'drop' that is to gather together the people. For it is written in the prophets thus: *And it shall come to pass that out of the drop of this people Jacob shall surely be gathered.*[229] For it befitted Him who came to gather not Jacob only, but also all the nations which, as the prophet says, were accounted as a drop in a bucket, to be made Himself as a drop in His self-emptying of the form of God, and so to come and gather the drop of the Gentiles and the drop of the remnant of Jacob alike.[230]

But in the Psalm 44 also it is said to the Beloved, to whom also the Psalm itself is addressed: *Myrrh and a drop and cassia perfume Thy garments.*[231] From the garments of the Word of God, therefore, which denote the teaching of wisdom, myrrh proceeds, a symbol surely of the death He underwent for humankind. The drop, as we said before, denotes His self-emptying of the form of God and His condescension in assuming the form of a servant. And cassia likewise, because this kind of plant is said to be nourished and to grow together where it rains incessantly, points to the redemption of mankind bestowed through the waters of Baptism.

This, then, is the sense in which the Bride, speaking in the course of this nuptial drama, says that her Nephew is to her as a sachet of a myrrh-drop abiding between her breasts. Understand the 'breasts,' as we told you before, as the ground of the heart[232] in which the Church holds Christ, or the soul holds the Word of God, fast bound and tied to her by the chains of her desire. For only he who with his whole intention and with all his love holds the Word of God in his heart, will be able to perceive the odour of His fragrance and His sweetness.

II

'A cluster of cyprus is my Nephew to me in the vineyards of Engaddi.' (1.14—Vg. 1.13)

A CLUSTER OF CYPRUS [233] IS MY NEPHEW TO ME IN THE VINEYARDS OF ENGADDI. As to the literal interpretation, the expression 'a cluster of cyprus' is somewhat ambiguous; for the word 'cyprus' is used for a fine cluster of grapes, and there is also a certain kind of foreign shrub called 'cyprus' which likewise bears a beautiful sort of fruit that grows in the same manner as a bunch of grapes. But as mention is made of the vineyards of Engaddi, the words seem to refer rather to the fruit of the vine. Engaddi, by the way, is a district of Judea where balsam trees, not vines, are mostly grown. The historical sense of the Bride's words to the maidens will therefore be as follows. She must be understood as saying to the maidens first: 'My spikenard has yielded me the odour of my Spouse, 'secondly: 'My Nephew has been made for me as a sachet of a myrrh-drop abiding between my breasts,' thirdly, that He is as 'a cluster of grapes from the vineyards of Engaddi,' which surpasses everything in the way of odours and of flowery scents, in order that the maidens, hearing her say these things, may be incited to an ever greater charity and love towards the Bridegroom. For that is why she names these things one by one and in this order; first the spikenard, then the drop of myrrh, and lastly the cluster of cyprus— that thus she may teach certain stages of advance in charity.

But now let us see what the spiritual meaning may be. If this thing that is called a cluster be taken as meaning the fruit of the vine, we note that as the Word of God is called wisdom and power and the treasure of knowledge, and many other things, so also is He called the true vine.[234] As, therefore, He makes those to be wise and understanding and strong in virtue, for whom He is made to be wisdom and understanding, but does so not all at once, but by certain stages and steps, according to the diligence and application and faith of these sharers in His wisdom and knowledge and power; so also, for those for whom He is made the true vine, He does not suddenly produce ripe grapes and sweet, nor does He all at once become for them the pleasant wine that cheers the heart of man.[235] Rather, He first gives them only the sweet fragrance of the flower; so that souls, attracted at the outset by the grace of His fragrance, may be able thereafter to endure the harshness of the tribulations and trials which are stirred up for believers because of the Word of God. Then, after that, He offers them the sweetness of maturity, until such time as He can lead them to the wine-presses where the blood of the grape is shed, the blood of the New Testament which is to be drunk on the festal day in the heavenly places, when the great feast is set.[236]

Thus, therefore, does it behove those to advance from stage to stage, who, having been initiated through the mystery of the vine and the cluster of grapes, are being borne onwards to perfection, and are hastening to drink of the cup of the New Testament that they have received from Jesus.[237]

If, on the other hand, 'cyprus' is to be taken as meaning a special sort of tree, the fruit and flower of which are said to possess not so much sweetness of odour as the power of warming and fomenting, we shall assuredly take it as denoting that power of the Bridegroom whereby souls are kindled to believe in and to love Him, the power that had touched the men who said: *Was not our heart burning within us, whilst He . . . opened to us the Scriptures?* [238]

Or surely, since this cluster is said to come from the vineyards of Engaddi, and Engaddi means 'the eye of my temptation,' [239] if there is anyone capable of understanding the truth of the saying that *the life of man upon earth is temptation*, and if he understands also how one is saved from temptation in God, and who so knows the nature of his own temptation that it can be said of him that *in all these things* he *sinned not with his lips before God*,[240] to such a one as this the Word of God is made 'a cluster of cyprus from the vineyards of Engaddi.'

We must observe, however, that the Bride's words are so framed as to make it clear that the spikenard, and the sachet of a myrrh-drop and the cluster of cyprus are for herself alone, as being one who has already risen to these points of progress. For that soul only is perfect, who has her sense of smell so pure and purged that it can catch the fragrance of the spikenard and myrrh and cyprus that proceed from the Word of God, and can inhale the grace of the divine odour.

BOOK THREE

(On Cant. 1.15–2.15—Vg. 1.14–2.15)

I

'Behold, thou art fair, My neighbour; behold, thou art fair.
Thine eyes are doves.' (1.15—Vg. 1.14)

BEHOLD, THOU ART FAIR, MY NEIGHBOUR; BEHOLD, THOU
ART FAIR. THINE EYES ARE DOVES. Now for the second time
the Bridegroom engages in conversation with the Bride.
The first time He spoke, He urged her to know herself,
telling her she was indeed the good one among women,
but that, unless she knew herself, she would suffer certain
things. And, as though she has come swiftly to knowledge
of herself in mind and understanding, He compares her
to His horses or horsemen with which He defeated the
chariots of Pharao. At the same time He compares her
cheeks to turtle-doves, because of her outstanding modesty
and the speed of her conversion; and her neck He likens
to necklaces of jewels.[1]

Now, however, He declares her fair, and fair not only
among women, as before, but as being neighbour to Himself; and then He honours her with even loftier praise by
telling her that she is fair not only when she is thus close to
Him, but fair also if she should chance to be away from
Him. This is made clear by the fact that after He had said,
'Behold, thou art fair, my neighbour,' He added simply
and without any qualification, 'Behold, thou art fair.'

In the former passage, however, He had not praised her

face, I think because she had not yet attained the insight of a spiritual understanding; but now He says: 'Thine eyes are doves.' The greatness of her advance is shown by the fact that she who formerly was called only the fair one among women, is now called neighbour as well as fair; and without doubt she receives the splendour of beauty from the Bridegroom Himself, so that, having once gained that loveliness, she will continue beautiful, even if she should chance to suffer absence from Him for a little while.

Her eyes, moreover, are compared to doves, surely because she understands the Divine Scriptures now, not after the letter, but after the spirit, and perceives in them spiritual mysteries; for the dove is the emblem of the Holy Spirit.[2] To understand the Law and the Prophets in a spiritual sense is, therefore, to have the eyes of a dove. So her eyes are called doves here; but in the Psalms a soul of this sort longs to be given *the wings of a dove*,[3] that she may be able to fly in the understanding of spiritual mysteries, and to rest in the courts of wisdom.

Indeed, if anyone can *sleep among the midst of lots,* that is to say, can be put there, and can there repose, and understand the reason for the lots, and discern the causes of the divine judgements, such a one is promised not only *the wings of a dove* with which to fly in spiritual understanding, but also *silver wings,* wings that are made beautiful with the adornment of speech and reason. The soul's *back* also is said to be of the colour of gold, and this denotes the steadfastness in faith and the stability in its teachings,[4] that are proper to the perfect.

So then, as Christ is called the Head, it seems by no means absurd to me to take the eyes of those who understand spiritually *according to the inward man* and have a spiritual judgement, as meaning the Holy Spirit.[5] And perhaps this is the reason why in the Law, just as a lamb is appointed as the victim for the people's purification at Passover, so are doves appointed for a man's purification when he first comes into this world.[6] But to speak of these things now and to discuss the different sorts of victims would involve a long digression ill-suited to the work we have in hand.

In regard to the passage before us, 'Thine eyes are doves,' let what we have already said suffice; it is as though He said: 'Thine eyes are spiritual eyes, seeing and understanding in a spiritual way.'

In the words, 'Behold, thou art fair, my neighbour,' there is perhaps a still deeper mystery. They can be understood as spoken of this present age, for even now the Church is fair when she is near to Christ and imitates Christ. The repetition, 'Behold, thou art fair,' can then refer to the age to come, wherein she will be fair and beautiful not only by imitation, but also with her own peculiar perfection; and His saying that her eyes are doves may be understood as meaning that the two doves of her eyes are the Son of God and the Holy Spirit.

And you must not be surprised at our calling Them both doves, since each alike is called advocate; just as John in the Gospel speaks of the Holy Spirit as the paraclete, which means advocate, so also in his epistle does he say of Jesus Christ that *He* is the advocate with the Father for our sins.[7] So too the two olive trees set on the right and left of the candlestick in the prophet Zacharias[8] are believed to denote the Only-begotten and the Holy Spirit.

2

*'Behold, Thou art good, my Nephew, behold, Thou art fair
indeed. Our bed is shady.'* (1.16—Vg. 1.15)

BEHOLD,[*] THOU ART GOOD, MY NEPHEW, BEHOLD, THOU
ART FAIR INDEED. OUR BED IS SHADY. It seems that the Bride
has now looked more closely at the beauty of her Spouse,
and has considered with her eyes that have been called
doves, the fairness and the beauty of the Word of God. For
of a truth nobody can perceive and know how great is the
splendour of the Word, until he receives dove's eyes—that
is, a spiritual understanding.

But the bed which she says she shares with the Bridegroom seems to me to denote the soul's body; although
the soul is still in the body, she has been considered worthy
to be admitted to the company of the Word of God. And
she says that it is shady—that is to say, not dry, but fruitful,
and as it were bushy with a thicket of good works. Thus
speaks the Bride, or the soul rather, she who has dove's
eyes.

But these people who only believe in the Bridegroom,
and have lacked power to see what beauty there is in the
Son of God, say: *And we looked, and He had no beauty nor
comeliness, but His appearance was unbeautiful and lacking
before the sons of men.*[9] The soul, however, who has made
good progress and has advanced beyond the rank of the

---

[*] Procopius, *Comm. in Cant. Cant.* 1.14 (MG 17.260 C): The Bride
only now for the first time seems to have looked more closely at the
beauty of her Bridegroom and by her 'dove' eyes to have perceived
how the Word excels in beauty. Then straightway she declares—
speaking in riddles—that her body is the couch shared by herself and
her Bridegroom. Her soul, while yet in that body, is deemed worthy of
communion with the Word. Paul, for instance, says: *Your bodies are*

maidens and the eighty concubines and the sixty queens,[10] *she* can say: 'Behold, Thou art beautiful, my Nephew, and fair indeed.' And if I, although still in the body, understand the great numbers of spiritual meanings, the sense of the Divine Scriptures that is woven together with such frequent obscurity, so that the fiercer heat that is wont to burn many and shrivel up their fruits, yet cannot darken me, neither can any power of temptation dry up in me the seed of faith—if this be so, then *I* can say: 'Our bed is shady.'

As for her speaking of 'our bed,' in the sense of the place of her body that she shares with the Bridegroom, you must understand this in the light of the figure that Paul also uses when he says that *our bodies are members of Christ.*'[11] For when he says 'our bodies,' he shows that these bodies are the body of the Bride; but when he mentions the 'members of Christ,' he indicates that these same bodies are also the body of the Bridegroom. If, then, these bodies are shady, as we said just now, in the sense that they are full of good works and leafy with the abundance of spiritual perception, then we can truly say of them that *the sun shall not burn thee by day, nor the moon by night.*[12] For the sun of temptation does not burn the righteous man, resting as he does beneath the shadow of the Word of God (the sun that does burn the righteous is not the sun that may be praised, but rather he who *transformeth himself into an angel of light*).[13]

---

members of Christ (1 Cor. 6.15). By the word 'your' he means that the body is the Bride's, by the words 'members of Christ,' that it is the Bridegroom's. The Bridegroom is 'shady,' she says, because of the thick-coming intuitions she has of His Word and Wisdom. And if in this her union the Bride be flourishing in both, it is not at all astonishing that under the guidance of the divine power also in matters of her body all her body's activity is proved good.

The Nephew, then, is said to be good and beautiful, and
the more closely He can be contemplated with the eyes of
the spirit, so much the lovelier and more beautiful is He
found. For not only will His own fairness and marvellous
beauty appear; but in the soul herself, as she looks at and
beholds Him, an immense glory and extraordinary beauty
of form will arise, according to the saying of the Apostle
who beheld the beauty of the Word of God: *For though our
outward man is corrupted, yet the inward man is renewed day by
day.*[14] Such a soul as this rightly shares her bed—that is, her
body, with the Word; for the divine power extends even
to bestowing favour on the body, when it implants in it the
gift of chastity or the grace of continence and of other
good works.

Think, moreover, whether we may not also call the
body that Jesus took a bed that is shared by Himself and
the Bride. Through it the Church has been allied to Christ
and has been enabled to become a partaker in the Word of
God.[15] We know this both from the fact that He is called
the mediator of God and men, and from the Apostle's saying
that *in Him we have access through faith . . . in the hope of the
glory of . . . God.*[16]

3

'*The beams of our houses are cedars, our rafters of cypresses.*'
(1.17—Vg. 1.16)

THE BEAMS OF OUR HOUSES ARE CEDARS, OUR RAFTERS [17]
OF CYPRESSES. This seems to be the Bridegroom's answer to
the gracious things previously uttered by the Bride. His
purpose in speaking is to teach her the nature of these
common dwellings, and the sort of timberwork that they

contain. This is the substance of the words, so far as the story goes.

It is plain, however, that Christ is describing the Church, which is a spiritual house and the House of God, even as Paul teaches, saying: *But if I tarry long, it is that thou mayest know how thou oughtest to behave thyself in the House of God, which is the Church of the living God, the pillar and ground of the truth.*[18] So, if the Church is the House of God, then— because all things that the Father has are the Son's [19]—it follows that the Church is the House of the Son of God.

There is, however, frequent mention of 'churches' in the plural; as, for instance, the passage which says: *We have no such custom, nor the churches of God.*[20] And again, Paul writes to *the churches of Galatia,* and John to *the seven churches.*[21] The Church or the churches, then, are the houses of the Bridegroom and the Bride, the houses of the soul and the Word; and in them there are beams of cedar. We read of some cedars of God, upon which the vine that was brought out of Egypt is said to have spread out its boughs and branches, as it says in the Psalms: *The shadow of it covered the hills and the branches thereof the cedars of God.*[22]

Obviously, then, there are in the Church some things that are called cedars of God. So, when the Bridegroom says, 'the beams of our houses are cedars,' we must understand the cedars of God to be those who protect the Church, and that among them there are some stronger ones that are called rafters. And I think that those who faithfully discharge the office of a bishop in the Church may fitly be called the rafters,[23] by which the whole building is sustained and protected, both from the rain and from the heat of the sun. And I think that, in the next place after these, priests are called beams. Moreover, the rafters are said to be of cypress, which tree possesses a greater strength and a sweetness of smell; and that denotes a bishop as being at once sound in good works and fragrant with the grace of teaching. And in the same way the beams are said to be of cedar, to show that priests ought to be full of the virtue of incorruption and the fragrance of the knowledge of Christ.[24]

4

'I am the Flower of the field and the Lily of the valleys; as the lily among the thorns, so is my neighbour among the daughters.' (2.1 and 2)

I AM THE FLOWER OF THE FIELD AND THE LILY OF THE VALLEYS; AS THE LILY AMONG THE THORNS, SO IS MY NEIGH-BOUR AMONG THE DAUGHTERS. It seems that He, who is at once the Bridegroom and Word and Wisdom, says these words about Himself and the Bride to His friends and companions. But according to the kind of interpretation that we have proposed to follow, Christ is to be understood as speaking in this way with reference to the Church, and to be calling Himself 'the Flower of the field and the Lily of the valleys.' We call a 'field' a level piece of ground that is under cultivation and is tilled by farmers; valleys, on the other hand, rather suggest stony and uncultivated places. So we can take the field as meaning that people which was cultivated by the Prophets and the Law, and the stony, untilled valley as the Gentiles' place.

Here,* then, among that people the Bridegroom was the Flower; but because the Law brought no man to perfec-

---

* Procopius, *Comm. in Cant. Cant.* 2.1 (MG 17.260 D–261 A): *I am the flower of the field, the lily of the valley.* By 'flower' He means

tion,[25] the Word of God could not there advance beyond the flower, nor achieve the perfection of fruit. In that valley of the Gentiles, however, He became the Lily. But what sort of lily? Surely just such a one as that of which He Himself says in the Gospels that the heavenly Father clothes it, and that *not even Solomon in all his glory was arrayed as one of these.*[26] The Bridegroom, then, becomes the Lily in this valley, in that the heavenly Father clothed Him with such a robe of flesh as never Solomon in all his glory had power to possess. For Solomon's flesh was not born spotless, without man's desire or woman's intercourse with man; nor was it innocent of any subsequent offence.

He shows us, moreover, why He who had been the Flower of the field, willed to be also the Lily in the valleys. For, though He had been long the Flower in the field, He makes no mention of any other flower as having come forth from that field in imitation and likeness of Himself. But, when He became the Lily in the valleys, forthwith His neighbour too is made a lily in imitation of Himself; so that it has been worth His while to have become the Lily, in order that His neighbour likewise—that is, every single soul that draws near Him and follows His pattern and example—may be a lily too.

So we will take His saying, 'as the lily among thorns, so is my neighbour among the daughters,' as denoting the

---

that which is on the way to becoming fruit. In that part of the earth called 'a field' the Bridegroom-Word is the 'flower' as giving promise for the future, for *when that which is perfect is come* (1 Cor. 13.10), the flower will change and become fruit. And since those upon earth make no further progress than to be what He calls 'the flower,' for this reason the Bridegroom became as a 'flower of the field.' For He *emptied Himself, taking the form of a servant* (Phil. 2.7) to the end that we might be able hereafter *to behold His glory* (2 Cor. 3.18).—For the

Church of the Gentiles, either because she has come forth among the infidels and unbelievers, as from among thorns, or else because she may be said to be placed in the midst of thorns because of the vexations of the heretics who clamour round her. And this last will seem the more exact interpretation, because He says: 'So is my neighbour among the *daughters*': He would not have used the term 'daughters' for those souls that had never come to faith at all. For heretics all begin by believing, and afterwards depart from the road of faith and the truth of the Church's teaching, as the apostle John also says in his epistle: *They went forth from us, but they were not of us; for, if they had been of us, they would no doubt have remained with us.*[27]

We can, however, also take this passage as referring to each individual soul. To a soul whose simplicity and evenness and equity entitle it to be called a field, the Word of God may be said to become the Flower, and to teach her the beginnings of good works. But for such as are already seeking deeper things and pondering matters less to be seen on the surface, souls who, either because of their singular modesty or else because of their outstanding wisdom, are as it were the valleys, for those He becomes the Lily, so that they too may become as lilies breaking forth in the midst of the thorns—that is to say, fleeing from those worldly thoughts and interests which in the Gospel are compared to thorns.[28]

---

loftier and smoother places called 'fields' He may be a 'flower'; but He is the 'lily' for places lower and more hollow than these.—Having said this, the Bridegroom compares His neighbour with the 'daughters,' the other souls who are as thorns compared with her. Such souls are not neighbour to the Bridegroom; but His neighbour is a lily shining in their midst.

5

'*As the apple tree among the trees of the wood, so is my Nephew among the sons; in His shadow I desired and sat, and His fruit was sweet in my throat.*' (2.3)

AS* THE APPLE TREE AMONG THE TREES OF THE WOOD, SO IS MY NEPHEW AMONG THE SONS; IN HIS SHADOW I DESIRED AND SAT, AND HIS FRUIT WAS SWEET IN MY THROAT. It was fitting indeed for the Bridegroom to speak about Himself, and to tell us what He was in the field, and what He was in the valleys; and concerning the Bride, who she was, and how she stood among the daughters. But, when the Bride replied, the fitting thing for her was not to speak of herself, but to be wholly occupied with wonder at her Spouse, and to confine herself to praising Him. So she compares Him to the apple tree.

But lest the similarity between the words should lead some simpler folk to think an apple tree (*arbor mali*) an evil tree (*arbor mala*) and take its name as derived from malice, let us for our part call it the 'melum tree' (*arborem meli*), using the Greek word which, as a matter of fact, is more familiar than *malum* to the simpler Latins. For it is better for us to offend the philologists than to put any difficulty in our readers' way when we expound the truth.[29]

She likens Him, then, to an apple tree (*arborem meli*), and

---

* Procopius, *Comm. in Cant. Cant.* 2.3 (MG 17.261 AB): *As the apple tree among the trees of the wood, so is my Nephew among the sons; beneath His shadow I desired and sat down, and His fruit was sweet in my throat.* It was fitting for the Bride, having become wholly possessed of the beauty of the Bridegroom, to say nothing concerning herself, but to add to what the Bridegroom said about Himself by likening Him to the 'apple tree' and the 'sons' at His side to the 'trees of the wood';

His companions to the other trees of the wood. She says that the Bridegroom resembles an apple tree (*arbori meli, etc.*) in such sense that she can say of herself that she 'desired and sat beneath His shadow,' and can affirm that 'His fruit was sweet in her throat.' And she appears to be addressing these words to the maidens, just as when the Bridegroom spoke before, He addressed His companions.

Now, however, let us see who it is whom, according to the mystery, the Bride calls the sons, whom the Bridegroom, so she says, surpasses, even as the apple tree surpasses the other trees of the wood; and let us see if, following the twofold interpretation given above about the daughters and the thorns, we can take the sons as meaning either those who were such aforetime and now are such no longer, or else the multitudes of heavenly ministers. For that which is written: *I have said, 'You are gods, and all of you the sons of the Most High,'* applies to all in the beginning; but a difference intervened in respect of what follows: '*But you like men shall die, and shall fall like one of the princes.*' [30] The latter, however, also has reference to this: *For who in the clouds can be compared to the Lord? Or who among the sons of God shall be reckoned as equal to Him?* [31]

The Bridegroom is among the sons, therefore, as the apple tree is among the trees of the wood, in that He bears fruit that not only surpasses all other fruits in taste, but also in fragrance, and thus appeals equally to the soul's two

---

and to say that in the excess of her longing she desired His 'shadow' and consigned what He had created to the deep of her mind. It seems that she says these things to the maidens, as the Bridegroom said the first words to the companions. These she calls 'sons' or companions whom by comparison with the Bridegroom she has likened to the fruitless 'trees of the wood,' or else (she describes them) as strangers to Him.

senses, taste and smell. For Wisdom furnishes her table for us with a variety of riches: she not only sets thereon the bread of life, she also offers us the Flesh of the Word.[32] And she not only mingles her wine in the bowl, she also supplies plenty of fragrant apples, apples so sweet that they not only yield their luscious taste to mouth and lips but keep their sweetness also when they reach the inner throat.

We can, then, take the trees of the wood as meaning those angels who have been the authors and promoters of every heresy; so that in this passage, when the Church compares the sweetness of Christ's teaching with the sourness of heretical dogmas and their barren and unfruitful doctrine, she describes as 'apples' the sweet and pleasant doctrines preached in the Church of Christ, but as 'trees of the wood' those that are asserted by the various heretics.

And the words of the Gospel, *Behold, now is the axe laid to the roots of the trees. Every tree therefore that doth not yield good fruit shall be cut down and cast into the fire,*[33] will be seen to apply to those unfruitful trees of the wood. Thus the Bride's Nephew is to her as an apple tree in the Church of Christ; but the various heretics, being unfruitful trees of the wood, are sentenced by the divine judgement to be cut down and cast into the fire.

The Bride, therefore, desires to sit down in the shadow of this apple tree: this is either the Church, as we said, under the protection of the Son of God, or else the soul fleeing all other teachings and cleaving to the Word of God alone; the Word whose fruit, moreover, she finds sweet in her throat by continual meditation on the Law of God, chewing as it were the cud thereof like a clean animal.[34]

But* as to the mention of that shadow under which the Church says that she desired to sit, I do not think it inappropriate to adduce in connection with it such passages as we can find in the Divine Scriptures, to help us to a worthier and more godly understanding of what this shadow of the apple tree denotes. Jeremias says in Lamentations: *The breath of our face, Christ the Lord, has been taken with us in our corruptions; to whom we said: 'Under His shadow we shall live among the Gentiles.'*[35] You see, then, how the prophet, moved by the Holy Spirit, says that life is afforded to the Gentiles by the shadow of Christ; and indeed how should His shadow not afford us life, seeing that even at the conception of His very body it is said to Mary: *The Holy Spirit shall come upon thee, and the power of the Most High shall overshadow thee?*[36]

As, therefore, at His body's conception the overshadowing was that of the Most High, His own shadow will justly give life to the Gentiles. And justly does His Bride the Church desire to sit beneath the shadow of the apple tree, in order, surely, that she may be made partaker of the life that is in His shadow. But the shadow of the other trees of the wood is such that he who sits thereunder may find himself sitting in the region of the shadow of death.[37]

And further, in order to make the passage before us plainer still, let us also look into what the Apostle means when he speaks of *the Law having a shadow of the good things*

---

* Procopius, *Comm. in Cant. Cant.* 3.3 (MG 17.261 BC): *Under His shadow she desired to sit down and she sat down.* Jeremias, too, says in Lamentations: *The breath of our face, Christ the Lord, has been taken with us in our corruptions; to whom we said: 'Under His shadow we shall live among the Gentiles'* (Lam. 4.20). For how should not His shadow have become the cause of our life after we had become free from the shadow of the Law (*for the Law had a shadow of the good things to come* [Heb. 10.1])

to come, and calls all the things that are written about feast days and sabbaths and new moons *a shadow of* good *things to come*—meaning, of course, the things that were done according to the letter; and in what sense he declares that all the rites of the ancients were *an example and shadow of heavenly things.*[38] If that is so, certainly it follows that all who were under the Law and had the shadow rather than the substance of the true Law, sat under the shadow of the Law. We, however, are strangers to their shadow; *for we are not under the Law, but under grace.*[39]

Yet, though we are not under that shadow which was cast by the letter of the Law, we are notwithstanding under a better shadow. *For we live under the shadow of Christ among the Gentiles.* And there is a certain progress in coming from the shadow of the Law to the shadow of Christ; since Christ is the Life and the Truth and the Way,[40] we must first be fashioned in the shadow of the Way and in the shadow of the Life and in the shadow of the Truth, and apprehend in part and in a glass and in a riddle, in order that later on, if we persevere in this Way that is Christ, we may be able to achieve the face-to-face apprehension of those things which formerly we had beheld in the shadow and in a riddle.[41] For no one will be able to reach the things that are true and perfect who has not first desired and longed to sit in this shadow.

Job says in the same way that *the whole life of man is a shadow,*[42] meaning, I think, that every soul in this life is

---

and were no longer *under the Law but under grace* (Rom. 6.14)? Though even now we are under a shadow, however different, for after the present life we shall no longer *see* truth *through a glass in a dark manner, but face to face* (1 Cor. 13.12). And the Bride will say, . . . *until the day break and the shadows retire* (Cant. 2.17). For *our life is a shadow* (1 Par. 29.15), and those who came from the Gentiles *sat in the shadow of death* (Matt. 4.16<Isa. 9.2), and the unbelievers still sit there.

shadowed by the covering of this gross body. So all who are in this life must of necessity be in the shadow in some sense.

Some, however, are sitting *in the region of the shadow of death*,[43] that is, those who do not believe in Christ. The Church, by contrast, says with confidence: 'Under the shadow of the Bridegroom I desired and sat,' although there was a time when anyone sitting under the shadow of the Law was protected from the rigours of heat and summer. That time, however, has passed. We must come now to the shadow of the apple tree; and, although one may avail oneself of another shadow, it seems that every soul, as long as she is in this present life, must needs have a shadow, by reason, I think, of that heat of the sun which, when it has arisen, immediately withers and destroys the seed that is not deeply rooted.[44] The shadow of the Law indeed afforded but slight protection from this heat; but the shadow of Christ, under which we now live among the Gentiles, that is to say, the faith of His Incarnation, affords complete protection from it and extinguishes it. For he who used to burn up those who walked in the shadow of the Law was seen to fall as lightning from heaven at the time of the Passion of Christ.[45] Yet the period of this shadow too is to be fulfilled at the end of the age; because, as we have said, after the consummation of the age we shall behold no longer through a glass and in a riddle, but face to face.[46]

I think there is like meaning in the passage: *Under the shadow of Thy wings will I rejoice.*[47] But later in this little book the Bride speaks thus: *My Nephew to me, and I to Him, who feedeth among the lilies, till the day breathe and the shadows be taken away.*[48] By these words she shows us that the time will come when all shadows will be removed, and the truth alone will abide.

But her saying, '*and His fruit was sweet in my throat,*' applies to the soul that has in its mouth nothing that is dead, nothing senseless, and is wholly unlike those of whom it is said that *their throat is an open sepulchre.*[49] For the mouths of such as bring forth words of death and destruction are called sepulchres, as also are all that speak against the true faith or make any opposition to the discipline of chastity, justice, and sobriety.

Those, then, are the people whose mouths are sepulchres and homes of death, whence words of death come forth. But the just man says: *How sweet are Thy words to my palate!* And another person who taught the words of life says thus: *Our mouth is open to you, O ye Corinthians, our heart is enlarged.* And yet another who opened his mouth to the Word of God says: *I opened my mouth and drew in my breath.*[50]

6

'*Bring ye me into the house of wine.*' (2.4a)

BRING* YE ME INTO THE HOUSE OF WINE. It is still the Bride who speaks, but her words are now addressed, I think, to the friends and intimates of the Bridegroom, whom she is asking to bring her into the house of gladness, where wine is drunk and a banquet prepared.[51] For she who had already seen the royal chamber[52] desires now to be admitted also to the royal feast, and to enjoy the wine of gladness.

We have already stated above that the friends of the

---

* Procopius, *Comm. in Cant. Cant.* 2.4 (MG 17.261 C): *Bring ye me into the house of wine.* She says this to the friends of the Bridegroom, the holy angels or apostles and prophets; it is almost as if she said, 'Unite me to the Body of Christ.'

Bridegroom should be taken as meaning the prophets and all who ministered the Word of God since the beginning of the world.[53] The Church of Christ and the soul that cleaves to the Word of God may both of them rightly ask these friends to bring them into the house of wine—that is to say, into the place where *Wisdom has mingled her wine in a bowl* and through her servants entreats all *the unwise* and *them that lack understanding*, saying: *Come, eat my bread and drink the wine that I have mingled for you.*[54]

This is the house of wine and the house of the feast, at which feast all who *come from the east and the west shall recline with Abraham and Isaac and Jacob in the Kingdom* of God.[55] To this house and to this feast the prophets lead the souls who hear and understand them; so also do the holy angels and the heavenly powers, who are *sent to minister for them who receive the inheritance of salvation.*[56]

This is the wine that is in view in the Psalms that bear the title *For the presses.*[57] This is the wine made from the Vine who says: *I am the true Vine*; His heavenly Father is the Husbandman who makes it in the press. This is the wine which those branches produced that abode in Jesus not only on earth, but also in heaven. For that is how I understand His saying that *every branch that abideth not in me can bear no fruit.*[58] For no one brings forth the fruit of this wine, save he who abides in the Word, and in wisdom, and truth, and justice, and peace, and all the other virtues. This is moreover the wine with which the just and holy rightly desire to be inebriated. I think too that it is on seeing these things in the spirit that Noe is said to have been drunken;[59] and David marvels at the cup of this feast and says: *And Thy cup which inebriateth, how goodly it is!*[60]

The Church, therefore, or the individual soul who longs for the things that are perfect, hastens to enter this house of wine, and to enjoy the teachings of wisdom and the mysteries of knowledge as the sweetness of a banquet and the gladness of wine.

We must however recognize the fact that besides this wine which is pressed from the dogmas of truth and mingled in Wisdom's bowl, there is another wine of an opposite nature with which sinners and those who accept the harmful dogmas of false learning wickedly get drunk. Of these Solomon says in Proverbs: *They eat the bread of wickedness and drink the wine of iniquity.*[61] We read also in Deuteronomy of this same wicked wine: *Their vine is of the vineyard of Sodom, and their vine-shoots of Gomorrha; their grapes are grapes of gall, and their cluster is one of bitterness; their wine is the rage of dragons and the rage of asps which is incurable.*[62]

But the wine that comes from the true Vine is always new; for, as learners advance, their understanding of the divine knowledge and wisdom is perpetually renewed. And that is why Jesus said to His disciples: *I will drink this wine with you new in the Kingdom of my Father.*[63] For the understanding of secrets and the revelation of mysteries through the wisdom of God is always being renewed, not to men only, but also to the angels and celestial powers.

7

'Set ye in order charity in me.' (2.4b)

SET YE IN ORDER CHARITY IN ME. The words are still the Bride's, and still addressed to the same persons, though we may perhaps include Christ's apostles among those to whom she is speaking now. Her saying, 'Set ye in order charity in me,' means this, therefore: Most certainly all men love something; and there is no one who has reached the age when one is capable of loving, who does not love something, as also we have shown sufficiently in the preface to this work. [64] But whereas in some people this love or this charity advances in due order and is suitably directed, with very many its advance is out of order. We say that charity is out of order in a person, when he either loves what he ought not to love, or else loves what he ought to love either more or less than it is right for him to do. In people of the latter kind charity is said to be inordinate; but in the former—and they are very few, I think—those, namely, who go forward on the way of life and turn not aside to the right hand nor to the left, [65] in those and those alone charity is ordinate, and keeps the order proper to itself.

Here now is an example of its order and its measure. In loving God there is no measure to observe, no limit, save only that you ought to give Him as much as you have got. For in Christ Jesus God is to be loved with the whole heart, and the whole soul, and the whole strength. So in this there is no measure. But for the love of one's neighbour there is a certain measure: *Thou shalt love they neighbour as thyself,* Scripture says. [66] If, then, you have either done somewhat less in the way of loving God than is within your capability and strength, or if you have not kept an even balance between yourself and your neighbour, but have made some differences, then charity is not ordinate in you, and is not keeping the order proper to itself.

But as we are discussing the order of charity, let us enquire more particularly whom we ought to love, and how much we ought to love them. For if, as the Apostle says, *we are members one of another,* [67] I think we ought to have towards our neighbours the sort of attitude that makes us love them, not as alien bodies, but as our own limbs. This fact of our being members one of another demands, therefore, that we shall have a similar and equal love for all.

In view, however, of the further fact that there are in the body some members that are *more honourable and comely,* and others that are more *uncomely and more feeble,* [68] I think that the balance of love ought to be adjusted according to the merits and honour of the members loved. So, if a person sets out to behave reasonably in all things and to control his actions and affections in accordance with the Word of God, I think that he should know and observe the order of charity with regard to every member severally.

To make plainer what we are saying, let us now take some rather clearer instances of this. If a man were to labour in the Word of God, [69] for example, and instruct and enlighten our souls, teach us the way of salvation, and deliver to us the rule of life, does it not seem to you that you have in him a neighbour indeed, but one much more worthy to be loved than is some other neighbour who does none of these things? The latter also must be loved, of course, because we are members of one body and made of the same stuff; but the former who, besides having the neighbour's claim on us which all other men have, gives us this greater ground for charity towards himself, in that he shows us the way of God and bestows health on our soul by the illuminations of the Word of God, ought to be loved much more.

Again, if someone, finding me going astray and on the verge of sinning with a woman, were to recall me to the light of truth, and snatch and withdraw me from that imminent ruin, and thus save me and deliver me out of the very jaws of everlasting death, does it not seem to you that that man should be loved, after God, with the selfsame fullness of charity, if that be possible, as that with which we love God? And that you may not think that we are going too far in saying this, listen also to what the Apostle Paul says of those who labour in the Word of God: *that you esteem them the more abundantly in charity for their work's sake.*[70]

Let us now look also at another order of charity, simply that which we are bidden to have towards our neighbours. If there be someone who lacks the grace of teaching and instruction and of preaching the Word of the Lord, yet is a man of holy life, blameless, unspotted, and *walking in all the commandments and justifications of the Lord without blame,*[71] do you think that such a person should be regarded as being in the same order of charity as he who does none of these things, simply because both equally are called neighbour? Should not this man, for the sake of his work and the merit of his life, be held in more abundant love for the sake of the work of his life, even as—to quote the Apostle [72] —that other who labours in the Word of God?

And there is still another order of charity: we are bidden also to love our enemies.[73] Let us then see whether in their case there will be only one sort of love, or whether the saying, 'Set ye in order charity in me,' will apply here as well. My own opinion is that the order of charity does apply here. For instance, there is someone hostile to me, who nevertheless is kind to others, modest, sober, observant of many of God's commandments to a certain extent, though erring humanly in some respects; and there is another person who likewise is our enemy, who is also the enemy of his own life and soul, ready for deeds of evil, quick to do acts of shame, with no thought of anything holy or religious. Does it not seem to you that some difference of love should be observed here too between these enemies?

Indeed I think that the examples cited have made it abundantly clear that there is one force of charity; but that there are many reasons for loving, and many degrees thereof, and that this is the reason why the Bride now says: 'Set ye in order charity in me': that is to say, 'Teach me the different degrees of charity.' And if there is anything more that needs to be said, we can bring forward the Apostle's injunction: *Husbands, love your wives as your own bodies, as Christ also loved the Church.*[74] Now then, husbands must love their wives, of course; but must they not also love other women in all purity and holiness? Or will the others not come under the heading of 'neighbours'? Are we to bestow love on a wife, or a mother, or a sister, if they are such as believe and cleave to God, and not bestow it on any other woman who has a neighbour's status too? Though this may seem strange, yet the order of the commandment does require that a chaste love should be given to these also; and even among those same female persons, to whom love ought to be given, a certain order in charity and a suitable distinction ought assuredly to be observed. And love ought indeed to be rendered with greater honour to a mother and, in the next degree, with a certain reverence none the less, to sisters too. But love to wives ought to be shown in a manner peculiar to itself and set apart from these. After the foregoing persons, however, love should, as we stated above, be rendered to every woman, in all purity, according to her merits and claims.

We shall follow the same principles in regard to a father, or brother, or other relatives. But to the holy persons who have begotten us in Christ,[75] and the pastors and bishops and the presbyters who are stewards of the Word of God, or those who minister well in the Church or surpass others in faith—how shall the affection of charity not be given, in proportion to their merits, far more generously to such, than it can be to those who have done none of the aforesaid things, or else have done them not without reproach? Is it possible, moreover, not to make a distinction in respect of charity between believing and unbelieving parents, and between believing and unbelieving brothers and sisters?

The Bride, surveying these differences and seeing that the soul in search of perfection needs to have knowledge about them all that she may assess the measure of charity due in every case, says to the Bridegroom's friends—to those, that is, who serve the Word of God—'Set ye in order charity in me'; that is to say, 'Teach me and tell me how I must observe the order of charity in each of these cases.' For all men, as we have already said, ought to be loved alike simply because they are men like ourselves; nay more, since we ourselves are rational, every other rational being ought to be loved equally by us. But, in respect of charity, there is something extra to be considered in regard to each person, alike as a man and as a rational being. If, for example, a man excels others either in his behaviour, or in his work, or in his intentions, or in his knowledge, or in his occupations, there is some measure of especial charity to be added to the general love that is his due, in return for each of these ways in which he excels, according to its merits.

But that we may have a higher authority for this, let us take an example from God Himself. *He loves* equally *all that are, and hates none of the things which He has made, for He did not make anything that He should hate it*; [76] yet He did not for this reason love the Hebrews and the Egyptians in a like way, nor Pharao as He did Moses and Aaron. Again, He did not love the other children of Israel as He loved Moses and Aaron and Mary, nor did He love Aaron and Mary in the same way as He loved Moses; but, although it is true, as we say, that *Thou sparest all, because they are Thine, O Lord, Thou Lover of souls, for the spirit of incorruption is in all things,*[77] nevertheless He who *has disposed all things in measure and number and weight,*[78] undoubtedly regulates the balance of His love according to the measure of each. For surely we cannot think, can we, that Paul was loved by Him in the same way when he was persecuting the Church of God, as he was when he was himself bearing persecutions and torments for her sake, and when he said that he was bearing *the solicitude for all the churches?*[79]

It is now important for us to introduce among those orders of charity some remarks also about the emotion of hatred, which is the disposition opposed to that of charity, for the Lord Himself says: *I will be an enemy to thy enemies, and I will be an adversary to thy adversaries;* and again: *If thou helpest a sinner, thou art also a friend of him whom the Lord hates.*[80] The explanation of these things surely is the same as that which underlies the words, *Honour thy father and thy mother,* and, *He that hateth not his father and mother,* etc.— namely, that obviously excess of love generates the opposite disposition towards God in those who oppose Him; since *there can be no fellowship between light and darkness and between Christ and Belial,* and *the believer and the unbeliever have not the same part.*[81]

Now that we have explained about these orders of charity to the best of our ability, it is easy to understand what the Bride—that is to say, the Church or the soul in pursuit of perfection—is asking the Bridegroom's friends to do for her. Having asked to be brought into the house of wine, where doubtless she had understood that among all the things that she had seen the grace of charity was best and first of all, and had learnt that that same charity was greater than all, and that charity alone never falls,[82] therefore she asks further that she may learn its order; lest perchance she should do something out of order and so receive some wound from charity, as she says later: *I have been wounded by charity*.[83]

But if we take these words as spoken to the angels by whom she asks to be instructed and protected, there will be nothing incongruous in such an interpretation, in view of what is said of the people of God: *Rejoice, ye nations, with His people, and may all the angels of God comfort them*; and as it is said in another place: *The angel of the Lord encampeth round about them that fear Him and shall deliver them*; and in yet another: *Despise not one of these least ones that are in the Church, for their angels always see the face of my Father who is in heaven*.[84] And in the Apocalypse of John the Son of God testifies to the angel of Thyatira of the charity which he ordered in the Church committed to his care; for it is written thus: *I know thy works and thy charity and faith and ministry and patience, and thy last works which are greater than the former*.[85]

It seems too that there is nothing incongruous in taking this passage as referring to the prophets who ministered the Word of God before the Bridegroom's coming; the Church will be desiring, in that case, to learn the order of charity from their teaching—that is, to be instructed out of the prophetical books. Neither will it be unsuitable if we should say that all the saints who have departed this life, still having charity towards those who are in this world, are concerned for their salvation and help them with their prayers and intercessions with God. For it is written in the

Books of the Maccabees thus: *This is Jeremias, the prophet of God, who always prays for the people.*[86]

Again, there will be nothing strange in our referring the words to the apostles, as we said before; for through them the whole Church of God, or the soul seeking God, is brought into the house of wine, as we noted above, and is filled with sweet odours and placed among apples, as we read in the following, and is taught the whole order and meaning of charity.

8

'*Strengthen me with ointments, encompass me with apples, because I am wounded by Charity.*' (2.5)

STRENGTHEN[*] ME WITH OINTMENTS, ENCOMPASS ME WITH APPLES, BECAUSE I AM WOUNDED BY CHARITY. In Greek the text reads: 'Strengthen me with *amoyrs*,'[87] naming the *amoyr* as a certain kind of tree; the Latins, thinking that it was the same as 'myrrh,' translated it as 'ointments.' The sequence of the narrative is, then, as follows. After the Bride has heard the words from the Bridegroom's own lips and has entered into the King's chamber, and into the house of wine and the place of feasting and wisdom, ⟨and⟩ has beheld therein the victims and the wine bowl mingled in His mysteries, she, being as it were amazed and smitten with wonder at all these things, begs of those same friends and companions of the Bridegroom that she may be strengthened and, being weak as it were, may lie down and be supported for a little while on an *amoyr* or apple tree.

---

[*] Procopius, *Comm. in Cant. Cant.* 2.5 (MG 17.261 CD): *Strengthen me with ointments, heap me up with apples, because I am wounded with love.* Symmachus edited thus: *Cushion me with grape-blossoms,* that is to say, with sweet-smelling trees bearing good bright-coloured fruit, the trees

For, being smitten with the wound of charity, she seeks the consolation of trees and woods. So much for the literal meaning.

But in order to extract the spiritual meaning from these facts we need the grace that Solomon was found worthy to attain from God, the grace of knowing the natures of all the things that are, of roots and trees and shrubs;[88] so that we too may know what is the property and nature of the *amoyr* tree, so that we may suitably adjust the spiritual explanation to the natural. But the only thing we have been able to learn about this tree is that it has a sweet smell only; it does not bear fruit. In regard to the apple tree, however, everyone knows that it bears not only fruit, but very sweet and pleasant fruit.

Very well, then. All men are called trees, whether good or bad, whether fruitful or unfruitful, even as the Lord says in the Gospel: *Either make the tree good and its fruit good, or make the tree evil and its fruit evil*; and again: *Every tree that beareth not good fruit shall be cut down and cast into the fire.*[89] So it seems that men fall into three classes: some who bear no fruit at all, and others who do bear; while among those that bear, the fruits are either bad or good. And here the Bride, that is, the Church of Christ, asks that she may be strengthened, and that she may recline upon a tree, an apple tree that bears good fruit; and her request is right and suitable. For it is by those who are fruitful and grow in good works that the Church is strengthened and supported.

But what does the Bride mean by wanting to be strengthened with *amoyrs*, unfruitful trees, rejoicing in

---

termed bad being either without fruit or with evil fruit. But some of the copies have, *Strengthen me with scentless ointments* [trees?]. We must understand the 'trees' as either the faithful (not indeed as being called *members* of her that *has not spot or wrinkle* [Eph. 5.27]), or else those who

their fragrance only? I think myself that by those who rejoice only in their fragrance and do not bear the fruits of faith, she means those persons of whom Paul, writing to the Corinthians, says that *they invoke the name of Our Lord Jesus Christ in every place of theirs and ours*.[90] In that they invoke the name of Our Lord Jesus Christ, they have a certain sweet odour in themselves from the very fact that they do so invoke it; but in that they do not approach the faith with all boldness and freedom, they are not bringing forth any fruits of faith. And we can take this passage as referring to the catechumens of the Church, by whose means the Church is to some extent strengthened. For she has no small confidence in them, and also a great hope that they too may become fruitful trees one day and may be planted in God's paradise by the Father, the Husbandman Himself. For it is He who plants such trees as this in the Church of Christ, which is the paradise of delights,[91] even as the Lord says: *Every plant which my heavenly Father hath not planted shall be rooted up*.[92]

The Church is, therefore, in the first place encompassed with apples, and she also takes her rest thereon. By those apples we must understand the souls who are being daily renewed *according to the image of Him that created them*.[93] For, since the sons of God are thus repairing His Image in themselves by the renewal of themselves, they are rightly called apple trees; because the Bridegroom Himself also was said just now to be 'as the apple tree among the trees of the wood.'[94]

And let it not surprise you that He should be called the

---

are strangers to the faith of Christ. Now Symmachus, in explaining the phrase *heap me up with apples*, reads *encompass me with apples*. For the Bride wants to rest with quantities of apples all around her—which, I think, are *the apple tree among the trees of the wood* (Cant. 2.3), namely,

apple tree, as well as the tree of life and various other things; seeing that He also bears the title of the true Bread, and the true Vine, and the Lamb of God, and many others. For the Word of God becomes all these things to each and every one according as the capacity or the desire of the participant requires; in just the same way the manna also, although it was one food, yielded its flavour to each person after his desire.[94a] So He does not offer Himself only as bread to those who hunger, and as wine to those who thirst, but He presents Himself also as fragrant apples to those who crave delights.

That, then, is the reason why the Bride, being already as one refreshed and amply fed, asks further to be stayed with apples, knowing that all delights are in the Word for her, as well as every food; and she passes these in review more particularly when she feels she has been wounded by the darts of charity.[95]

If there is anyone anywhere who has at some time burned with this faithful love of the Word of God; if there is anyone who has received the sweet wound of Him who is the chosen dart, as the prophet says; if there is anyone who has been pierced with the loveworthy spear of His knowledge, so that he yearns and longs for Him by day and night, can speak of nought but Him, would hear of nought but Him, can think of nothing else, and is disposed to no desire nor longing nor yet hope, except for Him alone—if such there be, that soul then says in truth: 'I have been wounded by charity.' And she has received her wound from Him of whom Isaias says: *And He hath made me as a chosen dart, and in His quiver hath He hidden me.*[96]

---

the Bridegroom—so that she may partake of their richness. *For I am wounded with a love-charm*, she says according to Symmachus, from the *chosen arrow*, according to Isaias (49.2).

It beseems God to strike souls with such a wound as this, to pierce them with such spears and darts, and smite them with such health-bestowing wounds, that, since *God is Charity*,[97] they may say of themselves: 'I have been wounded by Charity.' And indeed in this as it were drama of love the Bride does say she has received the wounds of Charity. And the soul who is aflame with longing for God's wisdom—a soul, that is, who has been able to behold the beauty of His wisdom—can say in the same way: 'I have been wounded by Wisdom.'[98] And another soul, contemplating the splendour of His might, and marvelling at the power of the Word of God, can say: 'I have been wounded by Might'; and such a soul, I think, was that one who said: *The Lord is my light and my salvation, whom shall I fear? The Lord is the protector of my life, of whom shall I be afraid?*[99] And yet another soul, enkindled by the love of His justice and contemplating the justice of the dispensations of His providence, says surely: 'I have been wounded by Justice.' And another, beholding the vastness of His goodness and lovingkindness, speaks in the same manner. But the one wound that includes all these is that wound of charity with which the Bride declares she has been wounded.

We must know, however, that as there are those darts of God which inflict the wound of salvation on the soul, so also are there *the fiery darts of the wicked one*[100] with which the soul who is not protected by the shield of faith is wounded unto death. Of these the prophet says: *Lo, the wicked have bent their bow, they have prepared their arrows in the quiver, to shoot in the dark at the upright of heart.*[101] It is the unseen demons whom in this place he calls the wicked that shoot from hiding; and these have certain darts—some of fornication, others of greed and avarice; and with these they wound as many as they can. They have also the javelins of boasting and vainglory. But all these are very subtle, so that the soul scarcely perceives that she has been pierced and wounded by them, unless she is *wearing the armour of God and standing* watchful and unmoved *against the deceits of the devil,* guarding herself constantly with *the shield of faith* and taking care to leave no part of her body naked of faith. And however many spears the demons have fashioned, even though they be fiery, even though they blaze with the flames of lusts and the fires of vices, if they find a man's mind fortified by faith, his complete faith extinguishes them all.[102]

9

'*His left hand is under my head, and His right hand shall embrace me.*' (2.6)

HIS LEFT HAND IS UNDER MY HEAD, AND HIS RIGHT HAND SHALL EMBRACE ME. The picture before us in this drama of love is that of the Bride hastening to consummate her union with the Bridegroom.[103] But turn with all speed to the life-giving Spirit and, eschewing physical terms, consider carefully what is the left hand of the Word of God, what the right; also what His Bride's head is—the head, that is to say, of the perfect soul or of the Church; and do not suffer an interpretation that has to do with the flesh and the passions to carry you away.

For the Bridegroom's right and left hands are the same in this place as those attributed to Wisdom in the Book of Proverbs, where the writer says: *Length of life is in her right hand, and in her left hand riches and glory.*[104] And, just as in this place you will not think that Wisdom is a woman because she appears under a feminine name, so also you must not understand the left and right hands of the Word of God in a corporeal sense, simply because He is called the Bridegroom, which is an epithet of male significance. Nor must you take the Bride's embraces in that way, simply because the word 'bride' is of feminine gender.

Rather, although the 'Word' of God is of the masculine gender in Greek, and neuter with ourselves,[105] yet all these matters with which this passage deals must be thought of in a manner that transcends masculine and neuter and feminine, and everything whatever to which these words refer. And this applies not only to the 'Word' of God, but also to His Church and to the perfect soul, who likewise is here called 'the Bride.' For thus says the Apostle: *'For in Christ there is neither male nor female, but we are all one in Him.'*[106]

The Divine Scripture expresses these things after the manner of human speech, for the sake of those who cannot understand them unless they are thus couched in terms to which they are accustomed. The words in which we hear them, therefore, will be well known and familiar; but our perception of them, if we give them the perception they deserve, will be of things divine and incorporeal. For, just as he who calls himself a lover of the beauty of wisdom will transfer the natural affection of charity that is in him to the pursuit of wisdom; so likewise here the Church that is the Bride begs her Bridegroom who is the Word of God to support her head with His left hand, but with His right hand to embrace the whole of her, and hold her body fast.

But it is in her left hand that Wisdom is said to hold riches and glory. And what riches has the Church, and what glory, save those that she received from Him who, *though He was rich, became poor*, that through His poverty the Church might be made rich? And what is her glory?

That, surely, of which He says: *Father, glorify Thy Son*; [107] meaning without a doubt the glory of the Passion. Faith in the Passion of Christ is, therefore, the glory and the riches of the Church that are held in His left hand.

I think, moreover, that the left hand of the Word of God ought to be interpreted as follows. There are in Him some dispensations wrought before the Incarnation, and some wrought by the Incarnation. That part of the Word of God which in the divine economy was exercised before He took flesh, can be regarded as His right hand; and that which functioned through the Incarnation can be called His left. It is for this reason that He is said to have *in His left hand riches and glory*; for through the Incarnation He won riches and glory—that is to say, the salvation of all nations. We are told, however, that *length of life is in His right hand*; and that doubtless points to the fact of that sempiternity of His, whereby the Word was God with God from the beginning. [108]

This left hand, then, the Church, whose Head is Christ, desires to have beneath her head, and she wills to have her head protected by the faith of His Incarnation. But she desires also that His right hand may embrace her—that is, that she may know and be instructed in those matters which were locked up in mysteries and secrets before the time of this dispensation which He wrought through the flesh. For we must think of all 'right-hand' things as being where there is included nothing of the grief of sinners, nor of the fall of weakness; and the 'left-hand' things as being of that time when He Who was Himself made sin and made a curse for us, healed our wounds and bore our sins. [109]

And although all those things support the head and the faith of the Church, they will nevertheless rightly be called the left hand of the Word of God. Some of them, moreover, He is stated to have endured contrary to that nature which is wholly right-hand, and wholly light and splendour and glory.[110]

10

'*I have entreated you, ye daughters of Jerusalem, by the powers and the forces of the field, whether ye have raised and roused up charity as far as He will.*' (2.7)

I HAVE ENTREATED YOU, YE DAUGHTERS OF JERUSALEM, BY THE POWERS AND THE FORCES OF THE FIELD,[111] WHETHER YE HAVE RAISED AND ROUSED UP CHARITY AS FAR AS HE WILL. The Bride is still speaking to the maidens, urging and exhorting them, and even adjuring them by the things which she knows that they hold dear and lovable, that— if so be they have begun to raise up charity, now lying down in them, and to awaken that which so far sleeps in them—they will raise it up and rouse it up, just so far as it shall please the Bridegroom, and will do nothing less with it than His will shall permit.

For herein lies the loving Bride's perfection, that she desires nothing to be done by anyone against the mind and will of her Beloved. And, so that they shall not be negligent or slack in doing this, they are entreated 'by the powers of the field'—that is, by the young trees and bushes that are in the field, and by its 'forces,' which surely means the things that have been sown in it. Let us then understand the text of this dramatic story in this sort of way, and let this be the construction that we put upon it.

Now let us enquire further the hidden meaning underlying the text. Every soul, especially a soul who is a daughter of Jerusalem, possesses a field all her own which has been given her by Jesus, through a kind of hallowed sharing in His merits. Such also was the field of Jacob, of which the patriarch Isaac, moved by its pleasantness, said in mystical language: *Behold, the smell of my son is as the smell of a plentiful field which the Lord hath blessed.*[112] So, as we said, every soul has her field; for her life and her manner of living are her field. In this field the diligent and industrious soul is very busy, and takes care to plant all the good dispositions and to cultivate all the powers of the mind; and not only the powers of the mind, but also the forces of works with which the activities enjoined by the commandments can be fulfilled.

Each soul, therefore, has, as we said, her field, which she tills and plants and sows on the lines that we have mentioned. But there is also one common field that belongs to all the daughters of Jerusalem together; of that Paul says: *You are God's husbandry.*[113] Let us take this field as meaning the common practice of the Church's faith and way of life, in which assuredly are heavenly powers and forces of spiritual graces. To the cultivation of this field every soul, who is now called a daughter of Jerusalem because she knows her mother is the heavenly Jerusalem,[114] must of necessity bring some contribution; and she must desire this to be made worthy of being a heavenly possession.

By the powers and the forces of that field, therefore, the Church declares that the maidens and those who have the beginnings of faith must raise and rouse up the charity of Christ, and says to them: 'Have you raised and roused up charity as far as He will?' Which is as much as to say: 'If you have reached the point where you are beginning to be influenced not *by the spirit of . . . fear*, but by *the spirit of adoption*, and have made such advance that *perfect love is casting out fear* from you,[115] and you are raising and exalting charity in yourselves, and waking it up, then you must raise and lift it up so far as it shall please *the Son of Charity*, even Him who is the *Charity of God*;[116] lest perchance, if you think that the standards of human charity are good enough, you should do somewhat less in the charity of God than is worthy of God.' For the sole standard of God's charity is that our love should be as great as He would have it be; for the will of God is always the same and never changes. Therefore no change nor termination ever finds place within the charity of God.

You must surely notice that she did not say, 'whether ye have *received* charity,' but 'whether ye have *raised it up*,' as though she would say, 'Charity is in you, certainly, but at present it is lying down and has not found its feet.' Again, she did not say: 'whether ye have *found* charity,' but 'whether ye have *aroused* it,' implying that it is within them, truly, but is inactive and dormant in them, until it finds someone to wake it up. I think that Paul was arousing this same sleeper in his disciples when he said: *Rise, thou that sleepest, and thou shalt lay hold of Christ.*[117]

II

'*The voice of my Nephew! Behold here He cometh leaping upon the mountains, skipping over the hills.*' (2.8)

THE* VOICE OF MY NEPHEW! It is advisable for us to remind you frequently that this little book is cast in the form of a play. The line that we have just now cited for consideration suggests something like this. The Bride was

---

* Procopius, *Comm. in Cant. Cant.* 2.8 (MG 17.264 AB): *The voice of my nephew!* Some have referred this to what precedes, but the Hebrew applies it out of its own context. And it is clear that the Bride while talking with the daughters of Jerusalem suddenly hears the voice of the

addressing herself to the maidens, the daughters of Jerusalem, when suddenly, as from afar, she perceived the Bridegroom's voice talking with some people. Breaking off what she was saying to the maidens, therefore, she turned her attention to catching whatever it was that she had heard, and said, 'The voice of my Nephew!'

You must understand, however, that at first, before He appeared before her eyes, the Bridegroom was recognized by the Bride by His voice alone. Afterwards, however, He appeared before her eyes, leaping upon certain mountains near that place where the Bride was, and skipping over the hills and mountains, not with great steps so much as with great bounds, after the manner of a hart or roe, and in this manner coming with all speed to His Bride.[118]

Understand that when He reached the house wherein the Bride was staying, He stood a while behind the house, so that at any rate His presence might be noticed; though as yet He would not enter the house openly and for all to see but, lover-like, would first look through the windows at the Bride.

Understand also that near the Bride's house some nets and snares had been set; so that if she or one of her companions among the daughters of Jerusalem should chance to go out at any time, they would be caught. The Bridegroom, moreover, had come to these nets, certain that He could not be caught in them; and, being stronger than they, He tore them and, having torn them, He stepped

Bridegroom talking to some people—quite a natural thing; and even as the Bride hears His voice He comes skipping upon the mountains and the hills lying near the place of the Bride, not unlike a young hart. Then in His eagerness to get to the Bride, He came near the house and stood behind it. Then with a leap he reaches the windows of the house, like a lover having in mind to peep in at her. Near the house where the Bride is, many nets have been spread to catch the Bride and those around

Summary *of* Drama

over them and also looked through them. And after achieving this work He says to the Bride: *Arise, come, my neighbour, my Bride, my dove.*

And He says this in order to show her by the very fact of what He had done, how boldly she herself should now despise the nets which the Enemy had spread out in her path, and that she should not fear the snares which she now sees torn by Him. And, in order to urge her still more cogently to hasten to Himself, He tells her: The whole time that seemed oppressive is now past, and the winter, whose incidence had been her excuse, has departed, and the unprofitable rains have ceased, and the time of flowers is come. 'So, do not delay to take the road that leads to me. For look, the farmers likewise, now that the time of spring has smiled upon them, are tending their vineyards and, amid the notes of other birds, the loud and welcome voice of the turtle-dove announcing spring is likewise heard. Yes, and the fig tree, sure of the mildness of spring, without anxiety puts forth her shoots; and the vines are so certain of the season's calmness, that they venture to produce their flowers and scents.'

All these things about the calmness of the season He points out to the Bride, that she with greater confidence may venture to set out upon the way that leads to Him. But He also describes the place where He desires her to rest with Him. There is a place, He tells her, that has been made most shady by the covering of a certain rock, which

---

her. The Bridegroom broke through these, as being stronger than they, and peeped through them. Now He calls the Bride to come near, emboldening her by His action to despise the nets as being already broken, and the time that had been made so difficult by them as having passed, which time He calls winter, bringing useless and excessive rain. He also takes her through the beauties of the present time, speaking of flowers in the spring and the pruning of the vines. He describes the

is near to the wall itself, or to the outwork part. He wants her to come to this place and, when the veil has been removed, there to behold His unveiled face, that face to face she may be known to her Bridegroom, and that He may not only see her face unveiled and free, but may also hear her voice there; for He is certain both that her face is beautiful and that her voice is sweet and a delight to hear.

We have anticipated these things and connected them with the preceding, so as not to leave the impression that we were disrupting the order of the play and the text of the narrative. And in thus anticipating we have reached the point in the story where He says: *For thy voice is sweet, thy countenance is fair.* Now, looking back to the place where we began, let us see what she means by saying, 'The voice of my Nephew!'

Christ, to begin with, is recognized by His Church by His voice alone. For He first sent her His voice in advance through the prophets, and so, although He was not seen, He was heard. And heard He was through the things that they proclaimed about Him; and the Bride, that is, the Church which was gathered together from the beginning of time,[119] heard His voice only, until such time as she saw Him with her eyes and said: BEHOLD, HERE HE COMETH LEAPING UPON THE MOUNTAINS, SKIPPING OVER THE HILLS. For* He leaped upon the prophetical mountains and the holy hills, those, namely, who in this world bore His image

---

voice of the turtle-dove and the green figs and the vines in flower and the place where He will rest with her, where He wanted her to come and appear to the Bridegroom with unveiled face, and where He wanted to let her hear His sweet voice.

* Procopius, *Comm. in Cant. Cant.* 2.9 (MG 87.2.1597 C): Or again, her word 'mountains' means the prophets, who were perfect in thought, seers of the truth; and, I think, the apostles also, since their

and His form. And, if you reckon the apostles also as the mountains upon which He leaps, as being higher than them all, and take the hills in the same way as meaning those whom in the second place He chose and sent, it will not be unfitting. For among these He is made *like unto a roe or a young hart*—to a roe, because its sight is keener than that of any other animal, and to a hart, because He comes to destroy the serpent.[120]

Now* every soul—if such there is who is constrained by love for the Word of God—if at any time it is in the thick of an argument about some passage—and everyone knows from his own experience how when one gets into a tight corner like this, one gets shut up in the straits of propositions and enquiries—if at any time some riddles or obscure sayings of the Law or the Prophets hem in the soul, if then she should chance to perceive Him to be present, and from afar should catch the sound of His voice, forthwith she is uplifted. And, when He has begun more and more to

---

nature is such that Wisdom enters into their souls. She terms them 'mountains' since they were the first to receive the light of the rising Sun. 'Hills' she calls those who are less capable of receiving the manifestation of the Spirit. You could say further that the 'mountains' are the things perceived in the Law, while 'hills' are the perceptions of the remaining prophets. Indeed, too, he who has beheld the Word in the New Testament sees Him *leaping upon the mountains*, but in the Old, *skipping over the hills*. Again, the Bridegroom is likened to a 'young hart' of the deer, not only because He destroys the serpents, but also because *He was born a child for us and given as a son to us* (Isa. 9.6) and *humbled Himself* (Phil. 2.8). A deer would have meant a full-grown animal.

* Procopius, *Comm. in Cant. Cant.* 2.8 (MG 87.2.1596 A–C): This passage as far as the words, *Thy voice is sweet and thy face is fair* (2.14), is for the clarification of what has been dramatically set forth. And it is clear that the Bride of the Word—the soul or the Church of Christ— lays hold of the 'voice' as divine before she understands it. We the faithful have the same experience when, before understanding the

draw near to her senses and to illuminate the things that are obscure, then she sees Him 'leaping upon the mountains and the hills'; that is to say, He then suggests to her interpretations of a high and lofty sort, so that this soul can rightly say: 'Behold, He cometh leaping upon the mountains, skipping over the hills.' [121]

In making these remarks, however, we have not forgotten that earlier [122] He has already spoken with the Bride as being Himself personally present. But, because—as we have often said—this little book contains a kind of play, sometimes things are said with reference to a Bridegroom who is present, and sometimes to one absent; and the interchange of the characters is so conducted that either sequence seems properly used. Thus, although the Bridegroom promises and tells His Bride—that is, His chosen disciples: *Behold, I am with you all days, even to the consummation of the world,* [123] He nevertheless tells her elsewhere in parables that the householder called his servants and distributed to each one his money to trade with, and departed. And again He says that He went away to seek a kingdom for Himself; and yet again it is said with reference to the absent Bridegroom, that *at midnight there was a cry made* of those who said, *The Bridegroom cometh!* [124]

The Bridegroom is thus sometimes present and teaching, and sometimes He is said to be absent; and then He is desired. And either of these will suit either the Church or the dutiful soul. For when He allows the Church to suffer

'voices' of the Law and the Prophets, we are amazed at their fullness of divine grace. It is the same with this expression, *The voice of my Nephew*: it is prophetic long beforehand of the coming of the Word; and when the Bride sees Him engaged in great contemplations after not having despised the lesser, she cries: *Behold, He cometh leaping upon the mountains, skipping over the hills!*

Throughout the whole story certain things are said to the Bride-

persecution and tribulations, He seems to her to be absent; and again, when she goes forward in peace and flourishes in faith and good works, He is understood as being present with her.

So also is it with the soul. When she is trying to under-stand something and desiring to know some obscure and secret matters, as long as she cannot find what she is looking for, the Word of God is surely absent from her. But when the thing she sought comes up to meet her, and appears to her, who doubts but that the Word of God is present, illuminating her mind and offering to her the light of knowledge? And again we perceive He is withdrawn from us and comes again, in every matter that is either opened or closed to our understanding.

And this state of affairs we endure until we become such people as He may condescend not only often to revisit, but to remain with. This is in full accordance with what He said when a certain disciple having asked Him, saying: *Lord, how is it that Thou wilt manifest Thyself to us, and not to the world?* The Saviour replied: *If anyone loves me, he keeps my word, and my Father loves him, and we will come to him, and will make our abode with him.*[125]

If, then, we too want to see the Word of God, the Bride-groom of the soul, 'leaping upon the mountains and skipping over the hills,' we must first hear His voice and then when we have heard Him in all things, we shall be able to see Him under the same conditions as those under

groom as present, others to Him as being sought by the Bride, just as in dealing with problems we are sometimes in a state of seeking, being at a loss as to the solution, while at other times we are in a state of enjoyment of the solution—that is, of the Bridegroom, the Word, shining brightly in our hearts. Then again, concerning some other things we are at a loss, and again He manifests Himself to us. And the Church when abandoned to trials desires Him, and He manifests Him-

which the Bride is said to have seen Him here. For although she herself saw Him before, she did not see Him
as she sees Him now, 'leaping upon the mountains and
skipping over the hills,' nor did she see Him leaning
through the windows or looking through the nets; but
rather it appears that on that first occasion she saw Him
in the time of winter. For He says now for the first time
that the winter is past.[126] The fact that emerges is, therefore, that He appears to His Bride all through the winter
—that is to say, in the time of tribulations and trials.

That visitation, however, whereby she is visited for a
little while and then left, in order that she may be tested,
and then sought again, so that her head may be upheld and
she be wholly embraced, lest she either waver in faith or
be weighed down in body by the load of her trials, is
different. And so it seems to me that the 'winter' was that
time when she asked for her head, that is, the crown of her
faith, to be held in the Bridegroom's left hand, and for
His right hand to embrace her whole body. And, on the
other hand, this vision that appears now from the mountains and hills, should denote, I think, the heights and
powers of spiritual graces. And that He is said also to look
forth through the windows seems to me to represent the
light afforded to the soul's perceptions; while the nets
which He tears and rends stand, I think, for the snares of
the devil; inasmuch as the time of temptation, like winter,
has now passed away.

The tokens of summer and spring are displayed too, as
is said in the Psalms: *Summer and spring, Thou madest*

---

self to her in His gifts of grace. Wherefore she says, *Behold, He cometh
leaping upon the mountains!* What is more, He comes upon the snares of
the Evil One close by the Church: He breaks them and teaches us to
tread them underfoot with contempt. By thus passing over all the

them.[127] Therefore, at last the Church has brought forth flowers of progress too, when her trials have been overcome and the business of pruning finished, as will be shown in the proper places when we come to the actual passage that deals with this.

'Behold, He cometh leaping upon the mountains, skipping over the hills.' We have already traced the course of the narrative above. Now we must see in what sense Christ comes to the Church leaping upon the mountains and springing forth [128] (for 'springing forth' is proper to the true sense rather than 'skipping') over the hills. For whereas Isaac increased by walking and marching on until he became very great,[129] and Paul advanced no longer by walking but by running, saying, *I have finished my course,*[130] Our Saviour and the Bridegroom of the Church is said neither to walk, nor yet to run, but to leap and to spring forth over these things.

For if you consider how in the space of a short time the Word of God has run through all the world that was possessed of false beliefs, and has recalled it to the knowledge of the true faith, you will understand in what sense He leaps upon the mountains—overcoming some great kingdoms with His leaps, that is to say, and inclining them to receive the knowledge of divine religion—and springs forth over the hills in that He swiftly subjugates the lesser kingdoms and leads them to the piety of true worship.[131]

And, as He leaps from place to place, from kingdom to kingdom, from provinces to provinces by the illumination of preaching, you will understand through him who said

winter of trial the Church learns to see the signs of spring and the approach of summer, about which we read in the Psalms—*the summer and the spring . . .* (Ps. 73.17): *The flowers have appeared* to her, and her perfect cleansing is at hand, called *the time of pruning.*

that *from Jerusalem round about as far as unto Illyricum* he *replenished the Gospel of Christ,*[132] in what sense the Bridegroom 'comes leaping upon the mountains and springing forth over the hills.'

This passage can, however, be taken in another sense too, as we remarked just now; for Moses wrote of Him, and so too the prophets foretold concerning Him.[133] This foretelling, of which we read in the Old Testament, has a veil on it, however; but when the veil is removed for the Bride, that is, for the Church that has turned to God, she suddenly sees Him leaping upon those mountains—that is, the books of the Law; and on the hills of the prophetical writings He is so plainly and so clearly manifested that He springs forth, rather than merely appears. Turning the pages of the prophets one by one, for instance, she finds Christ springing forth from them and, now that the veil that covered them before is taken away,[134] she perceives Him breaking out and emerging from individual passages in her reading, and bursting out of them in a manifestation that is now quite plain.

I believe that it was for this reason that Jesus Himself, when He came to be transfigured, was not on some plain, nor in a valley, but went up a mountain and was there transfigured;[135] you are to understand from this that He always appears on mountains or hills, to teach you too, lest you should ever seek Him elsewhere than on the mountains of the Law and the Prophets. And you will find many passages in Scripture indicating that mountains are holy. Thus He says in the Psalms: *The foundations thereof are in the holy mountains*; and again: *I have lifted up my eyes to the mountains, from whence help shall come to me*[136]—we receiving help in tribulations from the meanings of the Divine Scriptures.

We can further take the mountains, upon which the Word of God is said to leap and to be borne more freely, as it were, as the New Testament, and may understand the hills, from which He sprang forth as one who had been long restrained and hidden, as the books of the Old Testament.

Further, in Jeremias the hunters and fishers who are sent to capture men for their salvation are said to capture them on mountains and hills; the passage runs: *Behold, I send many fishers and many hunters, and they shall capture them upon every mountain and upon every hill.*[137] I think myself that this prophecy is to find its fulfilment rather in the future, at the consummation of the age; so that when, according to the Gospel parable, the angels have been sent forth at harvest time to separate the wheat from the tares,[138] he who has lived on a higher plane and followed a more lofty way of life may be found on the mountains or hills, and not in the low-lying places, nor in localities where he might be confused with the tares. Rather, he will be situated in the region of higher understanding and the loftiness of faith, ever cleaving to the Word of God, who leaps on the mountains and springs forth on the hills. And this is also stated, with the same meaning, by another parable in the Gospel: *If any is on the housetop, let him not come down to take anything out of the house.*[139]

And the extraordinarily rich saying of the verse before us may suggest yet another meaning. For it is possible to call every whole-hearted believer in God a mountain or a hill, according to the quality of his living and the extent of his understanding. Though such a one was formerly a valley, as Jesus advances in him in age and wisdom and grace, *every valley shall be filled*; for of such it is said that *they that trust in the Lord shall be as Mount Sion*, and of

Jerusalem it is said that *the mountains are round about her.*[140] But all such as are proud and haughty like mountains and hills shall be brought low; because *everyone that exalteth himself shall be humbled, and he that humbleth himself shall be exalted.*[141]

For this reason I think that Our Saviour likewise, since He Himself is said to be *a stone cut out of the mountain without hands,* that *became a great mountain,* can rightly be called the Mountain of mountains, in the same way that He is called the King of kings and the Priest of priests.[142]

But in order to include a third interpretation, let us return to the subject of the individual soul. If there are some who are more able to receive the Word of God, souls who have drunk the water given them by Jesus, and if this water has *become in them a fountain of living water springing up into life everlasting,*[143] then such as these, in whom the Word of God bursts forth in frequent and abundant perceptions like ever-flowing streams, have become mountains and hills by virtue of their life and knowledge and teaching. And the Word of God is fitly said to leap on them, and to spring forth from them, through the outpouring of their teaching, as *a fountain of living water springing up into life everlasting.*

12

'*My Nephew is like a roe or a young hart upon the mountains of Bethel.*' (2.9a)

MY NEPHEW IS LIKE A ROE OR A YOUNG HART[144] UPON THE MOUNTAINS OF BETHEL. The roe or hart is mentioned because these are clearly included among the animals that are accounted clean in Deuteronomy; the passage reads as follows: *These are the beasts that you shall eat: the calf and the lamb of the cattle, and the he-goat of the goats; the hart and the roe and the gazelle and the wild goat and ibex and giraffe.*[145] Moreover, there are in the Divine Scriptures many places where a holy man is likened to a hart; as for instance where we read in the Psalm: *As the hart panteth after the fountains of water, so my soul panteth after Thee, O God.*[146]

In the text that we have taken from Deuteronomy, however, we should not overlook the fitness of the order observed in enumerating the clean beasts: the calf comes first, then the lamb, and thirdly the he-goat. But among those which, according to the same Moses, are not offered at the altar, he puts the hart first, the roe second, and then writes the remaining animals in turn.[147] The reason for this arrangement will become plain and clear to those to whom the Holy Spirit has granted a fuller spiritual grace in respect of the gift of knowledge.

Yet it seems fitting that we who are under obligation to speak about the hart and the roe in the course of our explanation of the verse before us, should to the best of our ability collect from the Sacred Scriptures the passages which have to do with these animals. The same Moses speaks of them when he is treating of those that might be eaten as meat when people wished, if they had not been offered at the altar—*like the roe or the hart*, he says.[148] There is a striking passage also in the twenty-eighth Psalm. Writing in order about the powers and the force of the voice of God, the writer speaks of the hart thus: *The voice of the Lord perfecting the harts*—that is, making the harts perfect—*and it will discover the thickets.* For just as the voice of the Lord is said to *divide the flame of fire* and to *shake the desert*, so also is He declared to *perfect the harts* and to *discover the thickets.*[149]

And in Job also we find reference to the hart, when the

Lord speaks to Job through the whirlwind and the cloud, saying: *Hast thou observed the time when the deer bring forth, or numbered the months when they are ready for birth? Hast thou eased their pangs or fed their young, or wilt thou send forth their offspring without pangs? Their children will break away and will be multiplied in birth; they will go forth, and they will not return.*[150] And to the foregoing passages we should add what we read in Proverbs as follows: *Let the hart of friendships and the fawn of graces speak to thee.*[151]

These are all the passages of Scripture about the hart that we are able to recall at present. We have quoted them that *we may speak not in the doctrine of human wisdom, but in the doctrine of the Spirit, comparing spiritual things with spiritual.*[152] Let us therefore call upon God, the Father of the Word, that He may make plain to us the secrets of His Word, and may transfer our perception from the doctrine of human wisdom and lift and raise it to the doctrine of the Spirit, to the intent that we may utter not the things that the ear of the flesh perceives, but those that are contained within the Spirit's will.

Paul the apostle teaches us that the invisible things of God are understood by means of things that are visible, and that the things that are not seen are beheld through their relationship and likeness to things seen.[153] He thus shows that this visible world teaches us about that which is invisible, and that this earthly scene contains certain patterns of things heavenly.[154] Thus it is to be possible for us to mount up from things below to things above, and to perceive and understand from the things we see on earth the things that belong to heaven. On the pattern of these the Creator gave to His creatures on earth a certain likeness to these, so that thus their great diversity might be more easily deduced and understood.

And perhaps, even as God made man to His own image and likeness, so also did He create the other creatures after the likeness of some other heavenly patterns. And perhaps the correspondence between all things on earth and their celestial prototypes goes so far, that even *the grain of mustard seed, . . . which is the least of all seeds,* has something in heaven whose image and likeness it bears; and so, because the nature of this seed is such that, *though it is the least of all seeds, . . . it nevertheless becomes greater than all herbs . . . so that the birds of heaven come and dwell in the branches thereof,* the likeness that *it* bears is not merely that of some heavenly pattern, but of the kingdom of heaven itself.[155]

In the same way, therefore, it is possible that other seeds too that are in the earth may have a likeness and relationship to something found in heaven. And, if this is the case with seeds, it is doubtless the same with plants; and if with plants, undoubtedly with animals, whether they fly or creep or go upon all fours.

And there is something further that can be discerned. The grain of mustard seed resembles the kingdom of heaven because the birds dwell in its branches, but that is not its only likeness. It is an image also of the perfection of faith, so that if a man had *faith as a grain of mustard seed,* and told a mountain to move away, then it would move away.[156] This being so, it is possible that other things also bear the appearance and likeness of things heavenly, not in one respect only, but in several.

And although in a grain of mustard seed, for example, there are several qualities that reflect the likeness of things heavenly, yet its last and final use is to serve the bodily needs of men. So with the other seeds and plants and roots of herbs, and even with the animals, it is possible to think that though they do serve the bodily needs of men, yet they also have the shapes and likenesses of incorporeal things; and thus by them the soul may be instructed and taught how to contemplate those other things that are invisible and heavenly.

And this, perhaps, is what the writer of the divine Wisdom means by saying: *For He hath given me the true knowledge of the things that are: to know the substance of the world and the virtues of the elements; the beginning and ending and midst of the times; the alterations of courses and the changes of seasons; the revolutions of the year and the positions of the stars; the natures of living creatures and the rages of beasts; the forces of winds and the reasonings of men; the diversities of plants and the virtues of roots; and all such things as are hid and manifest have I learned.* [157]

Let us see, then, if from these words of Scripture we can get more light and evidence upon the things that we have set out to discuss. For when that writer of divine Wisdom had enumerated all things one by one, he says finally that he has received knowledge of things hidden and things manifest. And he doubtless shows by this that each of the manifest things is to be related to one of those that are hidden; that is to say, all things visible have some invisible likeness and pattern. Since, then, it is impossible for a man living in the flesh to know anything of matters hidden and invisible unless he has apprehended some image and likeness thereto from among things visible, I think that He who made all things in wisdom so created all the species of visible things upon earth, that He placed in them some teaching and knowledge of things invisible and heavenly, whereby the human mind might mount to spiritual understanding and seek the grounds of things in heaven; so that taught by God's wisdom it might say: *The things that are hid and that are manifest have I learned.*

In the same way the writer has knowledge also of *the substance of the world,* not only of its visible and corporeal substance, which is *manifest,* but also of that incorporeal and invisible essence that is *hid* from us. He knows *the elements* of the world too, not the seen ones only, but the unseen too, and he knows *the virtues* of both.

And as to what he says about *the beginning and the end and the middle of the times,* he is speaking of the beginning of the visible world, a beginning which Moses put at not quite six thousand years ago;[158] the middle is a term relative to the total count of time; and the end is that for which we hope, when *heaven and earth shall pass away.*[159] But in the knowledge of hidden things the beginning is that which he understands, whom the wisdom of God has taught, that which no times nor ages can comprehend; the middle is the things that are going on now, and the end is the things that are yet to be—that is, the perfecting and consummation of the universe. Yet all these hidden things can be understood and deduced from the things that are seen.

Moreover, he relates *the alterations of courses and the changes of seasons and the revolutions of the year* of the things that are seen to the unseen changes and alterations of incorporeal things. And *the revolutions of the* temporal *years* of our present estate he relates to those more ancient and eternal years after the manner of him who said: *I had in my mind the eternal years.*[160] Nor will he who has merited to have this knowledge of *things hid and manifest* hesitate to relate *the positions of the stars* that are clearly seen to those which are hidden; and he will tell us that a certain race of holy persons, tracing descent chiefly from Abraham, is *as the stars of heaven.* [161] And, in accordance with his know-ledge of things hidden, he will further pronounce the glory of the future resurrection to be stars; and in this he will be following him who said: *One is the glory of the sun, another the glory of the moon, and another the glory of the stars; for star differeth from star in glory. So also is the resur-rection of the dead.* [162]

I should like you to take his mention of *the natures of animals and the rages of beasts* in the same way. For without a good knowledge of the natures of animals the Saviour would never have said in the Gospels: *Tell that fox*; nor would John have said of certain people that they were serpents, *a brood of vipers*; nor yet would the prophet say of some that *they are become as stallions*; nor another, that *man, when he was in honour, did not understand; he is com-pared to the senseless beasts, and is become like to them.* [163] Again, he who said: *Their madness is according to the likeness of a serpent, as that of the deaf adder that stoppeth her ears,* [164] had carefully studied *the rages of beasts.*

And when he mentions *the forces of the winds*, he will mean on the visible side the winds and breezes of the air, and on the invisible the forces of the unclean spirits, which Paul also calls *the winds of doctrine*. [165] It follows from these things that he both knows after a bodily manner *the reasonings of men* which come *from the human heart*, [166] and also recognizes without sight those beings that suggest bad and wicked thoughts to men; as it is written in the Gospel: *When the devil had put it into the heart of Judas Iscariot to betray the Lord . . .* , [167] and as is said in Proverbs: *If the spirit of him that hath power ascend upon thee, leave not thy place, because right reason restrains great sins.* [168] Good thoughts, however, also have their instigator; wherefore it is written in the Psalms, I think: *Blessed is the man whose help is from Thee, O Lord, in his heart he hath disposed to ascend;* and again: *The thought of man shall give praise to Thee, and the remainders of the thought shall keep holiday to Thee.*[169]

So, as we said at the beginning, all the things in the visible category can be related to the invisible, the corporeal to the incorporeal, and the manifest to those that are hidden; so that the creation of the world itself, fashioned in this wise as it is, can be understood through the divine wisdom, which from actual things and copies teaches us things unseen by means of those that are seen, and carries us over from earthly things to heavenly.

But this relationship does not obtain only with creatures; the Divine Scripture itself is written with wisdom of a rather similar sort. Because of certain mystical and hidden things the people is visibly led forth from the terrestrial Egypt and journeys through the desert, where there was a biting serpent, and a scorpion, and thirst, and where all the other happenings took place that are recorded.[170] All these events, as we have said, have the aspects and likenesses of certain hidden things. And you will find this correspondence not only in the Old Testament Scriptures, but also in the actions of Our Lord and Saviour that are related in the Gospels.[171]

If, therefore, in accordance with the principles that we have now established all things that are in the open stand in some sort of relation to others that are hidden, it undoubtedly follows that the visible hart and roe mentioned in the Song of Songs are related to some patterns of incorporeal realities, in accordance with the character borne by their bodily nature. And this must be in such wise that we ought to be able to furnish a fitting interpretation of what is said about the Lord perfecting the harts,[172] by reference to those harts that are unseen and hidden.

For what perfection would come to those visible harts from the voice of the Lord? Or what teaching ever comes down to them from the voice of the Lord? But if we were to look for the spiritual harts, of which the corporeal animal possesses the form and image, you would find that they can be brought to the height of perfection by the voice of the Lord.

We must notice also how it became the Lord to guard the births of these harts,[173] and how fitting it was that He should stand by, offering His services as healer when they brought forth, until they were delivered of such sons as should oppose and chase the race of serpents, in a manner worthy of the divine majesty; also what sort of deer they are whose bringing to birth it beseems the Lord to guard that they may not miscarry, whose months it beseems Him to count till their time to give birth is come, and over whose travail pangs He keeps a fitting watch, so that their offspring may not come to nought, but that their birth may be perfect, and they may be in labour only until such time as Christ be formed in them.[174]

The Lord Himself, then, feeds the fawns of deer like these, that is, of those who pour out their thoughts on the Lord, that He Himself may feed them and guard them in the pangs of birth, when by the fear of the Lord they have conceived in their womb, and have given birth, and have brought forth the spirit of salvation.[175] The Lord Himself looks after travail pangs such as these. And He also sends forth their griefs that they may go and weep, bearing their seed, and may share the griefs of men, and be scourged along with men,[176] lest haply pride get hold of them.

These same harts also snatch away their offspring,[177] as Scripture says. For those whom they have begotten through the Gospel they tear away from the chains of sin and the snares of the devil, that they will be no longer held enchained to his will. These also will be multiplied and, as the Scripture says, will not return. For they will not imitate Lot's wife, they will not return backward; for they know that a man who puts his hand to the plough will not be fit for the kingdom of heaven if he looks back; no, they will always forget the things that are behind, and press on towards those that are before.[178]

Such, then, are the harts whom the voice of the Lord makes perfect. And what is the voice of the Lord save that which is contained in the Law and the Prophets, and reaches even to John who was *the voice of one crying in the wilderness*? And John's own voice, that said: *Prepare ye the ways of the Lord, make straight the paths of our God,* made harts perfect that they might be *perfect in the same mind, and in the same knowledge.* For one who is such says with reason: *As the hart panteth after the fountains of waters, so my soul panteth after Thee, O God.*[179]

And as for *the hart of friendships,* who else should this be but He who destroys the serpent that had beguiled Eve and by spreading the poison of sin in her with his inbreathed encouragement had infected the whole of her posterity with the contagion of the Fall, He who came to loose in His own flesh the enmities which the baneful mediator [181] had brought to pass between God and man?

The fawn of graces, however, can be taken as denoting the Holy Spirit from whom those who thirst and long for God win spiritual graces and celestial gifts.

Now we have said all this in order to make clearer the reason why the Bride compares her Nephew with a young hart. And if you would enquire further why He is compared to a *young* hart, and not, as elsewhere, to the hart itself, do note the fact that, *though He was in the form of*

God, a Son was given to us and a Child was born to us, whose power was upon His shoulder.[182] He is a fawn, for He was born a little child for us. And perhaps the harts may be understood as some of the saints, such as Abraham and Isaac and Jacob and David and Solomon, and all from whose seed Christ came according to the flesh. Those harts the Lord's voice did indeed make perfect, and their fawn is He who was born as a child of them according to the flesh.

I am moved also by a passage in the hundred and third Psalm which reads: *The high hills for the harts.*[183] We have indeed remarked already, with reference to the harts, that they may be taken as meaning the saints, who came into this world in order to destroy the poison of the serpent. But let us see now what the high mountains are which appear as being reserved for the harts alone, and which none can scale unless he be a hart. My own opinion is that it is knowledge of the Trinity that is called high mountains; no one can achieve possession of that, unless he be made a hart.

But these same mountains that here are called high mountains in the plural, in other places are termed a high mountain in the singular, as Isaias says: *Get thee up upon a high mountain, thou that bringest good tidings to Sion; lift up thy voice with strength, thou that bringest good tidings to Jerusalem.*[184] For that which in the former place is understood of the Trinity because of the distinction of Persons, is here understood as the One God by reason of the unity of Substance.

Let that suffice about the young hart. Now let us see why the Nephew is compared also to a roe or little fallow deer. If we look to the Greek, this creature has received its name from its keen power of sight.[185] And who is there who sees as Christ sees? For He alone it is who sees or knows the Father. For, although it is said of the pure in heart that they shall see God, they will doubtless see Him only by Christ's revealing;[186] for it is a further part of the roe's nature that it not only sees and perceives most acutely itself, but also bestows the power of sight on others. For those who are skilled in medicine assert that there is a certain fluid in the viscera of this animal which dispels dimness from the eyes and stimulates defective vision. Deservedly, therefore, is Christ compared to a roe or fallow deer, since He not only sees the Father Himself, but also causes Him to be seen by those whose power of vision He Himself has healed.

But you must not take this talk of 'seeing the Father' in any bodily sense, or think that God is visible. The sight by which God is seen is not of the body, but of the mind and spirit. Our Saviour Himself marks this distinction in the Gospel[187] by the word that He employs; for He did not say that no man *saw* the Father save the Son, but that no man *knew* the Father save the Son. And finally, to those to whom He gives the power of seeing God, He gives the Spirit of knowledge and the Spirit of wisdom, that by the same Spirit they may see God. And for that reason He told His disciples: *He that hath seen me hath seen the Father also.*[188]

But we shall surely not be so silly as to think that he who saw Jesus in the body, saw the Father too in the same way. For were that so, we should find the hypocritical Scribes and Pharisees, and Pilate who scourged Him,[189] and all the people who cried *Crucify, crucify Him,*[190] seeing the Father when they saw Jesus in the flesh; and that would obviously be both ridiculous and profane. For just as when crowds were pressing Him along with His disciples, none of those who thus crowded and jostled Him is said to have touched Him, save only she who, vexed with an issue of blood, came and touched the hem of His garment, and He bore witness to her alone, saying: *Somebody hath touched me, for I felt virtue is gone out of me*; [191] so also, though there were many who saw Him, none of them is said to have seen Him, save he who recognized that He was the Word and Son of God, in whom at the same time the Father is said to be recognized and seen.

Let us not miss this further point, however, that He is compared to a roe or a fawn in the first place, though a hart is obviously a larger animal than is the roe. Look at this closely; does not the reason for it lie perhaps in the fact that while the salvation of believers depends upon two things, their understanding of the faith and the perfection of their works, it is the element of faith—likened, as we have said, to a roe by reason of its power of sight and contemplative insight—that is taken as the first step in salvation, whereas second place is given to perfection of works, which is represented under the figure of the hart, that conquers and destroys the poison of serpents and the wiles of the devil?

The Bride, then, says that her Nephew is like to a roe or a young hart on the mountains of Bethel. Bethel means the House of God. [192] So the mountains that are in the House of God can be taken as meaning both the books of the Law and the Prophets, and also those of the Gospels and apostolic writings. It is by means of these that the faith of God is beheld and also the perfection of works is learned and fulfilled.

13

'Behold, He stood behind our wall, leaning against the windows, looking through the nets. My Nephew answered, and He says to me: "Arise, come, my neighbour, my fair one, my dove. Lo, the winter is past, the rain is gone, the flowers have appeared in our land. . . . The fig tree hath put forth her green figs, the vineyards have yielded their sweet smell."' (2.9b–13b)

BEHOLD, HE STOOD BEHIND OUR WALL, LEANING AGAINST THE WINDOWS, LOOKING THROUGH THE NETS. MY NEPHEW ANSWERED, AND HE SAYS TO ME. When I consider the difficulties of finding out the meaning of the words of Scripture that we have here adduced, it seems to me that I am in like case with a man who pursues his quarry by means of the power of scent, such as a wise dog has. For sometimes it happens that when the hunter, following a hot trail, thinks that he has come close to the hidden lairs, he is all of a sudden forsaken by the track-marks. And, having urged his hound to pursue the scent more carefully,[193] he goes back along the same trails that he had traced before, until he finds the place where his quarry, now thoroughly aroused, has secretly betaken itself on to another trail. When the hunter finds this, he follows it up with more alacrity, more sure now of his prey and more certain that he is on the right tracks. So, when the tracks of the explanation that we thought to find have in some way failed us, we likewise hope that after a little search and after pursuing a plainer sort of explanation than appeared possible before, the Lord our God may deliver the prey into our hands, and that we, preparing and seasoning it with the salt of the reasonable word,[194] after the knowledge of our mother Rachel, may be found worthy to obtain blessings from our spiritual father Jacob.[195]

This is the reason why it seems needful, as we said, to go back and briefly unravel the former explanation, so that it may be shown which is the clearer meaning. I take it, therefore, that at the beginning of the drama before us [196] the Bride is standing out of doors at a place where two ways meet, and for love of her Spouse is looking this way and that, to see if perhaps He may be coming, and maybe is in sight. But so long as she does not know from which direction He is likely to come, she is unwilling either to set out on any road or to stay indoors.

She stands outside, therefore, and, moved with longing for Him, says: *Let Him kiss me with the kisses of His mouth.* But when the Bridegroom has arrived, she says: *Thy breasts are better than wine,* and that which follows up to the place where the Scripture says: *We will run after Thee.* After that, the Beloved receives the Bridegroom's answering love, and is brought into His chamber; *the King has brought me into His chamber,* she says. The rest of what is written after this, however, she speaks as from within the chamber, to the Bridegroom in the presence of the maidens who attend on the Bride, and to the companions who attend on the Bridegroom.

The Bridegroom, however, is to be understood as a husband who is not always in the house, nor is He in perpetual attendance on the Bride, who stays in the house. Rather, He frequently goes out, and she, yearning for His love, seeks Him when He is absent; yet He Himself returns to her from time to time. It seems, therefore, that all through this little book we must expect to find the Bridegroom sometimes being sought as one who is away, and sometimes speaking to the Bride as being present with her.

But the Bride herself, because she has seen many and great splendours in His chamber, asks further that she may be brought *into the house of wine*. Having entered this and looked around, because the Bridegroom her husband has not tarried in the house, she goes out once again, anguished anew by love for Him, and goes all round the house, and in and out of it, looking in all directions for her Bridegroom's return. And then all of a sudden she sees Him, overtopping the crests of the nearby mountains with great leaps, and so descending to the house, where the Bride is yearning and burning for His love.

The Bridegroom, however, on reaching the wall, stands a while behind it, considering something, as a person will, and turning it over in His mind. Then, being Himself moved now with something of love for the Bride and availing Himself of His height, which reaches to the windows of the house—and these windows are furnished in part with what is called network—since He, when He leans against them, is taller than they and reaches to their upper parts which, as we said, are divided off by network, He looks through these nets and speaks to the Bride, saying: ARISE, COME, MY NEIGHBOUR, MY FAIR ONE, MY DOVE, etc.[197]

This is the sequence of events which, as we remarked before, seemed to us very difficult to sort out and explain; and I think that the foregoing analysis of the dialogue will have made it clearer.

The spiritual interpretation, however, is not so difficult and hard to come by.[198] For the Bride of the Word, the soul who abides in His royal house—that is, in the Church —is taught by the Word of God, who is her Bridegroom, whatsoever things are stored and hidden within the royal court and in the King's chamber. In this house, *which is the*

Church of the living God,[199] she becomes acquainted also with the cellar of that wine which is extracted from the holy wine-presses, the wine that is not only new, but also old and sweet—that is, the teaching of the Law and the Prophets.[200]

And when she has been adequately trained in that, she receives unto herself the Word Himself, who was God with God in the beginning.[201] He does not always stay with her, however, for that for human nature is not possible: He may visit her from time to time, indeed, and yet from time to time she may be forsaken too by Him, that she may long for Him the more. But—taking the meaning of the verse before us—when she is visited by the Word, He is said to come to her *leaping upon the mountains,*[202] that is, revealing to her the meaning of high and lofty truths of heavenly wisdom in such wise as to effect the building up of *the Church, the house of the living God, the pillar and ground of the truth;*[203] and then He stands near or behind the wall, so that He is neither wholly hidden, nor yet wholly in open view. For the Word of God and the word of knowledge does not appear as set in public places where everyone can see, nor is He to be trampled underfoot of men;[204] nay rather, He is found when He is sought for, and found, as we said, not in the open courtyard, but covered over and as it were hiding behind the wall.

But the soul, which is said to be 'in the Church,' is understood not as being situated within the buildings which the walls enclose, but rather as being placed within the bulwarks of faith and the edifice of wisdom, and covered over with the lofty gables of charity. What makes a soul to be in the house of the Church is, therefore, good conduct and belief in right doctrines. And there are rooms in this house, which are severally called the chamber, and

the house of wine, or go by similar names according to the
degrees of graces and the diversity of spiritual gifts.

So, therefore, the wall likewise is a part of this house and
it can be taken as denoting the stability of doctrines: it
is beneath this wall that the Bridegroom is said to stand,
and in these doctrines He is so great and tall, that He over-
tops every building and looks upon the Bride—that is, the
soul. But He does not show Himself openly and wholly to
her yet; rather, looking at her through the nets, as it were,
He encourages and urges her not to sit idle in there, but to
go to Him outside and try to see Him—no longer through
windows and nets, nor *through a glass in a dark manner*; but,
going out to Him, to see Him *face to face*.[205] For now,
because she cannot yet behold Him thus, He stands not in
front of her, but at her back, and behind the wall.

Moreover, He also leans through the windows, which
doubtless were open to admit the light and to bring light
into the house. Leaning and looking through those windows, then, the Word of God calls on the soul to rise and
come to Him.

We* can take the windows as meaning the bodily
senses through which life or death gains entrance to the
soul; for that is what the prophet Jeremias means when,
speaking of sinners, he says: *Death is come up through your
windows*.[206] How does death come up through windows?
If the eyes of a sinner should *look on a woman to lust after
her*; and because he who has thus looked upon a woman
has committed adultery with her in his heart,[207] then

---

* Procopius, *Comm. in Cant. Cant.* 2.9 (MG 87.1600 D–1601 A):
By 'windows' we should understand the senses by which in the case of
sinners death enters in (Jer. 9.21); but in the case of the soul lovingly
disposed towards Him, the Word 'peeps' in upon her need when she
is strongly influenced by the senses and has snares laid by the 'net' in

death has gained entrance to that soul through the windows of the eyes.

Similarly, when a person hears some piece of vanity, and especially the vanity of the false knowledge of perverted teachings, then death enters that soul through the windows of the ears. When, on the other hand, a soul, seeing how the world is decked out, perceives the Creator of all in the beauty of His creatures and marvels at His works and praises their Maker, to this soul life enters through the windows of the eyes. And also, when she listens to the Word of God and takes delight in the reasonings of His wisdom and knowledge, to her the light of wisdom enters through the windows of her ears.

So the Word of God, looking through these windows and fixing His regard on the Bride-soul, exhorts her to arise and come to Him, that is to say: to forsake things bodily and visible and to hasten to those that are not of the body and are spiritual.[208] For *the things which are seen are temporal, but the things which are not seen are eternal.*[209]

Thus also is the Spirit of God said to go around and seek for worthy souls, such as can be rendered fit for Wisdom to inhabit.[210] But that He is said to 'look through the nets' of the windows doubtless points the fact that so long as the soul is in the house of this body, she cannot receive the naked and plain wisdom of God, but beholds the invisible and the incorporeal by means of certain analogies and tokens and images of visible things. And this is what is meant by the Bridegroom looking at her through the nets of the windows.

---

her upper room. Coming up to these, the Bridegroom 'peeps' through them, calling the Bride to Himself away from the senses to the invisible and incorporeal; this is obvious from the words with which He invites her to Himself, *Arise, come!*

If, however, we are to expound the passage with reference to Christ and the Church, then the house in which the
Church was dwelling is the writings of the Law and the
Prophets. For there too is a king's chamber, filled with *all
the riches of wisdom and knowledge*; there too is a house of
wine—the teaching, whether mystical or moral, that
cheereth the heart of man.[211]

When Christ was coming, therefore, He stood awhile
behind the wall of the house of the Old Testament. He
was standing behind the wall, in that He was not yet
showing Himself to the people. But when the time is come,
and He begins to appear to the Church who sits inside the
house, that is, within the letter of the Law, and to show
Himself to her through the windows of the Law and the
Prophets, that is, through the things that had been foretold
concerning Him, then He calls her to come forth and
come outside to Him.

For,* unless she comes out, unless she comes forth and
advances from the letter to the spirit, she cannot be united
with her Bridegroom, nor share the company of Christ.
He calls her, therefore, and invites her to come out from
carnal things to spiritual, from visible to invisible, from the
Law to the Gospel. And therefore He says to her: 'Arise,
come, my neighbour, my fair one, my dove.'

And if we may anticipate somewhat of that which we
shall have to say later on, because we do not want to lose a
meaning that has just occurred to us, perhaps that is the

---

* Procopius, *Comm. in Cant. Cant.* 2.10 (MG 17.264 C): 'Arise,'
He says, 'from things of the senses to things spiritual, that thou mayest
understand them by means of the things by which thou beholdest them.
For *the winter is past, the rain is gone.*' We should say that the rain is the
time before the Incarnation, when God gave commandment to the
clouds to rain down (Job 37.6) the word of the Law and the Prophets;
but that this stopped, since *the Law and the Prophets were until John*

reason why He tells her further: LO, THE WINTER IS PAST, THE RAIN IS GONE: [212] He thereby both indicates the actual time of the Passover, for He suffered when winter was past and the rains had spent themselves, and also signifies on the spiritual side that there were rains upon the earth up to the time when the Lord endured His Passion. For up to that time the Lord was giving command to the prophet-rains to pour the shower of the Word upon the earth. [213] But because the prophets functioned only until John the Baptist, [214] the showers are rightly said to have gone away and departed.

The prophetical showers ceased, however, not to the loss of believers, but for the greater profit of the Church. For what need is there of showers, when *the river maketh the city of God joyful*, when *a fountain of water springing up into life everlasting* [215] is found in every faithful heart? What need is there of showers, now that THE FLOWERS HAVE APPEARED IN OUR LAND, and since the coming of the Lord THE FIG TREE, that formerly was barren, is no longer cut down? [216] For now she HATH PUT FORTH HER GREEN FIGS. So too THE VINEYARDS HAVE YIELDED THEIR SWEET SMELL. Wherefore a certain member of that vineyard said: *We are the good odour of Christ unto God* in every place, *in them that are saved and in them that perish*. [217]

As we have remarked above, however, we have dealt with these matters before we reached their actual place in the Scripture, fearing lest perhaps the meaning, which was

---

(Luke 16.16); and it is spring and summer after the Incarnation, when there was no longer need of rain, when—thanks to the presence of Christ—*flowers appeared in the land*. And from the time of His Incarnation the fig tree is not cut down, the one that was barren in the former time; for now *it has put forth green figs* and *the vines are in blossom*. Wherefore one of the branches says, *We are the good odour of Christ unto God* (2 Cor. 2.15).

obvious to us at the moment, should escape our memory. Now, therefore, let us go back and consider in what sense He is said to 'look forth through the nets.'

It is written: *For nets are spread not unfairly for birds*; and again, the just man, if he have fallen into sin, is commanded to *flee as a doe from the snares, and as a bird from the nets.*[218] The life of men, then, is full of the snares of deadly offences, full of the nets of fraud, which he who is called *Nemrod, the giant hunter against the Lord,*[219] spreads for the human race. For who is in fact that giant, save the devil, who rebels even against God? So the snares of temptations and the craftily contrived gins of the devil are called nets. And, because the Enemy had spread these nets everywhere and had trapped almost everyone in them, it was needful that somebody should come who should be stronger than they and stand out above them and should destroy them, and thus clear the way for those who followed Him. Therefore is the Saviour also tempted by the devil[220] before He could enter into union and alliance with the Church; so that, conquering the snares of temptations, He might look through them and through them also call her to Himself, thus teaching and showing her beyond all doubt that the way to Christ leads, not through idle ease and pleasure, but through many trials and temptations.

There was, therefore, none other who could overcome these nets. *For all have sinned*, as it is written; and again, as Scripture says: *There is no just man upon earth that hath done good and hath not sinned;*[221] and again: *No one is free of uncleanness, not even if his life be of but one day.*[222] Therefore Our Lord and Saviour Jesus Christ alone is He *who did no sin*; but the Father *made Him to be sin for us,* that *in the likeness of sinful flesh and of sin He might condemn sin.*[223]

So He came to these nets; but He alone could not be

caught in them. Instead of that, when He has torn and trampled them, He so emboldens His Church that she too dares to trample now upon the snares, and to pass over the nets, and with all joy to say: *Our soul hath been delivered as a sparrow out of the snare of the fowlers; the snare is broken, and we are delivered.*[224] Who rent the snare, save He who alone could not be held by it?[225] For, although He suffered death, He did so willingly, and not as we do, by necessity of sin; for He alone was *free among the dead.*[226]

And, because he was *free among the dead,* when He had conquered him *who had the empire of death,*[227] He brought forth the captives that were being held by death.[228] And He did not raise only Himself from the dead; He also raised, together with Himself, those who were held by death, and made them *to sit with Him in the heavenly places.* For *ascending on high, He led captivity captive,*[229] not only bringing forth the souls, but also raising their bodies, as the Gospel testifies: *Many bodies of the saints . . . were raised, . . . and appeared to many, and came into the holy city of the living God, Jerusalem.*[230]

We have adopted the foregoing as a secondary explanation of the nets. It is for the reader to judge which of the two best suits the mystical sense of the words.

[BOOK FOUR][231]

14

'*Arise, come, my neighbour, my fair one, my dove; for lo, the winter is past, the rain is gone and has departed to itself, the flowers have appeared on the earth, the time of pruning is come, the voice of the turtle-dove is heard in our land, the fig tree hath put forth her buds, the vines in flower have yielded their sweet smell.*' (2.10b–13a)

ARISE, COME, MY NEIGHBOUR, MY FAIR ONE, MY DOVE; FOR LO, THE WINTER IS PAST, THE RAIN IS GONE AND HAS DEPARTED TO ITSELF, THE FLOWERS HAVE APPEARED ON THE EARTH, THE TIME OF PRUNING IS COME, THE VOICE OF THE TURTLE-DOVE IS HEARD IN OUR LAND, THE FIG TREE HATH PUT FORTH HER BUDS, THE VINES IN FLOWER HAVE YIELDED THEIR SWEET SMELL. We have already described the arrangement of the drama; now let us consider what we are here to understand the Word of God as saying to the soul that is worthy and prepared for Him, or what Christ is to be understood as saying to the Church.

Forthwith, then, let the Word of God speak first to this fair and noble soul, to whom He has appeared by means of her bodily senses—that is, through her reading of Scripture and hearing of doctrine—as it were, through windows, and to whom He has shown how tall and great He is; in order that He might speak to her in the words just cited, leaning towards her, and then calling her to come out of doors and, being removed from the bodily senses, to cease to be in the flesh, that so she may merit to hear : *But you are not in the flesh, but in the spirit.*[232]

For the Word of God would not otherwise say that she

was His neighbour, did He not join Himself to her and become one spirit with her.[233] Nor would He call her fair, unless He saw her image renewed day by day.[234] And, did He not perceive her to be able to receive the Holy Spirit, who descended on Jesus at the Jordan in the form of a dove,[235] He would not say to her, 'My dove.' For she had conceived the love of the Word of God and was desiring to come to Him by a swift flight, saying: '*Who will give me wings like a dove, and I will fly and be at rest?*[236] I will fly with my affections, I will fly with my spiritual perceptions and rest, when I have understood *the treasures of His wisdom and knowledge.*'[237]

For I think that just as those who accept the death of Christ and mortify their members upon earth are made partakers of the likeness of His death,[238] so also those who receive the power of the Holy Spirit and are sanctified by Him and filled with His gifts, themselves become doves, even as He Himself appeared in the form of a dove. And so, uplifted on the Holy Spirit's wings, they fly from earthly and corporeal places to celestial ones.

To show that the time is opportune for these things to happen, He has, moreover, logically inserted: 'For lo, the winter is past, the rain is gone.' The soul is not made one with the Word of God and joined to Him,[239] until such time as all the winter of her personal disorders and the storm of her vices has passed; so that she no longer vacillates and is *carried about with every wind of doctrine.*[240] When, therefore, all these things have gone out of the soul, and the tempest of desires has fled from her, then the flowers of the virtues can begin to burgeon in her; then* the time of pruning also comes to her. And, if there be

---

* Procopius, *Comm. in Cant. Cant.* 2.10–13 (MG 87.2.1605 C): *The time of the pruning*—of the putting away of the superfluous things.

anything superfluous and of small use in her affections and perceptions, it may be cut back and recalled to the buds of spiritual understanding.

Then★ also will she hear 'the voice of the turtle-dove,' which surely denotes that wisdom which the steward of the Word speaks among the perfect, the deep wisdom of God which is hidden in mystery.[241] This fact is indicated by the mention of the turtle-dove; for this bird spends its life in the more hidden and remote localities, away from crowds; it loves either mountainous wastes, or the secret parts of the forests, is always found far from the multitude, and is a stranger to crowds.

And what else is there that fits the opportuneness of this time and its delightfulness? 'The fig tree,' He says, 'hath put forth her buds.' The spirit of man, of which the fig tree is a figure, does not yet bear the fruits of the spirit— love, joy, peace, and the rest;[242] but it is beginning now to put forth buds of them.

Indeed, different trees are generally understood in the Church as meaning the individual souls of the faithful, of whom it is written: *Every tree that my heavenly Father hath not planted shall be rooted up.* And again Paul, who calls himself *God's coadjutor* in *God's husbandry*, says also of himself: *I have planted, Apollo watered*; and so too the Lord in the Gospels: *Either make the tree good and its fruit good.*[243] Just so, as the different trees are understood in the Church as meaning the individual souls of the faithful, are the various powers and virtues in the individual soul understood under the figure of sundry kinds of trees. There is,

★ Procopius, *ibid.*: *The voice of the turtle-dove.* Surely too He speaks of the turtle-dove as of the unutterable and unknown wisdom; for this creature is a lover of solitude, whose voice is heard by those still girt with their earthly body.

then, in the soul a certain fig tree that puts forth its bud; and there is also a vine that flowers and yields its sweet smell. The Husbandman, who is the heavenly Father, purges the shoots of this vine, that they may bring forth much fruit.[244] But according to him who said, *We are the good odour of Christ in every place,*[245] this vine first rejoices the nostrils with the sweetness of the odour yielded by its flowers. So the Word of God, seeing these beginnings of the virtues of the soul, calls her to Himself, bidding her hasten and come forth and cast aside all things corporeal, and come to Him and be made a sharer in His perfection.

This, then, is the reason why on this first occasion He says to her: 'Arise,' implying that even now she is lying down and reclining amid things corporeal; and she, forthwith obeying Him when He calls and doing what He bids, is praised by Him and hears: 'My neighbour and my dove.'

And after this, lest she be frightened at the storms of temptations, He tells her that 'the winter is past, and the rain has gone over and departed to itself.' Well did He signify the natures of vices and sins in a single marvellous saying, when He said that this kind of winter and of rains that fall upon us from the offence and storm of vices had 'departed to themselves,' thus indicating that sins have no being. For when a man's vices leave him, they are not gathered together to form some other being, but take themselves away and, being dissolved into themselves, they vanish and are reduced to nothing. And therefore He said that it 'has departed to itself.'[246]

Tranquillity, then, comes to the soul when the Word of God appears to her, and sin ceases to be. And so at last, when the vineyard is in flower, the virtues and the orchards of good fruits will begin to bud.

But now suppose once more that Christ is speaking these words to the Church, and is representing the whole duration of this present age within the circle of the year.[247] He would then be describing as 'winter' the period in which the hail and storms and the other catastrophes of the ten plagues chastised the Egyptians; or that in which Israel was engaged in diverse wars,[248] or even the time of her resistance to the Saviour Himself when, caught in the storm of unbelief, she was overwhelmed in the shipwreck of faith. So, now that *by their offence salvation is come to the Gentiles,*[249] He calls the Church of the Gentiles to Himself, and says to her: 'Arise and come to me, for the winter which overwhelmed the unbelievers and held you down in ignorance, has passed. And the rain too has gone—that is to say, no longer will I bid the prophet-clouds to pour the rain of the Word upon the earth;[250] but the voice of the turtle-dove, the very Wisdom of God, shall speak on earth and say: "*I myself that spoke, I am here.*"[251] The flowers, therefore, of believing peoples and of budding churches have appeared on the earth. And★ the time of pruning, through the faith of my Passion and Resurrection, also has come.'

For sins are lopped and cut away from men when remission of sins is given in Baptism. The voice of the turtle-dove is heard indeed, as we have said, not just through the various prophets; it is the voice of God's own wisdom that is heard on earth. And the fig tree is sprouting; which may be taken as referring to the fruits of the

---

★ Procopius, *ibid.*: This (time) is the time of His Parousia, in which the bodily excrescences of the Law and the history in the Prophets must receive the circumcision of the Spirit, so that the better part may survive. Further it is the appointed time for the pruning away of sins and their remission through the rebirth of Baptism.

Holy Spirit that are now for the first time disclosed and revealed to the Church; or to the letter of the Law, which before Christ's coming was closed and bound up and covered over with a sort of overlying carnal interpretation, whereas, as a result of His presence and coming, a bud of spiritual understanding has been put forth from it, and the fresh and living meaning that was concealed in it, has now appeared. And in consequence of this the Church, which was concealed by Christ in the 'fig tree,' that is, in the Law, appears not as barren and as pursuing the letter that kills, but as following the flowering and life-giving Spirit.[252]

Yes, and the vines also are said to be in flower, and to have yielded their sweet smell. The various churches too that are found all over the world can certainly be called flowering vines and vineyards. *For the vineyard of the Lord of hosts is the house of Israel, and the man of Juda, His pleasant plant.*[253] These vineyards, then, are said to flower when they first come to faith; but when they are adorned with the sweetness of godly works, then they are said to have yielded their sweet smell.

And I think it is not without reason that He says 'their sweet smell,' and not *a* sweet smell: it was to show that there is in every soul a potential force and a freedom of the will, by means of which it has the power to do all things good. But this inborn good had been beguiled by the Fall, and perverted to sloth or wickedness: when it is amended by grace and restored by the teaching of the Word of God, then assuredly it yields that odour which God the Creator had originally implanted in it, but which the guilt of sin had taken away.

The vines or vineyards can, moreover, be taken also as denoting the heavenly and angelic powers which bestow their sweet smell on men—that is to say, the benefit of teaching and instruction whereby they instruct and imbue souls, until they reach perfection and begin to be able to comprehend God.[254] In the same way the Apostle also, when writing to the Hebrews, says: *Are they not all ministering spirits, sent to minister for them who shall receive the inheritance of salvation?* [255] And for this reason men are said to receive from them first the bloom, as it were, and the sweet smell of good things, but to look to receive the actual fruits of the vine from Him who said: *I will not drink . . . of the fruit of this vine until I shall drink it new with you in the kingdom of my Father.*[256]

These perfect fruits must then be hoped for from Himself; but the beginnings of them, and the sweetness of progress, so to speak, can be ministered by the heavenly powers, or at any rate by those who said, as we remarked above: *For we are the good odour of Christ* in every place.[257]

There is, however, another way in which we may understand the passage before us: we can say that it is a sort of prophecy given to the Church, to call her to the promised blessings of the future. She is told to 'arise,' as though the consummation of the age were already reached and the time of resurrection come.[258] And, because this word of command forthwith seals the work of resurrection, she is invited into the Kingdom, as being now, by virtue of the resurrection, brighter and more splendid, and is bidden: 'Come, my neighbour, my fair one, my dove, for the winter is past'—winter here denoting surely the storms and tempests of this present life and the blasts of temptation with which human life is racked.

This winter, then, is past with its rains, and has 'departed to itself'; for everyone did what he did in this life 'to himself.' The flowers, which have appeared on the earth, we may take as the beginning of the future promises. And take the time of pruning as *the axe laid to the root of the trees* at the consummation of the age, that it may *cut down every tree that bringeth not forth good fruit*.[259] But in the voice of the turtle-dove, which is heard in that land of promise, you must see Christ teaching in His own Person, seen *face to face*, and no longer *through a glass and in a dark manner*.[260]

The fig tree, moreover, that puts forth its buds, may be taken as the fruit of the whole congregation of the just. And those holy and blessed angelic powers with whom all the elect and blessed—who will themselves *be as the angels of God*[261]—will be associated by virtue of the resurrection, they are the flowering vines and vineyards that impart to every soul her fragrant odour, and the grace which she received from her Creator at the first and now, after losing it, has again recovered. And with the sweetness of their celestial fragrance they drive away at last the stench of the mortality and corruption, that the soul has laid aside.

15

'*Arise and come, my neighbour, my fair one, my dove; in the shelter of the rock by the outwork show me thy face, and let me hear thy voice; for thy voice is sweet, and thy face is fair.*' (2.13b–14)

ARISE AND COME, MY NEIGHBOUR, MY FAIR ONE, MY DOVE; IN THE SHELTER OF THE ROCK BY THE OUTWORK SHOW ME THY FACE, AND LET ME HEAR THY VOICE; FOR THY VOICE IS SWEET, AND THY FACE IS FAIR. In the sequence of the drama before us the Bridegroom who has come to His Bride leaping upon the mountains and springing forth upon the hills, says to her now for the second time,[262] as He looks forth at her and sees her through the windows: 'Arise, come, my neighbour, my fair one, my dove.' But now He goes a step further, indicating to her the place whither she is to come; this place is situated under a covering or roof of stone. And this same place is to be found, not by the wall, but by some outwork of the wall. An outwork is so called when, beyond the walls that surround a city, there is another wall; the outwork, therefore, is a wall in front of a wall.

After this, speaking as though the Bride were veiled and covered for the sake of reverence, the Bridegroom asks her, when she comes to that place which He has just specified as being more secluded, to lay aside her veil and show her face to Him. And, because the Bride was keeping silence out of her great reverence, the Bridegroom desires further that He may sometimes hear her voice and take pleasure in her words; He bids her let Him hear her voice. It appears, however, that her face is not altogether unknown to Him, neither is He ignorant of her voice; but that some time has elapsed since He saw her face or heard her voice.

That seems to be the implication of the drama before us. The statements that the flowers have appeared on the earth, and that the voice of the turtle-dove is heard, and that the trees have budded, tell us further that the season of spring is now with us. Therefore He calls upon the Bride, who has doubtless sat indoors all winter, to come forth now, as at a fitting time.

But these things seem to me to afford no profit to the readers as far as the story goes; nor do they maintain any continuous narrative such as we find in other Scripture stories. It is necessary, therefore, rather to give them all a spiritual meaning.

First, then, you must take the winter of the soul as the time when she is still tossed with the waves of her passions and battered by the storms of her vices and the strong blasts of malignant spirits. So long as she is in the thick of these, the Word of God does not exhort her to come forth; rather, He would have her hold herself close and guard herself and shield herself on every side against these harmful blasts of the malignant spirits. She gets no flowers of zest from the Divine Scriptures then, nor do the secrets of the deeper wisdom and the hidden mysteries sound as by the turtle-dove's voice. Her sense of smell likewise receives no favour, as from the flowering vines, neither does her vision find delight, as in the budding fig tree: during the storms of temptations it is all that she can do to keep safe and guarded from falling into sin.

But if she does contrive to get through these unscathed, then the winter is past, and spring has come to her. For spring for her is when repose is given to her soul and calmness to her mind. Then* the Word of God comes to her, then He calls her to Himself, and bids her come forth, not only from the house, but from the city itself—in other words, she must forsake not only fleshly vices, but also everything bodily and visible that the world contains. For we have already demonstrated plainly that the city is a figure for the world.[263] The soul, therefore, is summoned forth outside the wall, and is brought to the outwork, when, forsaking and leaving things seen and temporal, she hastens towards those that are unseen and eternal.[264]

She is shown, however, that the way thereto must be followed beneath the cover of the rock, and not out in the open. And that she may not suffer the sun's heat and per-

---

* Procopius, *Comm. in Cant. Cant.* 2.13 f. (MG 17.264 D–265 A): He wishes the soul to pass beyond sense objects; He calls the world of the senses the wall as it were and 'outwork' of the city. The soul which will have fellowship with the Word must then be in the 'shelter of the rock,' not only outside the city-wall, but also outside the 'outwork';

haps become tanned again and say once more: 'The sun hath looked askance at me,' therefore she takes the way beneath the cover of the rock. But He will not have this covering made for her of branches, or canvas, or skins; He will have her covering made of *rock*—that is, the firm and solid teachings of Christ. For Him St. Paul declares to be a rock when he says: *And the rock was Christ.*[266]

If, then, the soul be shielded and covered with the doctrine and the faith of Christ, she can come safely to that secret place wherein she may *behold the glory of the Lord with open face.*[267] We may well believe that that covering of the rock is safe, since Solomon also says of it in Proverbs that the tracks of the serpent cannot be detected on the rock. This is what he says: *There are three things that are impossible for me to understand, and a fourth that I do not know: the tracks of an eagle in flight, the ways of a serpent on the rock, the paths of a ship at sea, and the ways of a man in youth.*[268] For no tracks of the serpent—that is, no marks of sin—can be found in this rock which is Christ, for it is He alone who did no sin.[269]

Having, therefore, availed herself of the covering of this rock, the soul comes safely to the place on the outwork— that is, to the contemplation of things incorporeal and eternal. David speaks of this same rock under another metaphor in Psalm Seventeen: *And He set my feet upon a rock and ordered my paths.*[270] Do not be surprised if with David this rock is as it were the ground and basis upon which the soul goes to God, while with Solomon it is the

---

so that, being near, she may with unveiled face behold the glory of the Lord, obeying His word, *Show me thy face.* But He desires also to hear her voice when she speaks, wondering at its sweetness. Now the 'outwork' is what Isaias calls the bulwark, saying, *He shall set a wall and a bulwark* (Isa. 26.1). He wants her, then, when she has gone forth from

covering of the soul that is set upon reaching the mystical secrets of wisdom; seeing that Christ Himself is at one time called the Way by which believers go, and again the Forerunner, as when Paul says: *Into which the forerunner Jesus is entered for us.*[271]

Like to these is the saying of God to Moses: *Lo, I have set thee in a cleft of the rock, and thou shalt see my back parts.*[272] That Rock which is Christ is, therefore, not completely closed, but has clefts. But the cleft of the rock is He who reveals God to men, and makes Him known to them; for *no one knoweth the Father, save the Son.*[273] So no one sees the back parts of God—that is to say, the things that are come to pass in the latter times, unless he be placed in the cleft of the rock, that is to say, when he is taught them by Christ's own revealing.[274]

And here, then, under the cover of the rock the Word of God invites the soul that has been made His neighbour, to this place on the outwork, as we said before, to contemplate the things that are eternal and unseen. And there He says to her: 'Show me thy face'—surely that He may see that nothing of the old veil remains upon her face, but that she can with fearless gaze behold the glory of God, so that she too may say: *And we saw His glory, the glory as it were of the Only-begotten of the Father, full of grace and truth.*[275]

But when she has become worthy to have it said of her, as also it was said of Moses, that *Moses spoke, and God answered him,*[276] then there is fulfilled in her that which He says: 'Make me to hear thy voice.' It is indeed high praise of her that is disclosed in that saying, 'Sweet is thy voice.'

---

bodily things, not only to be on the wall—which I reckon to be the word to describe the boundary of this world—but also to be clinging to the outwork, and this is the word for the extreme end of corporeal things and the beginning of the incorporeal.

For thus also said the most wise prophet David: *Let my speech be sweet to Him.*[277] And the voice of the soul is sweet when it utters the word of God, when it expounds the faith and the doctrines of the truth, when it unfolds God's dealings and His judgements.

If, however, silly talk or smart jests or vanity proceed out of her mouth, or the idle word for which account is to be rendered on the Day of Judgement,[278] that voice is neither sweet nor pleasant. From this voice Christ turns away His ear. And therefore every perfect soul *sets a watch before her mouth, and a door round about her lips,* that what she utters may ever be seasoned with salt, and so be gracious to those who hear it,[279] and that the Word of God may say of her: 'Thy voice is sweet.'

He says further: 'Thy face is fair.' If you understand what Paul means by 'face' when he says, *We all . . . with unveiled face,* and again when he says, *But then face to face,*[280] you will perceive what manner of 'face' it is that is praised by the Word of God and described as fair. It is, without a doubt, the sort of face that is daily being renewed *according to the Image of Him who created it, not having spot or wrinkle or any such thing,* but is *holy and without blemish,* even as the Church which Christ *has presented to Himself*[281] —in other words, the souls who have reached perfection. And all of these together make up the body of the Church.

This body truly will appear as beautiful and comely, if the souls of which that body is constituted persevere in all the comeliness of perfection. For, as the soul when in a rage makes the bodily visage distorted and wild, but gives to it a peaceful and kindly look when it continues in calm tranquillity, so also the face of the Church is declared to be comely or ugly according to the virtues and aspirations of her believers, even as it is written: *A cheerful countenance is a token of a heart that is in prosperity*; and again in another place: *A glad heart maketh a cheerful countenance; but by grief of mind the face is cast down.*[282] The heart is glad when it has within it the Spirit of God, whose first fruit is charity, and the second, joy.[283] I think it is from these facts that certain secular sages have formed the opinion that only the wise man is fair, whereas every bad man is ugly.[284]

It remains for us to give a somewhat fuller explanation about the word 'outwork.' This, as we said above, means a wall in front of a wall, and that is expressed also in Isaias like this: *He shall set a wall, and a wall round about.*[285] The wall is the rampart of the city; but the other wall, in front of or around that one, denotes larger and stronger fortifications. This shows us that when the Word of God calls out the soul, and leads her forth from bodily concerns and physical perceptions, He desires to teach her about the mysteries of the age to come, and thence to find defence for her; so that she, being fortified and encompassed by the hope of things to come, may in no wise be overcome by decoys, nor wearied by tribulations.

Now let us consider in what sense these words are spoken by Christ to the Church, which is to Him a neighbour and fair, but fair to nobody except to Himself alone; for that is what He implies by saying, '*My* fair one.' Christ then, arouses her, and proclaims the Gospel of the Resurrection to her, and hence says: 'Arise, come, my neighbour, my fair one.' Moreover, He gave her *the wings of a dove*, after she had slept *among the midst of lots.*[286] For the Church was called between the two callings of Israel; that is to say, first Israel was called, and afterwards when Israel had stumbled and fallen, the Church of the Gentiles was called. But when the fullness of the Gentiles has come in, then will all Israel, having been called again, be saved.[287]

So, *among the midst of* these two *lots* the Church sleeps; and for this reason He gave her *the wings of a dove covered with silver*, which denotes the flights of reason through the gift of the Holy Spirit, and He covered *the broad of her back with the freshness of gold*, as some read, or, as the text of others reads, *with the paleness of gold*;[288] and this may point to the fact that the later calling of Israel, which the Apostle says is yet to be, will be not in the keeping of the Law, but in the preciousness of faith. For when faith blossoms in the virtues, it begets a freshness like to that of gold.[289]

The Church, however, may be said to sleep, or rest, *among the midst of lots*, in that she is in the midst between the two Testaments; and her wings are silvered over with the understanding of the Law, but the gold on the broad of her back stands for the bountiful gift of the Gospel.

To this Church, therefore, Christ says: 'Come, thou my dove, and be under the covering of the rock,' thus teaching her to keep under cover, lest any assault of temptation should befall her, and to walk in the shelter of the shadow of the rock, saying: *The breath of our face, Christ the Lord, . . . to whom we said, 'Under His shadow we shall live among the Gentiles.'*[290]

She walks thus veiled and covered, however, because she *ought to have a power over her head, because of the angels.*[291] But when she has reached the outwork place, that is, the state of the age to come, there He says to her: 'Show me thy face, and let me hear thy voice; for thy voice is sweet.' He would have the voice of His Church to be heard, because everyone that shall have confessed Him before men, him will He also confess before His Father who is in heaven.[292]

'For thy voice is sweet.' Who would not admit that the voice of the Catholic Church is sweet in her confession of the true faith; whereas the voice of the heretics, who speak not the doctrines of the truth, but blasphemies against God and *iniquity on high,*[293] is harsh and unpleasing? In the same way the face of the Church is fair, but that of heretics is hideous and ugly; if indeed anyone is able to discern this beauty of face—if he is *spiritual,* that is to say, and a person who knows how to sift all things out. For with ignorant and sensual men the fallacies of falsehood appear more beautiful than do the dogmas of the truth.[294]

As to the outwork in this passage, we can, moreover, add this, that the outwork may be the bosom of the Father, whence the Only-begotten Son declares all things and tells his Church whatsoever things are hidden in the secrets of the Father's heart. Wherefore also one that was taught by Him said: *No man hath seen God at any time; the Only-begotten Son who is in the bosom of the Father, He hath declared Him.* Thither, therefore, does Christ call His Bride, alike to teach her about all things that are with the Father, and to say: *I have made known to you all things which I have heard of my Father,* and yet again to say: *Father, I will that where I am, they also . . . may be with me.*[295]

15

'*Catch us the little foxes that destroy the vines, and our vine-yards will flourish.*' (2.15)

CATCH US THE LITTLE FOXES THAT DESTROY THE VINES, AND OUR VINEYARDS WILL FLOURISH. There is a change of characters in the drama here: the* Bridegroom is speaking

---

* Procopius, *Comm. in Cant. Cant.* 2.15 (MG 17.265 AB): These words the Bridegroom says to His friends, either to the angels or to the holy men, as many as are teachers of the Church. His orders are for the safety of the vines, so that when the evil powers which destroy the

now no longer to the Bride, but to the companions, and telling them to catch the little foxes that lurk in the vineyards when they are just coming into bud, and do not let the vines develop their flowers.

But we must search out these matters by the spiritual interpretation, as we have done from the beginning. And I think that if you take these words as referring to the soul who joins herself to the Word of God, the foxes must be understood as the opposing forces and the wicked powers of demons who by means of base thoughts and perverted notions destroy the bloom of the virtues of the soul and ruin the fruit of faith.[296] According to the promise of the Word of God who is *the Lord of hosts*,[297] therefore, command is given to the holy angels, who are *sent to minister for them who receive the inheritance of salvation*,[298] to catch in every soul such thoughts as these that have been put into her by the demons; so that when these have been driven away, the flowers of virtue may be brought forth. Their catching of the bad thoughts consists in their suggesting to the mind that those thoughts come not from God, but from the Evil One, and in imparting to the soul the power to discern the spirits; so that she may understand which thought is according to God, and which thought is from the devil.

But so that you may know the thoughts which the devil sends into the heart of man, look at what is written in the Gospel. *The devil*, it says, *having now put into the heart of Judas Iscariot . . . to betray Him. . . .*[299] So there are thoughts like this which are insinuated into the hearts of men by the

beginning of the growth of the fruit have been caught, the vines may be able to advance from bloom up to the perfection of fruit, being husbanded by God; though owing to their free will they can either bring forth fruit or refuse to do so. Or some men may be taken as demons. But because the Divine Providence fails not, lest human freedom should be disrupted by such insolence as this and there should be no just cause for judgement, the care of men is committed to the kind angels and the friendly powers, that when the foxy deceivers begin to invade the soul, they may support her with the help of their right hands.

This, then, is why it is said: 'Catch us the little foxes.' Suitably indeed He bids them to be caught and taken while they are still little. For as long as a bad thought is only beginning, it is easily driven from the heart. But if it comes again and again, and goes on for long, it surely leads the soul to agree with it; and, once agreed to and entrenched in the heart, it is certain to result in the commission of sin. It must, therefore, be caught and driven out while it is still incipient and small; otherwise, when it has grown up and become a matter of habit, it can no longer be driven out.[300]

Thus Judas too had a beginning of evil in his love of money; and that was for him a 'little fox.' But the Lord, seeing the soul of Judas as a flowering vineyard that was being damaged by it and wishing to catch it and drive it away, committed purses of money to his care; so that, possessing what he loved, he might no longer covet.[301] But he, for all that he had freedom of choice, did not embrace his Physician's wisdom, but in self-indulgence chose to give himself over to that counsel which was destroying his soul, rather than to that which served its healing.

If, however, we would understand these words with reference to Christ and the Church, the words will appear

---

'foxes,' when by their bitter heterodoxy they put stumbling-blocks in the path of those beginning to run well; the Lord wants them to be caught while they are still small, before they advance to yet greater impiety. For if a fox grows up without being caught by the friends, he

as addressed to the teachers of the Church, giving them orders about catching the foxes that are destroying the vineyards. We can take the foxes as the perverted teachers of heretical dogmas, who by the artfulness of their arguments lead the hearts of innocent people astray and destroy the vineyard of the Lord, so that it does not bear the flower of orthodox belief. Command is given, therefore, to the Catholic teachers to make haste to rebuke and to restrain these foxes while they are still little and only beginners in false doctrine, and to subdue and capture the gainsayers of the word of truth with demonstrations of the truth.

For, if they have tolerated them and indulged them at the outset, *their speech spreadeth like a canker*[302] and will become incurable; so that many are found who, deceived by them, presently begin to take up arms on their behalf, and to defend the authors of the error that they have received. It is fitting, therefore, to catch the little foxes and to refute the cunning fallacies of the heretics with positive statements of the truth straight away at their very beginnings.[303]

In order, however, to clarify further both the explanations that we have given, let us collect from the divine books whatever mention of this animal is made therein. In Psalm Sixty-Two we find the wicked spoken of like this: *But they have sought my soul in vain, they shall go into the lower parts of the earth; they shall be delivered into the hands of the sword, they shall be the portions of the foxes.*[304]

Moreover, in the Gospel according to Matthew the Saviour's answer to the scribe who had said to Him:

---

can be hunted by the Bridegroom alone; but when they are only beginning to work their evil deeds, they are also easily caught by His friends, and He naturally says, 'little vineyards,' for the foxes have no power against great ones.

Master, I will follow Thee whithersoever Thou goest, is this:
*The foxes have holes and the birds of the air nests, but the Son
of Man hath not where to lay His head.*[305] And in the same
way, in the Gospel according to Luke, to those who said
to the Lord: *Depart and get Thee hence, for Herod hath a mind
to kill Thee,* Jesus replies: *Go, tell that fox, 'Behold, I cast out
devils and do cures to-day and tomorrow and on the third day
I shall be consummated.'*[306]

Samson also, in the Book of Judges, when his wife, who
was of the race of the Philistines, had been taken away from
him, says to his father: '*I am innocent this time with regard to
the foreigners, for I am going to do you evil.' And Samson went
and caught three hundred foxes; and he took torches and tied
them tail to tail and he put a torch between two foxes' tails. And
he set fire to the torches and sent them forth through the
foreigners' standing corn; and he set fire to all their standing
corn and their stubble-fields, and to their vineyards and olive
groves.*[307]

Again, in the Second Book of Esdras, where Tobias the
Ammonite is hindering the building operations of those
who had returned from captivity, and preventing them
from building the Temple and the wall, he says to the
Allophyli: *Will they indeed sacrifice and eat what they have
offered in this place? Will not the foxes go up and destroy the
wall that they are building with stones?*[308]

These are all the passages from the Sacred Scriptures that
we can think of at the moment, which contain mention of
this animal; from them the discerning reader may gather
whether what we have given here is an apt interpretation
to explain the passage before us that says: 'Catch us the
little foxes.' And, though it may be tedious to explain in
detail each of these examples that we have adduced, we will
nevertheless touch briefly on them, as far as we are able.[309]

First, then, let us look at the sixty-second Psalm, where, because the wicked were persecuting the soul of the just, the Psalmist sang as follows: *But they have sought my soul in vain, they shall go into the lower parts of the earth; they shall be delivered into the hands of the sword, they shall be the portions of foxes.* Herein it is clearly shown that the bad teachers who desire to deceive the soul of a just man with vain and foolish words, are said to go into the lower parts of the earth; insomuch as their wisdom is that of the earth, and they speak *from* the earth and descend into its lower parts— that is, into the depths of folly.

For I think that people who live after the flesh are said to *be* earth and to dwell *on* the earth,[310] because they do harm only to themselves; whereas those who interpret the Scriptures in an earthly and carnal manner and deceive others by teaching in that way, are said to *enter into* the lower parts of the earth, from the very fact that they produce such babblings and arguments of carnal and earthly wisdom. For surely the offence of those who teach earthly things is greater than that of those who live earthly-wise, and a heavier doom awaits them in the future, even as it is foretold in this same place that *they shall be delivered into the hands of the sword*, perhaps that *flaming sword, turning every way.*[311]

But let us see in what sense they also become *the portions of foxes.* Every soul is either the portion of God or the portion of someone who has received power over men. For *when the Most High divided the nations and separated the sons of Adam, He appointed the bounds of the nations according to the number of the angels of God; and Jacob became the portion of the Lord.*[312] As, then, we all agree that every soul is either in God's portion, or in someone else's, and since our freedom of will makes it possible for anyone to go from one portion to another—to God's portion, if the change be for the better, and to that of the demons, if it be for the worse —then this mention in the Psalm of those who have sought in vain for the soul of the just and will be the portion of foxes is as much as to say that they will be the portion of the worst and wickedest demons; it will thus be all the baleful and cunning powers by which the deceptions and frauds of the false wisdom have been introduced, that are figuratively termed foxes.

And people who are led into this error and will not consent to the sound words of Our Lord Jesus Christ and to that doctrine which is according to godliness,[313] but suffer themselves to be deceived by such beings, these people will become the portion of such foxes, and will go with them into the lower parts of the earth. They are the same also as those among whom those foxes, to which we referred just now, are said in the Gospel to have holes, but among whom the Son of Man has no place to lay His head. Herod also must be thought of as being called a fox, because of his deceptive shrewdness.

But I find it very difficult to furnish an explanation of this image or figure in relation to Samson, of whom it is recorded that he caught three hundred foxes and tied them together by their tails, and put burning torches between the tails and sent them through the foreigners' fields of standing corn, thus setting these on fire along with the stubble-fields and olive groves and vineyards. Let us try to knock something out of it, however, as far as we are able: so let us take the foxes as false and perverted teachers, as in the explanation given above. We will then suppose that Samson, who represents a true and faithful teacher, catches these foxes with the word of truth, and ties them tail to tail—that is to say, he confutes them by setting the holders and teachers of different views against each other; and, by taking syllogisms and propositions out of their own words, he sends out the fire of the conclusion into the foreigners' corn, and with their own arguments burns up all their fruits and the vineyards and olive groves of the evil brood.

With regard to these foxes that differ from and disagree with one another, however, the number three hundred itself signifies that there are three kinds of sins. For every sin is committed either in deed, or in word, or by the consent of the mind.[314]

Neither must we ignore entirely what we said is written in the Second Book of Esdras. There, when the Holy of Holies was in building—that is, when the faith of Christ and the mysteries of His saints were in process of establishment, the enemies of truth and the opponents of the faith, who are the wise of this world, seeing the walls of the Gospel rising without literary art or philosophical skill, say scornfully that these things can easily be destroyed by the cunning of words, through crafty falsehoods and the arguments of dialectic.

Let what we have said about these things, as far as the small space available permitted, suffice for the present. We must return now to the subject before us. In the Song of Songs the Bridegroom is seen to bid the powers friendly to Himself to catch and to rebuke the adverse powers which lie in ambush for the souls of men; lest these, who lurk like foxes in their holes in people who have offered themselves to follow up these matters, should destroy their budding faith and the flower of their virtue under the pretext of some secret and hidden knowledge. And, so that they may be more easily silenced and rebuked, it is commanded that these foxes be caught while they are still little, and have only just begun to exercise their abominable persuasion. For maybe if they grow up and become big foxes, the Bridegroom's friends will no longer have the power to catch them, and only the Bridegroom Himself will be able to do it.

And, too, some holy doctors and teachers of the Church receive the power of catching foxes, even as they have received *the power to tread upon serpents and scorpions*; for so it has been given them to have power *upon all the power of the enemy*.[315] And one of these powers of the enemy is certainly the fox that destroys all the vineyards, and is bidden to be caught while it is small, even as also in the hundred and thirty-sixth Psalm he is called *blessed, that takes and dashes the little ones* of Babylon *against the rock*, and suffers not the Babylonian outlook to grow and increase in itself, but, while it is only beginning, takes and dashes it on the rock; for then it is easily destroyed.[316]

This, then, is the sequence of the interpretation of 'Catch us the little foxes that destroy the flowering vineyards.' His saying '(for) *us*' means '(for) me, the Bridegroom, and the Bride'; or else 'for me and you, who are my companions.'

It can, however, be taken thus: 'Catch us the foxes'; and then, following a pause, 'that are destroying the little vineyards,' so that 'little' is taken as referring not to the foxes, but to the vineyards.[317] The implication then will be that little vineyards are liable to destruction, whereas big ones are not; that is to say, some little souls, and such as are beginners, being not strong and sturdy yet, are liable to be injured by opposing forces; as it is said in the Gospel: *If anyone shall scandalize one of these little ones*.[318] This shows that it is not the tall and perfect soul that can be caused to stumble, but the little, unformed one, as we read in the

Psalm: *Much peace have they that love Thy name, and to them there is no stumbling-block.*[319]

In the same way you can see that any little vineyard, any soul that is only a beginner, can be injured by foxes—that is to say, by evil thoughts and debased teachers, whereas a strong and perfect soul cannot. But if these foxes are caught by good teachers and driven out of the soul, then she will go forward in the virtues and flourish in the faith. Amen!

PART TWO

THE HOMILIES

FROM THE LATIN TRANSLATION BY ST. JEROME

PROLOGUE

Jerome to the Most Blessed Pope Damasus:[1]

While Origen surpassed all writers in his other books, in his *Song of Songs* he surpassed himself.[2] In ten full volumes, containing nearly twenty thousand lines, he expounded first the version of the Seventy, then those of Aquila, Symmachus, and Theodotion, and finally a fifth, which he tells us that he found on the coast near Actium.[3] And this exposition of his is so splendid and so clear, that it seems to me that the words, *The King brought me into His chamber*,[4] have found their fulfilment in him. I have passed over that work, for it would require far too much time and labour and expense worthily to render into Latin such a mighty theme. It is not strong meat that I offer here; instead of that, with greater faithfulness than elegance I have translated these two treatises which he composed for babes and sucklings[5] into the speech of every day, to give you just a sample of his thinking, so that you may reflect how highly his great thoughts should be esteemed, when even his little ones can so commend themselves.

THE FIRST HOMILY

On the beginning of the Song of Songs to the
place where the writer says: UNTIL THE KING RE-
CLINE AT HIS TABLE.

1. As we have learned from Moses that some places are
not merely holy, but *holy of holies*,[1] and that certain days
are not sabbaths simply, but are sabbaths of sabbaths: so
now we are taught further by the pen of Solomon that
there are songs which are not merely songs, but SONGS
OF SONGS. Blessed too is he who enters holy places, but far
more blest the man who enters the holy of holies! Blessed
is he who observes the sabbaths, but more blest he who
keeps sabbaths of sabbaths![2] Blessed likewise is he who
understands songs and sings them—of course nobody sings
except on festal days—but much more blest is he who
sings the Songs of Songs! And as the man who enters holy
places still needs much to make him able to enter the holy
of holies, and as he who keeps the sabbath which was
ordained by God for the people still requires many things
before he can keep the sabbath of sabbaths: so also is it
hard to find a man competent to scale the heights of the
Songs of Songs, even though he has traversed all the songs
in Scripture.

You must come out of Egypt and, when the land of
Egypt lies behind you, you must cross the Red Sea if you
are to sing the first song, saying: *Let us sing to the Lord, for
He is gloriously magnified.*[3] But though you have uttered
this first song, you are still a long way from the Song of
Songs. Pursue your spiritual journey through the wilder-

266

ness, until you come to *the well which the kings dug*,[4] so that there you may sing the second song. After that, come to the threshold of the holy land, that standing on the bank of Jordan you may sing the song of Moses, saying: *Hear, O heaven, and I will speak, and let the earth give ear to the words of my mouth*![5] Again, you must fight under Josue and possess the holy land as your inheritance; and a bee must prophesy for you and judge you—*Debbora*, you understand, means 'bee'—in order that you may take that song also on your lips, which is found in the Book of Judges.[6] Mount up thence to the Book of Kings, and come to the song of David, when he fled *out of the hand of all his enemies and out of the hand of Saul, and said, 'The Lord is my stay and my strength and my refuge and my saviour.'*[7] You must go on next to Isaias, so that with him you may say: *I will sing to the Beloved the song of my vineyard.*[8]

And when you have been through all the songs, then set your course for greater heights, so that as a fair soul with her Spouse you may sing this Song of Songs too. I am not sure how many persons are concerned in it; but, as far as God has shown me in answer to your prayers, I seem to find four characters—the Husband and the Bride; along with the Bride, her maidens; and with the Bridegroom, a band of intimate companions. Some things are spoken by the Bride, others by the Bridegroom; sometimes too the maidens speak; so also do the Bridegroom's friends. It is fitting indeed that at a wedding the bride should be accompanied by a bevy of maidens and the bridegroom by a company of youths. You must not look without for the meaning of these; you must look no further than those who are saved by the preaching of the Gospel. By the Bridegroom understand Christ, and by the Bride the Church *without spot or wrinkle*, of whom it is written: *that*

He might present her to Himself a glorious Church, not having spot or wrinkle or any such thing, but that she might be holy and without blemish.[9] In the maidens who are with the Bride you must recognize those who, although they are faithful, do not come under the foregoing description, yet are regarded none the less as having in some sense obtained salvation—in short, they are the souls of believers. And in the men with the Bridegroom you must see the angels and those who have *come unto the perfect man.*[10] We have thus four groups: the two individuals, the Bridegroom and the Bride;[11] two choirs answering each other—the Bride singing with her maidens, and the Bridegroom with His companions. When you have grasped this, listen to the Song of Songs and make haste to understand it and to join with the Bride in saying what she says, so that you may hear also what she heard. And, if you are unable to join the Bride in her words, then, so that you may hear the things that are said to her, make haste at least to join the Bridegroom's companions. And if they also are beyond you, then be with the maidens who stay in the Bride's retinue and share her pleasures.

These are the characters in this book, which is at once a drama and a marriage-song. And it is from this book that the heathen appropriated the epithalamium, and here is the source of this type of poem; for it is obviously a marriage-song that we have in the Song of Songs.[12] The Bride prays first and, even as she prays, forthwith is heard. She sees the Bridegroom present; she sees the maidens gathered in her train. Then the Bridegroom answers her; and, after He has spoken, while He is still suffering for her salvation, the companions reply that 'until the Bridegroom recline at His table'[13] and rise from His Passion, they are going to make the Bride some ornaments.

2. We must consider now the actual words with which the Bride first voices her prayer: LET HIM KISS ME WITH THE KISSES OF HIS MOUTH.[14] Their meaning is: 'How long is my Bridegroom going to send me kisses by Moses and kisses by the prophets? It is His own mouth that I desire now to touch; let Him come, let Him come down Himself!' So she beseeches the Bridegroom's Father saying: 'Let Him kiss me with the kisses of His mouth.' And because she is such that the prophetic word, *While thou art yet speaking, I will say, 'Lo, here am I!'* [15] can be fulfilled upon her, the Bridegroom's Father listens to the Bride and sends His Son.

She, seeing Him for whose coming she prayed, leaves off her prayer and says to Him directly: THY BREASTS ARE BETTER THAN WINE, AND THE ODOUR OF THY PERFUMES BETTER THAN ALL SPICES.[16] Christ the Bridegroom, therefore, whom the Father has sent, comes anointed to the Bride and it is said to Him: *Thou hast loved justice and hated iniquity: therefore God, Thy God, hath anointed Thee with the oil of gladness above Thy fellows.*[17] If the Bridegroom has touched me, I too become of a good odour, I too am anointed with perfumes; and His perfumes are so imparted to me that I can say with the apostles: *We are the good odour of Christ in every place.*[18]

But we, although we hear these things, still stink of the sins and vices concerning which the penitent speaks through the prophet, saying: *My sores are putrefied and corrupted because of my foolishness.*[19] Sin has a putrid smell, virtue exhales sweet odours. Look up examples of them in the Book of Exodus; you will find there stacte, onyx, galbanum, and so on. Now these are to make incense; in addition, various perfumes, among them nard and stacte, are taken for the work of the perfumer.[20] And God who made heaven and earth speaks to Moses, saying: *I have filled them with the spirit of wisdom and understanding, that they may make the things that belong to the perfumer's art*; [21] and God teaches the perfumers. If these words are not to be spiritually understood, are they not mere tales? If they conceal no hidden mystery, are they not unworthy of God? He, therefore, who can discern the spiritual sense of Scripture or, if he cannot, yet desires so to do, must strive his utmost to live not after flesh and blood, so that he may become worthy of spiritual mysteries and—if I may speak more boldly—of spiritual desire and love, if such indeed there be. And as one sort of food is carnal and another is spiritual, and as there is one drink for the flesh and another for the spirit, so there is a love of the flesh which comes from Satan, and there is also another love, belonging to the spirit, which has its origin in God; and nobody can be possessed by the two loves. If you are a lover of the flesh, you do not acquire the love of the spirit. If you have despised all bodily things—I do not mean flesh and blood, but money and property and the very earth and heaven, for these will pass away [22]—if you have set all these at nought and your soul is not attached to any of them, neither are you held back by any love of sinful practices, then you can acquire spiritual love.

We have put this here, because the opportunity arose to say something about spiritual love. And it is for us to follow Solomon's injunction, and still more His who spoke through Solomon concerning wisdom, saying: *Love her, and she will keep thee safe; enfold her, and she will exalt thee; render her honour, that she may embrace thee.* [23] For there is a certain spiritual embrace, and O that the Bridegroom's more perfect embrace may enfold my Bride! [24] Then I too shall be able to say what is written in this same book: *His left hand is under my head, and His right hand will embrace me.*[25]

3. 'Let Him kiss me,' therefore, 'with the kisses of His mouth.' The Scriptures are wont to use the form of command, rather than that of wish. We have, for instance, *Our Father who art in heaven, hallowed be Thy name,*[26] instead of 'O that it may be hallowed!'; and in the passage before us we read 'Let Him kiss me with the kisses of His mouth,' rather than 'O that He would kiss!'

Then she sees the Bridegroom. Fragrant with sweet oils He comes; and He could not otherwise approach the Bride, nor was it fitting for the Father to send His Son to the marriage in any other wise. He has anointed Him with divers perfumes, He has made Him the Christ,[27] who comes breathing sweet odours and hears the Bride declare: 'Thy breasts are better than wine.' The Divine Word rightly has different names for the same thing, according to the context. When a victim is offered in the Law, and the Word wants to show exactly what is meant, it says: *The little breast that is set apart.*[28] But when someone reclines with Jesus and enjoys full fellowship of thought with Him, then the expression is, not *little breast*, but *bosom.*[29] And again, when the Bride speaks to the Bridegroom, because it is a marriage-song that is beginning, the word used is not *little breast*, as in the sacrifice, not *bosom*, as in the case of the disciple John, but *breasts*—'Thy breasts are better than wine.'

Be you of one mind with the Bridegroom, like the Bride, and you will know that thoughts of this kind do inebriate and make the spirit glad. Wherefore, as *the inebriating chalice of the Lord, how surpassing good it is!*[30]—so are the breasts of the Bridegroom better than any wine. 'For Thy breasts are better than wine'—this is how in the midst of her prayers she addresses herself to her Spouse—'and the odour of Thy perfumes is above all spices.' Not with one perfume only does He come anointed, but with all. And if He will condescend to make my soul His Bride too and come to her, how fair must she then be to draw Him down from heaven to herself, to cause Him to come down to earth, that He may visit His beloved one! With what beauty must she be adorned, with what love must she burn that He may say to her the things which He said to the perfect Bride, about *thy neck, thine eyes, thy cheeks, thy hands, thy body*, thy shoulders, thy feet![31] God permitting, we will think about these questions, and consider why the Bride's members are thus differentiated and a special meed of praise accorded to each part; thus, when we have thought it out, we may try to have our own soul spoken to in the same way.

'Thy breasts,' then, 'are better than wine.' If you have seen the Bridegroom, you will know that what is spoken here is true: 'Thy breasts are better than wine, and the odour of Thy perfumes is above all spices.' Many people have had spices: the queen of the South brought spices to Solomon,[32] and many others possessed them; but no matter what any man had, his treasures could not be compared with the odours of Christ, of which the Bride says here: 'The odour of Thy perfumes is above all spices.' I think myself that Moses had spices too, and Aaron, and each one of the prophets; but if I have once seen Christ and have perceived the sweetness of His perfumes by their smell, forthwith I give my judgement in the words: 'The odour of Thy perfumes is above all spices.'

4. THY NAME IS AS PERFUME POURED FORTH.[33] These words foretell a mystery: even so comes the name of Jesus to the world, and is 'as perfume poured forth' when it is

proclaimed. In the Gospel, moreover, a woman took an alabaster vessel containing precious ointment of pure spikenard and poured it on Jesus' head, and (another) on His feet.[34] Note carefully which of the two women poured the perfume on the Saviour's head: the *sinner* poured it on His feet, and she who is not called a sinner poured it on His head. Notice, I say, and you will find that in this Gospel lesson the evangelists have written mysteries, and not just tales and stories. And so *the house was filled with the odour of the ointment.*[35] We must take what the sinner brought with reference to the feet, and what the woman who was not a sinner brought with reference to the head. Small wonder that the house was filled with fragrance, since with this fragrance all the world is filled!

The same passage speaks of Simon the leper and his house. I think the leper is the prince of this world,[36] and that the leper is called Simon: his house it is that at Christ's coming is filled with sweet odours, when a sinful woman repents and a holy one anoints the head of Jesus with sweet perfumes.

'Thy name is as perfume poured forth.' As perfume when it is applied scatters its fragrance far and wide, so is the name of Jesus poured forth. In every land His name is named, throughout all the world my Lord is preached; for His 'name is as perfume poured forth.' We hear the name of Moses now, though formerly it was not heard beyond the confines of Judea; for none of the Greeks makes mention of it, neither do we find anything written about him or about the others anywhere in pagan literature.[37] But straight away, when Jesus shone upon the world, He led forth the Law and the Prophets along with Himself, and the words, 'Thy name is as perfume poured forth,' were indeed fulfilled.

5. THEREFORE HAVE THE VIRGINS LOVED THEE.[38] Because *the charity of God is poured forth in our hearts by the Holy Spirit*,[39] the mention of pouring forth, which is made here, is apt. As the Bride says the words, 'Thy name is as perfume poured forth,' she sees the maidens. When she made her petition to the Bridegroom's Father, and while she was talking directly to the Spouse Himself, the maidens were not present; but a band of virgins appears even as she is praying, and, praising them, she says, 'Therefore have the virgins loved Thee, AND HAVE DRAWN THEE.' And the maidens answer: WE WILL RUN AFTER THEE IN THE FRAGRANCE OF THY PERFUMES.[40]

How fine a touch it is that the attendants of the Bride do not as yet have the Bride's own confidence! The Bride does not follow behind, she walks side by side with the Bridegroom; she takes His right hand, and in His right hand her own hand is held. But the handmaidens follow after Him. *There are threescore queens, and fourscore concubines, and young maidens without number. One is my dove, my perfect one, she is the only one of her mother, she that conceived her hath no other one.*[41] 'After thee,' therefore, 'we will run into the fragrance of thy perfumes.'

It was entirely appropriate that these words, 'we will run into the fragrance of thy perfumes,' were used of lovers; they accord with *I have finished the course*, and *they that run in the race all run indeed, but one receiveth the prize*[42]— which prize is Christ. And these maidens who, as we know, are standing without because their love is only just beginning, are like *the friend of the Bridegroom, who standeth and heareth Him, and rejoiceth with joy because of the Bridegroom's voice*.[43] The maidens undergo a like experience: when the Bridegroom enters, they remain without.

But when the Bride, the fair, the perfect one who is

without spot or wrinkle, has entered the Bridegroom's chamber, the secret place of the King, she comes back to the maidens and, telling them the things that she alone has seen, she says: THE KING BROUGHT ME INTO HIS CHAMBER.[44] She does not say: 'He brought us'—using the plural—'into His chamber'; the others remain without, the Bride alone is brought into the chamber, that she may see there dark and hidden treasures and may take back word to the damsels: 'The King brought me into His chamber.'

Further, when the Bride has gone into the Bridegroom's chamber and is seeing there the riches of her Spouse, the maidens—the goodly company of those who are learning to be brides—sing together joyfully while they await her coming, saying: WE WILL BE GLAD AND REJOICE IN THEE.[45] They are glad because of the Bride's perfection, for there is here no envy in respect of virtues; this love is pure, this is love free from fault.

'We will be glad and rejoice in thee. WE WILL LOVE THY BREASTS.'[46] She who is greater is already enjoying the milk of those breasts, and she says in her joy: 'Thy breasts are above wine.' But these, because they are young maidens only, defer their joy and gladness; their love also they defer and say: 'We will be glad and rejoice in thee. We will love'—not 'we love,' but 'we will love'—'Thy breasts MORE THAN WINE.'[47] Then they say to the Bridegroom, 'EQUITY HAS LOVED THEE':[48] they praise the Bride by calling her Equity, as denoting the sum of her characteristic virtues—'Equity has loved Thee.'

6. The Bride then makes the maidens this reply: I AM BLACK AND BEAUTIFUL, O YE DAUGHTERS OF JERUSALEM—we learn now that 'daughters of Jerusalem' is what the maidens are—AS THE TENTS OF CEDAR, AS THE CURTAINS OF

SOLOMON. LOOK NOT AT ME, FOR THAT I AM BLACKENED;
FOR THE SUN HAS LOOKED DOWN ON ME.[49]

Beautiful indeed is the Bride, and I can find out in what
manner she is so. But the question is, in what way is she
black [50] and how, if she lacks whiteness, is she fair. She has
repented of her sins, beauty is the gift conversion has bestowed; that is the reason she is hymned as beautiful. She is
called black, however, because she has not yet been purged
of every stain of sin, she has not yet been washed unto
salvation; nevertheless she does not stay dark-hued, she is
becoming white. When, therefore, she arises towards
greater things and begins to mount from lowly things to
lofty, they say concerning her: *Who is this that cometh up,
having been washed white?* And in order that the mystery
may be more clearly expressed, they do not say *leaning
upon her Nephew's arm,* as we read in most versions—that
is to say, *epistērizoménē,* but *epistēthizoménē,* that is, *leaning
upon His breast.*[51] And it is significant that the expression
used concerning the bride-soul and the Bridegroom-
Word [52] is *lying upon His breast,* because there is the seat of
our heart. Forsaking carnal things, therefore, we must
perceive those of the spirit and understand that it is much
better to love after this manner than to refrain from love.
She *cometh up,* then, *leaning on her Nephew's breast*; and of
her, who at the Canticle's beginning was set down as
black, it is sung at the end of the marriage-song: *Who is
this that cometh up, having been washed white?*

We understand, then, why the Bride is black and beautiful at one and the same time. But, if you do not likewise
practise penitence, take heed lest *your* soul be described as
black and ugly, and you be hideous with a double foulness
—black by reason of your past sins and ugly because you
are continuing in the same vices! If you have repented,

however, your soul will indeed be black because of your
old sins, but your penitence will give it something of what
I may call an Ethiopian beauty. And having once made
mention of an Ethiopian, I want to summon a Scriptural
witness about this word too. *Aaron and Mary murmur
against Moses, because Moses has an Ethiopian wife.*[53] Moses
weds an Ethiopian wife, because his Law has passed over
to the Ethiopian woman of our Song. Let the Aaron of the
Jewish priesthood murmur, and let the Mary of their
synagogue murmur too. Moses cares nothing for their
murmuring; He loves His Ethiopian woman, concerning
whom it is said elsewhere through the prophet: *From the
ends of the rivers of Ethiopia shall they bring offerings*, and
again: *Ethiopia shall get her hands in first with God.*[54] It is
well said that she shall get in first; for, as in the Gospel the
woman with the issue of blood received attention before
the daughter of the ruler of the synagogue,[55] so also has
Ethiopia been healed while Israel is still sick. *By their
offence salvation has been effected for the Gentiles, so as to make
them jealous.*[56]

'I am black and beautiful, O ye daughters of Jerusalem.'
Address yourself to the daughters of Jerusalem, you member of the Church,[57] and say: 'The Bridegroom loves me
more and holds me dearer than you, who are the many
daughters of Jerusalem; you stand without and watch the
Bride enter the chamber.' [Let no one doubt that the
black one is beautiful, for all she is called black. For we
exist in order that we may acknowledge God, that we may
tell forth songs of a song, that we may be those who have
come from the borders of Ethiopia, from the ends of the
earth, to hear the wisdom of the true Solomon.][58] And
when the Saviour's voice is heard thundering out the
words: *The queen of the South shall come to judgement and*

shall condemn the men of this generation, because she came from
the ends of the earth to hear the wisdom of Solomon, and behold,
a greater than Solomon is here,[59] you must understand what is
said in a mystical sense: the queen of the South, who comes
from the ends of the earth, is the Church; and the men of
this generation whom she condemns, are the Jews, who
are given over to flesh and blood. She comes from the ends
of the earth to hear the wisdom, not of that Solomon about
whom we read in the Old Testament, but of Him who is
said in the Gospel to be greater than Solomon.

'I am black and beautiful, O daughters of Jerusalem,
black as the tents of Cedar, beautiful as the curtains of
Solomon.' The very names accord with the Bride's comeliness. The Hebrews say that *Cedar* is the word for darkness
—'I am black,' therefore, 'as the tents of Cedar,' as the
Ethiopians, as Ethiopian tents; and 'beautiful as the curtains of Solomon,' which he prepared as adornments of the
tabernacle at the time when he built the Temple with the
utmost care and toil. Solomon was rich indeed, and no
one surpassed him in any branch of wisdom. 'I am black
and beautiful, O daughters of Jerusalem, as the tents of
Cedar, as the curtains of Solomon. Look not at me, for
that I am blackened.' She apologizes for her blackness; and,
being turned to better things through penitence, she tells
the daughters of Jerusalem that she is black indeed, but
beautiful for the reason which we gave above, and says:
'Look not at me, for that I am blackened.' 'Do not be
surprised,' she says, 'that I am of a forbidding hue; the
Sun has looked down on me. With full radiance His bright
light has shone on me, and I am darkened by His heat. I
have not indeed received His light into myself as it were
fitting that I should, and as the Sun's own dignity
required.'

By their offence salvation has been effected for the Gentiles.
And again: *Through the unbelief of the Gentiles is the know-*
ledge of Israel. You find both these texts in the Apostle.[60]

7. THE SONS OF MY MOTHER HAVE FOUGHT AGAINST ME.[61]
We must consider in what sense the Bride says: 'The sons
of my mother have fought against me,' and at what time
her brothers launched this attack. You have only to look
at Paul, the persecutor of the Church,[62] to see how a son of
her mother fought against her. The persecutors of the
Church have repented, and her opponents have turned to
their sister's banners and have preached the faith which
they formerly sought to destroy. Foreseeing this, the Bride
now sings: THEY HAVE CONTENDED AGAINST ME, THEY HAVE
MADE ME THE KEEPER IN THE VINEYARDS; MY VINEYARD
I HAVE NOT KEPT.[63] 'I, the Church, the spotless one,'[64]
she says, 'have been appointed keeper of many vineyards by my mother's sons, who once had fought
against me. Harassed by the responsibility and care involved in guarding many vineyards, I have not kept my
own.'

Apply these words to Paul or any other of the saints who
care for the salvation of all men, and you will see how he
guards others' vine-plantations while not guarding his
own; how he himself bears loss in some respects so that he
may gain others; and how, though he was free as to all, he
made himself the servant of all that he might gain all,
being made weak to the weak, a Jew to the Jews, as
subject to the Law to those who are so subject,[65] and so
forth—how, in a word, he can say: 'My vineyard I have
not kept.'

The Bride then beholds the Bridegroom; and He, as
soon as she has seen Him, goes away. He does this frequently throughout the Song; and that is something

nobody can understand who has not suffered it himself. God is my witness that I have often perceived the Bridegroom drawing near me and being most intensely present with me; then suddenly He has withdrawn and I could not find Him, though I sought to do so.[66] I long, therefore, for Him to come again, and sometimes He does so. Then, when He has appeared and I lay hold of Him, He slips away once more; and, when He has so slipped away, my search for Him begins anew. So does He act with me repeatedly, until in truth I hold Him and go up, 'leaning on my Nephew's arm.'

8. TELL ME, THOU WHOM MY SOUL HAS LOVED, WHERE THOU FEEDEST, WHERE THOU LIEST IN THE MIDDAY.[67] I am not asking about other times, I ask not where Thou feedest in the evening, or at daybreak, or when the sun goes down. I ask about the full day-time, when the light is brightest and Thou dwellest in the splendour of Thy majesty: 'Tell me, Thou whom my soul has loved, where Thou liest in the midday.'

Observe attentively where else you have read about midday. In the story of Joseph his brethren feast at noon;[68] at noon the angels were entertained by Abraham,[69] and there are other instances besides. You will find if you look into it, that Holy Scripture never uses any word haphazard and without a purpose. Who among us, do you think, is worthy to attain the midday, and to see where the Bridegroom feeds and where He lies at noon? 'Tell me, Thou whom my soul has loved, where Thou feedest, where Thou liest in the midday.' For, unless Thou tell me, I shall begin to be a vagrant, driven to and fro; while I am looking for Thee, I shall begin to run after other people's flocks and, because these other people make me feel ashamed, I shall begin to cover my face and my mouth. I am the beautiful Bride in sooth, and I show not my naked face to any save Thee only, whom I kissed tenderly but now. 'Tell me, Thou whom my soul has loved, where Thou feedest, where Thou liest in the midday, LEST I HAVE TO GO VEILED BESIDE THE FLOCKS OF THY COMPANIONS.'[70] That I suffer not these things—that I may need not to go veiled nor hide my face; that, mixing with others, I run not the risk of beginning to love also them whom I know not—tell me, therefore, where I may seek and find Thee in the midday, 'lest I have to go veiled beside the flocks of Thy companions.'

9. After these words the Bridegroom warns her, saying: 'Either know thyself, that thou art the Bride of the King and beautiful, and made beautiful by me because I have presented to myself *a glorious Church, not having spot or wrinkle*;[71] or understand that if thou hast not known thyself nor grasped thy dignity, thou must endure the things that follow.' What may these be?

IF THOU HAVE NOT KNOWN THYSELF, O FAIR ONE AMONG WOMEN, GO FORTH IN THE STEPS OF THE FLOCKS AND FEED—not the flocks of sheep, nor of lambs, but—THY GOATS.[72] He will set the sheep on the right hand and the goats upon the left,[73] assuredly. 'If thou have not known thyself, O fair one among women, go forth in the steps of the flocks and feed thy goats AMONG THE SHEPHERDS' TENTS.' 'In the steps of the flocks,' He says, 'wilt thou find thyself at the last, not among the sheep, but among the goats; and when thou dwellest with them thou canst not be with m that is, with the Good Shepherd.

10. 'TO MY COMPANY OF HORSEMEN AMONG PHARAO'S CHARIOTS HAVE I LIKENED THEE.[74] If thou wouldst understand, O Bride, how thou must know thyself, think what it is to which I have compared thee. Then, when thou

hast recognized thy likeness, thou wilt see that thou art
such as must not be disgraced.'

What then is the meaning of these words: 'To my
company of horsemen among Pharao's chariots have I
likened thee'? I myself know that the Bridegroom is
likened to a horseman in the words of the prophet: *Thy
riding is salvation*; [75] so thou art compared to 'my company
of horsemen among Pharao's chariots.' As different is the
company of horsemen that belongs to me, who am the
Lord and drown the Pharao and his generals, his riders and
his horsemen in the waves—as different, I tell you, is my
cavalry from Pharao's horses as thou, the Bride, art better
than all daughters, and thou, the soul belonging to the
Church, art better than all souls that are not of the
Church.[76] 'To my company of horsemen among Pharao's
chariots have I likened thee.'

He next describes the beauty of the Bride in terms of
spiritual love: THY CHEEKS ARE AS THE TURTLE-DOVE'S.[77]
He praises her face, and is kindled to admiration by her
rosy cheeks. A woman's beauty is considered to reside
supremely in her cheeks. So let us likewise take the cheeks
as revealing the beauty of the soul; by lips and tongue,
however, let the intelligence be represented to us.

THY NECK IS AS A NECKLACE.[78] Thy neck, that is to say,
even when unadorned is of itself as much an ornament as
is the little necklace called *hormískos*,[79] that virgins are
wont to wear.

After these things the Spouse takes His repose. *He has
reposed as a lion, and as a lion's whelp He has slept*, so that in
due course He may hear: *Who shall arouse Him?* [80] While
He reposes, His companions the angels appear to the Bride
and comfort her with these words: 'We cannot make thee
golden ornaments—we are not so rich as is thy Spouse,

who gives thee a necklace of gold; we will make thee likenesses of gold, for gold we have not got. Yet this also is matter for rejoicing, if we make likenesses of gold, if we make studs of silver. WE WILL MAKE THEE LIKENESSES OF GOLD WITH STUDS OF SILVER; [81] but not for always, only until thy Spouse arises from His rest. For, when He has arisen, He Himself will make thee gold and silver, He will Himself adorn thy mind and thy understanding, and thou shalt be rich indeed, the Bride made perfect in the House of the Bridegroom, to whom be glory for ever and ever. Amen.'

THE SECOND HOMILY

From the place where it is written: MY SPIKENARD
SENT FORTH ITS ODOUR, to that in which it says:
FOR THY VOICE IS SWEET AND THY FORM IS COMELY.

1. God, the Maker of the universe,[1] created all the
emotions of the soul for good;[2] but because of the way in
which we exercise those emotions, it often happens that
things which are good by nature lead us into sin through
our bad use of them. One of the emotions of the soul is
love; and we use this emotion of love well if its objects are
wisdom and truth. But when our love descends to baser
levels, then we love flesh and blood. Do you, then, who
are spiritual,[3] listen in a spiritual manner to these words of
love that are sung, and learn to direct your soul's emotion
and the ardour of natural love to better things, according
to the saying: *Love her, and she shall preserve thee; encompass
her, and she shall exalt thee.*[4]

Husbands, love your wives, says the Apostle. But he does
not stop with saying, *Husbands, love your wives.* Rather,
because he knew that even the love of husbands for their
wives can be dishonourable, and yet was aware that their
love is God's good pleasure, he taught us in what manner
husbands should love their wives by adding to *Husbands,
love your wives* the further clause *as Christ also loved the
Church.*[5]

We have made these remarks by way of introduction to
the matters which we must later discuss.

2. The friends of the Bridegroom, then, 'while the King
takes His repose'—for in resting *He slept as a lion and as a*

lion's whelp[6]—had promised the Bride that until He should arise, they would make her likenesses of gold and silver; for they, unlike the Bridegroom, have no actual gold. And because the Bridegroom's Passion has been to some extent foretold in other words, the Bride, who has herself perceived a certain adumbration of the Passion in the words 'we will make thee likenesses of gold with studs of silver, while the King takes His repose,'[7] makes answer not unreasonably: 'MY SPIKENARD SENT FORTH ITS ODOUR. A SACHET OF A MYRRH-DROP IS MY NEPHEW TO ME: HE SHALL ABIDE BETWEEN MY BREASTS.'[8]

Now how are we to connect what was said before, 'while the King is at His repose,' with this which follows, 'My spikenard sent forth its odour'?[9] The Gospel says that *there came a woman having an alabaster box of ointment of pure and precious spikenard*; it is the holy woman I am speaking about now, not the sinner. For I know that Luke spoke of a sinner, but Matthew and John and Mark did not do so.[10] Not the sinner, therefore, but the holy woman, whose name John added—it was Mary—came with an alabaster box of pure and precious ointment, and poured it over Jesus' head. And thereupon, when Judas only, not all of the disciples, was indignant and said that it could have been sold for three hundred pence and given to the poor, Our Master and Saviour answered: *The poor you have always with you, but me you will not always have with you. In doing this she has anticipated the day of my burial. So wheresoever this gospel shall be preached, that also which she has done shall be told for a memorial of her.*[11]

She, therefore, in pouring her ointment on the head of the Lord, fulfilled the type of that which is said here: 'My spikenard sent forth its odour.' Do you likewise take spikenard; so that you too, when you have moistened

Jesus' head with fragrance, may boldly say: 'My spikenard sent forth its odour,' and may hear His answering word: *Wheresoever this gospel shall be preached, that also which she has done shall be told for a memorial of her*, your deed also having been proclaimed among all the nations.

But when will you do this? If you have become as the Apostle and have said: *We are the good odour of Christ . . . in every place in them that are saved.*[12] Your good works are your spikenard. But if you sin, your sins will exhale a foul odour; the penitent says with truth: *My sores are putrefied and corrupted because of my foolishness.*[13] The Holy Spirit does not have in mind to speak here of the spikenard we see with our eyes, nor did the Evangelist write of visible ointment; it is the spiritual spikenard, the spikenard that sent forth its odour, that is meant.

3. 'A sachet of stacte'—that is, of a drop or trickle of myrrh [14]—'is my Nephew to me.'

We read in Exodus that myrrh, onycha, cassia, and galbanum were at God's command compounded into incense, into the chrism for priests.[15] If you, therefore, see my Saviour descending to earthly and lowly things, you will see how one small drop flowed down to us from mighty power and majesty divine. The prophet also sang about this drop: *And it shall be that, from the drop of this people, Jacob that is to be gathered shall be gathered together.*[16] And just as the coming of Our Saviour in flesh is denoted under another figure by the stone that was cut out without hands from the mountain [17]—for He who came down to earth was not the whole mountain, nor could human weakness be portrayed in terms of such; but He was a stone from the mountain, a stone of stumbling and a rock of offence [18] that came down into the world—so, under another figure, He is here called a drop.

Indeed it was fitting, since all the nations are reckoned *as a drop of a bucket*,[19] that He who was made all things for the salvation of all, also should become a drop, that He might set them free. For what was He *not* made for our salvation? We were destitute, and He *emptied Himself, taking the form of a servant*.[20] We were *a foolish and a senseless people*, and He was made *the foolishness of preaching*, so that *God's foolishness* might be made *wiser than men*. We were weak, and *the weakness of God* was made *stronger than men*.[21] So, because all the nations *are as a drop of a bucket and are counted as the smallest grain of a balance*,[22] He too became a drop, so that through Him the odour of stacte might distil from our garments, according to that which is said to the Bride in the forty-fourth Psalm: *Myrrh and stacte and cassia perfume thy garments, from the ivory houses: out of which the daughters of kings have gladdened thee in thy glory*.[23]

'A sachet of a myrrh-drop is my Nephew to me.' Let us consider what is meant by the term Nephew.[24] It is the Church who speaks; which Church is we ourselves, gathered from out the nations. Our Saviour is the son of our sister—that is, of the Synagogue; for Church and Synagogue are verily two sisters. The Saviour, therefore, is the son of sister Synagogue, as we have said: He, being the Husband, the Bridegroom of the Church, is thus the Nephew of His Bride.

'A sachet of a myrrh-drop is my Nephew to me: He shall abide between my breasts.' Who is so blessed as to have the Word of God as guest in the seat of his heart,[25] between his breasts, in his bosom? Such indeed is the meaning of what is sung here, 'He shall abide between my breasts'; *if the paps of thy virginity have not been bruised*,[26] the Divine Word shall dwell between them. It was fitting in a marriage-song to speak of paps rather than of bosom. And it is clear why the words, *if the paps of thy virginity have not been bruised*, have been adduced to explain the other thing, the text, 'He shall abide between my breasts.' The Divine Word is He who 'shall abide between thy breasts'; that is why I quote Ezechiel: *If thy paps have not been bruised*. For in that passage the voice of the Lord which reproves Jerusalem says, among other things, to her: *In Egypt . . . thy paps were bruised*. The breasts of the chaste are not bruised; but the paps of harlots are wrinkled with folds of loose skin. The breasts of the chaste are firm and round and rosy with virginity; such receive the Bridegroom-Word and say: 'He shall abide between my breasts.'

A CLUSTER OF CYPRUS IS MY NEPHEW TO ME. [27] The beginning of a discourse is its bud; and the beginning of *kuprismós*—that is, of blossom, is the Word; wherefore she says: 'A cluster of cyprus'—that is, of blossom—'is my Nephew to me.' The cluster of cyprus is not for all; it is for those who are worthy of the flower that He is. There are different grapes for the others; only to her who is both black and beautiful does He offer Himself in the fairness of a flower. 'A cluster of cyprus is my Nephew to me': she says not merely, 'A cluster of cyprus is my Nephew,' but she adds 'to me,' so as to teach us that He is not a cluster of cyprus for everyone.

But let us see in what districts this cluster of the Bride's is found. It is found IN THE VINEYARDS OF ENGADDI, which means 'the eye of temptation.' [28] It is in the vineyards of the eye of temptation, then, that my Nephew is a cluster of cyprus to me. The eye of temptation is in our present state; indeed we abide in temptation in this world, and *the life of man upon earth is temptation*. [29] As long as we remain in the light of this sun, we are in the vineyards of Engaddi; but, if we are found worthy later on to be transplanted thence, it will be our Husbandman who thus transfers us. Nor must you doubt the possibility of being thus transferred from the Engaddi vineyards to better situations; our Husbandman is now, from frequent meditation, skilled in transplanting the vine. *Thou hast brought a vineyard out of Egypt: Thou hast cast out the Gentiles and planted it. . . . The shadow of it covered the hills: and the branches thereof the cedars of God.*[30] And we will take it that the Bride spoke these things which we have explained, telling thereby her love and her reception of the Bridegroom who comes to be her guest, and how, when He comes, 'He shall abide between her breasts' and in the secret chamber of her heart.

4. The Bridegroom addresses Himself to her again and says: 'BEHOLD, THOU ART FAIR, MY NEIGHBOUR, BEHOLD, THOU ART FAIR; THINE EYES ARE DOVES.' And she speaks to the Bridegroom thus: 'BEHOLD, THOU ART FAIR, MY NEPHEW.'[31] She does not add 'my neighbour.' But when He addresses her with 'Behold, thou art fair,' He adds 'my neighbour.' Why does she not say: 'Behold, Thou art fair, my neighbour,' but only 'Behold, Thou art fair'? Why does He say not only 'Thou art fair,' but 'Thou art fair, my neighbour'? The Bride is not fair if she has been far away from her Spouse; she becomes beautiful only when she is united with the Word of God. It is with reason, then, that He now teaches her she must be near Him and not depart from His side. 'Behold, thou art fair, my neighbour, behold, thou art fair. Indeed the beginning of your fairness is in your nearness to me; but once you have begun to be fair, you are fair absolutely, without my calling you my neighbour further. Behold, thou art fair, my neighbour, behold, thou art fair.'

Let us consider also another commendation of the fair one, so that we too may strive to become as is the Bride.

'Thine eyes are doves.' *Whosoever shall look on a woman to lust after her* and *commit adultery with her in his heart,*[32] has not the eyes of a dove. And if anyone has not a dove's eyes, he enters the house of his brother when he is in misfortune, not regarding that which is commanded in Proverbs: *But go not into thy brother's house when thou art in misfortune.* (Aquila gets the true meaning of the Hebrew word, which the Seventy rendered as 'unfortunate,' by putting *aporeōnta*—that is, witless.[33]) But he who has dove's eyes has an upright outlook and is deserving of mercy; indeed, having an upright outlook, he follows after mercy. Moreover, who does have this upright view of things save he who beholds with a chaste look and pure eyes? So please do not understand what I have said only with reference to eyes of flesh, although it may not be unprofitable to take it as including these. Enter rather into your own inmost heart and seek diligently with your mind for other eyes,[34] which also are illumined by God's command—for *the commandment of the Lord is lightsome, enlightening the eyes*[35]—and strive and work zealously to understand in a holy manner all these things that I have said; and, because you have dove's eyes, seek to hear things that are like *the Spirit* who Himself *descended in the form of a dove.*[36]

If you understand the Law spiritually, your eyes are those of a dove; so too if you understand the Gospel as the Gospel means itself to be understood and preached, seeing Jesus as *healing all manner of sickness and infirmity* not only at the time when those things happened in the flesh, but also at the present day, and realizing that He not only came down then to men, but comes down and is present here to-day; for, *Behold, I am with you all days, even to the consummation of the world.*[37]

'Thine eyes are doves. Behold, thou art fair, my neighbour, behold thou art fair. Thine eyes are doves.' Hearing
these praises of herself, the Bride responds to the Bridegroom with answering praises. Not that by such praise she
would bestow on Him something He does not yet have:
rather, with understanding of the loveliness that she is
contemplating, she says: 'BEHOLD, THOU ART FAIR, MY
NEPHEW, AND BEAUTIFUL INDEED; OUR BED IS SHADY.'[38]

I ponder the bed on which the Bridegroom reposes with
the Bride; and, if I am not mistaken, it is the human body.
We see that the paralytic who was lying on a bed and was
bidden by the Saviour's voice to take up his couch and go
into his house, before he could be healed, was lying on the
feeble body of his own limbs; which body was subse-
quently made whole by the power of God. That is how I
understand *Take up thy couch and go into thy house.*[39] For the
Son of God had not come down from heaven to earth to
give orders about beds, or to forbid a person getting up
from sickness to depart without his bed, saying as He did:
Take up thy couch and go into thine house. So do thou too
whom the Saviour has healed, *take up thy couch and go into
thy house*; and, when the Bridegroom comes to you, His
Bride, and has lain down with you on it, then say to Him:
'Behold, Thou art fair, my Nephew, and beautiful indeed;
our couch is shady. Behold, Thou art fair, my Nephew.'
He Himself is both fair and shade-giving; of a truth, *the sun
shall not burn thee by day, nor yet the moon by night.*[40]

5. 'THE BEAMS OF OUR HOUSES ARE OF CEDAR'[41] are the
words of a number of people speaking together. It seems
to me that it is the men with the Bridegroom, whom we
mentioned above, who make this statement about houses
roofed with cedar and raftered with cypress trees; since
instead of the shrub shall come up the cyprus, and instead of the

nettle shall come up the myrtle tree.[42] When, therefore, you enquire about the nature of these timbers and grasp the fact that cedar is incorruptible and cypress of surpassing fragrance, you yourself must strive so to roof your house that it may be said of you also: 'The beams of our houses are of cedar, AND OUR RAFTERS OF CYPRESS TREES.'

6. After this the Bridegroom says: 'I AM THE FLOWER OF THE FIELD AND THE LILY OF THE VALLEYS.'[43] For my sake, who was in the valley, He came down to the valley; and, coming to the valley, He became the lily of the valleys in place of *the tree of life that was* planted *in the paradise of God,*[44] and was made the flower of the whole field—that is, of the whole world and the entire earth. For what else can so truly be the flower of the world as is the name of Christ? 'His name is as oil poured forth'[45] and 'I am the flower of the field and the lily of the valleys' are the same thing put in different ways, and both are spoken with reference to Himself.

Then, praising the Bride, He says: 'AS THE LILY AMONG THORNS, SO IS MY NEIGHBOUR AMID THE DAUGHTERS.'[46] The lily cannot be compared with the thorns among which it often grows; and in like manner 'my neighbour' is before all the daughters a lily amid thorns.

Hearing these words, the Bride makes reply to the Bridegroom; and, perceiving yet another pleasant thing about Him, she breaks forth into praise. The odour of ointments is pleasant and soothing to the senses, certainly; but it is not such as to make delightful eating. There is, however, something that is excellent alike in taste and smell, something, that is to say, which delights the palate with its sweetness and at the same time pleases the nostrils with its fragrance; it is the apple, and it is the apple's nature to possess both these properties in itself. The Bride, in consequence, wishing to praise not only the fragrance of the Word, but also His sweetness, says: 'AS THE APPLE AMONG THE TREES OF THE WOOD, SO IS MY NEPHEW AMID THE SONS.' [47] All timbers, all trees, are reckoned as unfruitful woods in comparison with the Word of God; everything that you have said is as a jungle when compared to Christ, and all things are unfruitful. For what can be called fruitful when it is compared with Him? Even the trees that seemed to be bowed down with fruit have been shown to be unfruitful when set beside His advent. 'As the apple among the trees of the wood,' therefore, 'so is my Nephew amid the sons; BENEATH HIS SHADOW I DESIRED AND SAT.'

How lovely it is that she says, 'Beneath His shadow I desired,' and not, 'Beneath its shadow I desire,' and not 'I sit,' but 'I sat'! Indeed, strictly speaking, we cannot converse with Him at first; rather, we enjoy at the beginning what may be called a sort of shadow of His majesty; and it is for that reason that we read also in the prophets: *The breath of our face, the Lord Christ, to whom we said: 'Under His shadow shall we live among the Gentiles,'* and pass over from one shadow to another; for *to them that dwelt in the region and shadow of death, to them light is arisen;* [48] so that our passing over is from the shadow of death to the shadow of life. Advances are always on this pattern: a person desires at the outset to be at least in the shadow of the virtues.

And I think myself that the birth of Jesus also originated *from*—not *in*—the shadow, but was consummated in the truth. *The Holy Spirit,* it was said, *shall come upon thee, and the power of the Most High shall overshadow thee.* [49] The birth of Christ took its inception from the shadow; yet not in Mary only did His nativity begin with overshadowing; in you too, if you are worthy, the Word of God is born. See, then, that you may be able to receive His shadow; and, when you have been made worthy of the shadow, His body, from which the shadow is born, will in a manner of speaking come to you; for *he that is faithful in a little will be faithful also in greater things.*[50]

'In His shadow I desired and sat.' You see she stood not always in the shadow, but went on thence to better things, saying: 'AND HIS FRUIT WAS SWEET IN MY THROAT.'[51] 'I desired,' she says, 'to rest in His shadow, but after His shadow had covered me, I was also filled with His fruits, and I say: "and His fruit was sweet in my throat."'

7. 'BRING YE ME INTO THE HOUSE OF WINE.'[52] The Bridegroom stood without, and was received by the Bride; that is to say, He reposed between her breasts. The many maidens are not such as to deserve to have the Bridegroom as their guest; to the multitude that is without He speaks in parables.[53] How much I fear lest perhaps we ourselves should be these many maidens!

'Bring ye me into the house of wine.' Why do I stay so long outside? *Behold, I stand at the gate and knock; if any man shall . . . open to me, I will come in to him, and will sup with him, and he with me.*[54]

'Bring ye me in.' And now the Divine Word says the same; see, it is Christ who says: 'Bring ye me in.' He speaks to you catechumens[55] also: 'Bring ye me in'—not only 'into the house,' but 'into the house of wine'! Let your soul be filled with the wine of gladness, the wine of the Holy Spirit, and so bring the Bridegroom, the Word, Wisdom, and Truth,[56] into your house. For 'bring ye me into the house of wine' can be said also to those who are not yet perfect.

8. 'SET YE IN ORDER CHARITY IN ME.'[57] It is a graceful phrase—'Set ye in order, . . .' For truly the charity of many

is in a state of disorder; they accord the second place in their loving to that which ought to have the first, and to that which should come second they give the first, and the thing that it behoves them to rank fourth in their affection they put third, and the rightful third again comes fourth. But the charity of the saints has been set in order.

To understand what is spoken here, 'Set ye in order charity in me,' I want to unfold some examples. The Divine Word wants you to love father, son, daughter. The Divine Word wants you to love Christ, and it does not tell you not to love your children, nor does it tell you that you should not be united in love with those who gave you birth. But what does it tell you? It tells you: 'You must not have a love that is disordered. You must not love your father and your mother first and me afterwards; you must not be possessed by love of son and daughter more than by love of me. *He that loveth father and mother more than me is not worthy of me.*[58] He that loveth son and daughter more than me is not worthy of me.'

Examine your consciences concerning your affection for your father, mother, brother; consider what manner of love you bear the Word of God and Jesus, and you will realize forthwith that you love son and daughter more than the Word, and have more affection for your parents than for Christ. Which among us, do you think, has progressed so far as to have chief and first of all his loves that of the Word of God, and to put his children in the second place? After this fashion you must love your wife also. *For no man ever hated his own flesh*; but he loves her as his flesh; *they two*, it is said, *shall be two*—not in one spirit, but— *shall be two in one flesh.*[59] Love God too, but love Him not as flesh and blood but as Spirit; for *he who is joined to the Lord is one spirit.*[60]

Charity is set in order, therefore, in the perfect. But to the end that there may be order also in our loves for one another, after our love for God we are commanded to love first our parents, then our children, and thirdly members of our household. But if there is a bad son and a good retainer, let the domestic take the son's place in our love. And so it shall come to pass that the charity of the saints is set in order.

Our Teacher and Lord, moreover, in laying down commands in the Gospel about charity added something special to every man's love, and gave understanding of the order to those who can hear the Scripture, saying, 'Set ye in order charity in me.' *Thou shalt love the Lord thy God with thy whole heart and with thy whole soul and with thy whole strength and with thy whole mind. Thou shalt love thy neighbour as thyself.*[61] He does not say that thou shalt love God as thyself, that a neighbour shall be loved with the whole heart, with the whole soul, with the whole strength, with the whole mind. Again, He said: *Love your enemies,*[62] and did not add 'with the whole heart.' The Divine Word is not disordered, He does not command impossibilities, and He does not say 'Love your enemies as yourselves,' but only, *Love your enemies.* It is enough for them that we love them and do not hate them; but a neighbour is to be loved *as thyself,* and God *with thy whole heart and with thy whole soul and with thy whole mind and with thy whole strength.*

If you have understood these things, and have carried out what you have understood, you have done the thing that is commanded in the Bridegroom's saying: 'Bring ye me into the house of wine; set ye in order charity in me.' Which among us, think you, is a man of ordered charity?

'STRENGTHEN ME WITH PERFUMES.'[63] One of the translators put 'with blossoms.' It is the Bride who is speaking now. 'COMPASS ME WITH APPLES.' With what apples? 'As the apple among the timbers of the wood, so is my Nephew among the sons.' Therefore 'compass me with apples, FOR I HAVE BEEN WOUNDED BY LOVE.'

How beautiful, how fitting it is to receive a wound from Love![64] One person receives the dart of fleshly love, another is wounded by earthly desire; but do you lay bare your members and offer yourself to the *chosen dart*, the lovely dart; for God is the archer indeed. Hear what the Scripture says of this same dart; or rather, that you may marvel even more, hear what the dart Himself says: *He hath made me as a chosen arrow, and in His quiver He hath kept me. And He said to me: 'It is a great thing for Thee to be called my servant.'*[65] Understand what the arrow says and in what manner He is chosen by the Lord. How blessed is it to be wounded by this dart! Those men who talked together, saying to each other: *Was not our heart burning within us in the way, whilst He opened to us the Scriptures?*[66] had been wounded by this dart. If anyone is wounded by our discourse, if any is wounded by the teaching of the Divine Scripture, and can say, 'I have been wounded by love,' perhaps he follows both the former and the latter. But why do I say 'perhaps'? I offer a clear explanation.

9. 'HIS LEFT HAND IS UNDER MY HEAD, AND HIS RIGHT HAND WILL EMBRACE ME.'[67] The Word of God has both a left hand and a right; Wisdom, though it is multifold in respect of the different subjects to be understood, is one in substance. Solomon himself taught about the left and right hands of Wisdom, saying: *For length and years of life are in her right hand, and in her left riches and glory.*[68] 'His left hand,' therefore, 'is under my head,' that He may cause me to rest, that the Bridegroom's arm may be my pillow

and the chief seat of the soul [69] recline upon the Word of God.

'His left hand is under my head.' It is not expedient for you to have pillows upon which mourning follows. It is written in Ezechiel: *Woe to them that sew pillows under every elbow!*[70] Do not sew pillows, do not seek elsewhere for rest for your head; have the Bridegroom's left hand under your head and say: 'His left hand is under my head.' When you have that, all the things His left hand holds will be bestowed on you; you will say with truth: *In His left hand are riches and glory.*

'And His right hand will embrace me.' Let the right hand of the Bridegroom embrace the whole of you. *Length indeed and years of life are in His right hand*; and for that reason *thou shalt have long life and many days upon the good land that the Lord thy God will give thee.*[71]

'I HAVE ENTREATED YOU, YE DAUGHTERS OF JERUSALEM, AMONG THE POWERS AND FORCES OF THE FIELD.' What does the Bride entreat of the daughters of Jerusalem? 'WHETHER YE HAVE RAISED AND ROUSED UP LOVE.[72] How long, O daughters of Jerusalem, O maidens, sleeps there in you the love that does not sleep in me, because I have received the wound of love?' But in you, who are many, and are also daughters of Jerusalem and maidens, the love of the Bridegroom sleeps. 'I have entreated you,' therefore, 'O ye daughters of Jerusalem, whether ye have raised,' and not only raised, but also 'roused up' the love that is in you. When the Maker of the universe created you, He sowed in your hearts the seeds of love. But now, as it is said elsewhere: *Justice has gone to sleep in her*, so now is love asleep in you, according to that further saying: The Bridegroom *rested as a lion, and as a lion's whelp.*[73]

In unbelievers and in those who are of doubtful heart,

the Divine Word is still asleep; but He is wakeful in the saints. He sleeps in those who are driven by storms; but He is roused by the voice of those who desire the Bridegroom to awake and save them. When He awakes, calm supervenes forthwith; the mountainous waves immediately subside, the adverse winds are rebuked, the madness of the waters falls silent. But, when He sleeps, then there is storm and death and despair.[74]

'I entreat you, therefore, ye daughters of Jerusalem, among the powers and forces of the field.' Of what field? Surely of that of which *the smell* is *of a plentiful field which the Lord hath blessed.*[75]

10. 'Whether ye have raised and roused up Love AS FAR AS HE WILL. THE VOICE OF MY NEPHEW: BEHOLD, HERE HE COMETH LEAPING UPON THE MOUNTAINS!'[76] It is the Church who speaks thus far, exhorting the maidens to be ready for the Bridegroom's coming; if so be He means to come and grant them speech with Him. So, while she is still speaking, the Bridegroom comes, and she points her finger at Him, saying: 'Behold, here He cometh leaping upon the mountains!' The soul of the Bride, you see, is so blessed and perfect, that she is quicker to see, quicker to contemplate the coming of the Word; perceiving also that it is to her own self that Wisdom and Love have come, she says to those who do not see: 'Behold, here He cometh!'

Pray that I too may be able to say: 'Behold, here He cometh!' For if I have the power to expound the Word of God, I also say 'Behold, here He cometh!' in a sense. But whither? Not where there is a valley, certainly, nor where the ground lies low. Whither then does He come? 'Leaping upon the mountains, SKIPPING ACROSS THE HILLS.' If you are a mountain, the Word of God leaps upon you;

if you have not managed to be that, but are a hill, which is of lower grade than a mountain, then He skips across you. Truly, how beautiful and fitting are the words! He leaps upon the mountains, which are greater; the hills, which are less great, He skips across. He does not skip across the mountains, nor does He leap upon the hills. 'Behold, here He cometh leaping upon the mountains, skipping across the hills!'

11. 'MY NEPHEW IS LIKE TO A ROE OR A YOUNG HART UPON THE MOUNTAINS OF BETHEL.'[77] These two animals are often named in the Scriptures; and, to give you ampler food for thought, they are frequently put together. *These are the beasts that you shall eat*, it says, and adds a little later: *the roe and the deer*.[78] In the book before us also the roe and the deer are named together; for there is a certain affinity and kinship between these animals. The roe, that is, the dorcas, has very keen sight; the deer is a slayer of serpents.[79] Which of us, do you think, is competent to explain the full meaning of this passage and this mystery as it deserves to be explained? Let us pray God to grant us grace to open the Scriptures and enable us to say how Jesus opened the Scriptures to us![80] Well, we have been saying that according to the natural scientists who study the characteristics of animals, the dorcas—that is, the roe—takes its name from a power that is inborn in it; it is called the dorcas because of its keen sight—that is, *para to oxyder-késteron*.[81] But the deer is the enemy of serpents, and wages war on them; with the breath of its nostrils it drags them out of caves, it destroys the bane of their venom and then enjoys them as food.

Maybe my Saviour is a roe in respect of His sight, and a deer in respect of His works.[82] And for what are these works? It is He that slays serpents, that kills adverse powers; so I will say to Him: *Thou didst crush the heads of the dragons in the water: Thou didst crush the heads of the dragon.*[83]

12. 'My Nephew is like to a roe or a young hart upon the mountains of the House of God'—for Bethel means the House of God.[84] Not all mountains are houses of God, but only those which are mountains of the Church. We do indeed find other mountains reared and rising up together against the knowledge of God, mountains of Egypt and the Allophyli.[85] Do you want to know why the Bride's Nephew 'is like to a roe or a young hart upon the mountains of Bethel'? Then be a Church mountain, a mountain that is the House of God; and the Bridegroom will come to you 'like a roe or a young hart upon the mountains of Bethel.'

She notices that the Bridegroom, who formerly abode on the mountains and hills, has drawn nearer; she represents Him as skipping and leaping. And then, knowing that He has come to her and to the other maidens, she declares: 'BEHOLD, HE IS AT THE BACK, BEHIND OUR WALL!'[86] If you have built a wall and made an edifice of God, He comes behind your wall.

'LOOKING OUT THROUGH THE WINDOWS.' One window is one of our senses; the Bridegroom looks out through it. Another window is another sense; through it He gazes with solicitude. For what senses are there through which the Word of God does not look out? And what 'looking out through the windows' means and in what way the Bridegroom sees through them, the following example will teach us. Where He does not look out, there is death found coming up, as we read in Jeremias: *Lo, death is come up through your windows.*[87] When you *look on a woman to lust after her,*[88] death comes up through your windows.

'BECOME VISIBLE THROUGH THE NETS.'[89] *Know that thou walkest in the midst of snares and passest beneath menacing battlements.*[90] Everything is full of nets, the devil has filled all things with snares. But if the Word of God comes to you and begins to appear through the nets, you will say: *Our soul hath been delivered as a sparrow out of the snare of the fowlers: the snare is broken, and we are delivered. Blessed are we of the Lord who made heaven and earth.*[91] The Bridegroom, then, appears through the nets: Jesus has made a way for you, He has come down to earth and subjected Himself to the nets of the world. Seeing the great throng of mankind entangled in the nets, seeing that nobody except Himself could sunder them, He came to the nets when He assumed a human body that was held in the snares of the hostile powers. He broke those nets asunder for you,[92] and you say: 'Behold, He is at the back, behind our wall, looking out through the windows, become visible through the nets!'

When He appears, you will say to yourself: 'MY NEPHEW ANSWERS AND SAYS, "ARISE, COME, MY NEIGHBOUR.[93] I have made a way for thee, I have torn the nets asunder; so come to me, my neighbour. Arise, come, my neighbour, MY BEAUTIFUL ONE, MY DOVE."'[94] Why does He say, 'Arise,' why, 'hasten'? 'I myself [, He says,] bore for you the fury of the storms, and received the force of the waterfloods that you deserved; *my soul was* made *sorrowful even unto death* on your account. I arose from the dead, having broken the arrows of death and loosed the fetters of hell.[95] Wherefore I tell you: 'Arise, come, my neighbour, my beautiful one, my dove. FOR BEHOLD, THE WINTER IS PAST, THE RAIN HAS DEPARTED, THE FLOWERS HAVE APPEARED ON THE EARTH. In rising from the dead I have curbed the storm and restored calm. And, because ac-

cording to the dispensation of the flesh I grew from a
virgin and the Father's will, and advanced alike in wisdom
and in age,[96] the flowers have appeared on the earth, THE
TIME OF PRUNING HAS COME.'[97]

Pruning is the remission of sins. For *every branch that
abides in me and brings forth fruit*, He says, *my Father purifies
that it may bring forth more fruit.*[98] Have fruit, and the former
things in you that were unfruitful shall be taken away.

'The time of pruning is come,' indeed, THE VOICE OF
THE TURTLE-DOVE IS HEARD IN OUR LAND. Not without
reason are *a pair of turtle-doves and two young doves*[99]
accepted in the sacrifices. For they are worth the same,
and you never find separate mention of just a pair of
doves, but a *pair of turtle-doves and two young doves.* The
dove denotes the Holy Spirit. But when the great and
more hidden mysteries are in question, and the things that
many people cannot grasp, then the Holy Spirit is represented under the appellation of a turtle-dove—of the bird,
that is to say, that always dwells on mountain ridges and in
the tops of trees. But in the valleys, in the things that all
men understand, He figures as a dove.[100]

Finally, because the Saviour deigned to assume human
nature and came to earth, and because there were many
sinners then in the Jordan area, the Holy Spirit does not
take the form of a turtle-dove, but becomes a dove,[101] and
dwells as the tamer bird among us for the sake of the
multitude of men. But He appears as the turtle-dove, for
instance, to Moses, and to one of the prophets (it does not
matter which),[102] when they retire to the mountains and
deserts and there receive the oracles of God. 'The voice of
the turtle-dove,' then, 'is heard in our land.'

'THE FIG TREE HATH PUT FORTH HER GREEN FIGS.' *From the
fig tree learn a parable: When the branch thereof is now tender*

and putteth forth leaves, know ye that summer is nigh.[103] God wills to tell us by this declaration that after the winter, after its storms, the harvest of souls has drawn nigh; and He says: 'The fig tree hath put forth her green figs, THE VINES ARE IN FLOWER, THEY YIELD THEIR SWEET SMELL.' They are breaking out into blossom, and the time is coming when there will be grapes.

13. 'ARISE AND COME, MY NEIGHBOUR, MY BEAUTIFUL ONE, MY DOVE!'[104] The Bride, who alone hears the Bridegroom, speaks the words that we expounded previously, and that not in the hearing of the maidens. But we want to listen now to what He says when speaking to the Bride: 'Arise and come, my neighbour.' He does not address the maidens, nor does He say 'Arise ye,' but 'Arise, come, my neighbour, my beautiful one, my dove; AND COME, MY DOVE, BENEATH THE SHELTER OF THE ROCK.' Moses too is set in the shelter of the rock, that he may see God from the back.[105] 'IN THE SHADOW OF THE OUTER WALL.' First come to that which is before the wall, and then you will be able to enter where the wall is 'of the rock.'

'SHOW ME THY FACE.' That kind of thing is being said to the Bride up to the present day, but up to now she has not dared to contemplate the glory of the Lord with unveiled face.[106] But, because she has already been adorned and prepared, 'Show me thy face' is said to her.

Her voice was not sweet enough as yet to deserve that He should say to her: 'LET ME HEAR THY VOICE.' When, therefore, she has learnt to speak (yes, *be thou silent and hear, Israel*),[107] and when she knows what she is to say, and her voice has become sweet to the Bridegroom, according to that saying of the prophet: *Sweet may my discourse be to Him*,[108] then the Bridegroom says to her: 'And let me hear thy voice, BECAUSE THY VOICE IS SWEET.'

If you have opened your mouth to the Word of God, the Bridegroom will say to you: 'Thy voice is sweet AND THY FACE IS COMELY.' Let us stand up together, therefore, and pray God that we may be made worthy of the Bridegroom, the Word, Wisdom, Christ Jesus, to whom is glory and empire for ever and ever. Amen.[109]

NOTES

LIST OF ABBREVIATIONS

ACW	Ancient Christian Writers (Westminster, Md.— London 1946–)
v. Balthasar	H. Urs von Balthasar, *Origenes, Geist und Feuer. Ein Aufbau aus seinen Schriften* (2 ed. Salzburg 1950)
Blaise-Chirat	A. Blaise—H. Chirat, *Dictionnaire latin-français des auteurs chrétiens* (Strasbourg 1954)
CSEL	Corpus scriptorum ecclesiasticorum latinorum (Vienna 1866–)
DACL	Dictionnaire d'archéologie chrétienne et de liturgie (Paris 1907–53)
DB	Dictionnaire de la Bible (Paris 1895–1912); Supplement (1928–)
DSp	Dictionnaire de spiritualité (Paris 1937)
DTC	Dictionnaire de théologie catholique (Paris 1903–50)
GCS	Die griechischen christlichen Schriftsteller der ersten drei Jahrhunderte (Leipzig-Berlin 1901–)
Lomm.	C. H. E. Lommatzsch, *Origenis opera omnia* (Berlin 1831–48)
LXX	Septuagint
N. (O.) T.	New (Old) Testament
OCD	Oxford Classical Dictionary (Oxford 1949)
PG	J. P. Migne, Patrologia graeca (Paris 1857–66)
PL	J. P. Migne, Patrologia latina (Paris 1844–55)
RAC	Reallexikon für Antike und Christentum (Stuttgart 1950–)
Rousseau	O. Rousseau, *Homélies sur le Cantique des Cantiques*, Sources chrétiennes 37 (Paris 1954)
Souter	A. Souter, *A Glossary of Later Latin to 600 A.D.* (Oxford 1949)
Vg.	Vulgate

INTRODUCTION

[1] W. Völker, *Das Vollkommenheitsideal des Origenes* (Tübingen 1931).

[2] A. Lieske, *Die Theologie der Logosmystik bei Origenes* (Münster i. W. 1938).

[3] H. de Lubac, *Histoire et Esprit. L'intelligence de l'Écriture d'après Origène* (Paris 1950) esp. chs. 2–4.

[4] J. Daniélou, *Origène* (Paris 1948; tr. into English by W. Mitchell, London–New York 1955).

[5] J. Lebreton, 'La source et le caractère de la mystique d'Origène,' *Annalecta Bollandiana* 67 (1949) 55–62.

[6] F. Bertrand, *Mystique de Jésus chez Origène* (Paris 1951).

[7] H. Crouzel, *Théologie de l'image de Dieu chez Origène* (Paris 1955). For further literature, see J. Quasten, *Patrology* 2 (Utrecht–Brussels–Westminster, Md. 1953) 100 f.

[8] See Jerome, *Ep.* 33.4 (CSEL 54.256.16): In Canticum Canticorum libros X et alios tomos II, quos super scripsit in adulescentia.

[9] PG 87.2.1545–1780; the Origen fragments of the catena are excerpted in PG 17.253–88.

[10] M. Faulhaber, *Hohelied-, Proverbien- und Prediger-Katenen* (Vienna 1902) 20 ff.

[11] Cassiodorus, *Inst. div. et hum. lect.* 70 (ML 70.1117 A): Quod idem (Cant. Cant.) Rufinus ... usque ad illud praeceptum, quod ait: 'Capite vobis vulpes pusillas exterminantes vineas,' *tribus libris* latinis explanavit. See Baehrens XXVI f.

[12] Cf. M. M. Wagner, *Rufinus, the Translator* (diss. Washington 1945) esp. 97 f. Still important, also for our opinion of Rufinus as a translator of the *Comm. in Cant. Cant.*, is the study by G. Bardy, *Recherches sur l'histoire du texte et des versions latines du De Principiis d'Origène* (Paris 1923).

[13] On this see especially Völker, *op. cit.* 18–20.

[14] F. Barth, 'Prediger und Zuhörer im Zeitalter des Origenes,' *Aus Schrift und Geschichte, Festschrift für Orelli* (Basel 1898) 27: 'Aber im ganzen haben wir doch den echten Origenes vor uns, und zwar in der reifsten Entwicklung seines theologischen Denkens' (quoted by Völker, *op. cit.* 18). On the subject of Rufinus as translator, see also Lieske, *op. cit.* 19–23 (where, 20 with n. 4 f., references to the Harneck—de Faye—Bardy controversy on the subject); de Lubac, *op. cit.* 41 f.;

R. P. C. Hanson, *Origen's Doctrine of Tradition* (London 1954) 43–7 (see n. 65 to the Prologue to the *Comm.*); H. Hoppe, 'Rufin als Übersetzer,' *Studi dedicati alla memoria di Paolo Ubaldi* (Milan 1937) 133–50.

[15] See below, the Prologue to the *Homilies*, addressed to Pope Damasus.

[16] Cf. W. Riedel, *Die Auslegung des Hohen Liedes in der jüdischen Gemeinde und in der griechischen Kirche* (Leipzig 1898); L. Welsersheimb, 'Das Kirchenbild der griechischen Väterkommentare zum Hohen Liede,' *Zeitschr. f. kath. Theol.* 70 (1948) 393–449; H. Lesètre, 'Cantique des Cantiques,' DB 2.193 f.

[17] A. v. Harnack, *History of Dogma* 2 (tr. by N. Buchanan, London 1894) 295 n., thought that the idea of the individual soul as the bride of Christ was taken by Origen from Gnosticism. This is refuted by C. Chavasse, *The Bride of Christ. An Enquiry into the Nuptial Element in Early Christianity* (London 1940) 172 ff.

[18] For Origen's thoughts on the Church as bride and mother, see J. C. Plumpe, *Mater Ecclesia. An Inquiry into the Concept of the Church as Mother in Early Christianity* (Washington 1943) ch. 5; where note also sketches of Origen's *Ecclesia ex circumcisione*, *Ecclesia ex gentibus*, the pre-existent Church, etc.

[19] See also *In Isa.* hom. 2.1 (GCS 33.250.25 f.): 'Domus David' *nos sumus Ecclesia Dei.*

[20] See F. J. Dölger, 'Christus als himmlischer Eros und Seelenbräutigam bei Origenes,' *Antike und Christentum* 6 (1950) 273–5.—For further information on Platonic and Neo-Platonic influence on Origen's thought, see, besides Lieske (180–208), de Lubac (150–66: Scripture and Philo), and Daniélou (87 ff.)—Hal Koch, *Pronoia und Paideusis. Studien über Origenes und sein Verhältnis zum Platonismus* (Berlin–Leipzig 1932); H. A. Wolfson, *The Philosophy of the Church Fathers* 1 (Cambridge, Mass. 1956) 270–80.

[21] See Dom C. Butler, *Western Mysticism* (2 ed. London 1927) 160; see also the excellent introductory essay in the book by v. Balthasar (cf. n. 30 below).

[22] Socrates, *Hist. eccl.* 5.22.

[23] Cf. the superscription in the MSS (GCS 35.2.15–17): Incipiunt omeliae Origenis in Lucam . . . dictae *in diebus dominicis.*

[24] Pamphilus, *Apol. pro Origene* (tr. by Rufinus) Lomm. 24.298.

[25] *Op cit.* 1–21.

[26] Cf. O. Bardenhewer, *Geschichte der altkirchlichen Literatur* 2 (2 ed. Freiburg i. Br. 1914) 132; so also Rousseau 8 f.

[27] Origen, *De princ. praef. Ruf.* 1 (GCS 22.4.1–3); regarding the difficulty of Rufinus' assertion that Jerome had made such a promise

in his own prologue to his translation of the *Homilies*, see Baehrens' introduction to his edition of the *Homilies* and *Commentary*—GCS 33.XIX f.

[28] R. B. Tollinton, *Selections from the Commentaries and Homilies of Origen* (London 1929) 79–87, 194–7.

[29] G. Bardy, *Origène* (2 ed. Paris 1931) 88 f., 244–9, 259–61, 269 f., 271–3, 276–80.

[30] H. U. v. Balthasar, *Origenes, Geist und Feuer* (2 ed. Salzburg 1950): cf. list 519 ff.

TEXT

PART ONE

THE COMMENTARY

PROLOGUE

[1] For *epithalamium*, with which this work begins, see Origen's discussion in § 1, near the end, of *Hom.* 1, with our n. 12.

[2] The WORD—Λόγος—for *Sermo* (*Dei*), for which Rufinus quite regularly uses *Verbum* (*Dei*). Jerome, too, alternates between the two words as terms for the divine Λόγος Christ. Cf. the observations by C. Mohrmann, 'Les origines de la latinité chrétienne à Rome,' *Vigiliae christianae* 3 (1949) 166-8, and 'Emprunts grecs dans la latinité chrétienne,' *Vig. chr.* 4 (1950) 205 f. Prof. Mohrmann shows from Tertullian (*Adv. Prax.* 5) that in North Africa it was usual to render λόγος with *sermo* (and this is supported by the existing witnesses of the African versions of the Bible); whereas the ancient European Biblical terminology preferred *verbum*, which was to carry the day (see Mohrmann in the article quoted last, 206).

[3] For Origen's mystical concept of the Church or the individual Christian soul as the bride of the Bridegroom Christ, cf. W. Völker, *Das Vollkommenheitsideal des Origenes* (Tübingen 1931) 100-16; A. Lieske, *Die Theologie der Logosmystik bei Origenes* (Münster i. W. 1938) 32 ff., 61 ff., 147 ff.; J. Daniélou, *Origène* (Paris 1948) 297-301; C. Chavasse, *The Bride of Christ* (London 1939) 172-6. The subject is also the burden of our Introduction.

[4] Cf. Heb. 5.12 and 1 Peter 2.2.

[5] Heb. 5.14. Note Origen's ascription (if this is what he wrote) of *Hebrews* to St. Paul, in confirmation of Eusebius' record, *Hist. eccl.* 6.25.11-14, of Origen's opinion of its Pauline character.

[6] It is the private interpretation of Scripture, apart from the tradition of the Church, that is condemned.

[7] The Greek word δευτέρωσις in the singular is the usual translation of the Hebrew word *Mishnah*, which, coming from a root meaning 'to repeat' or 'do again' because of the method of teaching, denoted the oral 'tradition of the ancients' mentioned in Mark 7.3, and codified and

written somewhere between 160 and 220 A.D. approximately in Origen's own lifetime. Here, however, the word is in the plural, δευτερώσεις, and seems to denote not the Mishnah as distinct from the Miqrā' or 'read' text of Scripture, but the four portions of the latter that formed a second and more advanced course of study for students. R. Connolly, however, in his Introduction to the *Didascalia Apostolorum* (Oxford 1929) lvii ff. cites this passage in Origen as though it was the Mishnah that is meant.—The four sections of Scripture mentioned in the following as reserved for later reading are also so identified by Jerome, *Comm. in Ezech.* I praef. (ML 25.17 A), where he adds that the age required was thirty. See also his letter to Paulinus, *Epist.* 53.8 (CSEL 54.460.17-461.1); here there is no reference to the Canticle of Canticles.

⁸ The reference in this passage is especially to Plato's *Symposium*; works bearing the same title and treating the same subject were written e.g. by Xenophon, Epicurus (lost), and others. Cf. U. v. Wilamowitz-Moellendorff, *Platon* (2 ed. Berlin 1920) 1.356 ff.

⁹ Ps. 67.12.

¹⁰ See Gen. 1.26 f. and 2.7. On this theme of a double creation of man, in which Origen is influenced by Philo, cf. H. Crouzel, *Théologie de l'image de Dieu chez Origène* (Paris 1955) 54 f., 148-53.

¹¹ 2 Cor. 4.16 and Rom. 7.22. Cf. also Eph. 3.16.

¹² Here follows the first of a number of fragments, most of them surviving in Procopius of Gaza, that reflect Origen's original text—see the Introd. 5 f. At first overlooked by Baehrens, the present fragment appears on p. LIII of his edition.

¹³ See Eph. 4.13.

¹⁴ 1 John 2.12-14.

¹⁵ 1 Cor. 3.1 f.

¹⁶ 1 Cor. 13.11.

¹⁷ Eph. 4.13.

¹⁸ Eccles. 2.14.

¹⁹ Matt. 13.43.

²⁰ Jer. 50.1 of the Hebrew (so Vg.) recension=27.1 of the LXX. Of the numerous occurrences in Jeremias of the formula, *Verbum* (*Sermo*, as here) *Domini quod* (*qui*) *factum est ad Ieremiam prophetam*, this is the only instance showing the addition *in manu* (*Hieremiae proph.*). It is wanting in the LXX, as is also the name of the prophet; hence Origen, citing from memory, adds, 'sive alterius cuiuslibet' (the formula, without the addition *in manu*, is also frequent in Ezechiel).

²¹ See Prov. 3.23 and Matt. 18.8.

²² See Ps. 72.2.

²³ See Isa. 26.17 f.

[24] Ps. 5.11; 54.10; 3.8 and 9.36.

[25] Cf. John 6.32 f., 41; and 4.13.

[26] Cf. John 15.1.

[27] Similarly, on such aberrations regarding life after the resurrection, Origen, *Comm. in Matth.* 17.35 (GCS 40.698 f.); *De princ.* 2.11.2 (GCS 22.184.5 ff.). For further instances of Origen's polemics against false and preposterous interpretations of eschatological texts in Scripture, cf. H. de Lubac, *Histoire et esprit. L'intelligence de l'Écriture d'après Origène* (Paris 1950) 102–4: in such passages Origen, long under a cloud because of the Origenistic controversies, appears more and more as a protagonist of orthodox interpretation of Scripture and a defender of the Church against heterodoxy, e.g. millenarianism.

[28] I Kings 2.5.

[29] See Exod. 23.26.

[30] Cupido, "Ερως, the god of love, the myth of whose conception and birth Origen quotes from Plato (*Symp.* 203 B–E) in his *Contra Celsum* 4.39 (see the recent translation by Chadwick, *Origen, Contra Celsum* [Cambridge 1953] 215).

[31] See Gal. 6.8.

[32] See I Cor. 15.49.

[33] Cf. Col. 1.15 f.—Origen has here taken up a most striking phenomenon in the works of mystical writers through the ages, the concept of the *vulnus amoris*, the 'wound of love.' In the present volume he treats the subject again in bk. 3 of the *Commentary* (see pp. 198 f., with n. 95), and again in *Hom.* 2.8 (where see also n. 64).

The commonplace in ancient Greek and Roman poetry of the youthful god Eros or Cupido—he has just been referred to by Origen —piercing the hearts of the love-smitten with his arrows of love, is of course well known. In art he was represented with the bow since the 4th century B.C.

As Dom A. Cabassut points out in his article, 'Blessure d'amour,' DSp 1.1728, there are numerous instances in Scripture in which God is represented as the Divine Archer who brings misfortune and pain upon His enemies by His darts (cf. DB s.v. 'Flèche,' 2.2285 ff.). On the other hand, God, as described here in the Canticle of Canticles, transfixes and wounds the soul wholly devoted to Him with His arrow of love—His own *Verbum*; and this passage in the Canticle (2.5, in the LXX: τετρωμένη ἀγάπης ἐγώ; Symmachus—cf. below, p. 198, end of the Procopius frg.: τέτρωμαι γὰρ φίλτρῳ, 'I am wounded with a love-charm,' to which Origen remarks, 'from the "chosen arrow" according to Isaias' [49.2]; cf. also F. Field, *Origenis Hexaplorum quae supersunt* 2 [Oxford 1875] 414 n. 15) has certainly served as the mainspring of inspiration for the concept and experience of the 'wound of love' from patristic times (besides Origen—e.g. Sts. Gregory of Nyssa, Augustine, Gregory the Great) to and beyond the period that produced the great Carmelite mystics, St. Theresa of Avila and St. John of the Cross. The reader will remember the classical sentence in Augustine's *Confessions* (9.2.3): '*Sagittaveras tu cor nostrum caritate tua, et gestabamus verba tua transfixa visceribus.*' For full historical and theological detail on the subject, see Cabassut, *art. cit.* 1724–9.

[34] Isa. 49.2. On the 'saving wound' see Origen's remarks on the last clause of Cant. 2.5 in the *Second Homily* 8 (p. 297). For Origen's intimate conception of the love that obtains between Christ Logos and the Christian of 'the inner man,' see the penetrating discussion by Lieske, *op. cit.* 51–61.

[35] See Ezech. 23.

[36] qui apud sapientes saeculi *cupido* seu *amor* dicitur, honestiore vocabulo *caritatem* vel *dilectionem* nominasse. On the choice of the words made here by the translator Rufinus, see H. Pétré, *Caritas. Étude sur le vocabulaire latin de la charité chrétienne* (Louvain 1948) 86–90.

[37] Cf. Gen. 24.67 and 29.17 f. (LXX: ἠγάπησεν, Vg.: *dilexit, diligens*).

[38] 2 Kings 13.1, 2, 14 f. (LXX: ἠγάπησεν—ἀγάπη, ἠγάπησεν; Vg.: *adamaret, deperiret*, propter *amorem* aegrotaret, *amore* quo *dilexerat*).

[39] See Prov. 4.6, 8. (*adama*, LXX: ἐράσθητι, Vg.: *dilige*).

[40] Wisd. 8.2. (LXX: ἐραστὴς ἐγενόμην, Vg.: *amator factus sum*).

[41] Cf. Cant. 5.8. (LXX: ἀγάπης, Vg.: *amore*).

[42] 1 John 4.7 f.

[43] John 16.28.

[44] Cf. 1 Cor. 1.24, 30, and John 1.1, 14.6.

[45] See 1 John 4.16 (12).

[46] See John 14.23.

[47] Cf. 1 Tim. 6.15 f.

[48] Cf. John 17.3.

[49] Cf. Luke 10.27, citing Deut. 6.5.

[50] Cf. Rom. 8.35 and 39.

[51] See Luke 10.37.

[52] 'Improper' here means simply 'not its own,' as does the *non proprie* of Rufinus' text.

[53] A conflation of 1 Cor. 8.6 and Rom. 11.36.

[54] See John 10.34 ff.

[55] Ps. 81.1. For Origen's interpretation of the *congregatio deorum*, see also *In Exod.* hom. 6.5 (GCS 29.196.17 ff.).

[56] Ps. 95.5. Not the images, but the demons that dwell in them are meant, Origen says elsewhere: *In Num.* hom. 27.8 (GCS 30.267.2 f.).

[57] Ignatius, *Rom.* 7.2: ὁ ἐμὸς ἔρως (not ἀγάπη!) ἐσταύρωται. J. A. Kleist, ACW 1.136 n. 22, remarks on the passage: 'I follow Origen's interpretation of this passage: *Comm. in Cant. Cant.* prol. Lightfoot and others understand ὁ ἐμὸς ἔρως as "my earthly passions."' On the passage see also F. J. Dölger, 'Christus als himmlischer Eros und Seelenbräutigam bei Origenes,' *Antike und Christentum* 6 (1950) 272–5.

[58] Matt. 22.34–40 and 19.18.

[59] See 2 Cor. 4.8 f., 17.

[60] See Rom. 5.5.

[61] See Gen. 29.18, 20.

[62] See 1 Cor. 13.4–8.

[63] Origen is allegorizing the thought of 1 Tim. 2.15. On the passage, see Lieske, *op. cit.* 36 f., 69. On both the Church and the soul as the bride of the Word Christ, see the Introd. 10–16.

[64] For this passage see the following: Matt. 11.27; John 15.26; 1 Cor. 2.11; 1 John 4.7 f.

[65] Note that the Book of Wisdom is not included among the Solomonic writings—here limited to three—accepted into the Canon. It may be questioned, however, whether we have Origen's true version, that is, did Rufinus perhaps make the exclusion? In the Introduction we have adverted briefly to the problem of Rufinus' faithfulness, or lack of it, as a translator of Origen; and there we have already referred to Hanson's recent study (*Origen's Doctrine of Tradition*) in which Rufinus does not fare very well as a translator. Hanson (45 f.) also singles out a passage near the end of the Prologue (see below, at n. 120) exemplifying the liberties which Rufinus takes with the original Greek message of Origen. Here the text reads: 'The Church of God has not adopted any further songs of Solomon to be read, and . . . the Hebrews, by whom God's utterances were transmitted to us, have in their canon no other than these three books of Solomon that we also have in ours.' If, however, we look at a passage in Origen's *De Principiis* (4.4.33: GCS 22.357.2 f.), we may be inclined to give Rufinus the benefit of the doubt and decide that in both passages of the Prologue he did not tamper with Origen's enumeration. There Origen speaks of the Book of 'Wisdom which is called Solomon's, a book which is certainly not held by all to be authoritative': *Sapientia quae dicitur Salomonis, qui utique liber non ab omnibus in auctoritate habetur.* But even in the Latin version Origen does not state clearly that he *himself* does not consider the Book of Wisdom as authoritative or canonical; moreover, how are we to know that Rufinus did not in this instance modify the original text to agree with his own Scriptural Canon, which (as for Jerome too) did not include the Wisdom of Solomon, but listed it among other

appendages in the Old Testament (cf. J. N. D. Kelly, in ACW 20.21 f.)?

We may mention here an explanation of the later passage in the Prologue (at n. 120)—and this, if it were acceptable, would make Rufinus appear less arbitrary as a translator. A Merk, 'Origenes und der Kanon des Alten Testamentes,' *Biblica* 6 (1925) 203 f., suggests that here Origen is referring only to those *cantica* or songs—*three*—(of the many songs) of Solomon that were accepted into the Canon, and that, though not denying its canonicity, he does not regard the Book of Wisdom as a song. But it seems quite impossible to read into the text quoted above (the first part of which reads in Latin: cum *neque Ecclesia Dei ulla extrinsecus Solomonis cantica* legenda susceperit) that Origen meant to label also Proverbs and Ecclesiastes as *cantica* or songs.

At any rate, in his present *Commentary* Origen quotes from Wisdom more than a dozen times as from a canonical part of Scripture. In quoting Wisd. 7.17–21, he introduces the text as coming from 'the writer of divine Wisdom,' and then, having quoted the text, he sets out to shed light upon 'these words of Scripture' (*his Scripturae sermonibus*); see below, bk. 3 at n. 157. For Origen's obvious acceptance elsewhere of the Book of Wisdom as of the Canon, see Merk, *loc. cit.*; L. Pirot-A. Clamer, *La Sainte Bible* 6 (Paris 1946) 379: a listing of passages; J. Ruwet, 'Les "Antilegomena" dans les œuvres d'Origène,' *Biblica* 24 (1943) 23–31, 57 f.; also 'Le Canon alexandrin des Écritures. Saint Athanase,' *ibid.* 33 (1952) 8 f., 11.

⁶⁶ The 'branches of learning' (*generales disciplinae*) taken together constitute philosophy, which Origen sometimes divides into three parts, sometimes into four, as here, according as he includes or does not consider 'Enoptics.' Cf. Hal Koch, *Pronoia und Paideusis, Studien über Origenes und sein Verhältnis zum Platonismus* (Berlin–Leipzig 1932) 247 f. The third of the four branches of learning mentioned here is commonly called in English either the contemplative or the theoretic. Neither of these terms is wholly satisfactory; for 'contemplative' suggests looking at God, as far as may be without intervening images, and 'theoretic' (θεωρητικός, as Origen calls St. Paul—*De or.* 24.2: GCS 2.353.25) has lost its original idea of 'beholding,' and carries an almost wholly intellectual meaning. But what Origen here calls the enoptic science is concerned with the unseen realities behind the seen. George Herbert says:

> A man that looks on glass
> On it may stay his eye;
> Or, if he pleaseth, through it pass
> And then the heaven espy.

The enoptician, if we may coin the word, the enoptic philosopher who is surely none other than what we call today the mystical theologian, does so please; he looks into and through everything to find the heavenly reality beyond it and within. So we have rendered 'enoptic' as 'inspective,' this being the nearest literal equivalent and unflavoured by different associations. Origen also calls the science 'Theology': θεολογεῖσθαι (cf. *Comm. in Gen.* 3 [Lomm. 8.45]), or 'Mystics': μυστικά (cf. *Comm. in Lam.* frg. 14 [GCS 3.241.3 f.]).

67 Originally a bit of Jewish apologetic (cf. Josephus, *C. Ap.* 2.168, 257), the claim that the ancient Jewish law and wisdom antedated the Greek, and that the latter was indebted to Moses and other Old Testament writers, was taken over and used as a commonplace by the Christian apologists and later writers: cf. Justin Martyr, 1 *Apol.* 44; Tatian, *Or. ad Graec.* 31; Theophilus, *Ad Autol.* 3.16 ff.; Origen, *C. Cels.* 4.21 (GCS 1.280 f.), 6.43 (2.113 f.); Augustine, *De doctr. christ.* 2.28, 43; *De civ. Dei,* 8.11; etc. See also below, n. 12 to *Homily* 1.

68 3 Kings 4.29 f. The heart is the seat of the understanding in Hebrew parlance, not that of the affections. 'Largeness of heart' means, therefore, a comprehensive intelligence.

69 In Greek: παροιμία < παρά—οἴμη, literally 'a song (or saying) beside.' *Māshāl,* the Hebrew word for proverb (*proverbium*), carries much the same idea, for it comes from a root meaning to be like, to represent, to compare, and so denotes a parable or simile.

70 John 16.25.
71 For what follows see Prov. 1.2–6.
72 Reminiscences of Ps. 1.2 and 36.30.
73 Cf. Prov. 1.24.
74 Ecclus. 1.26 LXX (=1.33 Vg.).
75 Eccles. 1.2.
76 Exod. 3.6.
77 See Gen. 12.1–4; ch. 22.
78 See Gen. 26.12 ff.
79 See Gen. 28.10, 17; 32.2. For the interpretation of 'Israel' as here given, see Origen, *In Gen.* hom. 15.3 (GCS 29.130.1 f.); *ibid.* 3 (131.3 ff.); *In Num.* hom. 11.4 (GCS. 30.83.20–2); Eusebius, *Praep. evang.* 11.6; etc. Philo, *De ebriet.* 20.82, explains the name as 'vision of God' (ὅρασις θεοῦ).

80 Cf. Gen. 22.9; 26.25; 33.20 and 35.7.
81 Cf. Heb. 11.9. In the *Homilies on Exodus,* 9.4 (GCS 29.244.3–6), Origen says rather delightfully: 'It is not for nothing that we are told that the fathers lived in tents. This is how I understand Abraham and Isaac and Jacob to have lived in tents: they fashioned a tent for God

within themselves, by the great glory of the virtues with which they decked themselves.'

[82] Or perhaps 'from the knowledge of inferior persons' (*de scientia inferiorum*)—i.e. such knowledge as inferior persons have—'to that of perfect persons' (*ad scientiam superiorum*).

[83] Cf. 2 Cor. 4.18.

[84] Cf. Exod. 30.29; Num. 4.47; Rom. 16.27.

[85] In the *Homilies on Numbers*, 5.2 (GCS 30.27.8–11) Origen says: 'When he (i.e. Moses) speaks of the works of the children of Israel, he says not "works of works," but simply "works"; but when he was talking about the functions of the Levites, he said not just "works," but "works of works"; for as some things are holy, while others are holy of holies, so too some things are works, and others are works of works.' See also *Comm. in Lev.* hom. 13.6 (GCS 29.477.12 ff.)

[86] In the *Commentary on the Epistle to the Romans*, 10.43 (Lomm. 7.457), Origen says of the expression 'unto the ages of ages' that 'by this term the Divine Scripture is wont to designate time that cannot be measured.'

[87] See Gal. 3.19.

[88] Cant. 1.2 (Vg. 1.1).

[89] Cf. Cant. 6.8.

[90] See Exod. 14.31–15.1.

[91] See *ibid*. 14.29 ff.

[92] See Num. 21.12, 16–18. The 'ravine (LXX—Vg. "torrent") of Zared'—Zared is the pausal form—is mentioned also in Deut. 2.13 f. The derivation of the name is dubious, but Origen must have had some reason for his *aliena descensio*.

[93] See *In Num.* hom. 1.2 (GCS 30.99.2 ff.).

[94] Cf. John 4.10 f.

[95] See Deut. 31.19 and 32.1–3. This canticle (32.1–43) occurs in the ferial Lauds of Saturday.

[96] See Judges 5.1–3 (1–31, the canticle).

[97] Origen is correct in his derivations here, as below in Hom. 1.1 (cf. n. 6 thereto): *debhōrāh* means a bee. and *bārāq* lightning. He makes a similar remark about the use of the bee's work in his *Homilies on Numbers*, 27.12 (GCS 30.278.8 f.). For further instances of the etymology, see Baehrens *ad loc*.

[98] Judges 5.12.

[99] These homilies, nine in number, survive in the translation by Rufinus: cf. the edition by Baehrens, GCS 30.464–522. For the present passage, see the fifth homily, entitled *De Debbora et Barac et Iahel et Sisara*.

[100] See 2 Kings 22.1-3; see 22.2.51 for the song, which, as Origen himself observes below, is substantially repeated in the Psalter as Ps. 17. It is strange that he passes straight on to this song from that of Debbora, omitting that of Anna, 'the Magnificat of the Old Testament,' in 1 Kings 2.1-10. With the whole list here, compare that in the First Homily, section 1.

[101] See 1 Par. 16.8 f. (the song, 8-36; 8-22=Ps. 104. 1-15, and 23-33 =Ps. 95.1-13; see below).

[102] Two songs from Isaias are recited in the Breviary, that from ch. 12 at ferial Lauds on Monday, and that from ch. 38 (the Song of Ezechias) at ferial Lauds on Tuesday. In the *First Homily* on the Song of Songs, however (p. 267 in this translation), the song of Isaias to which Origen refers is that of the Vineyard in ch. 5; so presumably that is the song that he means here.

[103] The word *canticum* represents the Greek ᾠδή in the titles of the Psalms, and ᾆσμα in that of the Song of Songs, both these being from the same verb, ἀείδω contracted to ᾄδω; while *psalmus* is of course a transliteration of ψαλμός. These words in their turn stand respectively for the Hebrew *shîr*, a song, and *mizmôr*, a song accompanied by instruments. The titles of several psalms include the words *shîr mizmôr*; where this occurs, Origen follows the LXX in taking the first word as being in the construct state, song-of, and the second as its complement. In point of fact, however, the first is in the absolute, and the second is connected with what follows. The title of Psalm 82, for instance, should thus be rendered: A Song: a Psalm of (*or* belonging to) Asaph, as it is in fact by Mgr. Knox in his recent translation of the Bible, and not: A Song *of* a Psalm. . . .

[104] That is, 119-133, each of which psalms bears the title *shîr hamma‘a-lôth*, A Song of Ascents. Scholars disagree as to the meaning of 'Ascents' and the purpose for which these psalms were composed. The Mishnah connects them with the fifteen steps that led up from the Court of the Women in the Temple to the Court of the Israelites; but the likeliest view is that they were pilgrim psalms, sung at the ascent of Mount Zion. See *A Catholic Commentary on the Bible* (London 1952) 336, 361d.

[105] Cf. Ps. 41.5.

[106] See the LXX version of the first verse of each of these three books.

[106a] This etymology of the name Solomon=*pacificus*, εἰρηνικός— 'the Peaceful, Peaceable, Peace-loving,' is repeated in the following and is frequently used as a title for Solomon's antitype Christ, in the first section of bk. 2 of the *Commentary*. For the etymology see also Philo, *De congr. quaer. erud.* 177; Origen, *In Lib. Iesu Nave* hom. 11.5 (GCS

30.365.20 f.). See also the Vg. version in Cant. 8.11: Vinea fuit *pacifico* (LXX: τῷ Σαλωμων).

[107] See Matt. 12.42. Origen also tells us in the *First Homily*, § 6 (p. 278 in this translation) that 'the queen of the South, who comes from the ends of the earth, is the Church, and the men of this generation, whom she condemns, are the Jews, who are given over to flesh and blood. She comes from the ends of the earth to hear the wisdom, not of that Solomon about whom we read in the Old Testament, but of Him who is said in the Gospel to be greater than Solomon.'

[108] Cf. 1 Tim. 6.15 and Phil. 2.6 f.

[109] Cf. 1 Cor. 1.30.

[110] See Heb. 12.22 f. and, for the following, Gal. 4.26.

[111] See Col. 1.20 and 1 Cor. 15.24–6.

[112] 2 Cor. 5.16.

[113] Cf. Luke 2.52.

[114] See Heb. 12.22, 4.14, and 1 Cor. 6.17. Here as elsewhere (see above, n. 5) Origen assumes the Pauline authorship of Hebrews.

[115] Cf. John 13.36.

[116] See Num. 2.32 f.

[117] Num. 3.5 f.

[118] Similarly, *In Lev.* hom. 5.3 (GCS 29.340.12–17).

[119] See Matt. 10.24 and Luke 6.40

[119a] Cf. 1 Cor. 15.24.

[120] See above, n. 65.

[121] See 3 Kings 4.29–32.

[122] The New Testament apocrypha, of which Origen speaks, are very numerous. There are apocryphal gospels, acts, epistles, and apocalypses: for a ready conspectus, cf. M. R. James, *The Apocryphal New Testament* (Oxford 1924). Speaking of heretics, Irenaeus, *Adv. haer.* 1.31.1 (Harvey), says that 'they produce an untold mass of apocryphal and spurious writings, which they themselves have gotten up for the purpose of bewildering those who have no understanding and are uninformed on the Scriptures of truth.' It is not precisely of this type of apocrypha that Origen writes here. Regarding the present passage, see Merk, *art. cit.* 201 f.; on Christian apocrypha in general, E. Amann, 'Apocryphes du Nouveau Testament,' DB Suppl. 1.460–533; also G. Bardy, 'Apokryphen,' RAC 1.518–20.

[123] Cf. Prov. 22.28.

BOOK ONE

This deals with Cant. 1.2-4 (Vg. 1.1-3). The Latin text, as given by Rufinus, is as follows:

1.2. (Vg. 1.1)   Osculetur me ab osculis oris sui, quia bona sunt ubera tua super vinum,

3 (2)   et odor unguentorum tuorum super omnia aromata. Unguentum exinanitum nomen tuum.

4 (3)   Propterea iuvenculae dilexerunt te, traxerunt te; post te in odorem unguentorum tuorum curremus. Introduxit me rex in cubiculum suum; exsultemus et iucundemur in te. Diligemus ubera tua super vinum. Aequitas dilexit te.

꠸   ꠸   ꠸

[1] *cum Verbo Dei.*—see the opening to the Prologue to the Commentary, p. 21, and n. 2 to the same. For the bridal concepts of the Church and the soul, see the Introd. 10–16.

[2] See 1 Tim. 2.8 f.

[3] Cf. 1 Cor. 14.33. 'The saints,' ἅγιοι, *sancti*, is a collective term used by St. Paul for the Christian faithful of both Jewish and Gentile provenance. In early patristic times, beginning with the Apostolic Fathers, the 'saints' are the living Church on earth, the *orthodox* Christians. Gradually the term disappeared, but it is still echoed when Augustine in his sermons addresses his hearers as *sanctitas vestra*. See H. Delehaye, *Sanctus. Essai sur le culte des saints dans l'antiquité* (Brussels 1927) esp. 1–59.

[4] See Matt. 22.1-4, with which compare Apoc. 19.6–9 and Col. 1.15.

[5] Cf. Gal. 3.19.

[6] A free reminiscence of Isa. 33.22.

[7] On this unfolding and development of higher knowledge or γνῶσις, see *Lieske, op. cit.* 45 f. Here, as Daniélou (*Origène* 299) puts it, God no longer instructs the soul through human teachers *from without,* but He Himself is the Instructor, teaching from within.

[8] Ps. 118.131.

[9] The kiss of peace was part of the Eucharistic liturgy from the earliest Christian times—see e.g. Justin, 1 *Apol.* 65—and survives to-day in the *pax* given at Solemn High Mass. It figured also in the liturgy of

Baptism and Confirmation, and it marked the neophyte's reception into the Christian fraternity. Cf. F. Cabrol, DACL 2.1 (1925) s.v. 'baiser,' 117–30; F. J. Dölger, *Der Kuss im Tauf- und Firmungsritual bei Cyprian von Karthago und Hippolyt von Rom,* *Antike u. Christ.* 1 (1929) 186–96; also K. M. Hofmann, *Philema Hagion* (Gütersloh 1938); and G. Dix, *The Shape of the Liturgy* (2 ed. Westminster 1945) 105–10.

[10] *principale cordis*=ἡγεμονικόν in the surviving Greek of Origen: see Lieske, *op. cit.* 64, 66 n. 35, 103 ff. (note esp. 103 n. 17 the numerous passages cited from Origen in the original, or in translation by Jerome or Origen; also de Lubac, *op. cit.* 158 n. 112; Blaise-Chirat, s.v. 'principale' no. 1). Describing it as 'the holy of holies, as it were, of the soul,' Lieske (103) most appropriately renders the Greek-Latin term with 'Tiefengrund der geistigen Seele' and 'Seelengrund.' A. Souter, *A Glossary of Later Latin to 600 A.D.* (Oxford 1949) s.v. 'principale,' renders—less aptly, it would seem—'chief seat.' Origen's ἡμῶν τὸ ἡγεμονικόν in *Exh. ad mart.* 33 is rendered 'the higher part of our souls' by Prof. J. J. O'Meara: ACW 19.173. In our *Commentary*, as in the *Homilies*, *principale cordis* (*animae*) is found a number of times—see the Index s.vv.

[11] Matt. 5.8 and Rom. 10.10.

[12] See John 13.23–5.

[13] *internis sensibus*; as distinguished from the literal or historical sense —the *interiora mysteria, interiora doctrinae spiritalis* (*In Exod.* hom. 11.2 f. —GCS 29.253.23 and 254.26 f.); cf. de Lubac, *op. cit.* 149.

[14] Cf. Col. 2. 3.

[15] *in principali cordis* (cf. n. 10) and again, *principale cordis*; see also in the following.

[16] See Lev. 10.14 f., where the Vg. speaks of *the breast also that is offered, and the shoulder that is separated.* See Origen, *In Lev.* hom. 7.3 (GCS 29.380.17 ff.).

[17] See Ps. 103.15.

[18] Matt. 5.8.

[19] See Gen. 9.20 and Isa. 5.1.

[20] Eccles. 2.1, 4 f. and 8.

[21] Luke 2.46 f.

[22] See Matt. 5.1, 21 f., 27 f.

[23] Matt. 11.19.

[24] See John 2.1–10.

[25] See 3 Kings 10.1, 4 f.

[26] See Luke 11.31.

[27] This story is in Jer. 35.

[28] Deut. 32.32 f.

[29] Cf. Ps. 104.33.

[30] Matt. 13.44.

[31] *tertia expositione*, that is, in the *spiritalis* (following the *litteralis-historicalis* and *moralis*) *sensus*—the mystical interpretation: cf. the Introd., p. 8 f.

[32] See Num. 6. The Hebrew word *nazir*, from root NZR, means consecrated or devoted, and has no connection with the root NÇR, to sprout or grow green, from which come the *nēçer* or shoot from Jesse's stem in Isa. 11.1 and—in spite of the spelling—the place-name Nazareth. The two roots are, however, closely similar in sound; so that in the Latin Bible Nazaraeus (so Rufinus here) does duty both for Nazirite and for Nazarene, and the former is misspelt Nazarite in the earlier English versions.

[33] Cf. Luke 1.15.

[34] See Origen's further note on this text in the last paragraph of the next section, p. 74.

[35] See Gal. 4.1 f., 3.25. The pedagogue, παιδαγωγός (literally, child-leader), was originally the *slave* who took the child to school. The Greek word frequently contains a tinge of the derogatory which is no longer felt in our modern-language adoption of it.

[36] See Gal. 4.4; 1 John 4.9 and Acts 10.38.

[37] See Heb. 5.1 ff.; 1 Tim. 2.5; 1 John 2.2 and Eph. 5.2, 27.

[38] Cf. Exod. 30.22 ff.

[39] Cf. Exod. 30.22–5.

[40] Cf. Origen's *In Ezech*. hom. 1.4 (GCS 33.329.10–12), where he says that perhaps Ezechiel's first vision took place in the fourth month and on the fifth day of the month, because the Lord took a body composed of the four elements and assumed also the (five) human senses.

[41] See Col. 1.18; Rom. 6.3–5, and Apoc. 17.14.

[42] Cf. Eph. 5.25–7.

[43] See Ps. 44.2. By the pigment he means what we should call the ink that flows freely from the pen (reed).

[44] See the account of Pentecost, Acts 2.1–4; also the Parable of the Tares and the Wheat in Matt. 13.24 ff., with which compare 2 Thess. 1.1–10.

[45] 'The pardonable number fifty,' *quinquagenarius veniabilis numerus*: cf. in Leviticus 25.10 the law of the fiftieth or Jubilee year, which provided for, among other things, a remission (or suspension) of debts. For this 'holy' or 'mystical number,' see also Philo, *De mut. num.* 228; Origen, *Comm. in Matt.* 11.3 (GCS 40.38.22–5); Clement of Alexandria, *Strom.* 6.87.2. For five as a mystical number with reference to the senses, see Philo, *De migr. Abr.* 204; Origen, *In Gen.* hom. 16.6 (GCS

29.143.11-14); etc. The mystical significance of numbers was developed especially at Alexandria, beginning with Philo. On the subject, see H. Lesètre, 'Nombre,' DB 4, 1677-97; also the literature listed by J. C. Plumpe, ACW 5.203 f.

[46] See Phil. 2.6 f.

[47] See Gal. 5.22 and Ps. 44.8 (Heb. 1.9).

[48] See the discussion of these preliminary studies in the Prologue, p. 40.

[49] See 1 Cor. 2.5 f. and Col. 1.26. Cf. de Lubac, op. cit. 77.

[50] This paragraph, which has reference to the text discussed in section 2, is very characteristic of Origen. For him, the Septuagint is the Old Testament *textus receptus* of the Church and its authority is incontestable. But this does not say that he held this Greek version itself to be divinely inspired, as was the tradition before him, notably at Alexandria. See Clement of Alexandria, *Strom.* 1.149.2 f.; and earlier, Philo, *De vita Moys.* 2.37. The Septuagint version could be in error. Cf. Daniélou, op. cit. 141 f. See also below, n. 3 to St. Jerome's Prologue to the Homilies.

[51] See 2 Cor. 2.14-16.

[52] Origen here combines ideas from Eph. 4.20-4 and 5.27 and 2 Cor. 4.16. The idea of man's creation in God's image (Gen. 1.26 f.), which is so basic in his thought and is dwelt on often in the pages to follow, also is in his mind.

[53] See Phil. 2.8; 1 Tim. 6.16 (and 1 John 1.14).

[54] See 1 Cor. 9.24.

[55] See Matt. 18.20, with which compare Acts 2.1 ff. and 4.32.

[56] See n. 48.

[57] See 1 Cor. 6.17 and John 17.21.

[58] In Cant. 6.7.

[59] See 1 Cor. 9.21.

[60] See John 1.14; 1 John 1.1 and Acts 13.26.

[61] Cf. 1 John 1.1, Heb. 6.4, and John 6.33 (6.52 ff.).

[62] Cf. 1 Peter 1.23 and 2.2; Rom. 14.2; Heb. 5.14 (where Rufinus has translated *pro possibilitate* for διὰ τὴν ἕξιν [Vg. *pro consuetudine*], which Origen has elsewhere).

[63] Cf. Exod. 1.41, 14.24, 15.22, 16.14; Ps. 77.25.

[64] Cf. Job 10.11.

[65] Cf. Matt. 25.21; Ezech. 28.13; Ps. 36.4. For the same etymology of Eden, cf. Origen, *Sel. in Gen.* (Lomm. 8.56). See also Philo, *Cher.* 12; Clement of Alexandria, *Strom.* 2.51.4.

[66] Cf. Prov. 2.5. The following reference is again (see n. 62) to Heb. 5.14.

⁶⁷ The language in this long sentence is somewhat compressed. The meaning is: If the bodily eye is healthy, it will see things as they are; if it is not, its vision will be falsified, and the mind's judgement on the object seen also will be at fault, and therefore a wrong action will ensue. The application of this principle to spiritual sight in what follows is quite clear, and leads back to the passage from 2 Cor. 2.14–6 cited at the beginning of the section.

⁶⁸ 1 Cor. 2.14, *animalis homo*, ψυχικὸς ἄνθρωπος.

⁶⁹ The texts cited are from Ps. 18.9; Matt. 13.9; 2 Cor. 2.15; Ps. 33.9; 1 John 1.1.

⁷⁰ With this paragraph compare Origen, *De Princ.* 1.1.9 (GCS 22.27. 1–8): 'Frequently the names of the sense organs are applied to the soul. Thus the soul is said to see with the "eyes of the heart" (Eph. 1.18), that is to say, by its faculty of understanding it performs some intellectual perception. So too it is said to hear with the ears when it arrives at more profound understanding. So also we say that it uses teeth, etc.'

⁷¹ Compare Isa. 40.29–31 (2 Cor. 2.16).

⁷² See Phil 2.6 f. again, and John 1.16.

⁷³ Cf. 1 Cor. 9.22.

⁷⁴ See 1 Cor. 2.16, 12, 9 (cf. Isa. 64.4); Col. 2.3.

⁷⁵ See 2 Cor. 12.1–4.

⁷⁶ Cf. Isa. 45.3.

⁷⁷ Ps. 44.10 and 15. The psalm is a nuptial ode.

⁷⁸ See Matt. 6.6 and Luke 19.26.

⁷⁹ Cant. 1.2 (Vg. 1.1).

⁸⁰ See Gal. 4.1 f. and 3.24 f.

⁸¹ See Gal. 4.4 and Luke 2.52.

⁸² It seems best to translate *aequitas* (=LXX εὐθύτης) by its English derivative, rather than by 'uprightness' or 'righteousness,' as the point of what follows is the contrast between equity and its opposite, iniquity.

⁸³ Cf. Col. 3.14 and 1 Cor. 13.

⁸⁴ John 14.15.

⁸⁵ We render *regula* as 'straight-edge' here, because a straight-edge is a metal ruler, that does not warp. For *directoria* (fem. adjective used as noun) in the present passage Souter gives 'regulation,' but 'rule' seems happier.

⁸⁶ See 1 Cor. 1.30; 2 Cor. 13.11; Eph. 2.14 and John 14.6. See also *In Lib. Jesu Nave* hom. 17.3 (GCS 30.404.6 ff.).

⁸⁷ Ps. 84.11.

⁸⁸ Isa. 61.10. For Christ *Sponsus-Sponsa*, see also *In Gen.* hom. 14.1 (GCS 29.122.4 f.).

BOOK TWO

This deals with Cant. 1.5–14 (Vg. 1.4–13). The text as given by Rufinus is as follows:

1. 5 (Vg. 1.4)   Fusca (*or* nigra) sum et formosa, filiae Hierusalem, ut tabernacula Cedar, ut pelles Solomonis.

   6 (5)   Ne videatis me, quoniam infuscata sum ego, quia despexit me sol.
   Filii matris meae dimicaverunt in me, posuerunt me custodem in vineis; vineam meam non custodivi.

   7 (6)   Annuntia mihi, quem dilexit anima mea, ubi pascis, ubi cubile habes in meridie, ne forte efficiar sicut adoperta super greges sodalium tuorum.

   8 (7)   Nisi cognoveris te, o bona (*or* pulchra) inter mulieres, egredere tu in vestigiis gregum, et pasce haedos tuos in tabernaculis pastorum.

   9 (8)   Equitatui meo in curribus Pharaonis similem te arbitratus sum, proxima mea.

   10 (9)   Quam speciosae factae sunt genae tuae tamquam turturis, cervix tua sicut redimicula.

   11 (10)   Similitudines auri faciemus tibi cum distinctionibus argenti,

   12 (11)   quoadusque (*or* usquequo) rex sit in recubitu suo. Nardus mea dedit odorem suum (*or* eius).

   13 (12)   Alligamentum guttae fraternus mihi, in medio uberum meorum manebit (*or* commorabitur).

   14 (13)   Botrus cypri fraternus meus mihi in vineis Engaddi.

✶ ✶ ✶

[1] As Baehrens observes *ad loc.*, this remark is by the translator Rufinus and has to do with the *Latin* versions of the text. 'The Hebrew for "black" (*sheḥôrāh*) denotes a ruddy hue from sunburning': S. M. Lehrman *ad loc.* in his commentary on the Song of Songs in *The Five Megilloth*, ed. A. Cohen (London 1952). The Greek and Latin versions both use intenser words, which somewhat obscure the meaning of the Hebrew.

[2] An echo of Matt. 6.29.

³ *Exercitio quaesita. Exercitium* (ἄσκησις) in Patristic Latin often means the practice of the virtues; cf. Blaise-Chirat s.v. § 2.

⁴ Sed redeamus *ad ordinem mysticum*: see above, n. 3 to the Prologue; also n. 31 to bk. 1. Note that in the following pages this mystical interpretation sees the Church in the Bride, then (beginning with p. 106) the individual member, the Christian soul. See Lieske, *op. cit.* 26 f. Or, as Origen clearly puts it here and in the following, the *primal* beauty of the Divine Image was never quite lost in God's Bride (-Church, or -soul): when she approaches her Bridegroom in the Word of God and adorns His Image in her through her faith and prayer, her works of penance and mercy, she receives beauty that is her *own*. Concerning this twofold beauty of the Bride, the beauty of the Image and its resemblance (likeness), see H. Crouzel, *L'image de Dieu chez Origène* (Paris 1955) 178 f., 217 ff.

⁵ See Rom. 11.28.

⁶ Cf. Ps. 44.11.

⁷ See Gen. 1.26 f. The restoration of *illud primum*, of that *primal* beauty is, in the mystical theology of Origen, the mission of the Christian soul; cf. Lieske, *op. cit.* 50 f., 59 f., *passim.*

⁸ See Gen. 25.13 and 16.11. See also Origen, *In Gen.* hom. 11.2 (GCS 29.8 ff.).

⁹ The curtains of the tabernacle are described in Exod. 25.2 ff.

¹⁰ See John 1.14; Col. 1.15; Heb. 1.3; Ecclus. 8.6; Rom. 2.3.

¹¹ See Num. 12.1 f.

¹² Matt. 12.42.

¹³ 3 Kings 10.1–10.

¹⁴ Matt. 12.42.

¹⁵ Josephus, *Antiquities of the Jews* 8.165–75. In the following, as Baehrens observes, Origen obviously confused the city Sheba (Saba) with the queen, as he referred to the further text in Josephus, *Antiq.* 2.249: 'Saba, a royal city of Ethiopia, which Cambyses later renamed Meroe, after his own sister,' The queen of Sheba is called (8.165) 'queen of Egypt and Ethiopia,' but in this he was mistaken: cf. the remarks *ad loc.* by H. St. J. Thackeray–R. Marcus in the Loeb Classical Library. On the queen and her people, cf. DB 5 s.v. 'Saba' Nos. 5 and 6.

¹⁶ Ps. 37.31–3.

¹⁷ Cf. Soph. 3.8–11. The LXX in v. 11 does not have 'Saba.'

¹⁸ These references are to Jer. 38(45).10 and 39(46).15.18.

¹⁹ Cf. Num. 12.1 f.

²⁰ Cf. Num. 12.3, 6–8.

²¹ Cf. Origen, *In Num.* hom. 6.4 and hom. 7 (GCS 30.35.17 ff.).

²² Cf. Matt. 12.42.

[23] 'Vision of Peace,' *visio pacis*, ὅρασις εἰρήνης—the popular etymology of the namè Jerusalem: see e.g. Philo, *De somn.* 2.250; Clement of Alexandria, *Strom.* 1.29.4; Origen, *In Lib. Iesu Nave* hom. 21.2 (GCS 30. 431.3 f.); etc.

[24] Cf. Eph. 2.14.

[25] See John 15.14 f.

[26] This is a remarkable tribute, coming as it does from the age of persecution, the tendency of which must have been always to disorganize.

[27] Cf. 1 Cor. 13.10, 12.

[28] See Prov. 9.1.

[29] John 4.34.

[30] One should not overlook the place Origen gives in his highly mystical interpretations of the Scriptures to the Christian liturgy and to the ministers of the external Christian cult. As Daniélou, *Origène*, esp. 42–52, states succinctly, Origen does not see clearly the importance of the sacramental economy in the life of Christianity, and his spiritualizing tendencies make him deprecate to some extent the essential external, visible aspects of Christian worship. He is groping his way—a pioneer theologian—and it was by no means a wholly *invisibilis ecclesia* for whom he was stretched on the rack, and for whom he prayed to be permitted to consummate his martyrdom.

[31] Gal. 3.27.

[32] A reminiscence of Ps. 103.15.

[33] For this paragraph, see Heb. 12.22; 1 Cor. 13.13; and 1 Cor. 2.9, which quotes Isa. 64.4.

[34] See Luke 10.39–42.

[35] See Eph. 2.14.

[36] Cf. Philo, *Quaest. in Gen.* 1.91: before the Deluge the limit of human life was fixed at 120 years—see Gen. 6.3; cf. also Josephus, *Antiq.* 1.75 and 1.149: in the latter passage it is said that man's life-span was gradually reduced up to the time of Moses, for whom and after whom it was limited to 120 years (Deut. 34.7).

[37] See Gen. 6.3 and Deut. 34.7.

[38] Cf. Matt. 6.1–4.

[39] See Ps. 67.32.

[40] Origen has Rom. 11 (esp. v. 11 f.) in mind here, and picks up the theme again two paragraphs later.

[41] See Soph. 3.11.

[42] See Ps. 50.19.

[43] John 6.37.

[44] Cf. Rom. 11.25 f.

[45] See Soph. 3.11.

[46] See n. 18.

[47] See Matt. 19.12, on which Origen himself had acted all too literally in his youth.—In this sentence, 'But I think . . . wickedness,' it is difficult to know whether the pronouns should be capitalized or not.

[48] Cf. Prov. 17.2. The Hebrew original of this name means 'servant of the king'—not 'kings.'

[49] See Jer. 39(46).16–18.

[50] Matt. 6.29.

[51] Cf. Exod. 26.7–13.

[52] Cf. Prol. to *Commentary*, n. 106a.

[53] See Heb. 8.2 and 9.24.

[54] Similar statements by Origen on the spread of Christianity: *De princ.* 2.7.2 (GCS 22.149.16); *C. Cels.* 7.26 (GCS 3.177.21 ff.), where he emphasizes this spread in the face of 'countless hindrances' to the religion founded by Jesus Christ.

[55] John 14.2.

[56] Cf. Cant. 8.5.

[57] The name Ethiopian—Αἰθίοψ—means Burnt-face. We may recall the mention of the mythical Ethiopians at the beginning of the *Odyssey* (1.23), where they are divided into nations inhabiting the unknown farthest east and farthest west. Since Herodotus they are thought of as a people living south of Egypt (in Nubia, north Abyssinia, etc.). Cf. F. Vigouroux, 'Éthiopie,' DB 2.2007–13; OCD s.v. 'Ethiopia.'

[58] Cf. Cant. 8.5

[59] The contrast between going down and coming up derives from Israel's going down to Egypt and coming up thence to the Promised Land. St. Ambrose, *De Abrah.* 2.13, says: 'Our mind goes down (into Egypt) when it ponders carnal things; it comes up when it desires things unseen.' See also Origen, *In Num.* hom. 27.3 (GCS 30.259 f.).

[60] Cf. Mal. 4.2. In a Messianic sense this sun—ἥλιος δικαιοσύνης —is identified with Christ many times in Origen's writings: cf. e.g. *In Lev.* hom. 9.10 (GCS 29.438.20–4); *Comm. in Ioann.* 3.1 frg. 34 (GCS 10.509.27 f.); *C. Cels.* 6.79 (GCS 2.150.15 f.); etc.—for further passages see F. J. Dölger, *Die Sonne der Gerechtigkeit und der Schwarze* (Münster i. W. 1919) 108 n. 4, within the section 100–10: 'Christus als Sonne der Gerechtigkeit.'

[61] Cf. Luke 21.36.

[62] Cf. Rom. 11.30 f. and 25.

[63] See Num. 20.17; Prov. 4.36; and Luke 1.6.

[64] See Matt. 5.14.

[65] John 1.9 f.

[66] Cf. Lev. 26.21, 23 f., 40 f. The alternate version 'crookedly'—
obliqui, obliquus—is added by Rufinus from pre-Jerome translations of
the Bible (so Baehrens *ad loc.*).

[67] Elsewhere—*In Exod.* hom. 13.14 (GCS 29.275.16 ff.)—Origen
speaks similarly concerning fire: 'Fire has a twofold power: one by
which it gives light, another by which it burns. . . .'

[68] See Exod. 9.12.

[69] See Exod. 1.14.

[70] See Exod. 2.23 f.

[71] Ps. 120.6.

[72] Cf. John 3.20.

[73] Cf. Deut. 4.24.

[74] Cf. John 1.5.

[75] '. . . have fought in me': *in me* (abl.)=ἐν ἐμοί of the LXX. The
Vulgate reads *contra me*='against me.'

[76] Gal. 4.21–6, and see Gen. 16.15 f. and 21.2 f. For the importance
of this passage in Galatians for the early rise and popularity of the idea
of the Church as Mother Church, see J. C. Plumpe, *Mater Ecclesia, An
Enquiry into the Concept of the Church as Mother in Early Christianity*
(Washington 1943) 1, 6–9.

[77] Gal. 4.31.

[78] 2 Cor. 10.4 f.

[79] The term *sophista* (σοφιστής) is often used in a pejorative sense
for *philosophus*, not only to designate a pagan philosopher, but frequently too in speaking of purveyors of heretical teaching: cf. e.g.
Tertullian, *Apol.* 47.2, and the passages collected by J. H. Waszink in
his edition (Amsterdam 1947) of T.'s *De anima* (28.2) p. 356 f.; see also
Blaise-Chirat s.v.

[80] Gen. 27.27.

[81] See Phil. 3.7–9.

[82] See Jer. 2.21 and Deut. 32.32 f.

[83] See 1 Tim. 2.14 f.

[84] See Eph. 5.32, Gal. 2.20, and Rom. 5.6, 8 f.

[85] Here we have a passage among many in Origen reflecting his
belief and teaching concerning guardian angels. The doctrine was not
new with him; it is found in Ps.-Barnabas, the *Shepherd*, and Clement
of Alexandria, and was based principally on Scriptural passages such as
Gen. 48.16 (Jacob's blessing of the sons of Joseph), Tob. 3.25 (the
archangel Raphael accompanying the young Tobias), Matt. 18.10 (the
Saviour speaking of the little ones and *their angels in heaven*), and Acts
12.15 (the angel of Peter). Origen states very simply (in the translation
by Rufinus), *De princ.* 2.20.7 (GCS 22.181.20–2): 'Each and every one

of the faithful, and be he the least in the Church, is said to be assisted by an angel, of whom the Saviour says that he sees the face of God the Father.' Origen (*Comm. in Matt.* 13.27 f. [GCS 40.254–9]) was likewise very much alive to the question: does each human person receive an angel as his especial guardian when he is born, or does God give him this angel only when he is baptized? On this subject see especially J. Daniélou, *Les anges et leur mission d'après les Pères de l'Église* (2 ed. Chevetogne 1953) ch. 7: 'L'ange Gardien'=tr. by D. Heimann (Westminster, Md. 1957) 68–82.

86 Cf. 1 Cor. 3.1; Eph. 6.11; Gal. 4.2.

87 See Matt. 18.10 and 19.4. The 'little ones' are said to see the Father's face, no doubt as represented by their angels.

88 Cf. 1 Cor. 8.6.

89 See Col. 3.9 and Ps. 103.15.

90 Ps. 44.10.

91 See Cant. 6.7 f.

92 See 1 Cor. 12.12–27.

93 See also Origen, *In Num.* hom. 20.3 (GCS 30.192.26 ff.).

94 Cf. Mark 6.34.

95 Rufinus' Latin reads *velamen habentes super caput*, which suggests a telescoping of 1 Cor. 11.10 and 15, with perhaps a reminiscence of 1 Peter 2.16.

96 Cf. Deut. 32.8 f.

97 See John 10.26 f.; Origen, elsewhere: *In Lev.* hom. 3.3 (GCS 29.305.9 ff.); *Comm. in Matt.* 20.44 (GCS 10.387.22 ff.).

98 See 1 John 4.7 f.

99 See Luke 10.27, citing Deut. 6.5.

100 For this and the quotations in the next two paragraphs see Ps. 22. Here in v. 1 'ruleth' (*regit*) probably represents Rufinus' choice from Old Latin versions (Vg. has the same) for LXX 'feedeth' (ποιμαίνει), which Origen reads where his Greek text survives. The new Latin Psalter published by the Biblical Commission (Rome 1945) reads 'Dominus *pascit* me.'

101 See John 10.7, 11, 9.

102 Ps. 45.6.

103 Cf. Gen. 18.1 f. See also Origen, *In Gen.* hom. 4.1 (GCS 29.51.1 ff.): 'There came to Abraham *three* men, *at midday*; to Lot *two* men, and *in the evening*. For Lot could not take the brilliance of the sun at noon, whereas Abraham was capable of absorbing the full effulgence of light....'—At the end of this paragraph Origen (or Rufinus) interprets the name *Mamre* (it has no *b* in Hebrew) as *a visione*, From Seeing. This awkward result is reached by connecting the word with

a noun from the root R'H, 'to see,' prefixed by the preposition *min*, the *n* of which becomes *m* before *r*. For the same interpretation of the name found repeatedly in Origen (cf. Baehrens *ad loc.*), see also Philo, *De migr. Abr.* 165.

[104] John 8.39.

[105] Rom. 13.12 f.

[106] See Gen. 43.16 and 25 f.

[107] Matt. 27.45; Luke 23.44 f.; Mark 15.33.

[108] See Gen. 1.27 f. and 24.

[109] 1 Cor. 2.7 f. and 12.

[110] See 2 Cor. 3.18.

[111] '*Scito teipsum*' vel '*cognosce teipsum*,' γνῶθι σαυτόν; the Latin version is more usually '*nosce te (ipsum)*'—cf. A. Otto, *Die Sprichwörter und sprichwörtlichen Redensarten der Römer* (Leipzig 1890) 245. The Greek is ascribed to the Spartan Ephor Chilon (6th cent. B.C.), one of the Seven Sages: see Diogenes Laertius 1.40; Pliny, *Nat. hist.* 7.119. The Greek version is used by Cicero in a letter to his brother Quintus—3.6.7.

[112] See p. 40 and n. 67.

[113] As in note 108. On the subject, see the study by Crouzel, as referred to in n. 4 to the present bk. of the *Comm.*

[114] See Matt. 25.32 f. Origen's use of parenthesis in this sentence is breath-taking, but no more so than St. Paul's, in Rom. 2, for instance, where vv. 13–15 interrupt the sequence of vv. 12 and 16.—The wanton antics of goats were a commonplace with pastoral and other writers: cf. Horace, *Carm.* 3.15.12; Ovid, *Met.* 13.791; etc.

[115] See Cant. 1.4 (Vg. 1.3).

[116] For the sin-bearing emissary goat or scapegoat, see Lev. 16.5 ff. See Origen's 10th homily *On Leviticus* (GCS 29.440 ff.).

[117] Origen usually treats of the Bride-Church and the Bride-soul separately and without confusion. Here he does not do so.

[118] 'of oneself,' *sui*, supplied by Baehrens.

[119] Cf. Phil. 3.13.

[120] See Rom. 7.15.

[121] Cf. 2 Cor. 9.7.

[122] This amplification of the text is an even more dizzying example of parenthesis than that referred to in note 114; but it seems impossible to translate it otherwise than as it stands. Remarking how dictation added further to the rapidity of the great Alexandrian's writing, R. B. Tollinton, *Selections from the Commentaries and Homilies of Origen* (London 1929) xiv, puts it succinctly—'Origen is no master of the considered style.' Even so, the present long passage is also an excellent

illustration—and this it is more important to note—of Origen's great conscientiousness in all matters touching the spiritual life and of the stress he places upon a constant and meticulous autopsy of one's spiritual self. Cf. M. Viller—K. Rahner, *Aszese und Mystik in der Väterzeit* (Freiburg i. Br. 1939) 74.

123 See Matt. 19.30.

124 Cf. Eph. 4.14.

125 Similarly, *In Exod.* hom. 9.4 (GCS 29.241.2 f.); *In Lev.* hom. 2.2 (GCS 29.290.26).

126 See John 10.11.

127 This is the LXX version of Osee 10.12. The Hebrew *nîrû lākhem nîr*, which occurs also in Jer. 4.3, means really 'Till you the untilled ground' (Vg.='Sow for yourselves in justice'), and is a figure for unaccustomed moral effort. The LXX keeps this meaning in the Jeremias passage, but the translator of Osee, apparently not knowing this rather rare root NYR, connected the expression with the common word *nîr* or *nēr*, a lamp, which comes from the root NWR. Believing that the prophet was speaking of lighting a lamp, he therefore intruded the words 'of knowledge' by way of explanation. Cf. C. H. Dodd, *The Interpretation of the Fourth Gospel* (Cambridge 1953) 155.

128 Cf. 1 Cor. 12.8.

129 See Matt. 11.27 (where undoubtedly Origen read the aorist ἔγνω for the present ἐπιγινώσκει); Luke 10.22; John 10.15; and Ps. 45.11.

130 Wisd. 7.17 f.

131 In *De princ.* 2.10.7 (GCS 22.181.13 ff.) Origen discusses 'the better part' of the soul 'which was made after the image and likeness of God,' and 'the other part . . . , the friend and lover of corporeal matter'; cf. *ibid.* 3.4.1 (262.23 ff.).

132 The problem of the origin of the human soul—which problem, he states, has not been sufficiently resolved by the teaching of the Church—is put very similarly by Origen in *De princ.* 1 praef. 5 (GCS 22.13.7–11); cf. also *C. Cels.* 4.30 (GCS 2.300.9–12); see H. Chadwick's note to the latter passage—*Origen: Contra Celsum* (Cambridge 1953) 206—also regarding the teaching on pre-existence of souls (favoured by Origen); also J. J. O'Meara in ACW 19.6, 216 n. 394, 224 n. 617.

133 As Tollinton, *Selections* 195 n. 1, remarks, Origen has mentioned three possibilities: traducianism (generation of the soul with the body), creationism, and pre-existence (or transmigration, infusionism), which latter Origen favoured; see the note preceding; also J. Quasten, *Patrology* 2.91 f. It was especially Origen's teaching of the pre-existence of souls, intimately bound up with the teaching of a serial restoration

of the visible world (*apocatastasis*), that caused endless doctrinal controversies (Origenism, Anti-Origenism) during the centuries following;
and it is this pre-existence that was anathematized first when finally, in
543, Justinian, following a synod convoked in Constantinople, issued
an edict condemning Origenism for ever.

134 An echo of 1 Cor. 15.53.

135 See Origen, *De princ.* 1.8.4 (GCS 22.101.4 ff.); *ibid.* 4.5.9 (362.5–9),
for which see Jerome's criticism, also of the translation of the work by
Rufinus, *Epist.* 124 (*Ad Avitum*).14; cf. F. Cavallera, *Saint Jérôme, sa vie
et son œuvre* (Louvain–Paris 1922) 1.313 f.

136 That is, schools of philosophy—*sectas philosophorum*, rendering,
no doubt, αἱρήσεις φιλοσόφων: cf. e.g. *C. Cels.* 8.53 (GCS 3.269.30),
and often. In Christian Latin, *secta* was in the beginning used side by
side with the borrowed *haeresis*; and while the latter gradually was
narrowed to the pejorative sense of 'heresy,' the former retained its
more general meaning, and even became a favoured word, e.g. with
Tertullian, to designate the Christian religion: *secta christiana, divina
secta, Dei secta*, etc.; cf. St. W. J. Teeuwen, *Sprachlicher Bedeutungswandel bei Tertullian* (Paderborn 1926) 120; H. Janssen, *Kultur und
Sprache—zur Geschichte der alten Kirche im Spiegel der Sprachentwicklung
von Tertullian bis Cyprian* (Nijmegen 1938) 110–15; also Blaise-Chirat
s. vv.

137 Cf. Cant. 6.7 f.

138 Cf. Luke 12.48.

139 Cf. Wisd. 6.6 f.

140 Here Origen the teacher speaks and his consciousness of the
serious obligations of those entrusted by the Church with the instruction and guidance of the faithful. See Lieske, *op. cit.* 20, 96, *passim*.
Regarding Origen's activity as a teacher, Lieske aptly remarks (51):
'One has only to compare the theology contained in the homilies, and
note with astonishment what wealth of theological thinking he ex-
pected his hearers to assimilate.' The teaching element will turn up
again a few pages further on.

141 See Lev. 20.10 and 21.9.

142 Cf. 1 Cor. 12.26.

143 References to Matt. 25.18, and to 1 Par. 2.3 and Gen. 38.7–9.

144 See 1 Cor. 2.6 and Deut. 32.8.

145 Cf. 1 Cor. 3.19.

146 Cf. 1 Cor. 2.12 and Rom. 8.15.

147 *Ibid.*

148 For the whole story, see Exod. 14.

149 Similarly, Origen, *In Exod.* hom. 6.2 (GCS 29.193.15–17): 'All

those who persecute the saints are neighing horses, and these have riders that drive them on—wicked angels.' Cf. also *Sel. in Ps.* 75.7 (Lomm. 13.16); also *C. Cels.* 4.32 (GCS 2.302.24-6): 'It is the demons that have incited emperor, senate, local governors, and populace against the Christians.' For the counterpart to Origen's thoughts on the mystical union of Christ and the advanced Christian soul—the union of the devil or demons with the lapsed or weak souls—see W. Völker, *Das Vollkommenheitsideal des Origenes* (Tübingen 1931) 105 n. 1; Lieske, *op. cit.* 149.

150 See 4 Kings 6.8 ff; the quotation, vv. 16–18.

151 See Hab. 3.8.

152 Cf. Matt. 11.30 (not Lam. 11.30, as Baehrens has it).

153 Apoc. 19.11–14.

154 See John 10.17 f. The word for 'life' is *anima* (so also in the Vulgate), ψυχή, which of course also means soul; and this meaning also is in Origen's mind—cf. n. 157 below.

155 See Col. 1.24 and Eph. 5.25–7.

156 Cf. 1 Tim. 1.15.

157 Here (cf. n. 154) we do translate *anima* as 'soul': it is the perfect soul of Christ that is the pattern for the many souls (*animabus*) that make up the Church.

158 1 Cor. 12.14–18 and 27.

159 Eph. 5.21–7 and 29 f.

160 For these thoughts—of the spotless Bride of Christ identified with the visible, historic Church on earth, of this hymned Bride seen as His own mystical body and members, of this mystical organism identified with the Church in her hieratic organization—see Lieske's exposition (*op. cit.* 86 ff.) of these and similar passages in Origen. See above, n. 140.

161 See also *In Lev.* hom. 2.2 (GCS 29.290.28). The conjugal fidelity of the dove was a commonplace among both pagan and Christian writers: cf. e.g. Aristotle, *Hist. anim.* 9.7; Pliny, *Nat. hist.* 10.52.104; Clement of Alexandria, *Strom.* 2.139.4; Tertullian. *De monog.* 8. Commenting on the passage last mentioned, W. P. Le Saint, ACW 13.161 n. 115, remarks: 'Modern zoologists give the dove a less edifying reputation.'

162 Cf. Matt. 11.29 f.

163 See Gen. 3.

164 See Phil. 2.8 and Rom. 5.19.

165 See Gen. 38.11 ff. This story taxes even Origen's powers of allegorization; he may well say that 'this mystery is not obvious to all' —though Thamar has a place in the genealogy of Christ: Matt. 1.3.

166 In the Prologue, p. 21.

167 See above, the Prologue, p. 46.

168 Cf. Matt. 4.1–11.

169 See Gal. 3.19 and Heb. 2.2.

170 See Gal. 4.2, 3.25, 4.4 f. and Cant. 1.2 (Vg. 1.1).

171 See, for example, Jos. 5.13–end and Judges 6.11 ff.

172 See Eph. 1.4 f. Here and in what follows, Origen very explicitly adverts to his doctrine of the pre-existent Church; of the Church, therefore, that 'existed already before the historical founding of the Church on earth by Christ. Indeed it existed from the time man was created, and even before' (cf. Plumpe, *Mater Ecclesia* 69 with n. 20, where the present passage is considered). Further instances in Origen: see below, p. 208 with n. 119; also *In Num.* hom. 3.3 (GCS 30.17.4 ff.): *ecclesia primitivorum*; etc. See also Lieske, *op. cit.* 33–6.

173 Ps. 73.2.

174 Hippolytus, *Comm. in Dan.* 1.17, has quite the same thought: the Church, he says, is the holy union of those who live in justice, the spiritual house of God built on Christ. Here there are many kinds of trees: the generation of the patriarchs in the beginning, the prophets, the apostles, the martyrs, virgins, teachers, bishops, etc. On this early theory of the pre-existent Church, see J. Beumer, 'Die altchristliche Idee einer präexistierenden Kirche und ihre theologische Anwendung,' *Wissenschaft u. Weisheit* 9 (1942) 13–22; Y. Congar, 'Ecclesia ab Abel,' Festschr. f. K. Adam (Düsseldorf 1952) 79–99; (for Origen) Plumpe, *op. cit.* 69 f.

175 Cf. Eph. 2.20.

176 Origen states the same in *De princ.* 1.3.6 (GCS 22.58.5); cf. also Clement of Alexandria, *Strom.* 1.135.3.

177 See Eph. 5.32.

178 Cf. Gen. 2.24.

179 Again, Eph. 5.32.

180 Cf. Eph. 5.25 f.

181 Heb. 2.14.

182 See Gen. 18.1 ff. See also Origen, *In Gen.* hom. 4.6 (GCS 29.57. 20–3).

183 See Exod. 3.1–6.

184 See also Origen, *Comm. in Titum* 3.10 (Lomm. 5.285 f.): 'A heretic . . . : everyone who professes to believe in Christ, but yet says that the God of the Law and the Prophets is one, the God of the Gospels another, and says that the Father of Our Lord Jesus Christ is not He who is proclaimed by the Law and the Prophets. . . .'

185 So in *Sel. in Ezech.* 16.13 (Lomm. 14.220). Cf. also *In Exod.* hom. 13.2 (GCS 29.270.23 ff.); *In Num.* hom. 9.1 (GCS 30.54.32 ff.): faith

=gold, making known the word of God=silver; *ibid.* hom. 26.2 (30.246.12–16): virtues and good works=gold.

186 Cf. Osee 2.8.

187 Ps. 11.7 and Prov. 10.20.

188 See Exod. 25.18 ff. for the cherubim, and v. 31 ff. for the candle-stick. For their interpretation, see Origen, *In Exod.* hom. 9.3 (GCS 29.238.9 ff.); *ibid.* 13.3 (29.273.9 ff.); *Comm. in Ep. ad Rom.* 3.8 (Lomm. 6.209).

189 See Gal. 3.19; Heb. 10.1; 1 Cor. 10.11.

190 See Heb. 9.11 and 24.

191 See Exod. 25–7, 30, 31, 37, and 38 *passim.*

192 Cf. Col. 2.18.

193 Cf. 2 Cor. 3.16.

194 1 Cor. 10.11.

195 See also Origen, *In Gen.* hom. 15.6 (GCS 29.134.22 f.); *De princ.* 1.6.1 (GCS 22.78.8 f.).

196 See Isa. 5.7 The second text seems to echo Apoc. 17.15, but Origen may have in mind Isa. 8.7 f. and/or Ps. 123.1–6.

197 See Ezech. 23.4.

198 Heb. 1.3.

199 See Matt. 27.51.

200 See Gen. 49.9, the blessing of Juda.

201 See Phil. 3.10; 2 Cor. 4.18; Col. 3.1 f.; 2 Cor. 5.16.

202 See 1 Cor. 10.1–4; John 6.31 ff. (1.29); 1 Cor. 5.7; Apoc. 5.6; Heb. 10.19 f.; etc.

203 See Num. 24.17, 7–9.

204 The LXX renders the Hebrew name *ʾagāg* (Agag) as Γώγ (Gog); and Origen connects this with Hebrew *gāg*, a roof (*tectum*). See also *In Num.* hom. 17.5 (GCS 30.164.11): 'Gog super tecta interpretatur.'

205 See the homily and paragraphs referred to in n. 204; also *Sel. in Num.* 24.7 (Lomm. 10.7).

206 See John 8.56.

207 Matt. 13.17.

208 See Gal. 4.2; Matt. 18.10; Heb. 5.12 and Luke 2.52.

209 Et fiunt ei parvulae 'distinctiones argenti': v. Balthasar (No. 638), taking *ei* as a dative of the agent and referring *parvulae* to *distinctiones*, renders 'und es glücken ihr kleine "Unterscheidungen von Silber."'

210 See Lev. 26.12.

211 Cf. Isa. 66.2.

212 Cf. John 14.23.

[213] See John 12.3.

[214] 2 Cor. 2.15. St. Paul has 'of Christ' after 'odour.'

[215] The quotation is from the Marcan story, Mark 14.6. Both Mark (14.3) and John (12.3) describe the nard as πιστική, early taken in the sense of 'genuine,' 'in the original,' though the Vg. has *pretiosus* in place of *pisticus* in Mark. Whether or not the Greek adjective derives from πίστις, Origen's interpretation presupposes such an etymology.

[216] See Cant. 4.13 f. The word translated 'shoots,' *shelāhîm*, means literally 'sendings forth,' and is exactly rendered by the LXX ἀποστολαί, and the Latin *emissiones*.

[217] See Matt. 13.45 f.

[218] See John 4.13 f., 7.37 f., and 6.35.

[219] Ps. 104.15. The word χριστός, like the Hebrew *māshîah* that it translates, means 'one who is anointed.' See also Origen in his *Commentary on John* 6.6.42 (GCS 10.115.15–20); also *C. Cels.* 6.79 (GCS 3.150.18–24)—here applied to those who teach and live the doctrine of Christ. See also among other passages Methodius of Olympus, *Symp.* 8.8, where the Church is in travail with, and gives birth to, Χριστοί, in baptism.

[220] Heb. 5.14.

[221] Here and in the following we should note the place that Origen gives in his teaching to the inner senses of the Christian soul. By God's generous giving the soul is endowed with a *sensorium* for the divine, which faculty, as v. Balthasar puts it (307), can be developed and improved to an infinite delicacy and precision, so as to report to the soul more and more unerringly what is the will of God in every situation. Parallel with this is the fact, as Origen points out, that Scripture employs sense terminology to describe God's own actions. To Origen this indicates the possibility of a spiritual, super-sensible experience; and this is also indicated to him by the great diversity of the inner life, the life of the soul, from man to man. Such diversity and infinitely multiplied individuality precludes government and direction by abstract legislation alone: here auxiliary guidance is offered in the inner *sensorium*, given by God's grace to each soul and combining for each boundless possibilities of inner sight, hearing, smell, taste, and touch. It is for the soul to develop these inner senses: to let them lose their sensitivity and die spells spiritual death (cf. v. Balthasar, *loc. cit.*; also Lieske 63 f., 103–9). Some idea of the importance of this doctrine in Origen's teaching may be obtained from the number of pages (308–63) it takes up in v. Balthasar's diligent collection of passages; and he rightly emphasizes (305) that in Origen's theory of the inner senses we have a core piece of all subsequent mystical theology.

[222] See John 1.1-4, 6.35 ; 1 John 1.1 ; John 1.14.

[223] The Greek version of v. 13 (Vg. 12) would seem to involve Origen and his Latin translators—and certainly the modern translator— in some difficulty. The Hebrew çerôr ham-môr means a small bundle or bag or sack (sachet) of myrrh, and implies the dried product. The LXX, however, while rendering the first word by ἀπόδεσμος, which also means a small bag or sack (sachet) that is suspended (from the neck by Hebrew women), translates the second by στακτῆς which comes from the root in στάζειν, meaning to ooze or trickle, and so denotes the liquid oil that oozes or exudes drop by drop from fresh myrrh. Probably one may interpret these drops or droppings of myrrh as meant in a somewhat congealed or solidified form—gum of myrrh (=σμύρνα: so Aquila and Symmachus in the present passage—cf. Field's Origenis Hex. 2.413) which is encased in the sachet worn: cf. E. Levesque in DB s.v. 'stacté.' The LXX, we may add to show the diversity of meaning given to the word, uses στακτή (Vg. stacte) for a number of products that have separate designations in Hebrew; e.g. labdanum (Gen. 37.25, 43.11), storax (Exod. 30.34), perfume in general (Isa. 39.2) ; cf. Levesque, art. cit.

In his translation of Origen's version of the present verse, Jerome (see below, Hom. 2.2 f. with nn. 8 and 14) gives three renderings: *fasciculus* (*alligamentum*—so more precisely Rufinus for ἀπόδεσμος), *stactes*, keeping the Greek word, and *fasciculus guttae* or *stillae*. Considering Jerome's faithfulness as a translator, we may be quite certain that to his Latin alternatives in 'id est *guttae* sive *stillae*' there corresponded in Origen's text two Greek alternatives meaning 'drop' for στακτή of the LXX. One of these undoubtedly was σταγών; as for the other, no guess need be hazarded from the great number of nouns (ψεκάς [Cant. 5.2], ῥανίς, ἰκμάς, etc.) used by the LXX to render 'drop' elsewhere. But in σταγών, also cognate with στάζειν, Origen had the common word for a *fluid* drop (of water, dew, blood, wine, etc.) and an excellent bridge from the στακτή of his text to the σταγών in both Micheas 2.11 and Isaias 40.15, which passages serve his interpretation of Cant. 1.13 both here in the *Commentary* and in his homily.

It may be remarked further that in the Vulgate *gutta* itself is used to designate an aromatic substance: cf. Ps. 44.9, which verse also serves Origen's exegesis in both passages (LXX: στακτή=aloes) ; and Ecclus. 24.21 (v. 15 in LXX: στακτή=myrrh?). And do we not read 'gutta percha' in our own English dictionaries?

Seen thus, in the entire context of Origen's exegesis and in the light of what must have already been traditional Scriptural terminology for Jerome and Rufinus, it is really only the modern translator to whom a 'bag or sack of a drop' is a strange anomaly of language. We render 'sachet of a myrrh-drop.'

Lastly, in our present section of the Commentary the translation by Rufinus uses *gutta* alone for στακτή, 'drop.' Did he leave away *stacte* and *stilla* as equivalents of the Greek in Origen? We cannot say, though the fragment quoted from Procopius at the bottom of p. 163 seems to make it probable that here Origen did not use any synonyms of στακτή as bridges to σταγών.

224 See Rom. 9.3–5.

225 The Latin words *continentia*, *constrictio*, and *nodositas* (for which last Souter s.v. gives the meaning 'complication' for this passage) all carry the idea of something tied and knotted up and so held together. What Origen condemns in the following exposition is heresy in the literal sense of choosing, taking one article of faith and isolating it from the whole to which it belongs.

226 See Num. 19.15.

227 See Origen, *In Lev.* hom. 3.3 (GCS 29.304.11–13): 'When one touches sin, . . . this is really what "to touch the unclean" means.'

228 See Dan. 2.34.

229 See Mich. 2.11 f., and n. 16 to the *Second Homily*.

230 See Isa. 40.15 and Phil. 2.6 f.

231 Ps. 44.9; *gutta*=LXX (and Vg.) στακτή, rendered 'stacte' and 'aloes' in the English versions.

232 See n. 10 to Book One.

233 The Hebrew word for 'cyprus' is *kōpher*; it denotes the henna, a shrub with fragrant whitish flowers that grow in grape-like bunches. The etymology of the word is dubious; but there are no less than three Hebrew roots consisting of the consonants KPR, one of them yielding the identical form *kōpher*, with the meaning of the price of ransoming a life. Origen might well have delighted in this, had he known of it. See Brown, Driver, and Briggs, *Hebrew and English Lexicon* (Oxford 1906) s.v.

234 See 1 Cor. 1.30 and 24 and Col. 2.3; John 15.1.

235 See Ps. 103.15.

236 There are echoes here of the language of Mark 14.24 f. and 15, but the basic idea is that of the Messianic Feast at the end of time (cf. Matt. 8.11, Luke 14.15–24, etc.).—A particularly attractive German translation of this section is given by Lieske, *op. cit.* 70 f.

237 By 'the mystery (*sacramentum*) of the vine and the cluster of grapes' Origen means that of incorporation into the Body of Christ, of membership in the Church, viewed as a whole and as the means to the final consummation of the divine purpose in creating and redeeming

man. What we call the sacraments of Baptism and the Eucharist are included in this, as means to the means; but they are not expressly in view.

[238] Luke 24.32.

[239] S. M. Lehrman, *ad loc.* in his commentary on the Song of Songs (see above, n. 1), says that the henna still grows at the modern Ain-jidy (En-gaddi) on the western shore of the Dead Sea, and that the steep rocks are frequented by wild goats. Origen's interpretation of the name can hardly be correct. The Hebrew word *'ayin* means both 'eye' and 'spring' or 'well'; the second part is almost certainly connnected with *gedhî*, a kid; En-gaddi is thus the spring where the goats are watered. There is, however, a root GDD, with the meaning of 'to cut into' or 'make inroads,' and Origen may have taken the notion of temptation out of that.

[240] See Job 7.1 and 1.22.

BOOK THREE

This deals with Cant. 1.15–2.15 (Vg. 1.14–2.15). The text, as given by Rufinus, is as follows:

1.15 (Vg. 1.14)	Ecce, es speciosa, proxima mea; ecce es speciosa; oculi tui columbae.
16 (15)	Ecce es bonus, fraternus meus, et quidem ecce es speciosus, cubile nostrum umbrosum.
17 (16)	Tigna domorum nostrarum cedri, trabes nostrae cypressi.
2. 1.	Ego flos campi et lilium convallium;
2.	sicut lilium in medio spinarum, ita proxima mea in medio filiarum.
3.	Sicut arbor mali inter ligna silvae, ita fraternus meus inter medium filiorum; in umbra eius concupivi et sedi, et fructus eius dulcis in faucibus meis.
4.	Introducite me in domum vini. Ordinate in me caritatem.
5.	Confirmate me in unguentis, stipate me in malis, quia vulnerata caritatis ego sum.

6.   Laeva eius sub capite meo, et dextera eius complectetur me.

7.   Adiuravi vos, filiae Hierusalem, in virtutibus et in viribus agri, si levaveritis et suscitaveritis caritatem, quoadusque velit.

8.   Vox fraterni mei. Ecce, hic venit saliens super montes, transiliens super colles.

9.   Similis est fraternus meus capreae vel hinnulo cervorum in montibus Bethel. Ecce, hic stetit post parietem nostrum, incumbens super fenestras, prospiciens per retia.

10.   Respondit fraternus meus et dicit mihi, exsurge (*or* surge) veni, proxima mea, formosa (*or* speciosa) mea, columba mea,

11.   quoniam ecce hiems transiit, pluvia abiit et discessit sibi,

12.   flores visi sunt (*or* apparuerunt) in terra, tempus putationis advenit, vox turturis audita est in terra nostra;

13.   arbor fici (*or* ficulnea) produxit germina sua (*or* grossos suos,) vites florentes dederunt odorem (*or* vineae dederunt odorem suum). Surge et veni, proxima mea, speciosa mea, columba mea,

14.   in velamento petrae iuxta promurale ostende mihi faciem tuam, et auditam mihi fac vocem tuam, quoniam vox tua suavis et facies tua speciosa.

15.   Capite nobis vulpes pusillas exterminantes vineas; et vineae nostrae florebunt.

ᵧ   ᵧ   ᵧ

[1] See Cant. 1.8-10 (Vg. 1.7-9).

[2] See Matt. 3.16, appearance of the Holy Spirit as a dove at Christ's baptism. On the '*columba Spiritus Sancti*,' see Tertullian, *De bapt.* 8. Representation of the Holy Spirit as a dove in ancient Christian art goes back to at least the first half of the 2nd century. Cf. H. Leclercq, 'Baptême de Jésus,' DACL 2.1.350-4.

[3] This and the quotation in the next paragraph are from Ps. 67.14, a *crux interpretum* if ever there was one, but there is nothing to be gained by discussing the possible meanings here.

[4] This *dogmatum stabilitas*, loyalty to the rule of faith—a favoured subject everywhere in Origen's writings—finds repeated expression in the following. Cf. H. de Lubac, *Histoire et esprit. L'intelligence de*

l'Écriture (Paris 1950) 63 and n. 115; P. Batiffol, *L'Église naissante et le catholicisme* (9th ed. Paris 1927) 371-7.

[5] There are echoes here of 1 Cor. 11.3, Rom. 7.22, and 1 Cor. 2.14 f.

[6] See Exod. 12.1 ff. and Lev. 12.1 ff.

[7] See John 14.16 f. and 1 John 2.1.

[8] See Zach. 4.2 f.

[9] Cf. Isa. 53.2 f.

[10] Cf. Cant. 6.7.

[11] 1 Cor. 6.15.

[12] Ps. 120.6.

[13] That is, Satan—cf. 2. Cor. 11.14.

[14] 2 Cor. 4.16.

[15] Once more the thought is expressed: the union of the Word of God with His earthly body in the Incarnation brought into being the mystical Corpus Christi His Church. For Origen's theology in this and related passages in his writings, see Lieske, *op. cit.* 38 f. and n. 1.

[16] See Col. 1.24; 1 Tim. 2.5; and Rom. 5.2

[17] Latin *trabes nostrae*. The Hebrew original is *rāḥîṭēnû*, a word occurring nowhere else in the O.T. and probably meaning either the panels between the beams or rafters or, as in later Hebrew, furniture.

[18] 1 Tim. 3.15.

[19] See John 16.15.

[20] 1 Cor. 11.16.

[21] See Gal. 1.2 and Apoc. 1.4.

[22] Cf. Ps. 79.9-11.

[23] Elsewhere, *In Gen.* hom. 2.4 (GCS 29.32.8 ff.), Origen, interpreting the hewn timbers of which the Ark was to be built (Gen. 6.14), says of them: 'These, I think, are the teachers in the church and the instructors and zealous workers of the faith.'

[24] As Lieske, *op. cit.* 84 f. and n. 3, remarks, here in the midst of Origen's mystical theology we have a remarkably clear identification of the Church as the mystical Bride of Christ with the historical, hieratic Church; and at the same time the concept of the several local churches constituting the one universal Church is assumed as an obvious reality.

[25] Cf. Heb. 7.19.

[26] See Matt. 6.28-30.

[27] 1 John 2.19.

[28] Cf. Mark 4.18 f.

[29] Here Rufinus is being even more than paraphrastic; Origen disappears for quite a stretch. The Greek of course does not have the homonymous problem which Rufinus touches here: *mālus* m. and f. and *mălus*, *mālum* and *mălum* (and *māla* sing. and pl. and *măla*). For

comparison of the Greek form *mēlum*, Baehrens (*ad loc.*) refers to Petronius, *Trimalch.* 56.

[30] Ps. 81.6 f.

[31] Ps. 88.7. The reference in this rather difficult paragraph is apparently to the fall of Lucifer. See Isa. 14.12 ff. and Origen's interpretation, e.g. *In Ezech.* hom. 1.3 (GCS 33.326.12 ff.).

[32] See Prov. 9.1 f. and John 6.32–59.

[33] Matt. 3.10.

[34] See Ps. 1.2 and Lev. 11.1–4. Origen writes, *In Lev.* hom. 7.6 (GCS 29.389.1–3): 'I think that he is said to "chew the cud" who gives his efforts to knowledge and meditates on the law of the Lord day and night.'

[35] Lam. 4.20. The 'Christ,' the 'anointed' (Knox, 'our anointed king'), in this verse is king Sedecias, the captive last king of Juda. It is a favourite verse with Origen, applying it Messianically in various ways (see below, n. 290); cf. Crouzel, *op. cit.* 139 f.

[36] Luke 1.35. Tollinton renders somewhat differently: '. . . that it is upon the nations that life is bestowed from the shadow of Christ, and how for us it is not His shadow that gives life. Also at the conception of His body it is said to Mary, "The Holy Spirit shall come. . . ."'

[37] An echo of Isa. 9.2, cited in Matt. 4.16.

[38] Heb. 10.1, Col. 2.16 f., and Heb. 8.5.

[39] Rom. 6.14.

[40] See John 14.6.

[41] See 1 Cor. 13.12.

[42] See Job. 7.1 f., but probably 1 Par. 29.15 was meant.

[43] See n. 37.

[44] See Matt. 13.6.

[45] The reference is to Our Lord's words in Luke 10.18.

[46] See again 1 Cor. 13.12.

[47] See Ps. 56.2.

[48] Cant. 2.16 f.

[49] Ps. 5.11.

[50] Ps. 118.103; 2 Cor. 6.11; Ps. 118.131.

[51] Origen's treatment of Cant. 2.4a in the following receives special consideration in the monograph by H. Lewy, *Sobria Ebrietas. Untersuchungen zur Geschichte der antiken Mystik* (Giessen 1929) 123–5. The concept expressed in the oxymoron 'sober intoxication' is found by Lewy to be central in Philo's mysticism. He further investigates the concept, especially as inspired by Philo, in the writings of the Fathers. The oxymoron is not found in Origen's existent writings, or as they survive through his translators, but the mystical idea of a 'divine

intoxication' (θεία μέθη) as the enjoyment of God is amply attested (Lewy 119–28).

⁵² See Cant. 1.4 (Vg. 1.3).

⁵³ See p. 148.

⁵⁴ See Prov. 9.1–5.

⁵⁵ See Matt. 8.11.

⁵⁶ See Heb. 1.14.

⁵⁷ That is, Pss. 8, 80 (81 in Hebrew), and 83 (84). The Hebrew is *'al-gittîth*. In the Midrash the noun *gittîth* is connected with the word *gath*, a wine-press, and taken as meaning a tune associated with a vintage song. The LXX follows this tradition, and renders ὑπὲρ τῶν ληνῶν. In the Targum, however, the word is connected with the place Gath, and taken as meaning a tune of Philistine origin.

⁵⁸ See John 15.1, 4.

⁵⁹ See Gen. 9.21.

⁶⁰ Ps. 22.5.

⁶¹ Prov. 4.17.

⁶² Deut. 32.32 f.

⁶³ A reference to Matt. 26.29.

⁶⁴ See Prol. p. 36.—The theme of the present section (see also below, *Hom.* 2.8)—the proper ordering of love, the establishing of a hierarchy of charity—is well adverted to by H. Pétré, *Caritas. Étude sur le vocabulaire latin de la charité chrétienne* (Spic. Sacr. Lov. 22, Louvain 1948) 89. The author, also remarking on the significance attached to the concept by other patristic writers, quotes St. Augustine, *De Civ. Dei* 15.22: 'Unde mihi videtur quod definitio brevis et vera virtutis, *ordo est amoris*; propter quod et in sancto Cantico Canticorum cantat sponsa Christi, civitas Dei: *Ordinate* in me caritatem.' See also *De doct. christ.* 1.27.28–30.33.

⁶⁵ See 4 Kings 22.2, Prov. 4.27, etc.

⁶⁶ See Mark 12.30 f., citing Deut. 6.4 f.

⁶⁷ See Eph. 4.25.

⁶⁸ Cf. 1 Cor. 12, esp. vv. 12–25.

⁶⁹ A reminiscence of 1 Tim. 5.17.

⁷⁰ 1 Thess. 5.12 f.

⁷¹ Like Zachary and Elizabeth in Luke 1.6.

⁷² 1 Thess. 5.13.

⁷³ See Matt. 5.43–8.

⁷⁴ See Eph. 5.25 and 28.

⁷⁵ St. Paul's phrase in 1 Cor. 4.15.

⁷⁶ See Wisd. 11.25.

⁷⁷ Wisd. 11.27 and 12.1.

[78] Wisd. 11.21.

[79] See 1 Cor. 15.9, 2 Cor. 4.9, and 11.28.

[80] See Exod. 23.22 and 2 Par. 19.2.

[81] See 2 Cor. 6.14 f., Exod. 20.12, and Luke 14.26.

[82] Origen has 1 Cor. 13.8 in mind.

[83] Cant. 2.5.

[84] See Deut. 32.43 (Origen's version of which differs also from the LXX); Ps. 33.8; and Matt. 18.10.

[85] Cf. Apoc. 2.18 f.

[86] See 2 Macc. 15.14.—The latter half of the present paragraph contains a remarkably clear exposition of one phase of the Church's teaching (see the Apostles' Creed since the 5/6 cent.) of the communion of saints—of the saints' or the Church Triumphant's active and availing interest in the *viatores*, the Church Militant. For Origen, see also *De or.* 11.1 (GCS 3.321 f.), *Comm. in Ioann.* 13.58 (GCS 10.289.22 ff.), etc.; cf. P. Bernard, 'Communion des saints,' DTC. 3.436–8.

[87] Rufinus: In Graeco quidam habet: 'confirmate me in *amoyris*.' The Septuagint, however, reads: στηρίσατέ με ἐν μύροις, which Rufinus has just offered as Origen's version—'strengthen me with ointments.' One does not know what to make of *amoyris*. The word baffled Baehrens (as it did other editors before him), who printed in his apparatus 'amyris (-um)?'. In the text offered by Procopius as that of Origen (cf. p. 195, bottom) it is said that Symmachus read ἐπανακλίνατέ με οἰνάνθῃ, 'cushion me with (grape) blossoms'; and it is further stated that some MSS have στηρίσατέ με ἐν ἀμύροις, 'strengthen me with scentless ointments (trees?)'; hence, probably, Baehrens' suggestion of *amyris*. Here we seem to have an indication of a confusion of Origen's script wrought by the free-translating and freely adapting Rufinus. See also below, *Hom.* 2.8 with n. 63.

[88] See Wisd. 7.20.

[89] Matt. 12.33 and 3.10.

[90] 1 Cor. 1.2. For the catechumens mentioned in the following, see n. 55 to the *Second Homily*.

[91] Cf. Gen. 2.8.

[92] Matt. 15.13.

[93] Col. 3.10.

[94] Cant. 2.3.

[94a] See Apoc. 2.7; John 6.31 f.; 15.1; 1.19; Exod. 16.12 ff.

[95] Origen has already taken up the subject of the mystical 'wound of love' in the Prologue (see pp. 29–32 with nn. 33 ff.) and he treats it again in *Hom.* 2.8 (where see also n. 64). A. Cabassut, 'Blessure d'amour,' DSp 1.1728, quotes what follows here as Origen's list of

tokens by which one may tell whether or not he has received the *vulnus amoris.*

[96] Cf. Isa. 49.2.

[97] Cf. 1 John 4.8.

[98] On the wounding darts of Wisdom and the other virtues personified as God, see also Origen, *Sel. in Ps.* 119.4. (Lomm. 14.108).

[99] Ps. 26.1.

[100] Cf. Eph. 6.16.

[101] Ps. 10.3.

[102] See Eph. 6.11–18.

[103] Most of the MSS add here: 'hence, in somewhat plainer language, she runs,' but Baehrens rejects this.

[104] Prov. 3.13, 16. Some few paragraphs further down this verse is quoted again, but with reference there to Our Lord.

[105] Of course it is again Rufinus, the translator, who speaks here.

[106] Gal. 3.28.

[107] See 2 Cor. 8.9 and John 12.28.

[108] See John 1.1.

[109] Cf. 2. Cor. 5.21, Gal. 3.13, and 1 Peter 2.24.

[110] Echoes perhaps of John 12.46 and Heb. 1.3.

[111] So the wording of the LXX, for which the Vg., agreeing with the Massoretic Hebrew, has 'by the roes and harts of field.' This great difference in text and meaning derived in part from the fact that the Greek translators worked from unpointed Hebrew texts.

[112] Gen. 27.27.

[113] 1 Cor. 3.9. Elsewhere—*In Num.* hom. 11.3 (GCS 30.81.5 ff.)—Origen speaks of human hearts as a field entrusted to the angels for cultivation.

[114] See Heb. 12.22 and Gal. 4.26 ff.

[115] See Rom. 8.15 and 1 John 4.18.

[116] See Col. 1.13 and 1 John 4.7.

[117] Cf. Eph. 5.14.

[118] Here and in the next paragraphs Origen reviews Cant. 2.9–14, before returning to v. 8, which is his present subject.

[119] Another intimation of Origen's idea of a pre-existent Church—see above, bk. 2, p. 149 and n. 172.

[120] See also below, *Hom.* 2.11, and *C. Cels.* 2.48 (GCS 2.170.20 f.). Pliny, *Nat. hist.* 8.114, claims that the hearing of deer is most keen when they raise their ears. He states also, *ibid.* 118, that stags track out the holes of snakes and draw them out by the breath of their nostrils. Cf. also Aelian, *De nat. an.* 2.9, 8.6.

[121] This may all be a clumsy sentence, but Origen is trying to express a profound experience.

[122] See Cant. 1.8 f. and 15 ff.: above, pp. 128, 140 and 169 ff.

[123] Matt. 28.20.

[124] See Matt. 25.14 ff. and Luke 19.12 ff.; Matt. 25.6.

[125] John 14.22 f.

[126] Origen is again looking ahead to vv. 9–14, in order to connect the 'winter' of v. 11 with the Bride's words in v. 6 in the next paragraph.

[127] See Ps. 73.17.

[128] That is, *exiliens* in place of *transiliens*.

[129] Cf. Gen. 26.13.

[130] 2 Tim. 4.7.

[131] This is an interesting view of how the spread of Christianity appeared in the middle of the 3rd century. That this spread was taken as most unique and as divine witness to its truth, was the common contemporary Christian view. Recall the celebrated passage in Tertullian's *Apology* (37.4), written in 197 A.D.: 'We are but of yesterday, and we have filled everything you have—cities, islands, forts, towns, exchanges, yes! and camps, tribes, decuries, palace, senate, forum. All we have left to you is the temples!' (tr. by Glover). In *Ad nat.* 1.8.9 the same author speaks of *non ulla gens non christiana*. In his apologetic treatise *Against Celsus* Origen writes (1.3) that Christianity 'would have been defeated by the combined force of so many unless it had overcome and risen above the opposition by divine power, so that it has conquered the whole world that was conspiring against it' (tr. by Chadwick). For these and numerous other passages by the same and other authors, see esp. A. v. Harnack, *Die Mission und Ausbreitung des Christentums in den ersten drei Jahrhunderten* (4 ed. Leipzig 1924) 2.529 ff.

[132] Rom. 15.19.

[133] See John 5.45 f. and Luke 4.16–21.

[134] See 2 Cor. 3.14–16.

[135] See Matt. 17.1 ff.; Mark 9.1 ff.; and Luke 9.28 ff.

[136] See Ps. 86.1 and 120.1. See also *In Ierem.* hom. 12.12 (GCS 6.98.8 ff.) for Origen's distinction between the 'mountains of light' (=the angels, prophets, Moses, the apostles) and (Jer. 13.16) the 'dark mountains' (=the devil, *the princes of this world, etc.*); also *In Num.* hom. 15.1 (GCS 30.130.24 ff.).

[137] See Jer. 16.16.

[138] Cf. Matt. 13.24 ff.

[139] Matt. 24.17.

[140] See Isa. 40.4 and Ps. 124.1 f.

141 See Luke 18.14. In the text this sentence appears as a parenthesis after 'every valley shall be filled,' and a new sentence begins at 'For of such it is said. ...' The parenthesis disrupts the sense so badly that we have ventured to change its place.

142 See Dan. 2.34; 1 Tim. 6.15; Apoc. 19.16; Heb. 4.14.

143 See John 4.14, with 10 f.

144 *hinnulo cervorum*—'a fawn of the deer.'

145 See Deut. 14.4 f.

146 Ps. 41.2.

147 Apparently the reference is to Deut. 12.15 and 22, where however the order actually is *roe-hart* (LXX in v. 22=hind); nor is there mention of 'the remaining animals.' In the following, referring again to the present passage, the writer observes the true (roe-hart) order.

148 *Ibid.*

149 See Ps. 28.7–9.

150 Cf. Job. 39.1–4.

151 Cf. Prov. 5.19.

152 See 1 Cor. 2.13.

153 See Rom. 1.20 and 2 Cor. 4.18. Origen is off now on a favourite theme—the image-likeness relationship of terrestrial and celestial things. Cf. Crouzel, *op. cit.* 125, 265 f., *passim*.

154 A reminiscence of Heb. 9.24.

155 For this paragraph see Gen. 1.26 f. and Matt. 13.31.

156 See Matt. 17.19.

157 Wisd. 7.17–21; see n. 65 to the Prologue.

158 '"initium" ait visibilis quidem mundi, quod *ante sex milia non integros annos* "initium" designat Moyses.' The number 6000 doubtless reflects the common expectation of Christ's second coming, the *parousia*; it is strange that the present passage has escaped the attention of scholars quite generally. Millenarianism or chiliasm in one form or another (the crasser types were combated especially by Origen—cf. *De princ.* 2.11) is present with Papias, Barnabas (cf. J. A. Kleist, in ACW 6.179 n. 160), Justin, Irenaeus, Tertullian, and—among others— in his earlier years, St. Augustine. Hippolytus of Rome, in his *Commentary on Daniel* 4.23 (GCS 1.240-4), sets forth clearly the computation by which the total of somewhat less than six thousand years taken as elapsed since the creation of the world was reached. God created all things in six days, and then, on the seventh, took His Sabbath rest. But *one day with the Lord is as a thousand years* (Ps. 89.4, 2 Peter 3.8). The first Sabbath was a type of the second, to be inaugurated by Christ's second coming from heaven, and to last for a glorious millenium of the reign of the saints with Him (Apoc. 20.4). The signs preceding and

presaging this second *parousia* of Christ—e.g. the universal preaching of the Gospel, the rise of false prophets, persecutions, etc.—seemed more and more ominously present. But the exact year and day of His second advent were not known. Yet Hippolytus, *ibid.* 24, with an exaggerated and 'an all too literal interpretation of sabbatic symbolism' (Daniélou 14—cf. below), establishes that Christ was born on December 25 in the year 5500 after the creation of Adam. Thus the day and hour of the end of the world were determined with fine precision! For an excellent study on the subject, also setting forth the Irano-Babylonian and Jewish precedents of Christian millenarianism, see J. Daniélou, 'La typologie millénariste de la semaine dans le christianisme primitif,' *Vigiliae Christianae* 2 (1948) 1-16.

[159] Cf. Matt. 24.35; Mark 13.31.

[160] Cf. Ps. 76.6.

[161] See Gen. 22.17.

[162] 1 Cor. 15.41 f.

[163] See Luke 13.32; Matt. 3.7; Jer. 5.8; Ps. 48.13.

[164] Ps. 57.5.

[165] Eph. 4.14.

[166] See Mark 7.21.

[167] See John 13.2 ff.

[168] Eccles. 10.4.

[169] Pss. 83.6 and 75.11.

[170] Cf. Deut. 8.15; but it is especially 1 Cor. 10.1-11 that Origen has in mind. In verse 11, *Now all these things* (i.e. the events of the Exodus and the wilderness way) *happened to them in a figure, and are written for our instruction* (πρὸς νουθεσίαν ἡμῶν) *upon whom the ends of the ages are come*—or, as Moffatt translates, 'the closing hours of the world have come,' and Knox, 'in whom history has reached its fulfilment'—the key words are HAPPENED and WRITTEN. The actual events of the terrestrial exodus of Israel from Egypt and her return to Canaan, recorded *passim* in Exodus, Numbers, Deuteronomy, and the beginning of Josue, were figures of the redemption and restoration of mankind. In St. Luke's account of the Transfiguration (9.28 ff.) Our Lord talks with Moses and Elias of the *exodus* (ἔξοδον) that He is to accomplish at Jerusalem.

[171] In the healing miracles, for instance, the individual healed in body is always a type of the whole human race that is to be healed in its entirety of evil as a whole.

[172] He has reverted now to the passage in Ps. 28.7-9.

[173] Now it is Job 39.1-4 again.

[174] See Gal. 4.19.

[175] There are echoes of Isa. 26.17 f. here.

[176] See Ps. 125.6 and 72.5 f.

[177] In the version of Job 39.4 cited above, p. 218, the offspring were the subject of the verb: *abrumpent filli eorum.* Here, however, they have become its object; *ipsi cervi abrumpunt natos suos*: the verb used in the LXX, ἀπορρηγνύναι, is transitive as a rule, occasionally intransitive.

[178] For the other echoes in this paragraph, see 1 Cor. 4.15; 1 Tim. 3.7; Gen. 19.26; Luke 9.62; Phil. 3.13 f.

[179] See Matt. 3.3; 1 Cor. 1.10; Ps. 41.2.

[180] We revert now to Prov. 5.19.

[181] *Noxius mediator,* the *fallax ille mediator* of St. Augustine's *Confessions* (10.42.67), as opposed to *the one mediator of God and man, the man Christ Jesus* (1 Tim. 2.5). In the *City of God* (9.9) the demons are the mediators between men and the gods.

[182] See Phil. 2.6 f. and Isa. 9.6.

[183] Ps. 103.18.

[184] Isa. 40.9.

[185] That is, δορκάς—connected with the verb δέρκομαι, perfect with present meaning δέδορκα='I see clearly,' 'see' (so in the *Iliad* 17.674 f.)—a type of gazelle: it has large bright eyes, hence its name in Greek. See also above, n. 120, and below, *Homily* 2.11 at n. 79.

[186] See John 6.46 and Matt. 5.8.

[187] See Matt. 11.27.

[188] John 14.9.

[189] John 19.1.

[190] Luke 23.21.

[191] See Luke 8.43–6.

[192] See Gen. 28.17, 19, 22, also Origen, *In Lib. Iud.* hom. 5.3 (GCS 30.493.9 ff.).

[193] *fixius impressis odoratibus*: like v. Balthasar (No. 216), I have found it necessary to add the hunting-dog. Perhaps *venator* itself should have been rendered thus, though in extant Latinity the noun appears to have been used for hunting animals only attributively (or in apposition) with nouns such as *canis* (Vergil, *Aen.* 12.751), *equus* (Statius, *Theb.* 9.685).

[194] *rationabilis verbi.*

[195] For the blessings of Jacob see Gen. 49. As to Rachel, it seems that Origen's memory has slipped, and that what he really has in mind is the story of Rebecca in Gen. 27. The general meaning is that Biblical exegetes are like hunters after game: when they have found their quarry, they have to cook it and serve it up.

[196] Having reached the middle of Cant. 2.10, Origen now goes back to 1.2 (Vg. 1.1) and in what follows he reviews all the intervening verses.

[197] That is, the rest of 2.10 and the next two verses.

[198] Origen now reverts to part of 1.4 (Vg. 1.3).

[199] 1 Tim. 3.15.

[200] Similarly, Origen, In Exod. hom. 2.2 (GCS 29.157.17 ff.).

[201] See John 1.1.

[202] Cant. 2.8.

[203] See 1 Tim. 3.15.

[204] See 1 Cor. 12.8 and Matt. 7.6.

[205] See 1 Cor. 13.12.

[206] Jer. 9.21.

[207] See Matt. 5.28.

[208] Drawing a contrast between Clement of Alexandria, who leads his true 'gnostic' to such heights of Christian perfection, yet himself remains earth-bound throughout, and his pupil Origen, W. Völker in his recent monograph, Der wahre Gnostiker nach Clemens Alexandrinus (Berlin-Leipzig 1952), most aptly quotes (218) the present line as typical of the glowing love of God and the ascetic life that he not only preached but also practised himself: relinquere corporea et visibilia et ad incorporea ac spiritualia properare.

[209] 1 Cor. 4.18.

[210] Cf. Wisd. 6.17.

[211] Cf. Col. 2.3 and Ps. 103.15.

[212] In this paragraph and the next Origen cites Cant. 2.11, 12, and part of 13. This passage is discussed more fully in the next section.

[213] Perhaps a reminiscence of Isa. 5.6. The (rain-)clouds mentioned in Jer. 10.13, Ps. 35.6 and 134.7, and Isa. 5.6 are interpreted by Origen as the saints: In Ierem. hom. 8.3 (GCS 6.58.11 ff.).

[214] See Luke 16.16.

[215] Cf. Ps. 45.5 and John 4.14.

[216] Cf. Matt. 21.19, conflated with 7.19 (cf. 3.10 and Luke 3.9).

[217] 2 Cor. 2.15.

[218] See Prov. 1.17 (where 'not unfairly'=non enim indigne=οὐ γὰρ ἀδίκως LXX) and 6.5. Elsewhere, In Num. hom. 7.6 (GCS 30.48.6 ff.), Origen speaks of the great deed of 'man, clothed in the flesh, weak and destined to die, wearing only the armour of Christ's faith and of His Word, routing the giants—the legions of the demons.'

[219] Cf. Gen. 10.8 f.

[220] See Mark 1.13, Matt. 4.1 ff., and Luke 4.1 ff. There is surely nothing lovelier in all Origen's work on the Song of Songs than this

thought that it is precisely through the nets of temptation that the Lord the Lover looks at His beloved.

221 See Rom. 3.23 and Eccles. 7.21.

222 See Job 14.4 f.

223 See 1 Peter 2.22, citing Isa. 53.9; 2 Cor. 5.21 and Rom. 8.3.

224 Ps. 123.7.

225 See Acts 2.24.

226 Ps. 87.6.

227 Heb. 2.14.

228 Cf. Heb. 2.15 and Eph. 4.8.

229 Cf. Eph. 2.6 and 4.8.

230 A conflation of Matt. 27.52 f. and Heb. 12.22.

231 See the Introduction, p. 4.

232 Rom. 8.9.

233 Cf. 1 Cor. 6.17.

234 See 2 Cor. 4.16.

235 Cf. Matt. 3.16.

236 Ps. 54.7.

237 Col. 2.3.

238 See Col. 3.5 and Rom. 6.5.

239 Another reference to 1 Cor. 6.17.

240 Eph. 4.14.

241 See 1 Cor. 2.6 f.

242 See Gal. 5.22 f.

243 See Matt. 15.13; 1 Cor. 3.9 and 6; Matt. 12.33.

244 Cf. John 15.1 f.

245 2 Cor. 2.15, 14.

246 This awkward rendering of *discessit sibi* is necessitated by the interpretation Origen puts upon it. It is not English, but then ἐπορεύθη ἑαυτῷ is hardly Greek, though it is a literal translation of the Hebrew *hālakh lō*, a common use of the ethic dative which might almost be translated here, 'has gone about its business.'

247 Similarly, *In Lev.* hom. 9.2 (GCS 29.419.30 f.), Origen interprets the ordinance in Lev. 16.34 bidding prayer *for all the children of Israel and for all their sins once in a year*: 'once in a year, that is, through this entire present age.'

248 See Exod. 7–12 *passim* for the plagues, and Josue–Kings *passim* for Israel's wars.

249 Rom. 11.11.

250 See Isa. 5.6 and p. 236 in the last section.

251 Isa. 52.6.

252 See 2 Cor. 3.6.

[253] Isa. 5.7.

[254] *capaces Dei.*

[255] Heb. 1.14.

[256] Cf. Matt. 26.29.

[257] Yet another reference to 2 Cor. 2.15.

[258] That is, the general resurrection, which will follow the second coming of Our Lord and precede the judgement. As the *Quicunque* says: 'At whose coming all men shall rise again with their bodies, and shall give account for their own works.'

[259] See Matt. 3.10 and 7.19.

[260] Cf. 1. Cor. 13.12.

[261] Cf. Matt. 22.30.

[262] The first time was in verse 10, for which see above, the beginning of section 14.

[263] Thus e.g. *In Num.* hom. 18.4 (GCS 30.175.30).

[264] See 2 Cor. 4.18.

[265] As in Cant. 1.6 (Vg. 1.5).

[266] 1 Cor. 10.4. According to many exegetes, St. Paul's reference is to the rabbinical legend (e.g. Targum *Ps.-Jonathan* to Num. 20.19) that the rock of Exod. 17.6 followed the Israelites in their wanderings through the desert and supplied them with water.

[267] See 2 Cor. 3.18.

[268] See Prov. 30.18 f.

[269] See 1 Cor. 10.4 and 1 Peter 2.22, citing Isa. 53.9.

[270] These words occur in Ps. 39.3, not in Ps. 17.

[271] See John 14.6 and Heb. 6.20.

[272] See Exod. 33.21–3. For Origen Christ is at once the Rock and the Cleft in the Rock. Was this anomaly what led the later mystics to interpret the clefts in the rock as the sacred wounds? See for example St. Bernard, *Sermons on the Song of Songs* 61 (ML 183.1070–4)= translation by a Religious of C.S.M.V., *St. Bernard on the Song of Songs*, [London 1952] 194–7, where (§ 3) he reproduces an unspecified source. Cf. also the petition 'Within Thy wounds hide me' in the *Anima Christi.*

[273] See Matt. 11.27.

[274] For parallel interpretations Baehrens refers to Plutarch, *De fuga et inv.* 165; Origen, *In Ierem.* hom. 16.2 (GCS 6.134.17 ff.); *In Exod.* 12.2 (GCS 29.265.15 ff.); *De princ.* 2.4.3 (GCS 22.131.6 ff.).

[275] John 1.14.

[276] Exod. 19.19.

[277] Ps. 103.34.

[278] See Matt. 12.36.

[279] Echoes of Ps. 140.3 and Col. 4.6.

[280] 2 Cor. 3.18 and 1 Cor. 13.12.

[281] Cf. 2 Cor. 4.16, Col. 3.10, and Eph. 5.27.

[282] Ecclus. 13.26 and Prov. 15.13.

[283] Cf. Gal. 5.22.

[284] A Stoic sentiment; though the parallel adduced by Baehrens in Ps.-Acro does not seem very close.

[285] Cf. Isa. 26.1.

[286] Ps. 67.14, the *crux interpretum* again. See above, n. 3.

[287] See Rom. 11.11, 25, 26.

[288] *in viriditate auri*, ut quidam legunt, vel, ut alii scriptum habent, *in pallore auri*: cf. Ps. 67.14; the latter reading is found in the Vulgate version of St. Jerome.

[289] Faith—*fides cordis*—is termed gold also in Origen's *In Exod.* hom. 13.2 (GCS 29.271.10) and *In Num.* hom. 9.1 (GCS 30.54.28 f.).

[290] Another reference to the beloved verse (cf. above, n. 35), Lam. 4.20.

[291] 1 Cor. 11.10.

[292] Cf. Matt. 10.32.

[293] A reminiscence of Ps. 72.8.

[294] See 1 Cor. 2.14 f.—For Origen's devotion and affection for the orthodox Church on earth, as here exemplified, see especially de Lubac, *op. cit.* ch. 2: 'Origène homme d'Église' (where, p. 65 and n. 133, the present passage is noted).

[295] The references in this paragraph are to John 1.18, 15.15, and 17.24.

[296] Wild beasts mentioned in the Bible are very commonly allegorized by Origen as demons who attack the inner man—his thoughts and desires. On this see Crouzel, *op. cit.* 197–206: 'Images bestiales'; collected from his works, these beasts form a veritable 'theological menagerie' (197)! See also S. Bettencourt, *Doctrina ascetica Origenis, seu de ratione animae humanae cum daemonibus* (Vatican City 1945) 49–51, 99.

[297] Cf. Ps. 79.20.

[298] Heb. 1.14.

[299] See John 13.2.

[300] For further parallels in Origen to this vivid presentation of the rôle played by evil thoughts in man's struggle to save his soul, see Bettencourt, *op. cit.* 76–9.

[301] Cf. John 12.6 and 13.29.

[302] 2 Tim. 2.17.

[303] For Origen's passionate concern for orthodoxy and his abhorrence of all heresy, see the passages marshalled by de Lubac, *op. cit.* 55 ff.:

'Piété et orthodoxie' (63, the present passage). See also R. Cadiou, *Origen: His Life at Alexandria* (tr. by J. A. Southwell, St. Louis–London 1944) 133 f.

[304] Ps. 62.10 f.

[305] Matt. 8.19 f.

[306] Luke 13.31 f.

[307] Cf. Judges 15.3-5.

[308] 2 Esdras 4.3. Allophyli='foreigners,' i.e. the Philistines; cf. below, n. 85 to *Homily* 2.

[309] For the subjects discussed in what follows, see the references given in the five notes immediately preceding.

[310] Cf. Apoc. 8.13.

[311] See Gen. 3.24.

[312] Deut. 32.8 f.

[313] An echo of 1 Tim. 6.3.

[314] See *In Exod.* hom. 6.3 (GCS 29.194.18 f.), where Origen has the same division of sin: 'Man's way of sinning is three-fold: sin is committed in deed, or in word, or in thought.' For Origen and his contemporaries, see F. Cavallera, 'La doctrine de pénitence au IIIᵉ siècle,' *Bull. de litt. ecclés.* (1930) 53.

[315] See Luke 10.19.

[316] See Ps. 136.9. The word translated 'outlook' is *sensum*. We might have rendered it as 'ideology.'

[317] Potest autem et ita accipi: *Capite nobis vulpes* et post distinctionem dici: *pusillas exterminantes vineas*. For *distinctio* as a márk of separation or interpunctuation, see Cicero, *De or.* 3.48.186.

[318] Matt. 18.6.

[319] Ps. 118.165.

PART TWO

THE HOMILIES

ST. JEROME'S PROLOGUE

[1] St. Damasus I, Pope from 366 to 384.

[2] This estimate of the commentary was not recanted when in his letter to Pammachius and Oceanus, written in 399, he defines his later opinion of Origen and cites the present passage (see Jerome, *Epist.* 84.7: CSEL 55.129.8 ff.=Labourt 4.133.12 ff.), after Rufinus had quoted it in the preface to his translation of the *Peri archon* of Origen (GCS 22.3.5 ff.); cf. F. Cavallera, *Saint Jérome, sa vie et son œuvre* (Louvain–Paris) 1.249–53.

[3] The *Septuagint* (δι ἑβδομήκοντα=The Seventy [i.e. translators], LXX) is the Alexandrian Greek version of the Hebrew Scriptures, and dates from the Ptolemaic period, about 250 B.C. It owes its name to the tradition, based on the so-called *Letter of Aristeas*, that it was made by 72 Jewish scholars, six from each of the twelve tribes, in 72 days. The story was further embellished by Philo and certain Church Fathers, but rejected by Jerome (*Praef. in Pent.*: PL 28.181 A). The version of Aquila, made about 128 A.D., was (according to Epiphanius, *De mens. et pond.* 14 f.: PG 43.260 f.) directed against Christian interpretations of the LXX; for though he had become a Christian while helping his relative, the emperor Hadrian, to build Aelia Capitolina on the ruins of Jerusalem, he apostatized when excommunicated for persistence in the heathen practice of astrology, and then became a Jewish proselyte. His version is literal to the point of absurdity. Theodotion, another proselyte or possibly a Jew by birth, lived later in the 2nd century than Aquila, and made a free revision of the LXX, superior to Aquila's in style, and based for the most part on the standard Hebrew text. Symmachus was an Ebionite leader, also of the 2nd century; he seems to have worked with Aquila's version before him, and to have used both the LXX and Theodotion's in his efforts to improve it. It was his aim to give the sense of the original in polished Greek. Eusebius (*Hist. eccl.* 6.16.2) quotes Origen as remarking that he had found two other versions, the anonymous *Quinta* and *Sexta*, the former at Nicopolis,

near Actium; and as it is known that Origen was in Greece in 231, it is natural to connect its discovery with that date. This version would probably be a relic of the early Christianity of Epirus. In the following sentence (§ 3) Eusebius adds that Origen also reports in the Hexapla of the Psalms that of the *Sexta* and *Septima* used by him he had found the one version in an earthen jar at Jericho under Antoninus, called Caracalla (211-17). Epiphanius on the other hand (*op. cit.* 18: PG 43.268) says that the *Quinta* was found in some jars near Jericho in the year 217, in which case it would probably be a Palestinian work, hidden during the persecution of Septimius Severus, who was in Palestine in 202 A.D.; he also says (*ibid.*) that the *Sexta* was discovered in some jars at Nicopolis under Severus Alexander (222-35 A.D.). In any case, Eusebius and Epiphanius agree that Origen found one of these manuscripts in a jar near Jericho in the early 3rd century. It is interesting to reflect that the 'Dead Sea Scrolls,' found in the same area in 1947, must have been already in their nearby hiding-place when Origen made his find or finds seventeen centuries before. For the whole subject of the versions, see H. B. Swete, *Introduction to the Old Testament in Greek* (2nd ed. Cambridge 1914) 1-58; L. Méchineau, in DB 4.97-123.

[4] Cant. 2.4.
[5] See Introd., p. 18.

THE FIRST HOMILY

This deals with Cant. 1.1-12a (=Vg. Title and 1.1-11a). The title (verse 1 in LXX) is not quoted entire; reference is made only to the words *Cantica Canticorum*. The text of the remainder of the passage, in Jerome's Latin, is as follows:

1. 2 (Vg. 1.1)	Osculetur me ab osculis oris sui, quoniam bona ubera tua super vinum,
3 (2)	et odor unguentorum tuorum super omnia aromata. Unguentum effusum nomen tuum.
4 (3)	Propterea iuvenculae dilexerunt te, et attraxerunt te. Post te in odorem unguentorum tuorum curremus. Introduxit me rex in cubiculum suum. Exsultabimus et laetabimur in te. Diligemus ubera tua super vinum. Aequitas dilexit te.

5 (4)	Nigra sum et speciosa, filiae Hierusalem, ut tabernacula Cedar, ut pelles Salomonis.
6 (5)	Ne intueamini me, quia ego sum denigrata, quoniam despexit me sol.
	Filii matris meae pugnaverunt adversum me; dimicaverunt in me; posuerunt me custodem in vineis, vineam meam non custodivi.
7 (6)	Adnuntia mihi, quem dilexit anima mea, ubi pascis, ubi cubas in meridie, ne quando fiam sicut cooperta super greges sodalium tuorum.
8 (7)	Si non cognoveris temet ipsam, o pulchra in mulieribus, egredere tu in vestigiis gregum, et pasce haedos tuos in tabernaculis pastorum.
9 (8)	Equitatui meo in curribus Pharao assimilavi te, proxima mea.
10 (9)	Genae tuae ut turturis, collus tuus monile.
11 (10)	Similitudines auri faciemus tibi cum stigmatibus argenti,
12 (11)	quoadusque rex in recubitu suo (or donec rex in cubitu suo).

ϒ   ϒ   ϒ

[1] Cf. Exod. 30.10, Lev. 10.17, etc.

[2] *Sabbata sabbatorum*, corresponding to the Greek of the LXX—Lev. 16.31; cf. *ibid.* 25.2, 26.35, *sabbatizare sabbatum*.

[3] The opening words of the Canticle of Moses after the crossing of the Sea in Exod. 15.1–21. This song is recited at ferial Lauds on Thursday in the Breviary.

[4] The Song of the Well in Num. 21.17 f.

[5] The Song of Moses in Deut. 32.1–43. This is said at ferial Lauds on Saturday.

[6] The Song of Debbora after the overthrow of Sisara is in Judges 5. For the etymology of the name, see also Origen's *In Lib. Iud.* hom. 5.2 (GCS 30.493.17); also above, n. 97 to the Prologue of the *Commentary*.

[7] The Song of David in 2 Kings 22 is substantially reproduced in Ps. 17.

[8] The Song of the Vineyard is in Isa. 5.1–7.

[9] Eph. 5.27.

[10] Eph. 4.13.

[11] The Latin is simply *unum et unam.*

[12] The Latin text reads: 'Ex quo et gentiles sibi epithalamium vindicarunt et istius generis carmen assumptum est, epithalamium

siquidem est canticum canticorum.' Epithalamia were written by Sappho, Theocritus, Catullus, Statius, etc. Christian poets in the West, such as Ennodius, Paulinus of Nola, and Venantius Fortunatus found inspiration in this type of poem. Cf. OCD s.vv. 'Epithalamium Greek,' 'E. Latin.' For an example of the common belief of Christian writers that pagan thought and literature were indebted to Moses and Solomon and the O.T. generally, see above, Origen's Prologue to his *Commentary on the Song of Songs* (p. 40 and n. 67).

[13] Cant. 1.12a (Vg. 1.11a).

[14] Cant. 1.2a (Vg. 1.1a).

[15] A conflation of Isa. 65.24 and 52.6.

[16] Cant. 1.2b and 3a (Vg. 1.1b and 2a).

[17] Ps. 44.8.

[18] Cf. 2 Cor. 2.14 f.

[19] Ps. 37.6.

[20] See Exod. 30.34 f.

[21] Cf. *ibid.* 31.3.

[22] Cf. Matt. 24.35.

[23] See Prov. 4.8.

[24] That is to say, his soul. See above, in Origen's *Commentary*, the development of this concept in detail; also the Introd., pp. 14-16.

[25] Cant. 2.6.

[26] Matt. 6.9.

[27] *Christus*, Χριστός (from χρίειν=to anoint)=The Anointed.

[28] Cf. Lev. 10.14. See Origen *In Lev.* hom. 7.3 (GCS 29.381.10).

[29] See John 13.25.

[30] Ps. 22.5.

[31] Cf. Cant. 1.10 (Vg. 1.9); 1.15 (Vg. 1.14); 7.1-6.

[32] Cf. 3 Kings 10.1, 2, and 10.

[33] Cant. 1.3 (Vg. 1.2).

[34] Cf. Matt. 26.6 ff., Mark 14.3 ff., and John 12.3 ff., which recount the anointing at Bethany; and Luke 7.37 ff., Jesus' anointing by the sinful woman (see n. 10 to *Homily Two*). On the similarities and divergences of the four accounts, see *A Catholic Commentary on Holy Scripture* (London 1952) 753 g.

[35] John 12.3. The detail is not given by Matthew and Luke.

[36] See John 12.31, 14.30, and 16.11. Simon the leper, identified as such by Matthew (26.6) and Mark (14.3), must not be confused with Simon the Pharisee in Luke (7.37, 40).

[37] This remark still holds good at the present day; for no pre-Christian mention of Moses by pagan writers or in ancient Egyptian documents has come to light since Origen's time.

[38] Cant. 1.4 (Vg. 1.3).

[39] Rom. 5.5.

[40] Cant. 1.4 (Vg. 1.3).

[41] Cant. 6.7 f.

[42] 2 Tim. 4.7 and 1 Cor. 9.24.

[43] John 3.29.

[44-48] Cant. 1.4 (Vg. 1.3). The maidens address the words, 'We will be glad and rejoice in thee,' to the Bride; the rest to the Bridegroom. For *aequitas dilexit te* (=LXX εὐθύτης ἠγάπησέν σε) the Vg. reads *recti diligunt te*.

[49] Cant. 1.5 f. (Vg. 1.4 f.).

[50] See n. 1 to bk. 2 of the *Commentary*.

[51] Cant. 8.5. 'Nephew' for *fratruelis* (LXX ἀδελφιδός), *fraternus* of Rufinus in the *Commentary*; the Vg. reads *dilectus*, 'beloved.'

[52] The WORD, Λόγος, for *Sermo*. Elsewhere Jerome uses *Verbum* also. See above, n. 2 to Rufinus' translation of the Prologue to the *Commentary*.—In the following, 'the seat of our heart'=*principale cordis*: see n. 10 to bk. 1 of the *Comm.*

[53] Num. 12.1.

[54] Cf. Ps. 71.8 and 10; also 67.32.

[55] Cf. Matt. 9.18 ff.

[56] Rom. 11.11.

[57] 'Member of the Church,' for *ecclesiasticus*, transliteration regularly made by Jerome and Rufinus of Origen's ἐκκλησιαστικός=a devoted, orthodox Christian. Usually employed as an adjective, the term constantly emphasizes the *right* faith as against the beliefs of pagans and heretics. It is also used in many ways to designate the organization (bishops, priests, faithful, etc.) and government of the universal Christian community. For Origen, see P. Batiffol, *L'Église naissante et le Catholicisme* (9th ed. Paris 1927) 371 ff.; the English translation of the same—*Primitive Catholicism*, by H. L. Brianceau (New York—London 1911) 309 ff.; for the Latin term see Blaise-Chirat s.v.; for Tertullian, St. W. J. Teeuwen, *Sprachlicher Bedeutungswandel bei Tertullian* (Paderborn 1926) 63, 69–72. See also the remarks and further literature by Dom Rousseau 77 n. 2.

[58] I follow Baehrens in taking this passage as a gloss.

[59] Matt. 12.42.

[60] See Rom. 11.11, 31. Origen adduces these texts as a commentary on the preceding section.

[61] Cant. 1.6 (Vg. 1.5).

[62] See Acts 8.3.

[63] Cant. 1.6 (Vg. 1.5).

⁶⁴ Cf. Eph. 5.27.

⁶⁵ Cf. 1. Cor. 9.19 ff.

⁶⁶ Very appropriately Rousseau (*ad loc.*) draws attention to this account—rare in the writings of the Fathers—of a personal mystical experience. For the personal element, see also above, at n. 24, and note its similarity to accounts by modern mystics. On the subject as occurring here and elsewhere in Origen, see F. Bertrand, *Mystique de Jésus chez Origène* (Paris 1951) ch. 5: 'Le contact du Sauveur.'

⁶⁷ Cant. 1.7 (Vg. 1.6).

⁶⁸ Gen. 43.16 and 25.

⁶⁹ Gen. 18.1. See n. 103 to bk. 2 of the *Commentary*.

⁷⁰ Cant. 1.7 (Vg. 1.6).

⁷¹ Eph. 5.27.

⁷² Cant. 1.9 (Vg. 1.8).

⁷³ Cf. Matt. 25.33.

⁷⁴ Cant. 1.9 (Vg. 1.8).

⁷⁵ Cf. Hab. 3.8.

⁷⁶ *Ecclesiastica anima, animabus quae non sunt ecclesiasticae*—cf. above, n. 57.

⁷⁷ Cant. 1.10 (Vg. 1.9).

⁷⁸ *Ibid.*

⁷⁹ The word ὁρμίσκος is a diminutive of ὅρμος, a chain, necklace, or collar. It is singular here, but plural in the LXX, as also in the Hebrew, where the word *harûzîm* comes from a root meaning 'to string together,' and so is best translated 'beads.'

⁸⁰ See Num. 24.9.

⁸¹ Cant. 1.11 (Vg. 1.10).

THE SECOND HOMILY

This deals with Cant. 1.12b—2.14 (=Vg. 1.11b—2.14). The text is as follows:

1.12b (Vg. 1.11b)	Nardus mea dedit odorem suum.
13 (12b)	Fasciculus guttae (*or* stactes) fratruelis meus mihi, in medio uberum meorum demorabitur (*or* commorabitur).
14 (13)	Botrus cypri fratruelis meus mihi in vineis Engaddi.

15 (14)	Ecce es speciosa, proxima mea, ecce es speciosa; oculi tui columbae.
16 (15)	Ecce es speciosus, fratruelis meus, et quidem pulcher; lectus noster umbrosus.
17 (16)	Trabes domorum nostrarum cedri et contignationes cyparissi.
2. 1	Ego flos campi et lilium convallium.
2	Ut lilium in medio spinarum, sic proxima mea in medio filiarum.
3	Ut malum in lignis silvae, ita fratruelis meus in medio filiorum; in umbra eius concupivi et sedi, et fructus eius dulcis in gutture meo.
4	Introducite me in domum vini, ordinate in me caritatem.
5 ·	Confirmate me in unguentis. Stipate me in malis, quia vulnerata caritatis ego.
6	Sinistra (or laeva) eius sub capite meo, et dextra eius complexabitur me.
7	Adiuravi vos, filiae Hierusalem, in virtutibus et viribus agri, si levaveritis et suscitaveritis caritatem, quoadusque velit.
8	Vox fratruelis mei; ecce hic venit saliens super montes, transiliens super colles.
9	Similis est fratruelis meus capreae vel hinnulo cervorum in montibus (or super montes) Bethel. Ecce hic retro post parietem nostrum, prospiciens per fenestras, eminens per retia.
10	Respondet fratruelis meus et dicit: surge, veni, (or propera) proxima mea, speciosa mea, columba mea,
11	quia ecce hiems transiit, pluvia abiit . . . ,
12	flores visi sunt in terra, tempus sectionis adest, vox turturis audita est in terra nostra;
13	ficus produxit grossos suos, vites florescunt, dederunt odorem suum. Surge, veni, proxima mea, speciosa mea, columba mea;
14	et veni, columba mea, sub tegmine petrae (or antemuralis). Ostende mihi faciem tuam, audire me fac vocem tuam, quia vox tua suavis est et adspectus tuus speciosus.

✣ ✣ ✣

[1] See Heb. 11.10.

[2] *animae motiones*; in the next sentence, *unus de animae motibus.* Alternatively, one might render *motiones* as 'movements' or 'motive forces.'

[3] A reminiscence of 1 Cor. 3.1.

[4] Prov. 4.6 and 8.

[5] Eph. 5.25.

[6] Cf. Num. 24.9.

[7] Cant. 1.11 and 12a (Vg. 1.10 and 11a).

[8] Cant. 1.12b and 13 (Vg. 1.11b and 12). See note 223 to bk. 2 of the *Commentary.*

[9] Mark 14.3.

[10] For this and what follows, see Matt. 26.6–13, Mark 14.3–9, and John 12.1–8. Obviously, here Origen sides with those commentators, ancient and modern, who regard the incident of the sinner reported by Luke 7.36–50, as distinct from that of the other Evangelists. See n. 34 to *Homily One.*

[11] Cf. Matt. 26.11–13 and Mark 14.7–9.

[12] Cf. 2. Cor. 2.15.

[13] Ps. 37.6.

[14] '*Fasciculus stactes*'—*id est, guttae sive stillae.* The last two nouns may be nominatives plural, in which case we should render 'that is, drops or trickles.' For the rest, see above, n. 223 to bk. 2 of the *Commentary.*

[15] Cf. Exod. 30.34 f. For the following, see also Origen, *In Lib. Iud.* hom. 8.4 (GCS 30.512.20–513.2).

[16] Mich. 2.11 f., Jerome rendering faithfullyt he LXX as given by Origen. The Vulgate version differs very considerably. As for Origen's use of the text from Micheas, see n. 223 to bk. 2 of the *Commentary.*

[17] See Dan. 2.34. See, in the same connection, bk. 2 of the *Commentary* at n. 228.

[18] Isa. 8.14; Luke 9.32 f.

[19] Cf. Isa. 40.15.

[20] Phil. 2.7.

[21] Cf. Deut. 32.6 and 1 Cor. 1.25.

[22] Phil. 2.7.

[23] Ps. 44.9 f.

[24] Jerome uses *fratruelis* (son of a mother's sister), Rufinus, in the *Commentary, fraternus* (a brother's son), for ἀδελφιδός in Origen's LXX. In the Vulgate, Jerome has *dilectus* (beloved) corresponding to ἀγαπητός of Symmachus.

[25] *in principali cordis*: see n. 10 to bk. 1 of the *Commentary.*

²⁶ The reference is to Ezech. 23.3, but Origen has the whole chapter in mind.

²⁷ See n. 233 to bk. 2 of the *Commentary*. The word κυπρισμός (cf. Cant. 8.12) in the following is not adverted to in the corresponding place in the *Commentary*.

²⁸ See n. 239 to bk. 2 of the *Commentary*.

²⁹ Cf. Job 7.1.

³⁰ Ps. 79.9 and 11.

³¹ Cant. 1.15 f. (Vg. 1.14 f.).

³² See Matt. 5.28.

³³ Prov. 27.10. The LXX has ἀτυχῶν, 'unfortunate.' Aquila's word, ἀπορεῶντα (for ἀποροῦντα), means literally 'wanting' or 'without resource,' and is used in the N.T. in such passages as Mark 6.20, Luke 24.4 and 2 Cor. 4.8 to express perplexity. If it be taken here as meaning 'at one's wits' end with distress,' it renders the original Hebrew very well; but *stultum* conveys a different sense. Baehrens thinks it likely that the whole sentence, set off by him in parentheses, is a complementary remark by the translator Jerome.

³⁴ Similarly, Origen, *In Ezech.* hom. 2.3 (GCS 33.345.3 ff.): 'Within us there are other eyes better than those we have in the body. . . .' See also *In Num.* 17.3 (GCS 30.157.25 ff.): 'In sinners it is not the eyes which are better that see, but those which are called "the sense of the flesh" (Col. 2.18) and which were opened by the counsel of the Serpent.'

³⁵ Ps. 18.9.

³⁶ Cf. Matt. 3.16.

³⁷ Matt. 4.23 and 28.20.

³⁸ The conclusion of Cant. 1.16 (Vg. 1.15).

³⁹ See Matt. 9.2 ff.

⁴⁰ Ps. 120.6.

⁴¹ These and the words cited at the end of the paragraph are from Cant. 1.17 (Vg. 1.16).

⁴² Cf. Isa. 55.13.

⁴³ Cant. 2.1. The first term is in Hebrew the *ḥabhaççeleth* of *shārôn*. The former word, which occurs only here and in Isa. 35.1, is variously understood as the lily, the narcissus, and the rose. Sharon is a proper name, probably denoting the coastal strip from Caesarea to Joppa. But it comes from a root meaning to be flat or straight; and both the LXX and the Vg. take it in the general sense of open field or plain. The *shôshannah* of the second phrase and the next verse denotes any lily-like flower, including the iris. It is mentioned again in Cant. 5.2, where a red variety is presupposed, and also in Osee 14.6.

[44] Cf. Apoc. 2.7.

[45] Cant. 1.3 (Vg. 1.2).

[46] Cant. 2.2.

[47] Cant. 2.3. Origen continues the verse at the end of the paragraph.

[48] See Lam. 4.20 and Isa. 9.2.

[49] Luke 1.35.

[50] Luke 16.10.

[51] The concluding sentence of Cant. 2.3.

[52] Cant. 2.4.

[53] Cf. Matt. 13.2 f. See also Origen, In Num. hom. 6.1 (GCS 33.51 f.):
When Moses heard God speak to him and teach him, he was *within*
the house; but when he spoke God's words to the people (e.g. Num.
11.24 ff.) that was not permitted within, he went *without*. In other
words: every teacher of doctrine is *within*, when he expounds the more
profound mysteries or when for 'the perfect' he sheds light on some
hidden aspect of God's wisdom (1 Cor. 2.6); but when he teaches the
simpler things that are sufficient for the ordinary believers, then he is
said to go *without*, to the multitude. This is further illustrated from
Paul's teaching. See also *Comm. in Matt.* 11.1 (GCS 40.1.3 ff.).

[54] Apoc. 3.20.

[55] This is one of two passages in the present volume in which
catechumens are mentioned. It is noteworthy that the present text in
which Origen addresses himself to the catechumens, occurs in a homily.
In the other passage, occurring in bk. 3 of the *Commentary* (p. 197),
Origen discourses about the catechumens, distinguishing them as trees
that do not yet bear fruit, from the faithful who have become good
trees, trees bearing the fruit of good works.

[56] See John 1.1; 1 Cor. 1.30; John 14.6.

[57] Cant. 2.4. On the subject of this paragraph, see also section 7 of
bk. 3, with n. 64.

[58] Matt. 10.37.

[59] Eph. 5.29 and 31.

[60] See Eph. 6.12 and 1 Cor. 6.17.

[61] Matt. 22.37 and 39.

[62] Matt. 5.44. For a similar gradation of love, see *In Num.* hom. 11.8
(GCS 33.91.19 ff.): love of God, love of neighbour (as of self), love
of enemy.

[63] This and the next two clauses are cited from Cant. 2.5. Origen
passes over the first two with little comment. 'Perfumes' is rather wide
of the mark for the Hebrew *ʾashîshôth*, which denotes a kind of raisin
cake. The translator referred to is identified as Symmachus in a text
attributed by Procopius to Origen—cf. above, bk. 3 of the *Commentary*,

p. 195 bottom (where see also n. 87). Jerome in the present passage leaves the Greek phrase untranslated: ἐν οἰνάνθῃ, lit. 'in the flowering (opening blossoms) of the grape.'

[64] 'Wound of love': this theme, a favourite with the mystical writers through the ages (cf. Rousseau's note *ad loc.*), is treated at greater length in the Prologue to the *Commentary* (see pp. 29 ff., where see also nn. 33 ff.) and again in the 3rd book (see at n. 95).

[65] Isa. 49.2 f. and 6.

[66] Luke 24.32.

[67] Cant. 2.6.

[68] Prov. 3.16, quoted also in the next two paragraphs.

[69] *animae principale*; cf. n. 10 to bk. 1 of the *Commentary*.

[70] Ezech. 13.18. In the context (vv. 17–23) the activities of false prophetesses are described; the 'pillows,' probably better translated as 'bands,' were sewn as amulets on to their consultants' wrists, thus symbolizing and ensuring the dispensers' power over them.

[71] Cf. Exod. 20.13. The 'many days' promised are eternity, the 'good land,' heaven.

[72] Cant. 2.7. For the text, see above, n. 111 to bk. 3 of the *Commentary*.

[73] See Isa. 1.21 and Num. 24.9.

[74] See Matt. 8.23 ff., the account of the storm that overtook the Lord and His disciples. Origen gives a graphic description of the tempest, applying the same lesson as here, in another homily: *In Matt.* hom. 3.1 (GCS 41.257 f.).

[75] Gen. 27.27.

[76] Cant. 2.7 f.

[77] Cant. 2.9.

[78] Deut. 14.4 f.

[79] See above, the *Commentary* bk. 3 at nn. 120 and 185.

[80] See Luke 24.32.

[81] παρὰ τὸ ὀξυδερκέστερον—the comparative degree of ὀξυδερκής ='sharp-sighted' (<δέρκεσθαι='to see clearly'). Perhaps Origen's etymology is not entirely 'fantaisiste' (Rousseau *ad loc.*); cf. n. 185 to bk. 3 of the *Commentary*.

[82] 'Forsitan Salvator meus *caprea* sit iuxta θεωρίαν, *cervus* iuxta *opera*.' Here Origen exemplifies the inseparable components of Christian life and perfection—θεωρία-πρᾶξις, the contemplative (*gnosis*) and the operative (works, virtues) life—by showing their presence in our model, Christ Himself. Völker, *Das Vollkommenheitsideal* 76 f., points to Origen's interpretation of an incident at the Transfiguration on Mount Tabor (*Comm. in Ioann.* 12.41 [GCS 40.163 f.]): Peter was

eager that they should continue in the vision he was privileged to see, but that was not to be. By leaving the vision and going down to serve His brethren once more, Our Lord demonstrated to him that the active life must always continue with the contemplative, that the βίος θεωρητικός and the βίος πρακτικός are inseparable.

83 Ps. 73.13 f.

84 See Gen. 28.10—end.

85 *Allophyli* (='of another tribe,' 'foreigners') : the LXX word for the Philistines, e.g. Judges 14.1 (once in the Vg.: Ps. 55.1). See also above, *Comm.* bk. 3 at n. 308.

86 This and the next two capitalized phrases are the continuation of Cant. 2.9.

87 Jer. 9.21.

88 Cf. Matt. 5.28.

89 Origen follows the LXX in reading διὰ τῶν δικτύων, 'through the nets.' The Hebrew word *ḥᵃrakkîm* occurs nowhere else in the O.T., but the Vg. is probably right in rendering *per cancellos*, 'through the lattices.' As in the following, in bk. 3 of the *Commentary* (p. 212), also Origen derives a very attractive meaning from the 'nets' through which the Bridegroom-Word looks forth on the beloved soul, for he equates them with the *laquei* or snares of temptation.

90 Cf. Ecclus. 9.20.

91 Ps. 123.7 f.

92 See also bk. 3 of the *Commentary* (p. 237), where Origen adds that these nets were broken when the Lord permitted Himself to be tempted three times by the devil; and that then He looked through these nets at His Bride, the Church. See also *De or.* 29.9 (GCS 3.385=ACW 19.117 f.) : Christ goes into the nets, looks through them, and speaks encouragingly to those who have been caught by them, that is, have entered into temptation.

93 From here to the end of the section the quotations are from Cant. 2.10–12 and the first part of 13.

94 In Jerome's translation the Bride has just been urged, 'Arise, come' —*Surge, veni*—true to the LXX's 'Ανάστα, ἐλθέ. For the moment the translator appears to be off his guard, for here *veni* has become *propera*, 'hurry,' which he adopted in the Vulgate; but presently, in the address to the Bride that follows, Christ the Bridegroom again exhorts her, *Surge, veni*.

95 Cf. Matt. 8.23 ff.; 26.38.

96 Cf. Luke 2.52. The text witnessing to the virginity of Mary Mother of God : *quia secundum dispensationem carnis ex virgine et voluntate Patris crevi. . . .*

[97] In his *Exhortation to Martyrdom* 31 (GCS 2.27=ACW 19.172) Origen describes the martyr's lot in quite similar language: first he passes through the storms and winter of trials and persecutions; then follows the 'blessed state of the martyrs ..., then will be realized the words of the Canticle of Canticles addressed to the Bride who has come through the winter's blasts: My beloved answereth and speaks to me: Arise, come, etc.'

[98] Cf. John 15.2.

[99] Cf. Lev. 5.7; 12.8; etc.

[100] Elsewhere—*In Lev.* hom. 2.4 (GCS 29.59.11-15)—Origen interprets thus: 'If equipped with your reading of Sacred Scriptures, *if by your meditating on them like a dove* (Isa. 38.14) and *by your meditation on the law of the Lord day and night* (Ps. 1.2) you convert a sinner from his errant life; if you induce him to cast off his wickedness and so return him to the simplicity of the dove, and if you prevail upon him to cling to the saints and to seek the fellowship of the turtle-dove, then you have presented to the Lord *a pair of turtle-doves or two young doves*.'

[101] See Matt. 3.16.

[102] Baehrens regards *quemlibet intellige* as an early scribal gloss. Origen does not mean to identify the prophet. The point is that Moses retired to the mountain, and a prophet, such as Elias or John the Baptist, might go to the desert. Origen is here once more touching upon his favourite distinction of those privileged souls in the Church who have already attained to mystical union with God, to γνῶσις, to perfection—they are the τέλειοι, for them it is the Spirit of the *turtle-dove* dwelling on the summits that communicates the *sermones Dei*; whereas the ordinary folk, the *hominum multitudo*, in the visible Church of Christ are ministered to by the Spirit of the common, tame dove. See Lieske, *op. cit. passim*, but especially 74 ff.

[103] Matt. 24.32.

[104] From here to the end of the Homily Origen is commenting on Cant. 2.13 (end) and 14.

[105] Cf. Exod. 33.21. Moses had requested the favour of seeing God's glory. He was not permitted to see God face to face—he could not have lived to tell it. But he was placed on a rock from which he could see God after He had passed.

[106] A reminiscence of 2 Cor. 3.14, 18.

[107] Cf. Deut. 27.9.

[108] Ps. 103.34.

[109] 1 Peter 4.11.

INDEX

INDEX

ANCIENT CHRISTIAN WRITERS

The Works of the Fathers in Translation

Edited by
J. QUASTEN, S.T.D., and J. C. PLUMPE, Ph.D.

Know Yourself — 128-139

Five Senses — 162, 167-168, 74-83,
  (discernment)
        181, 198, 208, 211, 233-4,
                244-6, 292, 304
        340

Allegorical interpretation — 8f.,
        218-228, 234

Emotions — 284